Social Divisions

Social Divisions

Edited by

Geoff Payne

#439/9617

SOCIAL DIVISIONS

Selection, editorial matter and Introduction © Geoff Payne 2000

Individual chapters (in order) © Geoff Payne; John Scott; Pamela
Abbott; David Mason; David McCrone; John A. Vincent; Stevi
Jackson and Sue Scott; Sue Scott and Stevi Jackson; Mark Hyde; Judy
Payne and Geoff Payne; Graham Crow and Catherine Maclean; Geoff
Payne; 2000

St. Martin's Press, Scholarly and Reference Division,
175 Fifth Avenue, New York, N.Y. 10010

First published in the United States of America in 2000

This book is printed on paper suitable for recycling and made from
fully managed and sustained forest sources.

Printed in Great Britain

ISBN 0–312–23611-5 clothbound
ISBN 0–312–23612-3 paperback

CIP information is available from the Library of Congress

With thanks to
Max Gluckman, Frank Jones and John Rex
for first interesting me in social cohesion and
social divisions

Contents

List of Tables and Figures

Tables

Figure

Notes on Contributors

Pamela Abbott is Pro-vice Chancellor of Glasgow Caledonian University, and formerly Professor and Director of Social Sciences at the University of Teesside. She has published extensively on women and social class, health inequalities and research methods and her current research is concerned with older people and social exclusion. Her publications include *Women and Social Class* (with Roger Sapsford, 1987) and *An Introduction to Sociology* (with Claire Wallace, 1996).

Graham Crow is a Senior Lecturer in Sociology at the University of Southampton where he has worked since 1983. His research interests include the sociology of households and communities, sociological theory and comparative sociology, and he is currently writing a book on Social Solidarities. Earlier publications include *Comparative Sociology and Social Theory* (1997), *The Sociology of Rural Communities* (1996) and *Community Life* (with Graham Allan, 1994).

Mark Hyde is a Lecturer in Social Policy in the Department of Social Policy and Social Work, University of Plymouth. His work on labour market disadvantage and poverty has been published in *Work Employment & Society, Sociological Research Online, Disability & Society* and *Critical Social Policy*. He is currently researching comparative social security and privatisation, and contemporary welfare reforms.

Stevi Jackson is Professor of Women's Studies and Director of the Centre for Women's Studies at the University of York. The more recent of her several books are *Feminism and Sexuality* (with Sue Scott, 1996) and *Contemporary Feminist Theories* (1998). Forthcoming books include *Concerning Heterosexuality* and *Childhood and Sexuality Revisited*. She is currently researching the impact of risk and adult risk anxiety on the everyday world of children.

David McCrone is Professor of Sociology at the University of Edinburgh, Convenor of its Unit for the Study of Government in Scotland and Co-director of the Governance of Scotland Forum. His research on identity and elections has been funded by the ESRC and the Leverhulme Trust. Among his publications are *Understanding Scotland* (1992), *The Sociology of Nationalism* (1998), *Politics and Society in Scotland* (with Brown, A. and Paterson,

L., 1998) and *The Scottish Electorate* (with Brown, A., Paterson, L. and Surridge, P., 1999).

Catherine Maclean has recently joined the University of Edinburgh where she is a Lecturer in Sociology. Her PhD examined social change and migration in remote rural areas through the study of a community in the northwest of Scotland. Her research interests include social and economic change in Scotland, the work–family interface, and rural life.

David Mason is Professor of Sociology, Associate Dean for Research and Head of the Graduate School in the Faculty of Human Sciences, University of Plymouth. He has worked on labour market and equal opportunity issues, and more recently on the recruitment of minority ethnic nurses and on diversity in the armed forces. His publications include *Theories of Race and Ethnic Relations* (1986) jointly edited with John Rex, and *Race and Ethnicity in Modern Britain*, 2nd edition (2000). From 1997 to 1999 he was joint Editor of *Sociology*, the journal of the British Sociological Association.

Geoff Payne is Professor of Sociology and former Dean of Human Sciences at the University of Plymouth. He has published *inter alia* on class, employment, health and community, including *New Directions in the Sociology of Health* (1990) with Pamela Abbott, and *Sociology in Action* (1994) with Malcolm Cross. He is currently working on industrial, occupational and class changes in post-industrial society.

Judy Payne is a Research Consultant and Honorary Research Fellow in Sociology at the University of Plymouth. Her previous work has included social exclusion, housing, social class, and health and deprivation. Recent publications include *Interpreting the Index of Local Conditions* (1995), *Researching Health Needs* (1999) and *50 Key Concepts in Social Research* (with G. Payne, 2000). She is currently doing research for the Plymouth Health Action Zone.

John Scott is Professor of Sociology at the University of Essex and Adjunct Professor of Sociology at the University of Bergen. He is author of numerous books and articles on stratification, theories and methods, and business organisation. His most recent book (jointly with James Fulcher) is *Sociology*. He has previously taught at Strathclyde and Leicester Universities, and is co-editor of *Sociology Review*.

Sue Scott is Professor of Sociology at the University of Durham. Her research on gender, sexuality and the body included membership of the Women, Risk and AIDS Project: she currently holds MRC and ESRC grants for work on sex education, and on children, risk, and parental risk anxiety. Her publications include *Body Matters* (with David Morgan, 1993), *Feminism* *and Sexuality* (with Stevi Jackson, 1996) and *Gender: a Sociological Reader* (with Stevi Jackson, 2000).

John A. Vincent is a Senior Lecturer at the University of Exeter. After gaining his doctorate in Social Anthropology from the University of Sussex, he has conducted research in India, Kashmir, Uganda, Bosnia, and Devon old people's homes. His publications include *Inequality and Old Age* (1995) and *Power, Politics and Old Age* (1999).

Preface

It was Catherine Gray, now Publisher for Macmillan's College Division, who first suggested that an interesting book could be put together about social divisions. That sounded an intriguing idea and when I began to talk to other sociologists, they seemed to think so, too.

As a result, I used part of a sabbatical leave at the University of Edinburgh to develop the proposal, getting together a team of contributors who would combine academic credibility with an active concern for explaining and communicating sociology. I knew that they all could write in a clear and engaging way, while the fact that most of us knew each other personally, as colleagues or co-authors, from meeting at conferences or working on committees, was an added bonus. It certainly helped me over the inevitable difficulties that are part of editing a set of newly commissioned pieces!

Apart, perhaps, from its first chapter, *Social Divisions* has not been primarily written as an introductory book *per se*, although it has been written to be engaging and accessible to a wide student readership in Higher Education and beyond. What we have in mind is the level of work typically found not at the very *start* of a sociology course, but which could equally well be used in an introductory or 'intermediate' stage of most university degree programmes. We have tried to deal with some challenging ideas in a systematic, clear and rigorous way, and this, combined with a breadth of topics and extensive bibliography, should mean that students (and even our fellow professional sociologists) will find some new insights in its pages. Many of its examples are taken from Britain, but the ideas and arguments are equally relevant in other 'industrial societies': our intention is that readers in other countries should be able to use and enjoy this book.

The contents have been organised so that while seeking to develop a coherence of its own, parts of the book can be taken out and used in other contexts. Even in British universities there is no uniformity in which parts of sociology are taught at each stage. There may perhaps be more overall consensus than most sociologists like to admit (as the data collected for the British Sociological Association's Working Party on the Undergraduate Curriculum by Jon Gubbay, and by David Jary's review of the documentation for the 1996 Teaching Quality Assurance, have shown). However, that does not translate into universal accord about where to place the *emphasis* in early modules of sociology, whether this is in 'straight' sociology courses, or in health studies, social policy, or social work. What should be the balance between sociological theory, social research methods, the 'Social Structure of Modern Britain' (or increasingly, 'Europe': see Spybey 1997), or the 'Cook's Tour' of major concepts and perspectives? The apparent similarities of current introductory texts hides a degree of variation in teaching (Bailey 1998).

Thus our choice of particular topics is not an attempt to prescribe the content of particular stages of sociology, but to assist those involved with making choices. Although there is a coherent perspective running through the book, each of the topic chapters (Chapters 2–11) is intended to be free-standing. They do follow a common format, but readers who wish to do so should be able to select those chapters that most interest them: the book is not designed to be read from cover to cover.

The three chapters on class, gender and ethnicity are deliberately longer than the others, because these three social divisions are centrally important in their own right, have been more extensively researched, and help to gain a purchase on the other divisions. Indeed, these three topics are what most sociologists would initially think of as 'social divisions'; as such they already have an established place in the curriculum. While recognising the centrality of 'the Big Three', one of the key purposes of this book is to advocate that the notion of social divisions should be extended, and to explore the significance of other social divisions. There is nothing revolutionary about such a view: new topics are always emerging from narrow specialisms to take a more substantial place in the sociological sun. Feminism, post-modernism, and cultural and social identity, for example, initially had to struggle for space alongside more traditional topics like classic sociological theory or social stratification. Whereas most courses at one time focused on the single social division of social class, now room has to be found for gender and ethnicity, if not other social divisions.

Our expansion of social divisions covers five areas that are of increasing consequence, in addition to class, gender and ethnicity as already explained. Both age, and sexuality, are in most people's eyes almost as important, whereas childhood, and disability, are good examples of well researched, sharply defined and challenging social divisions, but ones that are still only now beginning to be part of the core curriculum. Nationalism is even more of a 'coming' topic, fired by devolution, civil strife close to home, and political choices about the EU, but as yet less widely taught.

The two later chapters on health and on community serve a slightly different purpose. While each social division can most readily be understood in its own right, social divisions inevitably overlap and impinge on one another. This raises some problems of interpretation, and rather than trying to deal with these in every chapter, a simpler solution is to demonstrate some of these interactions by looking more closely at two specific areas. Health and community are research fields in which social inequalities and the processes of social division have been well documented, but which also allow us, in their different ways, to explore how other divisions overlap and manifest themselves in ordinary life. Neither health nor community can best be thought of as social divisions *per se*, but they do illuminate the nature of social divisions as they are normally encountered, both in our daily lives, and as social problems requiring sociological explanation. In this way, these two chapters form a concluding section with the final chapter on social cohesion.

A larger volume would have found room for other topics, as explained in the Introduction. Global divisions have been omitted as being of a different order from those encountered, as it were, within a society. Some discussion of global divisions and globalisation can, however, be found in the chapters on nationalism and ethnicity. Nor is consumption given its own chapter, but like probably the major topic omitted – poverty – it is indirectly covered in other chapters. The main reason for this at first sight surprising omission is that consumption and poverty may divide, but they are largely the *outcome* of other processes and social divisions, not least aspects of class, gender, age and health. It will be in these latter chapters that financial well-being or its lack is mainly considered. I hope that not too many readers' 'favourite' topics prove to have been left out.

Social division, in whatever set of examples chosen, is something more than just a useful principle around which to assemble a number of reports about major facets of contemporary society. The cumulative effect of reading each chapter is to produce a sense of a strong, coherent perspective, a way of thinking about social conditions and the social order. The contributors did not necessarily start with this in mind nor would they all equally subscribe to the theoretical implications of this distinctive approach, now that it is being more explicitly articulated, particularly as in Chapter 12. The idea that social division represents a distinct sociological standpoint of some significance certainly became clearer during the process of developing the book. As editor, I was the person best placed to see this emerging from the volume as a whole, and so must take full responsibility for any shortcomings in representing the overview that resulted.

Indeed, the individual chapters are not totally dependent on the concluding overview, and can stand alone. *Social Divisions* can thus be seen as working on three levels. At its most basic, it is a collection of chapters, each dealing with a topic of major concern in sociology. Second, it has been designed as a source book to support individual interests or a variety of teaching programmes. In addition, it also offers a particular perspective for making sense of society.

To the extent that we achieve these three goals – and of course, the reader must be the final judge of that – the outcomes owe much to the publishers and reviewers for their support and advice. The contributors to the book are due my thanks for their good-natured co-operation and willingness to write to specification.

I would also like to thank other colleagues who offered comments on ideas and drafts, in particular Sue Hemmings. I am grateful to the University of Plymouth for my period of sabbatical leave, and to the staff of the Department of Sociology, University of Edinburgh, for giving me a temporary home. My special thanks go to Judy Payne, whose assistance with the technical aspects of the production was invaluable, and whose intellectual collaboration and personal support continue to be a major source of inspiration.

GEOFF PAYNE
Plymouth

CHAPTER 1

An Introduction to Social Divisions

GEOFF PAYNE

It is impossible even to begin to think about *people* without immediately encountering 'social divisions'. We automatically perceive other human beings as being male or female, black or white, older or younger, richer or poorer, sick or well, or friend or foe. In forming a perception of them, we place them in pigeon-holes, adapting our behaviour and attitude to them in terms of the slots into which we have placed them.

The categories we use, even those like 'older', 'female', 'fit' or 'white', which might at first sight seem to have a purely biological basis, are actually socio-logical labels. The *meaning* we bring to the labels depends on the cultural significance we have learned to attach to them during our lives up to this moment. The origins of the definitions we use; the ways in which separation between one category and another have been created and are maintained; the extent of inequalities that exist between groups; how people come to think about their own identity; and the consequences of this for future action, all these are sociological. 'Age', 'gender', 'health', 'ethnicity' and 'class', and so on are the 'social divisions' that shape society. If we are to make coherent sense of our own lives, let alone understand what is going on in our society and why society as a whole operates as it does, the idea of 'social divisions' is one of the most useful and powerful tools available.

This chapter goes back to basics, deliberately setting out to explain the idea of social divisions in very simple terms. This means reflecting on the nature of social life as sociologists see it, and our assumptions about contemporary society. The later chapters develop this simple introduction into a more detailed and advanced treatment. The full meaning and implications of a 'social divisions approach' are then brought out in the final chapter.

What are 'social divisions'?

In one sense, social divisions are so self-evident as hardly to need a formal definition. You do not have to be a professional sociologist to see that society is not only made up of many separate individuals, but that some of these individuals are similar to one another, and so can be differentiated from other people. In some cases, the differences between sets of people are sharply marked, with major contrasts of social conditions and 'life chances' (the chances during a person's lifetime of sharing in society's material and cultural rewards – income, employment, education, health, and so on).

However, if we need to explain why some things are social divisions whereas other differences are not, the picture is suddenly less clear. The variety of situations in which we can use the idea of social divisions means that it does not lend itself to a simple, short definition. For instance, a division does not necessarily separate people into *two* parts: sometimes we need to think of several distinct categories, as for example when noting differences between minority ethnic groups. Social divisions also often overlap, so that an explanation of people's employment positions may mean exploring how far class, gender, ethnicity, age or disability, for example, are contributing factors, in different combinations, to what we can observe happening. Some divisions are sharper than others. Some of them will seem more important than others, although such evaluations will change with time and will also vary from reader to reader.

It follows that, rather than starting with a full scale complex definition, it is probably more helpful to explore the dimensions of 'social division' in more detail. This will be done mainly by using concrete examples, like class, gender, and so on to indicate what we mean by social divisions. At this stage a preliminary sketch of the main features of a definition of social divisions will suffice. (Alternatively, readers who would feel happier starting with an abstract definition might first like to look at the opening pages of the concluding chapter of the book.)

When we talk about social divisions, we mean those substantial differences between people that run throughout our society. A social division has at least two categories, each of which has distinctive material and cultural features. In other words, one category is better positioned than the other, and has a better share of resources because it has greater power over the way our society is organised. Membership of a category is closely associated with a social identity that arises from a sense of being similar to other members, and different from other categories. This affects how people conduct their social interactions. Movement from one category to another is not easy.

However, social divisions are not 'natural': they are the outcome of previous social interactions, events, decisions and struggles. They are 'socially constructed', so that while there are always social divisions, their precise form varies from society to society. Although the distinctions between categories are strong and tend to be longlasting, they are not fixed for all time.

It may help to distinguish between social divisions and several similar terms used in sociology. *Social inequalities* refer to the differences in people's shares of resources (not just money, but chances of health, education, and so on). Such differences are often graduated over a wide range, rather than clearly defining two or more *categories*. Thus while as we saw in our earlier definition, social inequality is part of the idea of social division, it is only one part. Social divisions are similarly related to *social stratification*, but stratification is a term better reserved for specialist discussions of class, status and power. In this case, we can regard social stratification as a subset of social divisions, the latter, wider term placing more emphasis on the many types of divisions, and their capacity to structure identity and interactions. On the other hand, social division is a more focused and restricted idea than *social differentiation*, a general term used to describe the increasing complexity of specialised roles and relationships that are evident as societies grow in size, develop more elaborate social institutions, and utilise new technologies in production.

Social division is therefore a 'middle-range' concept, that offers a way of thinking about society as consisting of intelligible components, based on a set of principles. In the past it used to be said that sociologists were only interested in 'social class', to the exclusion of all other divisions. Over the last quarter of a century, gender and ethnicity both became more central to sociological research. Even more recently other divisions, such as sexuality, and national identity, have become prominent in the sociological repertoire. This growth of new sociological interests (and its associated tendency for increased competition between sociologists to define 'what sociology is *really* about') reflects the way most people's senses of personal identity had begun to draw more strongly on a *range* of social factors (Isin and Wood 1999). This in turn is a product of new ways of life replacing older, more traditional ones associated with former class structures.

In dealing with identity, the emphasis in this book is placed rather on what is shared by people as a social identity, in the sense of what identifies them and brings them together as a group, rather than on personal identity or individual differentiation. The idea of identity is important, but secondary to that of division. It would of course be possible to develop the discussion of identity much further, but that would go beyond the scope of the present book (for a very thoughtful discussion, particularly in the context of ethnicity, see Jenkins 1996).

A common feature of all these older and newly prominent social divisions is that everyone in society is involved: we all have a class, an age, an ethnic identity and so on. Each social division is 'universally inclusive': we all sit on one side or the other of each division, in this category or that, whether it seems to matter much to us or not. A person may not at this precise moment be, say, 'ill', but that is only because that person currently occupies the associated mirror-image category that goes with it: in this case, 'well'. When or if this person becomes adult or ill, her or his currently passive awareness of the social divisions of age or health is likely to be increased!

It is also true that a reconsideration of the other examples given so far will show that social divisions tend to divide people into 'better' or 'worse' categories. Social divisions result in social inequalities. Those in the 'better' categories have more control over their own lives, usually more money, and can generally be seen to lead happier lives. Those occupying the better positions often take their advantages for granted, but nonetheless, social divisions are still all about advantage and disadvantage. They are therefore also about who has the *power* to create and maintain this situation in which inequalities persist.

It follows from this that the various social divisions often connect and overlap, re-enforcing inequalities (although for ease of presentation we shall need to discuss each of the social divisions in its own right, and normally one at a time). In any one situation, a particular social division may assume greater importance, but people do not exist in a social world where only class, or only gender, or only ethnicity matters. It is not that there is a single category which is distinctive. All of us have multiple-membership in a number of such groups, so that depending on one's standpoint, people may be different in one context, but similar in another. Personal links with people in one category may sometimes be at odds with one's differences from them owing to membership of some category on another social division.

The particular combination and balance of memberships also matter. For example, to be white, middle class, male and healthy is not only different from being black, working class, female and sick, but also different from being black, middle class, male and healthy. In other words, as well as looking at each division separately, we need to consider how the various divisions seem able to work in specific combinations and, in a somewhat less coherent way, also work together as a whole to make up what we know as 'society'.

One purpose of studying sociology is to discover the nature of these unequal divisions and categories of people that together add up to a society. How have they come about, how do they relate to one another in a structured way, and what are the consequences of such social divisions? The idea of 'social divisions' addresses the distinctions between sets of people, and also the question that lurks behind such variation: if there are all these differences, why do they continue to operate as they do, and what prevents a society (in most cases) from splitting up into warring factions?

Social divisions as a way of thinking about society

Although this is a book that is mainly about the social inequalities and systems of social divisions that make up contemporary society, a useful starting point for that discussion is the 'individual' and 'social groups'. On the face of it, the most obvious division is between you, the reader, as an *individual* and the rest of human kind. One of the great perceptual paradoxes of life is that humans are at the same time individual entities as well as 'social animals'. Each of us is a physically separate being, with an independent consciousness, experiencing in her or his own particular way a physical world populated with other humans, all different from us but largely behaving in ways that are intelligible to us. Each of us feels unique: one's emotions about, understanding of, and reactions to, new encounters are the outcome of a discrete set of previous experiences that each person, and that person alone, has accumulated.

Yet at the same time, our day-to-day life is a social one. Our very survival depends on a complex, largely invisible, taken-for-granted web of group activities that produce, deliver and regulate the production and consumption of goods and services. We cannot exist in isolation from one another, even after we cease to be infants dependent on our families for support. Just as we pigeon-hole other people, and adapt our own behaviour towards them, so too do *they* adapt to *us*, in a continuing creative process.

It is true, of course, that a very small number of people live as hermits, but such a tiny minority does not challenge our basic observation about our social nature. Even in the much more common cases of people living as 'single person households' – a growing trend in recent years – they still have contact with the outside world. Most people who 'live on their own' in fact work or study outside of the home, in organisations. They do so in densely populated towns and cities, meeting other people as they buy food and clothes or engage in leisure pursuits, and indirectly connecting with other people by electronic and print media. Even if they live alone, many have family and relatives as a potential support. A feeling of loneliness is not the same as being alone or divorced from society; rather it confirms our social nature. The unfortunate cases where there is a real problem of isolation, and too little human contact, only prove the point that we prefer and expect to organise our lives on a collective basis of meeting with, and depending on, other people.

In practice, 'we' lead 'our' lives in social groups defined by what we have in common that is different from other groups; belonging to this one, but not that one; in this society rather than another. Our personal sense of identity draws on how we routinely interact with the members of our groups: it is a *social* identity. We share sets of values and attitudes, a 'culture'. We take our cues for action from those who share that culture through membership of 'our' group, or against those who belong to the 'other' groups, with their rival values and beliefs.

It is not just being a member that counts: *not* being a member of another category is just as important. We define who 'we' are in terms of who we are not. Our encounters with 'others' point to their differences from 'us' and help us to identify our own distinctiveness. 'Our team', 'our gang', 'our kind of music', 'our part of the country' make sense in contrast – and sometimes active opposition – to 'others'.

This does not mean that we mix exclusively with other members of a particular category or that all social interactions with other people are the same. For instance, our impersonal exchanges with shop assistants are not the same as the intense personal involvement with one's family (despite the mandatory cheerful 'Hello!' at the check-out, which has resulted from recent research that customers prefer to be greeted as if they were 'people' with a known identity rather than treated as anonymous punters). Acquaintances are not friends. Nonetheless, even the most minimal of social transactions are still orderly and governed by learned and regularised conventions. The social divisions that define both the *shop assistant* and us as *customers* (for example, in terms of class, gender, age, or ethnicity) set 'rules' for how we may interact.

We do not have to meet face-to-face for rule-driven constraints, inequalities and power to come into play. In the more usual situation where members of a social category do not meet or closely interact as a 'social group', the looser 'category' that is formed as part of the process of social division still imposes constraints on our individual actions. It places us inside a social structure. The common bond of a social identity, which is a mechanism for this, is not exclusively dependent on direct interpersonal interaction with other members of the category. It may equally well be a product of a more abstract awareness of shared circumstances and interests.

To take an example, when we talk about national identity or sexuality, we are dealing with social divisions that separate very large numbers of people, that are complex, and that extend well beyond the individual's direct personal experience. Over and above direct contact, we sense that we also belong to larger, notional categories of people who do not meet together. These 'imagined communities' provide us with identities in terms of which we define ourselves, and others define us (for example as belonging to a particular age group).

The connections between the large-scale and the small-scale categories work both ways: just as we may experience the grand social divisions through localised contacts, so too do the divisions determine our often unconscious selection of friends and mates, careers and places to live. These are overwhelmingly chosen from people like ourselves, on one or more division (for example, most marriages are between people from the same social class). Whatever our reactions to this fact, it is inescapable that we can most easily select for close relationships those whom we are most likely to meet. To the extent that societal arrangements define and physically separate young from old, men from women, upper class from working class, and so on, it is simply much more difficult to mix with people who are different from ourselves, even if that is what we want to do. The case of personal and sexual relationships between young adults, where members from different categories of the social divisions of gender and sexuality *are* meeting, mixing and mating, illustrates how *difficult* cross-boundary contact can be. Even at this most personal of levels, social interaction is still structured and segregated: mixing is still not an open and free process.

As this example also shows, when people from both sides of the social divide meet, their social interactions are rule-bounded. Indeed, not only are they rule-bounded, but the rules establish a social inequality between participants. Membership of a category offers social advantages or disadvantages, *vis-à-vis* members of a matching category. This makes membership of some categories more desirable than others. What reader would seriously argue that it is less advantageous to be young, fit, white and upper class, than to be old, ill, black and working class? People on the 'right' side of the social division line take precedence over others, once their identities are known. Social divisions reflect the imbalance of power between categories: they are *hierarchical*. This is why some forms of social difference are more important than others, and warrant the title 'social division'. Of course other kinds of social difference do exist, and can confer a sense of identity, without being social divisions.

Thus the social divisions with which this book deals are not the small-scale ones, such as a gang, a family, or a work group, nor are all shared consumer lifestyles – like 'surfing' or 'clubbing' – counted as social divisions. Groups may thus be interesting for what they tell about wider processes, without being the core focus in a social division approach. This is not to ignore the fact that when major social divisions such as class or gender are encountered, they are normally *experienced through* membership of smaller collectivities. Divisions are often encountered indirectly, through participation in, say, a group of co-workers or students, and it is within such groups that we are likely to develop face-to-face relationships and social interactions based on the underlying principles of division. However, this process makes most sense when it is seen as the *outcome* of the underlying social division.

Social divisions as 'social rules'

Broader and less tangible social divisions share with smaller, more concrete groups the characteristics of recognisable behaviour patterns and sets of attitudes. For the most part, unwritten rules of conduct apply. 'The rich man in his castle, the poor man at his gate' of the Victorian hymn expressed the imperative that the lower orders should 'know their place' – and keep to it. A more up-to-date set of rules for proper conduct, this time for older people, is cunningly thrown into relief by Jenny Joseph's well-known poem in which she threatens that as an old woman she will:

> wear purple,
> With a red hat which doesn't go, and doesn't suit me.
> And I shall spend my pension on brandy and summer gloves
> And satin sandals, and say we've no money for butter.
>
> (Joseph 1987: 229)

Older women (and note how the poet is defining a role in terms of both age *and* gender) should not run their sticks along the railings, spit, swear in the street, press alarm bells, eat excessive quantities of sausages, or any of the other things included in her poem that other categories of person may do. Despite the poetic threat to begin acting 'out of character' before she grows old, in an interview in the *Guardian* (1998), Joseph has since lamented the continued conformity of her own real life.

Similarly, in his fascinating book about life in a northern English city in the early 1960s (barely more than a generation ago), Jackson (1968) combines compassion with sociological insight to describe the details of the routine daily lives of 'ordinary people' working in the Mill, getting into Grammar School, meeting in the Coffee Bar or 'the Club', standing on the Terraces, or using gossip with family, friends and neighbours to express the right and wrong way of doing things. The book still makes a wonderful read, but it does so now as a *social history*. It is an account of a world we have lost. It tells us about living with greater certainties and more clearly patterned and predictable life experiences, governed by much sharper sets of social conventions specifying how people were expected to lead their lives. It shows how class and other divisions prescribed people's lives.

As post-modern writers have demonstrated, many such 'rules' have lost their force since the break-up of the old monolithic industrial social classes and their traditional ways. Even those rules, and the more subtle ones that have replaced them, should not be thought of as fixed, prescriptive, absolute laws of nature. They are there to be bent or broken. This operates at a variety of levels. Feminists have challenged male dominance, gay groups campaign for the lowering of the age of consent, patients ask for second medical opinions, and young children try to stay up past their bedtimes. As groups and as individuals, people seek to change their social positions in major and minor ways.

That does not mean that rules do not exist, but rather that the codes of conduct around social divisions, although structured and constraining, will not always be encountered in a precise and rigid form. Sometimes they will be implicit, and at others explicit. Conflicts of interests are sometimes played out in nationwide struggles to mobilise state support for particular pieces of single issue legislation, and subsequently in the courts. Equally, disputes can arise between two people from different categories whose lives together throw up contradictions in what they believe is 'the right thing' for 'people like us' to do. There is no uniform way to encounter the 'rules' that are intrinsic to social divisions.

Nonetheless, exploring social rules and their infractions helps us to identify boundaries and continuities in social divisions. A focus on social divisions offers an organised way of seeing and thinking about society; a 'perspective' for finding out what is going on and understanding social outcomes. It enables us to describe and to explain our social world, starting from the position that society is not a neatly integrated, tidy, consistent and, in particular, simple thing. Nothing in human society is 'given', fixed for all time or absolute. All social arrangements are worth examining, whether we are seeking explanations as specialists in sociology, or as students of health, welfare or social policy who want to use sociology's concepts and methods to situate our own work. Social divisions are important cleavages in society that affect us all. Social divisions are not just about society at a national or global level, but about what separates one individual from the next.

Social divisions in a post-modern world?

The relative importance of the various social divisions is then both situationally imposed by those around us and personally selected by ourselves. In the past there have been periods when the social behaviour expected as a result of major social divisions was much more clearly defined and conformed to more uniformly. Although individual lives involved unique personal autobiographies, their broad shape was socially determined. Sons followed fathers 'down the Pit'. Daughters became wives and mothers. Old people did not wear purple with red hats.

These certainties (or constraints, depending on how one wishes to see them) are starkly illustrated by photographs of male workers in northern

industrial cities, going home from the shipyards or factories in the 1930s and
40s, at trade union or political meetings, or 'on the Terraces'. Their uniformity
of social condition is symbolised in their 'uniform'. Scarcely one does not
wear a flat cap and a 'muffler' (the muffler was a small scarf worn at the neck
because British 'working men' – as distinct from 'white-collar' office workers
or American denim-clad 'blue-collar' manual workers – could not wear collars
on their weekday work shirts that would get dirty, worn and in any case be
uncomfortable). Today, what we wear to and from work, or at leisure, is more
likely to be an individual statement about how we want people to see us, in
terms of more specific personal identities or memberships of other categories.

The older rigidities can be exaggerated. Not all workers lived in northern
industrial towns, worked in heavy industry, or followed their local football
team. The upheaval of the late stages of the Industrial Revolution, two World
Wars, the Great Depression, massive technological changes in transport,
housing and engineering production, the wholesale creation of new types of
occupations, together with political and social welfare reforms, make it difficult to talk convincingly about a single period of 'modernity', even in the first
half of this century. How much more difficult to see a coherent period
reaching back to the fifteenth century (Kumar 1978; Hall *et al.* 1992). Calls
to see our world as 'post-modern' are frequently based on an over-simplistic
understanding of history.

Nonetheless, there are significant differences between an earlier 'modern
period' of pre-war mass production and the social arrangements that went
with it (see Chapter 2) and our contemporary society. In particular, it is
generally accepted that, for most people, life in the first half of this century
involved far fewer *choices* of behaviour. Our own society, with its media access
to other cultures and ways of life, and its greater separation of workplace,
home and leisure, is less prescriptive. With national economies becoming
increasingly interconnected in the process of globalisation, new possibilities
have been opened up as our secure, localised, little worlds and fixed positions
in a traditional labour market have been eroded.

The shift from manufacturing production to a services economy destroyed
old jobs and created new ones. As a result of this 'occupational transition', the
proportion of people working in manual jobs has since halved. Most women
with young children are now in paid employment. Most of us stay on in
education well past the minimum school leaving age, because more jobs now
require advanced skills. Our experiences are broader and our encounters with
different ways of life more common, but we have a greater sense of uncertainty about the future in the face of these new circumstances. The old
localised and relatively rigid patterns have declined.

By contrast, the more fragmented society of our own times offers greater opportunities (and for most people, the money) to select from a multitude of styles, groups and identities. We have greater opportunities to select, from among the partial social identities that social divisions give, the particular version we want. Consumption and lifestyle can be manipulated. In a 'global society' we like to believe that we have a new freedom, that we can 'be what we consume'.

We can distinguish two processes here. On the one hand, the contemporary world cannot be explained simply as a set of nations or localities, because multinational corporations have established a world economy of production and consumption as part of the boom in world trade since the mid-1960s. Goods are designed, produced as parts in factories and by suppliers around the world, assembled in one country and marketed in all the others. Increasingly, national boundaries do not contain a whole production process, so that it cannot be controlled by a single country. These changes, together with satellite communication systems, international tourism and sports, and the recognition of 'global issues' like the environment and health (for example AIDS), have led towards a homogenisation of our cultures and lifestyles. In this sense, we are *less* divided from each other: we are all consumers of a world economy, in which national differences are less important (although of course huge differences in *per capita* income and life expectancy between 'rich' and 'poor' nations remain).

On the other hand, our patterns of consumption provide ways of introducing new differentiations between ourselves. Within the underlying tendency for multinational corporations' products to be no longer designed for local markets (the 'European Car', the 'World Car'), and for more and more of our lives to be 'commodified' into patterns of consumption involving purchases under the influence of marketing, we can manipulate our own consumption to build and signal our identities. Rising affluence and shorter working hours leave more money and time to consume goods and leisure activities. Better-off groups can use 'positional' goods as markers to display their distinctiveness. Some writers, such as Saunders (1990) and Dunleavy (1980) have even suggested that new lines of social division can be drawn to mark 'consumption cleavages' between home-owners and renters, between those still dependent on core social welfare services (housing, state schooling, the NHS, welfare benefits) and the rest, and between those who work in the public sector and others. At the same time, these potential new cleavages are weakened by less wide-scale differentiations, as we can exercise a greater choice over what we consume or do, acting out our daydreams through our purchases and fashions.

This freedom of action has to be balanced by the recognition that even our choices operate within frameworks. Those in poorly paid, insecure, unskilled manual jobs cannot easily 'choose' to lead the life of, say, the computer nerd or the salsa queen, let alone become cosmopolitan jet-setters: these lifestyles cost money. Other groups are constrained by non-material factors. The physically disabled are disabled from having access to vast tracts of the buildings in which consumption lifestyles are acted out. Women cannot simply behave like, and 'pass' as, men. These various social divisions may be complex, but they remain powerful discriminators. It is for this reason that this book does not take globalised consumption patterns, or 'consumption cleavages' to be major social divisions. Globalisation and consumption are important in their own right, but social life is still far from being totally homogenised.

Because we do still live in a fragmented world, our knowledge of others is necessarily incomplete. We may all be members of one 'society', but we live our lives as members of large, imagined categories or groups with boundaries between them: middle class and working class; men and women; young and old. On the other hand none of us belongs only to a single category: we belong to a whole series of such identities. While within limits we can manipulate these identities according to our particular circumstances of the moment, it is membership of, and identification with, groups that makes up social life. Social divisions, then, blur not only because each is not a dichotomy, nor because a post-modern world offers a bedazzling variety of choices, but also because overlapping social divisions shape people's lives.

The complexity of social divisions

In his influential book, *The Sociological Imagination*, C. Wright Mills made two important distinctions: between 'personal troubles' and 'public issues', and between 'individuals' and 'history'. In the first case, Mills is making the point that we can interpret what happens to us in life either on a personal basis, or as part of a wider social process. To be unemployed is a genuine problem for somebody, whether it is 'their own fault' or not. If we were talking about one unemployed person among a city population of 100,000 all in paid employment, we might look to personal circumstance to understand (and possibly remedy) the individual's misfortune. But in times of high and rapidly rising unemployment, such as in the 1980s under a Conservative government, it is not credible to blame well over three million people for being themselves the cause of their condition, and to expect each one to seek individual remedies. In those latter years, unemployment began to assume the status of a social division.

Similarly, 'history' is not simply the record of kings and queens, but of social and economic movements and changes. Mills does not want us to forget the individual, but rather also to see the importance of the social processes that shape each life. He is concerned with systems, but sees systems as also made up of people with differing amounts of power. By addressing the inter-play of systems and people, he seeks to avoid the two extremes of a sociology exclusively of individuals, and a sociology of social structures where the people are just pre-programmed robots (1970: 15–17).

The similarities between Mills' sociological perspective and the one outlined so far in this chapter are obvious. If anything, we have so far stressed the individual and small groups more than Mills did, but that will be balanced by what follows. The contributors to this book start from the powerful forces that tend to constrain and influence us, rather than the things that we can directly control ourselves. The emphasis tends to be on the patterned way we are shaped, rather than on the way we can modify our own actions. However, whereas Mills made his point in terms of two dichotomies, with a neat contrast between personal and public, and between individual and history (which made them sharper, easy to remember, and therefore all the more influential), the idea of social divisions is a little more complicated.

In the first place, we have seen that there are not one or two social divisions, but many. Mills' 'public issues' category is greatly sub-divided. This book deals with eight major social divisions, but there are others that could legiti-mately claim a chapter in a bigger volume: poverty, religion, kinship, political affiliation, educational qualifications, consumer lifestyle, to name just half a dozen more (and which, indeed, are discussed as aspects of the major divi-sions in later chapters). The selection here is the outcome of a combination of personal judgements about which are the most important (and which there-fore largely determine what is happening in some of those omitted) and which topics loom large in sociology, as indicated by its core curriculum.

To take an example, at first sight it may seem surprising that there is no chapter in this book on 'social exclusion'. To be socially *excluded* sounds, on the face of it, to be something akin to being socially *divided* off from sets of other people and ways of life. However when we unpack the notion of social exclusion, we soon discover that it is a political shorthand for the conse-quences of poverty, and the particular New Labour policy approach designed to provide 'joined-up' administrative solutions. At the time of writing, most exclusion research has presented statistical accounts of lack of resources, but little sociological analysis of who is being actually excluded from what, and whether it is the resource deficit *per se* that is producing these effects (Room 1995; Levitas 1998; Lee and Murie 1999). In as far as we currently have explanations of exclusion, they are mainly couched in terms of employment, class, ethnicity, disability, gender, community structures and health inequalities. In other words, to explain social exclusion, we must first start with an understanding of the social divisions that produce it, and in turn are reinforced by processes of exclusion. There is therefore no chapter devoted to social exclusion, as the main topics for each chapter make up what are the major social divisions in contemporary society.

This means that the picture of a divided society we draw is a complex one. In practice, we can artificially simplify it by dealing mainly with one division at a time, bringing together ideas and evidence about its particular set of categories from the extensive specialist research carried out by sociologists in each of our selected areas in turn. This enables us to explore each division in some depth, and see the richness of its details.

The plan of the book

We can begin to demonstrate these points by looking at the titles of the chapters in this book, which indicate the range of key social divisions, starting with sociology's 'big three' of social class, gender and ethnicity, and going on to include national identity, age, childhood, sexuality, disability, health and community. Each of the chapters discusses the ideas we use to think about these divisions, together with the material, status and even mundane inequalities between the categories. However, we shall also see that it is not possible to keep each division tidily in its own chapter. On the one hand, class, gender and ethnicity are themes running throughout the book. It is not an accident that these three come as the first chapters, and that each is longer than the later contributions.

On the other hand, the chapters on health and community in particular involve consideration of the other social divisions. While health and illness, or rural and urban locations, are valid social divisions in their own right, health and community can also be seen as 'arenas' in which the consequences of the various social divisions are acted out, and come together in people's lives. The effect these have on our various senses of social identity is not always straightforward.

It is also the case that the social conditions we are trying to analyse have changed considerably, not least in the last few decades, a point that John Scott makes strongly in his discussion of class and stratification (Chapter 2). The vocabulary of 'social class' (the idea of upper, middle and working classes) did not emerge until the eighteenth and early nineteenth centuries. Manual workers have decreased from over 80 per cent of the workforce before the First World War to less than 45 per cent in the 1990s. The intermediate classes of professionals, managers and white-collar workers have grown and seen their work position radically changed, while what was called 'Society'(the exclusive, expensive social life of a small upper-class set) disappeared in the 1950s.

This does not mean that 'class is dead'. Drawing on an explanation of Weber's original conception of social stratification, Scott demonstrates continued *class* differentials in material conditions, security of employment, health, and life expectancy. Arguing that, when most people today talk in popular parlance of 'class', they are actually referring to status and lifestyle, he presents a distinctive occupations-based account of the three main class groupings – the subordinate (manual, wage-paid) classes; the intermediate (salaried or self-employed) classes, and the 'advantaged classes' (of capital and property owners, and employers). This shows that despite social change, the social division of class survives in new forms. Occupational transition, culture, identity and consumption may blur the picture, but it is the underlying class situations that still determine life chances.

Occupations also loom large in Pamela Abbott's analysis of gender, which she develops through a discussion of current patterns of work, education and poverty, and how they link with class and ethnicity. Work is pivotal to the position of women, representing both the public domain from which they have been largely excluded, an arena in which the struggle for equal pay and against the 'glass ceiling' is carried on, and in the form of unpaid, domestic work, representing much of the day-by-day oppression of women by men. She demonstrates a variety of gender-based material inequalities, concerning employment and pensions, state benefits, labour market access, 'home life' (in which mothers are the first 'to go without'), and the poverty of the lone parent family, as the products of a patriarchal system of social division which, although more oppressive of women, constrains men as well.

The strength of her analysis is the integration of past and present ideologies and conceptions of female roles, with contemporary social inequalities. This is exemplified both in terms of the development of sociological ideas, and in the way *improving* school performance by *girls* has recently been re-problematised as the *declining* performance of *boys* as a precursor to their youth unemployment. The 'natural' role of women, and 'gender segregation', take on a particular significance when seen as related aspects of social division, interacting with ethnicity and class. As she comments on this interconnection, in the past:

> it was mainly middle-class women who were excluded from paid employment, while in the late twentieth century, Afro-Caribbean women are most likely to experience public patriarchy and Muslim/British women private patriarchy. (Chapter 3)

Thus whereas at first sight one might expect gender to be exclusively a social division of two halves, Abbott unpacks much of the complexity of its categories. We have already observed that ethnicity is far more complicated than a simplistic dichotomy, and David Mason's chapter – carefully examining the notion of ethnic identity, and demonstrating differences between the ethnic groups, and their various experiences of discrimination – can be seen as a natural partner to the chapter on gender. It also draws a deliberate contrast to Scott's account of class: we cannot start from material circumstances, argues Mason, because:

> only in situations of extreme segregation will these kinds of information offer us good clues to people's ethnic status and, even then, few would argue that these characteristics represent the essence of their ethnicity. (Chapter 4)

In other words, while unemployment, earnings, type of work, and location are important (and duly documented in his chapter) the real issue lies in the meaning of ethnic identity. This not only requires an appreciation of where, historically, ideas of 'race' and 'ethnicity' have come from, and been adapted in this country, but also how discrimination has played a part in shaping identities. As the Fourth Policy Studies Institute Report found, 'black' teenagers define themselves as much in terms of job, education or religion, as any physical characteristics – but tend to think of themselves of 'black' when they are in contact with white people. Despite the disadvantaged positions of the minority ethnic groups that he describes, Mason is, on the whole, optimistic about the prospects for ethnic identity to be negotiable and open to change, not least as social conditions evolve and new senses of identity – the black *woman*, my *religion*, our *specific* minority ethnic group – enter the sociological and public consciousness.

This discussion of ethnic identity leads naturally into the next chapter. National identities are bound up with ethnicity but as David McCrone shows, this needs to be seen in terms of political and historical processes. The physical boundaries of a society may be governed as a single state, but those living there may have a sense of identity with only one part of it. Using contemporary events, he asks under what conditions do people call themselves, say, 'British' rather than English, Welsh, or Scots, or for that matter, say they are from 'Yorkshire' or 'the Highlands'. These expressions are markers of social division – and indeed, so much so that they form the basis for political mobilisation – which are not so much to do with material differences as with cultural symbols and 'imagined communities'. McCrone is therefore less concerned with tangible material differentials across geographical areas, than explanations that draw on political ideas. He locates the nationalism issue in the lack of fit between 'nation' and 'state', a problem of no small significance whether illustrated by governance and devolution, or by the violence of civil unrest in Northern Ireland, Yugoslavia, or other parts of Europe.

The following five chapters can be seen as a set. They present further examples of social divisions, around processes that superficially seem to be physical or biological. In each case an alternative sociological analysis is developed, challenging common sense assumptions, and using the idea of social divisions to explore the current social positions of those in the less-advantaged categories. In so far as these chapters can also be thought of as equivalent examples of social divisions, readers may choose to follow their own interests, by concentrating on particular topics.

Chapter 6 deals with age as a principle of social organisation, and in particular with old age. All human societies have used age as a basis for distinguishing groups: we operate with a potentially confusing range of concepts – chronological age, cohort, generation, age group, and so on. John Vincent draws on history and anthropology to explain the differences between these terms, and how demographic changes have set up new tensions within families between older and younger members. The divisions between the two, and among different groups of older people, are demonstrated through sharp contrasts of material circumstances. Together with his concerns with gender and class differences among the elderly, this connects directly into current social policy debates over how future pensions are to be financed. Vincent also addresses the social construction of ageism. His discussion of how our ideas shape our views of the older citizens echoes that of disability in a later chapter.

There is also a natural link to Stevi Jackson and Sue Scott's chapter on childhood, the other end of the age range. Here, too, the idea of 'childhood' is not taken as a given, but systematically explored as a social construction. Most earlier research (including that influential in the caring professions) has adopted a psychological development, or preparation for adulthood, model. This has not taken children's own experiences of being divided off into a subordinate position properly into account. Our own pre-Industrial Revolution history, when children were more integrated into work, have been forgotten, which adds to our ethnocentric view of children as needing to be protected from 'growing up too fast', and the 'evils of the adult world'. The authors' sociological framework allows an extensive discussion of current issues about child safety, abuse, parental powers, and the confusing transition points into 'maturity'. Together with the comparisons of ethnic and class differences in models of childhood, this section will be of particular interest to those with a vocation interest in the well-being of children.

The same authors develop a similar analysis in respect of sexuality in Chapter 8. Their first task is to dismantle the idea that heterosexuality is 'natural', 'normal', or universally the same. Sexuality is socially constructed, through institutions such as (male-dominated) marriage, and through the meanings and feelings that arise in and from social interactions. What is regarded as sexuality and sex depends on the society in which it exists: what is regarded as acceptable or deviant is largely a matter of power relations. Class and ethnic divisions mean there is no single shared 'normality'. Using examples such as sex education, the sex industry, and current fashions to think of the 'successful self' in sexual terms, Scott and Jackson argue that normative heterosexuality, rather than being a simple biological process, makes more sense as a form of gender-based control. Instead of seeing sex as 'special area' of human life, it needs to be re-integrated into the mainstream of social life.

The idea of integration, together with access, dominates Mark Hyde's chapter on disability. The disabled 'have unique and particularly intense experiences of deprivation' (Chapter 9); economically disadvantaged, excluded from mainstream social activities and stigmatised. In making a strong case for disability to be seen as a key social division, Hyde argues that disabled people's social exclusion comes not from their disability, but from the way society interprets it primarily as a medical problem. An alternative social model, and different social arrangements, would release disabled people from the sharp social division they currently encounter. Access to education and jobs would reduce dependency on welfare and 'charity', and offer an escape from the poverty that is so frequently associated with disability. Access to the political process has the potential to bring about change, not least as a mechanism by which to challenge negative stereotyping. Access to places – and many disabled people do not fit the stereotype of being wheelchair-bound – would reduce the physical division between the disabled and not-disabled.

The discussion of the social circumstances of the disabled leads naturally to the wider issue of health. This is one of the areas in which there is a long history of social inequality research, with an extensive debate about how health and (particularly class-based) inequality are related. Here, the purpose of the chapter is not simply to show that divisions exist, but to demonstrate the *interplay* of social divisions, and how there can be competing explanations of what people experience in their everyday lives. Judy Payne and Geoff Payne set this discussion in the context of 'the new public health', arguing that a medical or 'life style' approach fails to address the connections between illness and the poverty, unemployment, bad housing and poor services that make up the daily experience of the more disadvantaged sector of society. They also attempt to extend the idea of social division from this structural and material view, considering the divisions between health workers and their clients, and between the ill and the well. The interconnection with the other social divisions runs through the analysis.

Graham Crow and Catherine Maclean's chapter on community is also one that brings a fresh look at social divisions, rather than treating 'community' as a social division *per se*. In this sense, like the health chapter, their contribution differs from the earlier chapters, although they too bring out the importance of identity, conferred by membership of a community (whether of place, occupation or imagined community of attachment). Studies of place-based communities have richly documented the 'us' and 'them' divisions between incomers and locals over housing and local politics, which mobilise class, ethnic and gender identities. But as with the other chapters, the authors try to escape conventional wisdom, drawing attention to the normative pressures of 'community', the prevalence of migration, and the significance for identification of the contacts with the outside world. As with the health chapter, but in a more inclusive way, they discuss 'life in the round', showing the shift and play of social divisions during the dynamics of daily life.

The Conclusion revisits the core idea of a social division approach. Using the earlier chapters it establishes a formal definition of social division, and addresses the questions of cohesion and continuity that divisions pose. A contrast is drawn between this and other perspectives from sociological theory. This is a more conceptual chapter, and while there is an element of reprise, no new data on divisions are introduced.

Social divisions begin to make sense once we know what is being divided up, how it is divided, and what are the results of the divisions for our lives. This collection of essays provides a framework for analysing society, and thinking critically about its major elements. It testifies to the range and quality of contemporary sociological research, demonstrating the relevance of sociology for understanding contemporary social conditions. If the combination of the chapters also helps us to escape from the narrow confines of small sociological compartments, into a broader view, so much the better. Despite its analytical tone, this is a book about engaging with the world. The point of the sociological analyses is to promote a better understanding of society and social processes, so that we can operate more effectively. As Albrow has observed, sociology has no reason to be ashamed in 'staking its claim to enhancing the competence of its students to meet the demands of living and working' (1993: 241).

CHAPTER 2

Class and Stratification

JOHN SCOTT

In our everyday lives, many of us use the language of class to refer to a social hierarchy and 'knowing your place' within it. Class is a matter of 'breeding' and of social background. It is reflected in our attitudes and our lifestyles, our accents, and our ways of dressing. For this reason, class has also come to be seen as something that is outmoded and old-fashioned. Class distinctions are tied to a world of tradition and subordination that no longer exists, and the language of class is incompatible with contemporary attitudes and values. Many journalists and social commentators hold this view. These writers see the persistence of class-ridden attitudes and the continued use of the word 'class' itself, as evidence that Britain has failed to adopt the more modern – or perhaps 'post-modern' – approach to life found in such apparently class-less societies as the United States.

Sociologists, on the other hand, have more often used the word class to describe *economic* divisions and inequalities, especially those that are rooted in *property* and *employment* relations: in other words a particular kind of social division. This has led them to question whether Britain actually is any more, or any less, of a class society than the United States or the countries of continental Europe and other parts of the world. All these societies are unequal societies – they show vast and continuing differences in income, wealth, and property ownership – and so all can be described, in these terms, as class societies. Other differences of culture, attitudes, and life style are not disregarded, but they are seen as pointing to quite different kinds of social division. In sociological analyses, therefore, the economic relations of class are often contrasted with cultural matters, in particular with 'status', those more visible 'styles of life' led by people, and which affect their standing in the community. What non-sociologists describe in the everyday language of class, sociologists describe in the language of status.

Not all sociologists take this point of view, of course. There are few things on which sociologists are unanimous. For some, especially in the United States, class should, in fact, be seen as a matter of culture and identity, and not a matter of underlying material inequalities. According to these sociolo-

20

gists, cultural change has indeed undermined the power and relevance of the language of class. 'Class is dead', it is a thing of the past, even though economic and other inequalities may persist.

Even if it were true that class is dead, and that we wished to argue for an alternative framework of analysis, we would still need to know what class was supposed to have been before we could confine it to the grave of history. Unfortunately, as we have already noted, class does not mean the same thing to everybody. There is a considerable task in clarifying the idea of class, before we can make an informed judgement on its importance or lack of importance as a social division.

Indeed, in any field, linguistic confusion is a recipe for misunderstanding. If progress in sociological understanding is to be made, and if sociologists are to contribute to public debates, there needs to be some common ground in the language and concepts that they use. We need concepts that will help us to understand the many inequalities in resources, health, and education that exist in contemporary societies. This will help us to see how they relate to other social divisions, such as those discussed elsewhere in this book; in particular, gender, sexuality, ethnicity, and age. We must also agree about which aspects of these inequalities can legitimately be described and analysed as aspects of class relations. Only then would it be possible to investigate whether these class inequalities and class differences are increasing or declining in importance in particular societies. This kind of investigation raises very directly the relationship between the *facts* of class and their *interpretation* by commentators and by those who experience them in their everyday lives.

This chapter therefore begins with a conceptual exploration of the terms required to make some sense of this kind of social stratification. This exploration returns to the works of the classic sociologists. It does this not for reasons of 'ancestor worship', but in order to recapture the important distinctions that they recognised and that have been lost in many contemporary debates over class and stratification.

Conceptualising class and stratification

Social inequalities are central to any understanding of social stratification; but social stratification itself consists of more than simply inequalities in life chances. The concept of social stratification as a particular form of social division emphasises the idea that individuals are distributed among the levels or *layers* of a social hierarchy because of their *economic* relations. These layers or 'social strata' are real social groupings, forged together through both their economic relations and their associated social relations and interactions; groupings that are able to reproduce themselves over time. Work in similar occupations, marriage, kinship, and informal interaction connect individuals together and build up boundaries that close one stratum and divide it off from another.

They are not simply statistical categories defined in an unequal distribution of resources. They are not just the 'top 10 per cent' or 'bottom 30 per cent' of a distribution of income and wealth. Social strata are a kind of social grouping. They are a particular form of what elsewhere (Chapter 1) has been called the 'categories' that comprise a social division. In this sense social stratification is a typical social division, but differing from others in that it is solidly based in economic relations.

The interconnections between social stratification and other divisions like gender, sexuality, ethnicity, and age are very complex. Social inequalities are invariably structured by all of these social divisions: inequalities are gendered, sexualised, racialised, and aged. On the one hand, each division has an independent importance in sociological analysis, as do relations of social stratification. Social exclusion and discrimination on the basis of gender and ethnicity, for example, generate inequalities in life chances.

On the other hand, this often operates through a process that combines exclusion in one division with exclusion in another, so that these other social divisions can become crucial conditions for the formation of social strata. This comes out clearly both in the other individual chapters in this book, and particularly in the chapters on health and community that deal with how social divisions interact in ordinary life. However, this does not mean that the social inequalities arising from other divisions should simply be equated with stratification. 'Social strata' as referred to in this chapter exist only when the economic and social relations of people tie them into larger, more complex and more permanent structures that take the form of a system of 'social stratification'.

To develop these arguments, I want to return to some distinctions made by Max Weber (1914, 1920) in his comparative investigations into economy and society. In two places in his work – in an early draft and in an incomplete re-draft of this – Weber set out an argument that has been massively influential in contemporary sociology. He identified three distinct aspects or dimensions to the distribution of power within societies. These are class, status, and authority or command. Weber's discussions concentrate on class and status and their relationship to 'party', which has led to the common misunderstanding that his three dimensions were class, status and party. His third dimension is better understood as 'authority', as I shall shortly show. This misunderstanding, due also in part to problems of translation, is not however my main concern here (a more extensive discussion of this particular point can be found in Fulcher and Scott (1999: Ch. 15) while the rest of this section draws on Scott (1996: Ch. 2)). My main concern is to distinguish the core elements and how they relate to social stratification, as set out in the next two sections.

For Weber, class, status, and authority are aspects of power, each of which has a separate effect on the production of life chances. He defined *class relations* as those that result from the distribution of property and other resources in capital, product, and labour markets. It is the possession or non-possession of economic resources that gives people a specific capacity or power to acquire income and assets and, therefore, to enhance their life chances in all sorts of ways. Company shares yield an investment income and can be sold at a profit on the stock market, while educational credentials or technical expertise may give people the opportunity to earn a higher income in the labour market. The distribution of economic resources, then, defines the various class situations that individuals can occupy in a society. A class situation exists wherever the distribution of resources is such that a particular category of individuals have similar abilities to secure advantages (and disadvantages) for themselves through the use of their marketable resources. A person's class situation is a causal component in determining both their life chances and the interests that they have in protecting and enhancing these life chances.

In setting out his view of class, Weber quite deliberately sought to build on Marx's work, much of which he took as valid. Marx saw property ownership, and especially property in the means of production, as the basis of class relations. For him, it was the ownership or non-ownership of factories, machines, and land that determined people's life chances and shaped their actions. Marx recognised just two principal class situations in contemporary societies, those of capitalists and proletarians. Capitalist class situations rest on the ownership and control of capital. Their occupants include industrial entrepreneurs, bankers, and landowners, as well as those who simply live on an income from company shares. Proletarian class situations, on the other hand, involve a lack of ownership and are based on the exercise of labour power as an employee. They include those of people involved in skilled work, manual labour, or office work; in other words, people involved in sets of similar types of occupations.

Debates largely within Marxism have modified this basic picture of two classes, leading to the recognition of lines of differentiation among capitalists and among proletarians, and to the identification of a whole array of 'intermediate' class situations. The proletarian class, being larger, has more obviously been subdivided, and arguments about the relative merits of how this subdivision should be carried out, and which resulting classification scheme of the class situations is best, have been extensive. The most important of these debates in recent work are covered in the debates surrounding the work of Wright (1985, 1989, 1997). These debates are very much in line with Weber's suggestion that it is necessary to recognise a great variety of class situations in any society. In later sections, I will show how it is possible to build on these ideas to investigate contemporary class divisions.

Differentiating class, 'status' and 'authority'

One of the things that Weber objected to in Marxism was its economic determinism. He pointed out that non-economic factors were important, alongside the economic, in determining life chances and, therefore, in shaping patterns of social stratification. The first of these non-economic factors that he discussed was status. He saw divisions of status as originating in the distribution of prestige or social honour within a community. People judge one another as superior or inferior in relation to the values that they hold in common, and so a person's status is their standing or reputation in the eyes of others. When people act in conformity with these values, they build up a good reputation and, therefore, a high status in their community. Those who deviate from these values are accorded a lower status and may be excluded from the benefits and advantages given to others.

Most typically, a person's status follows from what Weber called the 'style of life'. The ways that people carry out the tasks that are associated with their occupations and their sex-gender roles, and the customs and practices that they follow as members of ethnic and other social groups define their particular and distinct styles of life (Chapter 4). Thus, manual workers, women or Asians may have a low status because of the way that their style of life is perceived and evaluated. 'Dirty' or routine work may be seen as undesirable or demeaning, a feminine style of life may be valued less highly than a masculine one, or the Asian way of life may be devalued.

What Weber called 'status' corresponds very closely to what in everyday life is often referred to by non-sociologists as 'class'. A style of life involves specific types of dress and bodily adornment, types and sizes of house, areas of residence, clothing, accent, methods of cooking and eating, and so on. These markers of social identity – symbols of status – are often of great importance. Much public discussion of 'class', however, tends to highlight status and to concentrate on its relatively minor and superficial aspects, so disregarding and disguising economic class.

However, for a more sophisticated and sociological analysis, we need to recognise that inequalities in life chances must be seen as reflecting the effects of *both* class and status situations. Status situation, like class situation, is a causal component in life chances. Class situations comprise the property and employment relations through which control over marketable resources is organised, while status situations are the communal relations through which prestige is given to a particular life style. Both operate to determine the life chances of individuals. An occupation, for example, involves both specific employment relations in the labour market *and* a particular level of occupational prestige (Parkin 1971). These two aspects of occupational position operate interdependently in determining life chances, and their separate effects can be difficult to disentangle. To claim that class and status should be seen as two separate and distinct dimensions of stratification is not to prejudge their relative importance. This is always an empirical matter. The distinction does, however, allow questions about the salience of class to be formulated with much greater clarity than is the case in much discussion of the subject.

Weber's third dimension of stratification is to be found in his discussions of authority and bureaucracy. Authority relations in states and business enterprises, he argued, involve relations of command in which one person is empowered to give orders to another. What Weber had to say on this can best be understood by introducing the concept of a 'command situation' to parallel his concepts of class situation and status situation. A command situation is a causal component in life chances that results from differentials of authority in formal organisations.

Weber's analysis of domination and authority gave him an acute understanding of the formation of ruling minorities in the top command situations of political, economic and other hierarchies, but, for all his insights, the conceptualisation of ruling minorities was one of the least developed parts of his sociology. His insights were independently developed, so far as social stratification is concerned, by Mosca (1896, 1923) and Pareto (1916: 1430). Their particular view was that the crucial social division was between a dominant minority and a subordinate majority. In other words, there were essentially two groups, a small one at the top of society, and a large one below it. They believed that this was an inevitable consequence of any social organisation of authority and that authority relations involve the formation of ruling minorities or what they called 'elites'. While we do not have to adopt their model of a society based on elites and masses, it illustrates how the delineation of class situation, status situation, and command situation is the crucial basis for any analysis of patterns of the social inequalities that comprise social stratification.

Occupations and social stratification

In the previous section, in distinguishing class, status and command in contemporary societies, I have already noted that occupations are central to the analysis of class and status situations. Occupations also lie at the core of structures of command. Occupations are positions in economic and social organisations in which each occupation has a different degree of authority, or lack of authority, over others. In all companies, government agencies, or charities, people in some occupations direct and manage the work of those in other occupations. Any particular occupation also rests on specific marketable skills or resources, and has a particular level of occupational prestige. *A sociological analysis of the class, status, and command situations of contemporary societies is, for many purposes, a mapping of the occupational structures.* Investigating social inequalities involves assessing the relative importance of class, status, and command in the life chances that are associated with particular occupations and groups of occupations.

Sociological research has used a variety of 'class schemes' to represent this, taking occupation as an indicator of class situation, in order to study classes as 'employment aggregates' (Crompton 1998: Ch. 4). This work is extremely important – and I make use of it below. It is sometimes held that the usefulness of particular class schemes and their advantages over others are to be judged on purely pragmatic grounds: whichever has the best *predictive* capacity for dealing with whatever is being studied is to be preferred (Erikson and Goldthorpe 1993. See the criticism in Morris and Scott 1996). However, the implication of my argument is that class schemes must by judged on theoretical as well as empirical grounds, and that they must be seen as more or less adequate attempts to offer a coherent and operational concept of class. It is Weber's framework that offers the best basis for this latter requirement.

A system of social stratification can be thought of as consisting of a number of separate social strata, layered one above another. Each social stratum contains people in similar distinctive class, status and command situations. Each stratum is a social group with boundaries marking off those inside from those outside. The group contains a cluster of social positions, with individuals moving both between these social positions and also interacting (or 'associating') with each other as they do so. They may modify their own and their children's social position by marriage or changing jobs ('circulating' within the boundary of their group). Through kinship and close intimate interactions such as leisure-time socialising and club membership, they associate with other people like themselves who make up their social stratum. For these reasons, both occupational mobility and patterns of association must be seen as central to strata formation.

These movements, on the one hand of individuals from one occupation to another, and on the other hand of interactions among those engaged in particular occupations, define the key boundaries within a system of social stratification. Occupational categories are a part of the same social stratum if there is easy and frequent movement between them. This might involve the lifetime mobility of individuals between types of occupations (called *intra*-generational mobility), or it might involve occupational movement between generations, for example from father to son (*inter*-generational mobility: see Payne 1989). Equally, it might involve frequent intermarriage between those in similar occupations, or their interaction with one another in leisure-time activities. Whenever these relations of circulation and association reinforce one another in such a way as to create regular and established patterns of connection among the people working in a set of occupations, the connected occupations form part of a single stratum.

Occupations fall into the same social stratum when they are connected through chains of frequent and relatively easy circulation and association. They fall into different social strata when they are connected – if at all – only through infrequent circulation and association. Boundaries between social strata exist wherever patterns of circulation and association produce divisions between categories of occupations. In sociological research, individuals are allocated to the occupations that combine together various class, status and command situations; rates of mobility and social interaction must be examined in order to uncover how those occupations are clustered together into social strata.

Marx held, for example, that the occupants of capitalist situations form a distinct social stratum because they circulate freely around the different forms of capital, because they are involved in extensive networks of intermarriage, and because their children are able to inherit accumulated capital and to enjoy the advantaged life chances that it generates. In the same way, he saw occupants of proletarian situations as forming a separate social stratum because they move from one type of work to another similar type, and from work to unemployment, they marry other workers, and their children have no choice but to try to enter paid employment.

One perennial topic in studies of stratification has been the question of whether the individual or the family household should be taken as the unit of analysis (Goldthorpe 1983; Abbott and Sapsford 1987; Scott 1994a). This debate has been fired in recent years by feminist criticisms of those conventional approaches to stratification that have allocated women to social classes according to the occupational position of their husbands (Stanworth 1984). Proponents of this approach claim that women's class attitudes and behaviour can be adequately 'approximated' by this method (Erikson and Goldthorpe

1993).This pragmatic argument offers little theoretical purchase on class, and its critics have rightly argued that women's work must be considered independently of men's work and must play an equal part in determining positions in a system of social stratification.

When considering the class, status, and command situations of individuals, it is of the utmost importance that each individual is classified on the basis of his or her own occupation. However, this is not the end of the matter. When considering the formation of social *strata* (rather than just the occupancy of class, status, and command *situations*), the social relations among members of family households cannot be ignored. Marriage connects or divides occupations from one another, and the question of which social stratum a person (man or woman) belongs to cannot be decided without reference to their various family relations. Households are formed through marriage or cohabitation, and it is within households that the educational and other opportunities that shape occupational mobility are generated. Households are also bases for the organisation of much free-time interaction. In all these ways, household membership is central to the allocation of individuals to social strata.

Class societies

Class, status, and command operate alongside one another, but their relative importance can vary a great deal. In contemporary capitalist societies, as we saw above, these all operate in and through the occupational division of labour and the associated system of property relations. One of the central features of the development of capitalist societies has been the way in which class situations have become, through the occupational system, the fundamental determinants of all other aspects of stratification. Status relations and command relations are, to a considerable extent, consequences of or reflections of class relations. It was for this reason that Weber thought it appropriate to describe contemporary capitalist societies as 'class societies'. A class society is one in which class situation is the most important determinant of the life chances of individuals. Weber contrasted class societies with 'status societies', where the most important determinants of life chances and the overall pattern of social stratification were status situations. Similarly, we can recognise 'command societies' where command situations are of paramount importance. These distinctions are important for comparative investigations, but they need not concern us here.

In a class society, social strata take the form of what Weber called 'social classes'. A social class is a cluster of households whose members owe their life chances principally to their property ownership or employment relations. It has been argued that the very language of 'class' developed in the eighteenth and nineteenth centuries as an attempt to grasp the new social relations that emerged with the increasing salience of class situations in capitalist industrial economies. The language of class was central to the recognition of 'social classes'. By the early nineteenth century, a recognition of capitalist societies as containing three social classes – an upper class, a middle class, and a working class – had become widely recognised.

The final conceptual point that needs to be made concerns class consciousness and class identity. All of us attempt to interpret and to understand the social world in which we live, and a central part of this social understanding is the attempt to interpret the social inequalities that we experience. Where people have life experiences in common, they are likely to develop a shared awareness and outlook on those experiences. Those who occupy the same class, status, or command situation and the members of a social stratum, then, are likely to develop a shared understanding of patterns of social stratification and the boundaries of social strata. This common awareness is most likely to result to the extent that people work together, live in the same neighbourhood, and engage in the same leisure activities. It is also influenced by the imagery conveyed in the mass media, although this is often mediated by personal, face-to-face contacts. This consciousness of social stratification (whether strong or weak) forms a central part of overall images of society, those cognitive maps that guide us in our relations with others.

What Marx and Weber called 'class consciousness' is that form of class awareness that develops in social classes and that, at its fullest, defines the interests that their members have in maintaining or enhancing their life chances. This will shape their political outlook and may lead them to form what Weber called 'parties' – conflict or interest groups of various kinds that give voice to their interests in political struggles. It is also likely to shape individual political action, and even in the absence of strong, class-based parties, a class consciousness may, for example, bring about a close association between social class position and voting.

The formation of a class consciousness is by no means automatic, as the awareness of social stratification may be only weakly developed or may be outweighed by other elements in social experience. One important aspect of investigations into social stratification, therefore, is the extent to which people's social imagery actually does centre on a sense of class identity. This means that we can add to the concepts that we have set out so far – principally those of social stratification based on economic relations, the differences between class, status and command situations, and the way occupations have been used to define strata – the ideas of identity and actions.

Mapping classes

We observed earlier that to understand class fully, we needed both clear concepts and a coherent way to operationalise them in research. The ideas just discussed have provided a not always explicit framework for the extensive discussion about how the class situations and social classes of contemporary Britain can be mapped in clear and reliable categories. Many different official and unofficial schemes have been proposed, by sociologists and non-sociologists alike. In these schemes, both the number of classes and their composition vary quite considerably. In most cases, the theoretical basis of the scheme is not spelled out, and few have been constructed along explicitly Weberian lines. It sometimes seems as if there is a huge gap between stratification theory and empirical research on social stratification, with the latter showing a bewildering variety of class maps. This has led some sociologists to suggest a radical revision of how stratification is conceptualised and measured. The Cambridge approach, for example, sees stratification as involving a continuous scale rather than discrete categories (Prandy 1991; Blackburn and Prandy 1997).

The range of disagreement can be seen quite clearly in the differences between two of the leading class schemes, those of E. O. Wright (1985) and Goldthorpe (1980). Wright's scheme – the most developed of a number that he has produced – contains 12 distinct class categories. These categories are defined by ownership and control of property, by organisational assets of authority, and by skills and education. These 12 categories are seen by Wright as a halfway house between the detailed listing of class situations and a briefer listing of real social classes, and they were intended to grasp broad differences in life chances in a large comparative study. Marshall *et al.* (1988) applied Wright's scheme to British data and showed that the classes ranged from a 'bourgeoisie' of property owners, accounting for 2.0 per cent of the population, to a 'proletariat' containing 42.9 per cent of the population. Between this bourgeoisie and proletariat was a whole range of propertied and non-propertied classes covering those working in various kinds of managerial, supervisory, and technical work.

Goldthorpe's scheme was an attempt to move closer to a true social class map, and he allocated class situations to seven separate categories. The extremes of this scheme were a 'service class' containing 25 per cent of the population and a class of non-skilled manual workers containing 22 per cent of the population (Erikson and Goldthorpe 1993). Unlike Wright, Goldthorpe did not incorporate substantial property ownership into his scheme, on the grounds that there were too few large property holders to figure in any national sample survey. Nevertheless, he recognised that, for some purposes, it was sensible to try to distinguish an 'elite' of property owners that would amount to a fraction of one per cent of the population. Goldthorpe has also modified his basic scheme in order to use it in the wide range of very different societies that he has investigated in comparative research. This enlarged scheme is less useful for investigations of any one society. Neither Wright nor Goldthorpe can be taken as having produced a completely accurate map of the class structure of contemporary Britain. Nevertheless, a wealth of secondary evidence suggests that Goldthorpe's basic scheme – modified by the inclusion of his eighth 'elite' category – does provide an approximation to an accurate mapping of contemporary social class boundaries.

The older and rival 'official' (that is, government-produced) schemes, however, are still widely used for a whole variety of purposes related to the investigation of life chances and life styles, and they are likely to continue in use for some time. In much of this chapter, these categories will therefore be the ones used. In many studies and especially in official statistics, two alternative sets of 'official' class categories have been used. These are the so-called 'Registrar General's scheme' and the SEG (Socio-Economic Groups) scheme. These are far from having the plausibility of the Goldthorpe scheme (not least because their origins and subsequent changes of detail were not grounded in a systematic sociological analysis), but they are nevertheless useful bases for mapping contemporary differences in life chances and life styles. Their particular attraction is that for many years they were the only schemes available to access data collected by the government's large-scale social surveys.

A significant advance in techniques of sociological research has recently been made with the introduction of a new official social class scheme that extends the Goldthorpe classification and integrates it with the Registrar General's and the SEG schemes. This scheme is the SEC, produced by David Lockwood and David Rose (see Rose and O' Reilly 1998), and it will soon allow a far more effective integration of official and sociological research into social class. Until it begins to be used in research, however, we must make do with the existing schemes.

The basic Registrar General's scheme contains five social classes, one of which (class III) is divided into manual and non-manual sections. In its most developed form, therefore, the Registrar General's classification contains six social classes. This scheme attempts to see class differences in terms of the skill and employment relations of occupations, and it combines this with an assessment of the social standing of the various occupations. The 17-category SEG scheme is more systematically economic in its basis, and in its 'collapsed' version also contains six social classes. These boundaries, however, are drawn at different points and they do not correspond to the Registrar

General's categories in a one-to-one way. The SEG scheme has sometimes been converted into a seven-category scheme by the subdivision of white collar workers by their grade. With numerous qualifications, it is possible to summarise the relationship between the various schemes as in Table 2.1.

Table 2.1   Social class schemes

Social classes		Goldthorpe categories	Registrar General categories	SEG categories
Advantaged classes				
	Capitalist class	'elite'		
	Service class	I, II	I	1, 2
Intermediate classes			II, IIIN	3a, 3b
	Petty bourgeoisie	IV		
	White-collar workers	III		
	Blue-collar elite	V		
Subordinate classes				
	Skilled manual	VI	IIIM	4
	Unskilled manual	VII	IV, V	5, 6

Changing class relations

We can use these class schema to map the shape and size of classes, and how these evolve. Class relations have not remained unchanged in British society. The structure of class relations itself is subject to change, and these patterns of change cannot be reflected in a fixed scheme of social classes. Nevertheless, the use of these categories in historical research does give some indication of how class relations have altered. A key element in this is the declining significance of the subordinate classes of manual workers. The subordinate classes amounted to over 80 per cent of the population in 1911, and in 1951 they still accounted for almost three quarters of the population. By 1981, however, they represented only just over a half of the population. Ten years later, they made up just 45 per cent of the population.

The decline in the number of manual workers, both skilled and unskilled, has been matched by a growth in the number of non-manual workers employed in the new service industries that have grown massively over the course of the century. Between 1911 and 1951, non-manual workers increased from just over 12 per cent to around a quarter of the population. By 1991 they made up 55 per cent of the population.

These figures, like all official statistics, must be treated with caution. However, they do give a general impression of the principal change in the system of social stratification. The key to understanding this change is what Payne (1987a; see also Clark 1940) has described as the 'occupational transition'. This term refers to the shift in occupational structure that occurs with developments in technology and the division of labour. Industrialism involved a shift from a structure of *primary sector* occupations (those in such industries as agriculture and mining) to one in which *secondary sector* occupations (those involved in the manufacturing of machinery and consumer goods from the products of the primary sector) played the leading part. Developments in manufacturing technology, however, led to the growth of technical and specialist occupations that require high levels of education and training. These occupations grew at the expense of purely manual work and, at the same time, there was an expansion in the *tertiary sector* of public service and commercial occupations concerned with distribution, banking, and insurance. The occupational transition, then, is one in which, successively, the primary, the secondary, and the tertiary sectors have been the most important bases of occupational differentiation.

The wider implications of these changes in the occupational division of labour have been widely discussed. For many observers, the changes point to a long-term development from an 'industrial' to a 'post-industrial' society, while others have described it as one aspect of a transition from a 'modern' to a 'post-modern' society. Whatever might be concluded about this, it is clear that the occupational transition has been associated with the development of forms of social structure in the second half of the twentieth century that are radically different from those that existed in the first half. The old pattern of social classes, their boundaries, and their forms of consciousness have all been transformed. The large, cohesive social classes that existed in the early twentieth century have developed into the more fragmented and divided classes that are entering the new millennium.

These changes in class relations will be discussed later in this chapter, but I would first like to look in some detail at the distribution of life chances across the social classes as they exist today. This will establish a benchmark from which the social changes of the twentieth century can be assessed. The data presented here come from the recent and valuable compilation produced by Reid (1998), where the evidence is discussed more fully.

Class and life chances in contemporary society

Tables 2.2 and 2.3 show the distribution of money, work, and property, as measured in relation to class situation. In each case, a sharp class gradient is apparent. Disposable income, for example, ranges from the £519 per week earned by professionals to the £213 per week earned by unskilled manual workers. The more detailed categorisation used for the distribution of income shows that the middle levels of the scheme do not form a neat and clear-cut hierarchy for all measures. Skilled manual workers, for example, earn slightly more per week than routine non-manual workers.

Table 2.2   Disposable income, share ownership, home ownership and pensions

SEG	Disposable weekly income (£) per household 1993	% of households owning shares 1988	% of owner occupiers	% of full-time workers in an employers' pension scheme 1994	
				Male	Female
1 Professional	519.6	55	89	74	67
2 Employers and managers	503.4	51	87	70	60
3a Intermediate non-manual	388.7	31	77	68	60
3b Lower non-manual	295.8				
4 Skilled manual	307.8	24	74	50	39
5 Semi-skilled manual	252.4	15	54	47	30
6 Unskilled manual	213.6	9	43	43	27

Source: adapted from Reid (1998): Table 4.3 on p. 84, Table 4.7 on p. 89, Table 5.5 on p. 105 and Table 6.18 on p. 149. Original data from *Family Expenditure Survey (income)* and *General Household Survey* (shareholdings, home ownership and pensions)

A similar gradient is apparent for the ownership of shares and for membership in a pension scheme. Level and continuity of income determines the chances that a person has to purchase property. In addition to inequalities in income-generating shares, there are marked inequalities in home ownership. Table 2.2 shows that the rates of home ownership are much lower for semi-skilled and unskilled workers than they are for all others. The rate for unskilled workers is half that found among professionals. Gender differences have rarely been explored in relation to class, but Table 2.2 brings out its importance. The proportion of women in pension schemes is lower, for each class, than it is for men.

A national survey in 1996 found that most people thought that a weekly income of £211 was necessary to avoid poverty, and it can be seen that the average for unskilled manual workers is only just above this level. Unemployment is a life experience that can push people into poverty, and Table 2.3 shows that unskilled workers are especially likely to become unemployed.

Table 2.3   Unemployment in 1996

RG	% unemployed	% unemployed for more than one year
I	3	0.9
II	4	1.2
IIIN	5	1.5
IIIM	8	3.6
IV	10	3.6
V	14	5.9

Source: adapted from Reid (1998): Table 5.10 on p. 111.
Original data from *Labour Force Survey*

Rates of unemployment are almost five times as high for these workers as they are for professionals and managers, and unskilled workers are also far more likely to remain unemployed for a year or more.

These class inequalities are reflected in the inequalities of health, life, and death documented in Tables 2.4 and 2.5.

Again, a clear – although far from perfect – class gradient is apparent. The proportion of babies with low birth weight, rates of infant mortality, rates of child mortality and life expectancy all show the same class gradient as found in income and property ownership, and these differentials in life chances persist into adulthood. Even less crucial aspects of health like long-term illness, eye, ear, and tooth problems (see also Chapter 10) have this gradient, as Table 2.5 shows.

In addition to these demographic life chances, class situation appears as a clear determinant of both housing and education. The proportion of those living in overcrowded housing and the proportion without central heating both show the familiar gradient (Table 2.6).

Table 2.4   Infant and child mortality and life expectancy

RG	% of babies underweight 1989–91	% infant mortality 1991	% child mortality 1979–83		Life expectancy 1991
			Male	Female	
I	4.8	0.51	0.033	0.033	} 72.5
II	5.1	0.53	0.034	0.031	
IIIN	5.9	0.61	0.041	0.036	} 70.6
IIIM	6.4	0.62	0.053	0.042	
IV	6.8	0.71	0.064	0.052	} 67.7
V	7.7	0.82	0.111	0.086	

Source: adapted from Reid (1998): Table 3.1 on p. 48, Table 3.2 on p. 49 and Table 3.18 on p. 77

Table 2.5   Adult illness and health problems

SEG	% with long-term illness, 1994		% with sight problems 1994	% with hearing problems	% with no natural teeth 1993
	Male	Female			
I	27	24	10	7	3
2	29	28	12	12	11
3	29	33	13	11	12
4	33	32	14	13	19
5	34	39	18	16	23
6	38	45	19	21	33

Source: adapted from Reid (1998): Table 3.4 on p. 52, Table 3.7 on p. 55. Original data from *General Household Survey*

Table 2.6   Housing deprivation

RG	% overcrowded, 1981	SEG	% without central heating, 1991
I	1.4	I	5
II	2.3	2	6
IIIN	3.6	3	15
IIIM	6.6	4	18
IV	8.0	5	24
V	9.6	6	28

Source: adapted from Reid (1998): Table 6.20 on p. 152, Table 6.22 on p. 154. Original data from Population Census

We also find the same pattern in the measures of educational achievement. Rates of attendance at private schools, where attendance depends on income, are predictably unequal, but so also are rates of higher education and the proportion of those leaving school with no formal educational qualifications of any kind.

Table 2.7   Education and qualifications

SEG	% with higher education	% with no qualifications	% attended private school
1	78	3	26
2	35	17	12
3	30	19	6
4	9	40	1
5	5	56	1
6	1	74	1

Source: adapted from Reid (1998): Table 7.1 on p. 161, Table 7.11 on p. 179. Original data from *General Household Survey*

Inequalities of life chances in education of the kind shown in Table 2.7 are especially important, as these are central to the reproduction of class relations. Chances of entering highly-paid occupations are closely related to educational achievement, which is, in turn, related to class situation as measured by occupation. This is the most striking result of research into social mobility (the movement between classes), the consequences of which are shown in Table 2.8.

Table 2.8   Social mobility in England and Wales: % of fathers' class in class destination

Fathers' social class	Respondents' social class (Goldthorpe scheme)							Total
	I	II	III	IV	V	VI	VII	
I	46	19	12	7	5	5	7	100 (680)
II	29	23	12	6	10	11	9	100 (547)
III	19	16	13	7	13	16	16	100 (687)
IV	14	14	9	21	10	15	16	100 (886)
V	14	14	10	8	16	21	17	100 (1072)
VI	8	9	8	6	12	31	26	100 (2577)
VII	7	9	9	6	13	25	32	100 (2126)

Source: Goldthorpe (1980), Table 2.2. N = 8575

These data, from the 1972 Nuffield study, show high levels of self-recruitment in each class. Over a half of men born with semi-skilled or unskilled fathers remained in manual work, with only 16 per cent entering professional or managerial work. Conversely, almost two-thirds of those born into professions and management families remained there, only 12 per cent taking up manual work. Despite apparently high levels of social mobility, class inequalities in chances of mobility remain strong, and they closely follow the other documented inequalities in material life chances.

These figures on inequalities in life chances are illustrative only – such inequalities are documented more comprehensively in Reid's (1998) own summary. My purpose in using them is to demonstrate that class situation, however this is measured, remains an important determinant of life chances in contemporary Britain. There is, for a number of key measures, a clear class gradient, and this has to be recognised in any discussion of the relevance of class analysis. Class differences persist and have, in many respects, become sharper. However, these are far less directly reflected in distinct differences of social status, and so they are less directly reflected in sharp differences of attitude and outlook. Class consciousness – at least as conventionally understood – is no longer a central feature of contemporary class relations. Traditional status values, that for so long defined the character of British class relations, have decayed. This has undermined the everyday use of the language of 'class', which I showed to rest, in fact, on 'status' differences in accent, dress, and social background.

Cannadine (1998) has convincingly shown that the language of stratification in Britain has drawn on three distinct and often contradictory images. These he terms the hierarchical, the triadic and the dichotomous. People draw on these to varying degrees and according to their social position (Lockwood 1966). They are rhetorical and interpretative devices that allow people to construct an understanding of the complex social structures in which they live. When thinking about the social stratification of their society, people are 'silently and easily shifting from one social vision to another' (Cannadine 1998: 165).

Hierarchical imagery has been dominant in social thought, especially in the form of a status hierarchy focused around traditional distinctions of education, dress, accent, ancestry, and other aspects of style of life. This imagery began its long-term decline in the inter-war years, when a tripartite imagery of upper class, middle class, and working class consolidated its position in the popular mind. For many in the working class of subordinate manual workers, this shaded into a dichotomous opposition between 'us' and 'them'.

In the second half of the twentieth century, social imagery became more complex and less clear-cut. The traditional imagery continued to decline as traditional and deferential values generally decayed with the decline of Empire and the sense of 'greatness' that went with it. The growth of consumerism and the encouragement of a greater diversity in lifestyles fragmented the tripartite and dichotomous images and encouraged the formulation of new hierarchical images in which spending power and consumption were the central elements. Such 'money models' of society established new and highly flexible forms of status division that mask, rather than solidify, underlying differences in economic resources. Class, as defined by Marx and Weber, remains the crucial determinant of life chances, and it shapes the opportunities that people have for pursuing particular lifestyles, but *it is less visible to people, who tend to define their positions in status terms.*

Subordinate classes

Having sketched the persistence of class differences, it is now possible to look in more detail at each of the classes in turn. This will involve taking a broadly historical perspective, examining the most important social changes that have taken place at the various *levels* of the system of social classes, as a means of understanding contemporary patterns and also recent debates about those patterns. It is not possible fully to understand class today without grasping how the classes have evolved, a social process that is arguably the key change in society. We will start with the subordinate, manual classes, followed by the intermediate 'middle' classes, before discussing the 'advantaged' or upper classes.

The employment relations that define the social position of the subordinate manual worker are those of the wage labour contract. Manual workers are engaged to work in exchange for a wage that is supposed to compensate them for their labour time. Most typically, this kind of work has been paid on a weekly basis, although large numbers of manual workers are employed on a part-time or casual basis for shorter periods. The limited autonomy allowed or expected for manual workers is apparent in the fact that their wages are generally calculated on an hourly basis, with employers exercising controls over both the time and the pace of their work.

The market situation of the manual worker, then, depends on the skills that they can bring to the labour market. Those skills that are in the greatest demand are likely to command a higher rate of pay than skills that are less in demand, and a significantly higher rate than unskilled labour. The major source of internal division within this class, then, has tended to be along the lines of skill (see Scott 1996 for an elaboration of this argument).

The employment relations of manual workers also involve them in distinct work situations. Within the occupational division of labour of the enterprise that employs them, they are in a subordinate position. They are subject to managerial authority over all aspects of their work. Manual workers in large organisations, such as car plants, engineering works, chemical plants, local authorities, banks, and so on (and formerly shipyards and coal mines) are subject to an extensive managerial hierarchy, the top levels of which may be far removed from them both socially and physically. Manual workers in smaller organisations, such as much light industrial and building work, farm work, and domestic service, are employed in smaller work groups and may have closer and more immediate contact with the managers who supervise their work. Cross-cutting the lines of skill, then, is a secondary line of internal division between those involved in large-scale and those in small-scale work situations.

Similarities in their conditions of employment – their involvement in a wage labour contract and their subordination to managerial authority – form these workers into a distinct class at the economic level. Unless lines of division by skill and work situation differences become particularly sharp, workers will form what Marx referred to as a 'class in-itself'. They are united by the shared economic conditions of propertylessness and subordinate employment, and by the life chances with which these are associated. Where internal divisions become marked and are reflected in differences in life chances – and I have documented some evidence for this in the previous section – it may make more sense to identify a number of different subordinate classes, or sub-classes, at the economic level.

The identification of economic class boundaries, however, is merely the first step towards the identification of social class boundaries. Those in various economically defined class situations form a single social class, it will be recalled, whenever mobility and association are easy and frequent among them. When a class in-itself is forged into a social class through the relations of mobility and association of its members, it is on the way to becoming what Marx described as a 'class for-itself'. In its fully developed form, a class for-itself has not only a real existence as a clearly bounded social class, but also has a consciousness of its own position and of its interests relative to other social classes. The class for-itself is most likely to act politically in pursuit of its collective interests.

For much of the nineteenth century, manual workers formed neither a class in-itself nor a class for-itself. They were, for the most part, employed in relatively small workshops where there were few opportunities for them to develop a consciousness and solidarity of themselves as members of a single class. At the same time, they were greatly divided by differences of skill

(Thompson 1968). From around the middle of the century, however, the scale of production began to increase and workers were brought together in larger and larger productive settings. The discipline of the factory became the common experience for manual workers (Foster 1974). Within large-scale factory systems of production, the occupational division of labour brought workers with different skills into closer contact with each other, and many forms of craft work underwent a process of de-skilling. Manual workers, while still differentiated by their skills, became more homogeneous in terms of both their market situations and their work situations.

This gradual forging of manual workers into a class in-itself was matched by high levels of mobility and association across the lines of skill within the working class during the nineteenth and early twentieth centuries. Manual workers were sharply separated from non-manual workers, and they were internally unified as a distinct social class. Very few manual workers or children of manual workers entered non-manual work, even at its lowest levels, and there were very few marriages across the manual/non-manual line (Savage and Miles 1994). On the other hand, skilled workers whose jobs disappeared with technological change had little option but to take up unskilled work. Consequently, unskilled workers and their children could sometimes enter semi-skilled work through on-the-job training, especially in times of economic growth and relative prosperity.

These relations of mobility and intermarriage closely linked workers in a particular locality to one another, although they were far less closely linked to similar workers in other localities. As a result, the great industrial towns and inner cities each became distinct, but structurally similar, communities of families dependent on manual work. It was in these conditions that the idea of a 'working class' took root. The proletarian communities were fertile seed beds for sentiments of class solidarity and for the forging of a shared consciousness of class.

By the inter-war years of the twentieth century, this process was well-developed. Contemporaries could refer to 'the working class', and everyone would know what this meant. Manual workers themselves embraced the label whole-heartedly and took it as their basic marker of social identity. The social institutions and agencies of the working-class community sustained this identity. The dense networks of kinship and friendship that tied together neighbourhood and place of work (Young and Willmott 1957) had a more formal expression in the shared leisure-time involvement in pubs and clubs, cinemas, and dance halls with which they were associated (Dennis *et al.* 1956; Jackson 1968), and in participation in trades unions, cooperatives, and the Labour Party. Through the first half of the century, the electoral strength of the Labour Party grew in parallel with the crystallisation of these working-class communities. Support for the Labour Party was seen as a natural reflection of the stronger and deeper-rooted local solidarity of a working-class community.

The degree of unity found in the working class until the middle of the twentieth century should not be exaggerated. Skill differences persisted, these were associated with differences in life chances, and they could often undermine class solidarity. Highly skilled male craft workers – those who had served an apprenticeship or some similar period of training – could generally command higher wages and had greater job security than their semi-skilled and unskilled counterparts. Many were also able to exercise a degree of authority at work as the foremen and supervisors of other manual workers. Their relatively high wages and their involvement in authority meant that there was a tendency for them to see their interests as distinct from those of unskilled workers (Gray 1981). As an 'aristocracy of labour', they were especially likely to be committed to ideals of self-help, getting-on, and respectability. One aspect of this respectability was that their wives withdrew from the labour market and took on full-time responsibility for domestic work and family obligations.

In a similar way, the persistence of small-scale production, often in small towns, meant that large numbers of manual workers were isolated from the mainstream of the labour movement. Their work situation encouraged a greater sense of identification with – or, at least, of accommodation to – their employers and managers. Isolated from the supportive institutions of the oppositional subculture, they were more likely to defer to the authority of their employers (Stacey 1960; Newby 1975).

At the other end of the scale there were large numbers of manual workers who lived in poverty and experienced long periods of unemployment. Casual work, a lack of skill, old age, and illness all made people susceptible to economic downturns that could push them below the poverty line (Booth 1901–2; Rowntree 1901). Poverty was the fate that could all-too-easily befall any manual working family. Once forced into poverty, their lives were degraded and demoralised, and they became the targets of moralising attack by respectable society – manual and non-manual alike – which saw them as the 'rough' and 'undeserving' members of society. The poor were not, however, a distinct social class, they were the lower level of the working class. The rise and fall of families across the poverty line ensured that there was no sharp separation between the poor and the rest of the working class.

The mainstream of the proletarian working class, therefore, coexisted with the small-town working class of deferential workers and workers who aspired to improve themselves within the system (Lockwood 1966; Parkin 1971; Bulmer, 1975). The lower levels of this working class formed a poor working class that amounted to 30 per cent of the whole population at its peak. The cultural division between the 'rough' and the 'respectable' working class, rooted in real economic differences, became a persistent theme in national politics.

Although there have been great changes, not everything has changed significantly since the middle of the twentieth century. Many of these changes had their roots in the early years of the century, while others are only just beginning to make themselves felt. It is undoubtedly the case, however, that the mid-century marked a watershed in the history of the working class.

The subordinate classes today

Manual workers, as I have shown, have come to account for a much smaller proportion of the population than was the case a century ago, and the economic boundary between manual and non-manual work has become less sharp and less salient. Changing technology has transformed much manual work. It has led to the collapse of whole industries and, through the resulting migration of workers in search of work, it has undermined and caused the disappearance of the stable working-class communities with which they were associated. The sociologists who first commented on these changes tended to see them as a process of 'embourgeoisement': a process in which manual workers, and society as a whole, were becoming more 'middle class' in character and outlook and, as a result, were abandoning old patterns of class solidarity and class politics (Zweig 1961; Klein 1965). These claims involved a serious over-statement of their case, and many of the changes that were occurring were misinterpreted. They did, nevertheless, highlight the quite critical changes in class structure that were taking place.

Manual workers were not becoming middle class, but many of them were becoming far better-off than earlier generations. The 1950s and 60s saw a real growth in manual worker incomes, and the general improvement in economic conditions allowed many more people to buy domestic consumer goods that were, in the past, available only to the privileged or were simply not available at all. 'Affluent' workers were able to buy houses, washing machines, cars, and televisions, and they were able to furnish their homes in much more comfortable ways than before.

This partial homogenisation of standards of consumption between manual and non-manual workers, however, was not matched by changes in their property and employment relations or in their life chances more generally. The conditions of work for manual workers remained inferior even to those of routine non-manual workers. Their work was dreary and monotonous, it was not a source of intrinsic satisfaction, they had less security of employ-ment, inferior pension and holiday provision, and few opportunities for promotion. They had often to move long distances to obtain this work. It was tolerated only because of the size of the pay packet – the higher their pay, the greater was their willingness to tolerate their inferior working conditions (Goldthorpe *et al.* 1969. See also Lockwood 1960; Goldthorpe and Lockwood 1963; Goldthorpe 1964; Devine 1992a).

Most importantly, consumer goods were acquired because of the opportu-nities that they opened up, and not because they were the status symbols of a middle-class lifestyle. It is still worth making the obvious point that people buy washing machines to wash clothes, televisions to provide entertainment, and cars to provide them with mobility. These things are not accumulated simply in order to make a claim to higher status. Indeed, status divisions, like class divisions, remain sharp. Manual workers do not regularly and frequently entertain non-manual workers at home, nor do they engage in many common forms of leisure-time associations with them. They have, in fact, been forced to become more 'home-centred', more concerned with the life chances and lifestyle of their own family, as they no longer have extensive working-class communities to support them in times of need.

'Affluence' was a cyclical phenomenon, not a permanent state, although levels of consumption have remained much higher than in the past. For a significant minority, however, poverty conditions have persisted (Townsend 1979). For some commentators, the poverty of the post-war period has been seen as indicating the emergence of an 'underclass' separate from the social class of subordinate manual workers (Murray 1984). The evidence does not support this claim.

In the first place, poverty is associated with other social divisions, particu-larly gender, age and ill health, as we shall see in Chapters 3, 6 and 10. Equally, as in the past, poverty remains an ever-present possibility for *all* manual workers, and its incidence is generally beyond their individual control. The collapse of a firm or an industry in an area of high unemploy-ment can throw workers at all levels of skill into protracted periods of poverty. On the other hand, those living in poverty are not necessarily condemned to a life of poverty. Many are able to obtain employment or better-paid work after a period of poverty, and there is, overall, a substantial turnover among those in poverty (Morris 1995). Those who do persist in poverty are, in partic-ular, the aged and the infirm, whose families and friends often do not them-selves live far enough above the poverty line to help them out. Poverty is a real and important problem in contemporary society, an inevitable consequence of the way that it operates, but the poor do not form an underclass that exists separately from the rest of the class of subordinate manual workers (Scott

1994b). Poverty is not a class situation *per se*, although aspects of it can be thought of as arising from many very poor people's lack of opportunities to sell their labour in the market (Payne *et al.* 1996).

Changes in consumption and the spending of income have largely concerned the extent to which a class of subordinate manual workers can be regarded as forming a class for-itself. Their market and work situations, and their associated life chances, remain distinct from those of other workers, and patterns of mobility and association still form them into a distinct social class, but these ties are neither so strong nor so intense as they were in the past. There is not the institutional support for the degree of class solidarity and cohesion that characterised the period before the Second World War and that persisted into the 1950s.

Instead of a class consciousness rooted in common cultural and political traditions and in participation in the labour movement, manual workers are today more likely to see their society, and their own position within it, in terms of a more open and flexible 'money model' of society that stresses relative spending power rather than political power. A focus on consumption and spending has made traditional class and status distinctions less relevant and has replaced them by new distinctions rooted in differences in consumption. To the extent that they see the language of class as relevant – and most will use it if given some encouragement by a researcher – it is not regarded as the *sole* or even the *most* relevant way of describing themselves.

People are likely to report themselves as being members of a large class that contains virtually the whole of society, only the very rich and the very poor falling outside it; that is, a tripartite model. Within the main class, people make distinctions on the basis of the income and standards of living that they believe people to have achieved. Their knowledge of the true extent of income differences, however, is generally very poor, and the correspondence between real conditions and perceived conditions is slight. Most manual workers feel that those who are better-off than themselves are not *that much* better-off, and so they look for only relatively modest improvements in their economic situation. They see the less well-off as being not much worse off than themselves, often tending to be unsympathetic towards welfare payments. For some, this central class is described as a 'middle class', while for others it is a 'working class'. For yet others – perhaps for a growing number – it is a sign of 'class-lessness': if almost everybody is in a single class, then 'class' distinctions are no longer relevant.

Subordinate manual workers, therefore, no longer *live* class in the same way as their counterparts did in the working-class communities of the past. This makes it more difficult to use the term 'working class' to describe them. They are a more fragmented social class than before, the differences between 'rough' and 'respectable', skilled and unskilled, proletarian and 'deferential' having become more visible and, at the same time, submerged in a larger pool of social identities. Despite the inferior life chances that were documented in the previous section, manual workers have neither the solidarity nor the consciousness that is needed to sustain a strong commitment to collective class action. This declining sense of class identity is one of the most important factors underlying the decline in the traditional Labour vote from the 1940s to the 1990s. If a greater percentage of manual workers supported Labour in 1997 than at any other time in the post-war period, this is evidence not of a resurgence of class consciousness but of the transformation of the Labour Party itself. New Labour's commitment to the 'classless' society commits the party to mobilising the support of those who see themselves in the large central class through pursuing the politics of the centre.

Intermediate classes

Just as the subordinate classes can be thought of as either a single block or as subdivided, the middle classes cover a range of positions. The three main segments of the intermediate classes comprise those who are employed in professional, managerial, administrative, and technical occupations; those who are self-employed; and those with small-scale property. The employment relations of the latter are distinguished from those of subordinate workers by the much greater autonomy and involvement in authority that their work situations involve and, for those at the more senior levels, by the possession of a longer-term 'service' contract of employment rather than a time-based labour contract. They are contracted to employ their skills in the service of an employer – generally a large-scale organisation – and they have a great deal of autonomy and discretion as to when and how they provide these services (Goldthorpe 1980). They are paid on a monthly, salaried basis, and they have significant additional benefits over and above their basic salary.

Self-employed workers, such as lawyers, accountants, doctors, and many business consultants, whether working alone or in partnership, exchange their professional services for a fee paid by their clients. By virtue of their self-employment, they, too, have considerable discretion and autonomy over the conditions under which they carry out their work, and they have much leeway in determining the level of their own fees. Small-scale property owners involved in the running of manufacturing or service businesses may, legally, be employees of their own businesses or they may be self-employed. In practice, however, it is their property that defines the petty bourgeoisie's market situation and allows them to earn an income.

These differences in market situations have meant that the intermediate classes have never had quite the degree of economic homogeneity achieved by subordinate manual workers. Nevertheless, there was a sharp economic gulf between the two classes. The intermediate classes were more closely linked to each other than they were to those who stood below them in the economic structure. This was matched by the sharpness of the social imagery that, for most of the nineteenth century, separated the 'middle class' – often called the 'middle classes' – from the mass of society.

The middle classes were the leading elements in the towns and cities, occupying positions of power in local councils and running the whole array of church, civic, charitable, and other voluntary associations (Morris 1990). Around the formal associations were formed extensive networks of interlocking committee memberships, informal meetings, and leisure-time activities. Their economic circumstances and life style sustained a cultural and political individualism that precluded any collective action except that in pursuit of sectional professional privileges and business interests. Individuals were to help themselves, and not expect the state to act on their behalf, although this self-help often involved the mobilisation of the informal social networks that abounded within the middle classes. In small towns across the country, this pattern persisted into the 1950s (Stacey 1960).

Internal differences within the intermediate classes did, however, sharpen towards the end of the nineteenth century. The numbers of doctors, lawyers, and teachers grew only very slowly in the years leading up to the First World War, as did the numbers of small property-owners. However, there was rapid and substantial growth in the number of managerial and clerical workers: the number of clerks was almost three times as high in 1911 as it was in 1880. Clerks accounted for 0.8 per cent of all male employees in 1851, but by 1911 they accounted for 5.7 per cent. By 1951, they formed 10.5 per cent.

While these clerks did not have the long-term service contract and the autonomy enjoyed by the old middle class, they did enjoy conditions of employment that were far superior to those of subordinate manual workers. They were generally recruited through the interpersonal connections that they or their families could mobilise, and their promotion depended on their maintaining good personal relations and loyalty to their employers (Lockwood 1958). These employment conditions secured them clear advantages in income and status over manual workers. Like the similarly expanding numbers of shop assistants, commercial travellers, and technicians, however, they remained at some distance from the established middle classes and tended to be defined as 'lower middle class' (Crossick 1977).

The continued growth in the numbers of clerical and managerial workers in the twentieth century further increased the diversity of the 'middle classes'.

A growth in the scale of management in large business enterprises produced a growing 'service class' of managers who became increasingly sharply separated from the equally large number of clerical workers whose working conditions were being transformed. Instead of being dependent on the mobilisation of personal contacts, clerks were more dependent on the educational qualifications that they could secure. The expansion of management, however, was also associated with a mechanisation of office work that progressively devalued the skills that these qualifications signified. Office work became more routine and, in many respects, more 'manual' than 'mental' in character (Braverman 1974). Promotion opportunities for clerks declined, while the work itself became more feminised (Holcombe 1973; Anderson 1976). By 1951, over a half of all clerks were female. The women who entered clerical work were often the wives or daughters of manual workers, further reducing the significance of the boundary between clerical work and manual work. Clerks were no longer so unambiguously 'middle class' as they had been in the nineteenth century, while the middle classes had become more exclusively professional and managerial in character.

The transformation of the middle classes, therefore, began much earlier than the changes experienced by subordinate manual workers. Nevertheless, the middle of the twentieth century does mark an important point of transition for the intermediate classes also. Economic competion has meant that small businesses have come under greater pressure from the large enterprises (in which the vast array of managers are employed), and the position of the petty bourgeoisie has consequently been much weakened. Small business owners have also had high levels of self-recruitment, and correspondingly much lower rates of mobility in and out of other intermediate class situations (Scase and Goffee 1982). The growth of large-scale enterprise has also transformed the position of many managerial and professional workers, forcing many of them to convert from self-employed to employed positions (Johnson 1972). Those in service locations have become more diverse. Particularly significant has been the growth of the public sector and of the 'semi-professionals' (teachers, social workers, nurses, and so on) employed within it. The vast growth of financial services in the 1980s has led to an expansion in the numbers of non-traditional service workers in insurance, pensions, and estate agency. At all levels, then, the intermediate classes have been tied to bureaucratised conditions of employment.

The class cohesion of the middle classes was always rather low: they formed a clearly bounded social class in relation to the working class, but they were internally divided by the relative difficulty of moving from propertied to employed and self-employed positions. Savage *et al.* (1992) have argued that this separation has become more marked in the second half of the twentieth century, and that the managerial, professional, and propertied sections of the intermediate classes are now sharply distinct from each other. The intermediate layers of the class structure have, like its subordinate levels, become more fragmented. This fragmentation at the intermediate levels has been along the lines of organisational assets, educational assets, and property assets.

As a result, traditional middle class individualism and civic power have weakened (Stacey *et al.* 1975). Those in the vast managerial bureaucracies – and especially those in the public sector bureaucracies – are more likely to consider collective action in pursuit of their interests. In place of the individualism of the old middle classes there has emerged the collectivism of the new middle classes.

The term 'middle class', however, may be less useful as a designation for those in these intermediate employment and property relations. The term 'middle class' as a self-description, as I have already shown, is as likely to be used by manual workers as it is by non-manual workers. Large bureaucracies, with their extensive professional and managerial hierarchies based on entry by educational qualification, technical competence, measured performance and competitive promotion, form the bases of intermediate class situations. This encourages their occupants towards the social imagery of an ostensibly open and 'classless' society. Intermediate class situations still exist, and they still enjoy life chances that divide them from subordinate manual and routine non-manual workers, but their self-perception – even when it employs the phrase 'middle class' – is not one that emphasises either their traditional status or a solidaristic class identity.

Advantaged classes

The advantaged classes are those who are involved in property and employment relations that give them ownership and/or control over large amounts of capital. Whether in the form of land, buildings, machinery, or financial securities, property is the key to their power. In some cases this involves the direct personal ownership of substantial property. This might be as the exclusive or part-ownership of a large integrated block of capital (such as a landed estate or a large business enterprise) or it might be the holding of diversified portfolio investments in a large number of different types of capital. In other cases, the class situation might involve an employment relation that defines a position of control over these kinds of assets. The chief executives of large enterprises, their part-time directors, and the investment managers of large financial enterprises are all able to use their control over capital to secure, directly or indirectly, significant advantages for themselves.

For much of the nineteenth century, there was a sharp separation between land and manufacturing as sources of class advantage. Landowners —closely linked to the financial sector – saw themselves and were seen by others as forming an 'upper class', rooted in the aristocracy and, more narrowly, in the peerage. Landed wealth was the source of the biggest fortunes (Rubinstein 1981), and it was the land-owning upper class that dominated the political machinery of the state (Guttsman 1963). Manufacturing capitalists, often provincial in their origins, became an increasingly significant category of wealth, but they were barely distinguished by their contemporaries from the vast mass of the middle classes. The social imagery of upper class, middle class, and working class made manufacturing capitalists virtually invisible as a class. Towards the end of the nineteenth century, land and industry came closer together. Peers and other landowners, who were experiencing a fall in the returns on their estates, became more willing to invest in industrial enter-prises and to sit on the boards of the large business enterprises that were formed from the 1880s in banking, insurance, and railways, as well as in manufacturing. A 'lord on the board' was an important marker of stability and probity in a more complex business environment. Through these connections, and through mobility and intermarriage, manufacturing capitalists came grudgingly to be accepted as part of the upper class (Thompson 1963; Stone and Stone 1984; Scott 1991).

The advantaged class at the turn of the twentieth century numbered just under 40,000 people, approximately 0.1 per cent of the population. Its posi-tion in society was confirmed more by its status than by any widespread recognition of its economic resources. The popularity of the Royal Family was central to this, as the monarchs were, as major landowners, core members of the class. Victoria, Edward, and the two Georges were well integrated into the advantaged class, and through the ceremony and glamour that were attached to royalty they ensured that the social class as a whole received a high level of public approval and at least overt deference. The cement that held together the increasingly diverse upper class as a distinct status group was the round of 'Society' activities: the dances, dinners, parties, and salons held by the aris-tocracy and other prominent families in their London and country homes (Weiner 1981; Rubinstein 1993; McKibbin 1998).

As it became less exclusively aristocratic, 'Society' became more ostenta-tious and more focused around glamour and frippery. The relaxation of tradi-tional standards helped to weld the diverse elements of the upper class together, but in the long-run Society was incapable of preventing the disinte-gration of the class in the face of this diversity. The institutions of Society became more open to sheer wealth and less able to impose a single style of life on all its members. This is clear in the informal social networks that were rooted in kinship and friendship and sustained through attendance at public schools and at prestigious Oxford and Cambridge colleges. These networks were important bonds of solidarity for the male members of this upper class, who could rely on the mobilisation of the social capital of their 'old boy networks'. As the century progressed, these networks were becoming weaker. They could no longer guarantee success for land-owning families, although they were still highly successful in the social placement of the sons of the aristocracy, and they could not meet the needs of those who were closer to the margins of the class. Advantaged class situations were becoming ever more business-based in character, and less exclusively landed. In parliament and government, in the public schools, in the old universities, and in the top levels of the military and the civil service, the upper class was beginning to lose its distinctiveness and its cohesion.

By the early 1950s, 'Society' had virtually ceased to operate in its traditional form, its demise having been hastened by war-time conditions. The advantaged classes could no longer really be defined as an 'upper class'. They formed, instead, a diversity of overlapping cliques and sets, an 'upper circle' rather than an 'upper class'. These cliques were very diverse. Some followed traditional country pursuits, some were involved in the media and entertainment, some were members of a 'jet set', and others simply kept to themselves and made their money.

This decay in the traditional status of the upper class – the death of the upper class – was the counterpart of the growing economic complexity of property and its management. The middle decades of the twentieth century saw a transition from the direct personal ownership of land and business that had prevailed in the nineteenth century to more indirect and impersonal forms of corporate ownership. The number of large personal shareholdings in major companies declined and there was a corresponding growth in the proportion of shares that were owned by financial enterprises such as insurance companies, banks, and pension funds (Scott 1997). In this situation, it was the directors and top executives who controlled the capital embodied in these enterprises.

These directors and executives were recruited disproportionately from those who were, individually, property owners, although new channels of mobility to advantaged class situations had been opened up. Wealthy families had diversified their assets by taking stakes in a large number of enterprises and by entrusting the management of these assets to the growing financial enterprises. At the same time, they were able to ensure their continuing control over the assets that generated their wealth by taking top board and management positions in them. Whether as rentiers, who depended passively on the management of their capital by others, or as active finance capitalists and finance executives, the propertied were able to secure a continuation of their advantaged life chances. Indeed, the demise of 'Society' made their privileges far less visible and, therefore, less open to attack, than in the past (Scott 1997: Ch. 8).

This trend has been described as a 'managerial reorganisation' of the capitalist class (Mills 1956). Business enterprises have become ever more closely tied together through the interweaving shareholdings and interlocking directorships of the big financial investors. The directors and executives of these enterprises are overwhelmingly drawn from a propertied background, although with a growing influx from management and the professions and whose children are, thereby, able to become the propertied inheritors of the next generation. The capitalist class of today combines personal wealth with top-level participation in corporate management.

Conclusion

I have tried to show that a Weberian approach to social stratification – and especially his distinction between class and status – allows us to understand both the contemporary contours of class division and the long-term processes that have brought them about. There has been a move away from a stable tripartite system of social classes (upper, middle, and working) to a more fragmented class structure in which the advantaged, intermediate, and subordinate levels are no longer so directly defined in status terms. It was the close association of class and status from the 1880s to the 1950s, underpinned by the economic conditions of the period, that allowed the formation of a stable system of social classes. In these circumstances, the members of the various classes readily accepted this in their own social imagery, class consciousness, and political action.

Economic change and the demographic changes that have gone along with it have destroyed this structure. These changes have long roots, but they have been especially marked since the 1950s. Class divisions still exist, but they are no longer so easily mapped into a tripartite imagery of social classes. There is still a sharp gradient of life chances, as shown in the evidence on health, mortality, housing, and education that I have presented in this chapter, but it is no longer so obvious exactly where the real social boundaries are to be drawn on this gradient. Boundaries are more fuzzy, less distinct. Indeed, it is not clear whether it is more useful to focus on the broadly defined advantaged, intermediate, and subordinate classes or on their internal divisions along the lines of their property and employment relations.

In this sense, class as a social division is a complex one that does not divide society neatly or conspicuously into two, three, or even the half-a-dozen categories of the Registrar-General's scheme. It is also true that, certainly compared to the past, many more individuals can move between classes during their lifetimes (Payne 1992). Other social divisions, not least gender and ethnicity, have become increasingly important to our sense of identity, as will be seen in Chapters 3 and 4. However, 'fuzziness' of boundaries, or complexity in the structure of subdivisions, does not necessarily invalidate the idea of social divisions.

The new complexity of multiple class situations should not disguise this fact. It would be wrong to mistake contemporary society's increased individual capacities to manipulate the cultural trappings of identity as meaning that class actually no longer matters. No amount of personal choice to 'mix and match' consumption behaviour or symbolic life goals will remove the underlying constraints of class situations. The fact that we encounter so much political rhetoric about 'classlessness', and the importance of individual choice or the latest fashion in 'achievement', does not mean that class has disappeared. Indeed, we should be asking in whose interests is it to propagate such myths?

Everybody does not have to believe in the existence of class, nor constantly think of themselves in terms of class identity, for class to be a social division. The system of class situations is not dependent on people's awareness of, or faith in, it. Social divisions do not always lead systematically to a sense of distinctive group identities, or to action with others on the basis of such shared personal social identities.

Despite lacking in visibility, and however imperfectly measured in the existing social classifications, class divisions remain central to social life in contemporary Britain. Of course, we recognise that in contemporary society, people are less likely spontaneously to describe their own experiences in the language of class. They search for more direct and specific determinants of their life chances to put alongside their recognition of class, and they recognise the independent part played by age, gender, and ethnicity. We do not, then, live in a 'classless' society, although we do live in a society whose members no longer spontaneously and unambiguously use the language of class as the obvious, taken-for-granted way of describing social inequalities. Class is not dead, but perhaps the monolithic social imagery of class has, indeed, had its day.

FURTHER READING

The most comprehensive and up-to-date overview of data on class differences is Ivan Reid's *Class in Britain*, London: Polity Press (1998). A summary of the debates over poverty and inequality, which brings together historical and contemporary studies, can be found in Scott, J. *Poverty and Wealth*, Harlow: Longman (1994). Geoff Payne's *Mobility and Change in Modern Society*, London: Macmillan (1987) is an excellent summary of the debates and trends in social mobility, while McKibbin, R. *Class and Cultures: England 1918–1951*, Oxford: Oxford University Press (1998) is a social history of earlier class differences that adds some life to the statistical bones. Finally, a very useful, balanced summary of the theoretical debates can be found in Crompton, R. *Class and Stratification*, 2nd edn, Cambridge: Polity Press (1998).

CHAPTER 3

Gender

PAMELA ABBOTT

Since the 1970s, sociology has attached greater importance to the distinctive positions of women and men. Assumptions about gender and gender differences are now seen as embedded in the structures and institutions of British and other societies, in our way of thinking and talking, in our beliefs and attitudes, and in employment, education, politics, the family, and leisure. In identifying gender as an important social division, sociologists are going beyond arguing that men and women have *different* roles in society, and are typically found performing different jobs. We are concerned with explaining them – to provide theoretical accounts based on the idea that these differences are *structural*, are predominantly *social in origin*, and that men, as a category, have more power than women as a category. While there are considerable differences in these various theoretical accounts (see for instance the discussion of 'patriarchy' below), men are seen as able to use their power to control resources, maintain their position of dominance *vis-à-vis* women and so are able to exploit women. However, although men are thus in a position of advantage, they also are structurally constrained by ideas of masculinity and what is expected as the correct way for a 'man' to behave.

Underlying gender divisions, there continues to be a view (generally unspoken) that the sexual division of labour and the inequalities between men and women are natural and immutable. This is reflected not only in the assumption that women should be responsible for domestic labour and child care, but in the occupational roles that are available to women (or those from which women continue to be excluded). There continues to be a view that women are naturally good at caring, at service work, at secretarial work and so on, and an expectation that when men do this work they will do it differently to women. The assumed natural basis for women being able to perform these occupational roles is also used to justify the low pay of female occupations, whether they are routine, non-manual or professional, in relationship to male occupations. Inequalities between men and women persist across the life course, from girls and young women being denied the freedoms enjoyed by their brothers, through inequalities in the labour market, to the poverty and dependency on the state for income and care that many older women experience.

Sociologists have challenged the view that gender divisions can be explained by biological differences between men and women. They argue that biology is an inadequate explanation and that we must look to social, cultural and structural reasons for the differential access that men and women have to power, wealth and privilege in modern industrial societies. Nevertheless, common sense views that men and women are innately different continue to structure the experiences of boys and girls, men and women, and the opportunities that are open to them in contemporary society. Gender identity is fundamentally ascribed at birth and structures our experiences from birth and the expectations that others have of us. Generally, the first, or at least second, comment made on delivery of a baby is its gender. This is marked in the hospital by the colour of band that is placed on the baby's wrist. In UK hospitals, boys have a blue band and girls a pink band. From that point on, they are regarded as fundamentally different and as boys or girls. This ascription at birth of gender is reflected in the clothing that they are subsequently dressed in, which in turn is a fundamental basis for our cues for social interaction and our expectations dependent on the assumed gender of the person that we are interacting with.

Dorothy Smith has argued that there is a distinct female life experience that is a reflection of the essentialist notions of what it is to be male or female. The notions of what femininity is, and what masculinity is, are used as the basis for interacting with girls/women and boys/men, both in terms of expectations, and the behaviour that is encouraged or discouraged and punished. Boys/men are expected to be domineering, aggressive, noisy and active, whereas girls/women are expected to be caring, quiet and less assertive. These very characteristics are then those that are seen to differentiate men and women in terms of employment. Characteristics associated with men are those that are said to be necessary for management positions within non-manual occupations and for skilled positions within the manual classification, whereas the 'natural' qualities of girls/women are seen to suit them for occupations which are accorded lower status and lower economic remuneration, such as nursing, teaching, care-work, waitressing, domestic work, and so on.

These differences between men and women now seem so obvious that it is easy to forget that until the 1970s, sociologists rarely considered gender divisions to be significant, focusing on mainly class and status differences. Indeed, it is possible to go beyond criticising sociology for ignoring the importance of gender divisions and argue that often *women* were ignored. Much sociological research focused on boys and men. Women were not even included in many samples and, where they were, gender was not seen as a significant variable for analysis. Even when differences between men and women were noted, these were usually seen as 'natural', that is as the outcome of biological differences. As Hartman (1981) indicated, sociology was at best sex blind and at worst sexist.

Changes in gender relations?

This chapter will argue that gender inequalities persist as a significant social division and will illustrate this by focusing on three areas: education, work, and poverty and social exclusion. The ascriptive principle of gender (our genders are something that we are born with) continues systematically to disadvantage women and deny them freedom and equality with men. In other words, structural constraints continue to limit the opportunities available to women in a masculine culture. At the same time, although men benefit from this relationship, the same masculine culture also imposes constraints on men.

This not to deny recent changes in men's and women's roles, as the latter have moved from the private sphere of the home into the public sphere of work and wider social involvement. However, there continue to be different expectations of the role of men and women – in particular, continuing evidence that women's entry into the public sphere actually increases their burden. That is, they are expected to take on more roles, worker as well as domestic labourer and mother, whereas men's major role remains that of bread-winner.

A recent Eurobarometer poll (1997: Fig. B) found that nearly 50 per cent of men, but only 30 per cent of women, thought that 'the jobs that need to be done to keep a home running such as shopping, cooking and cleaning' were shared equally between themselves and their husband/wife/partner. Wetherall *et al.* (1987), in researching attitudes to gender and equality among students, found that they thought that there should be an equal division of labour between men and women in marriage, but still maintained that child care remained a woman's ultimate responsibility.

As women move into the public sphere, control by men in the home is replaced by control in the workplace or by the state (Abbot and Ackers 1997). This is exemplified in the role of office wife/secretary, mother/primary school teacher, and in wife/mother/tart/female flight attendant (Pringle 1989; Tyler 1997). In other words, the servicing work that women have traditionally undertaken for men in the private sphere becomes part of the work they are expected to perform in the public sphere. Men employed in the same jobs are not expected to undertake this work. So secretaries are expected to perform wifely duties for their male bosses, primary school teachers have to 'mother' their classes of children, while flight attendants are seen as being there to 'serve' the need of male passengers. Women are expected to relate to men in the public sphere in the same way as they do in the private sphere.

This is not to suggest that women are passive victims. Women do struggle to resist male power and this is evidenced by the considerable gains that women have made in the last 20 to 30 years, not least in western societies. Gender relations have been transformed: girls are now doing as well, if not better, in the English educational system than boys. Women (including married/cohabiting women) are increasingly in paid employment with some women challenging men for the 'top' jobs. Women are no longer largely confined to the domestic sphere – women are part of the 'public sphere' of paid employment and politics.

One reaction to this has been a concern that male dominance – that is, masculinity – is being challenged. Working-class boys are taking on new masculine identities in situations where the normal transition for boys is from work to (un)employment, where they see their male relatives without paid employment and their mothers as the bread-winner often engaged in low paid service work. In this situation some of the most powerful 'truths' of gender – that men are bread-winners, and women housewives and mothers and economically dependent on men, have been exploded. In the face of this uncertainty about what it is to be a man there is now a variety of masculinities rather than one hegemonic understanding.

Many areas with high levels of social deprivation have witnessed the construction of an exaggerated masculinity where to 'be a man' is to engage in activities such as joy-riding, burglary and arson. Nevertheless, there remains a value on maleness which involves the routine harassment of girls and women, homophobia, and a rejection of what are seen as female characteristics (Mac an Ghail 1994). Boys continue to take on masculine identities within which they see themselves as dominant, as more powerful than, and as controllers of, women. In particular, working-class lads continue to be 'sometimes/always sexist, homophobic and often explicitly racist' (Dixon 1996). For middle-class boys, the role adopted is one of intellectual masculinity (an apparent effortless success: Power *et al*. 1998). The culture of masculinity also perpetuates a kind of domineering manhood – the definition of masculinity that boys take on has femininity as the subordinate term. Boys therefore 'need' to dominate girls in order to demonstrate that they are 'real men'.

An alternative position has suggested that women are increasingly rejecting their 'natural' roles as wives and mothers. This is seen as an important factor in explaining male unemployment, the rise in crime and divorce rates and the lower educational achievement of some young men. However, feminist sociologists have argued that these New Right and Christian 'sociologists' –

Murray, Marsland, Cox – are doing no more than simply blaming women for social problems (Abbott and Wallace 1992).

Although the initial focus of much feminist sociological work was considering gender divisions, they have also come to recognise the importance of divisions among women (and men) based on race, ethnicity, age, social class and sexuality (Phizacklea 1983; Crompton and Mann 1986; Arber and Ginn 1991). As Guillaumin has pointed out:

> women, blacks and other dominated social groups are not categories existing of and by themselves... they are constituted in the context of social relations and dependence and the process of sexualisation and racialisation... functions so as to allocate humans within specific social categories and positions. (1995: 17, 19)

In recent years, it has been increasingly argued that differences between men and women are no longer as great as they were. Young women are doing as well, if not better, than young men in the formal education system, and women are competing on more equal terms with men in the labour market. However 'in Europe inequalities between women and men remain substantial in a large number of areas' not least in employment and public policy (Eurobarometer 1997: 3).

Feminist sociologists have pointed out that these inequalities apply within academic circles as well as outside. The work of nineteenth- and early twentieth-century female sociologists, in particular that which recognised the centrality of gender analysis, has been erased from the sociological cannon (Lengermann and Niebragge-Brantley 1998). Who now has regard for Harriet Martineau, forgotten as the first translator of Comte; Marianne Weber, a sociologist in her own right but reduced to the status of Max Weber's wife; Jane Adams and the other Chicago sociologists who published in the *American Journal of Sociology*, but who came to be regarded as 'social workers'; or Beatrice Webb, whose own contributions became merged with her husband as 'The Webbs'? These are examples of the way in which the power of men in privileged positions can be used to determine what is to count as important and significant knowledge and the work of women in the process becomes discounted. This process has been referred to as the construction of a 'man-made world' – knowledge produced by women has either been ignored, marginalised, or erased from history (Abbott and Wallace 1996).

Nineteenth- and early twentieth-century sociologists accepted biological explanations for gender division, or rather, in the terms of Sydie's book title, *Natural Woman, Cultural Man*, attributed female behaviour to women's physical characteristics whereas men were seen as dealing in logic, reason, intellect, and so on. Contemporary sociologists have generally sought to replace this gendered explanation of gender by *sociological* explanations. An important starting point for this was the distinction between sex, meaning biological differences – anatomical and hormonal – and gender, meaning socially constructed expectations and behaviour.

> Gender refers to the varied and complex arrangements between men and women encompassing the organisation of reproduction, the sexual division of labour, cultural definitions of femininity and masculinity. (Bradley 1996: 203)

Beck (1992) refers to the 'omni-dimensionality' of the inequality between men and women.

Gender is a social category – a lived relationship between men and women – which structures every aspect of our daily lives. It is both cultural and material – men are able to control women not only by marginalising them in discourse, but by men's exercise of political, economic, social and physical power. Gender is also a 'script' – we have to learn how to *do* gender, that is, behave in gender appropriate ways. All gender behaviour is an act, a performance. As Jan Morris has said about her own transition from male to female,

> There seems to be no aspect of existence, no moment of the day, no contact, no arrangement, no response, which is not different for men and women. (1974: 140)

Explaining gender divisions

I have already pointed out that gender divisions have traditionally been seen as natural, inevitable and therefore immutable. This acceptance that different roles, associated statuses and access to scarce resources are based on natural differences went unquestioned, not only by the founding male sociologists, but in academic sociology until the 1960s. While some sociological work did explicitly accept biological argument, most omitted a gender analysis – assuming either that men and women experienced the social world in the same way, or that gender differences were natural and/or of no interest or importance. As Simone de Beauviour has pointed out, women have been defined as 'other':

> She is defined and differentiated with reference to men and not he with reference to her. She is the incidental, the inessential, as opposed to the essential. He is the subject, he is the Absolute. She is the Other. (1949, translated 1972: 16)

However, in the 1960s and 70s, women began to express a dissatisfaction with sociology; to argue that the sociological imagination was a male one – it did not speak to the experiences of women. Despite its claim to neutrality, sociology had a male bias. Dorothy Smith (1979) argued that this was because women's concerns and experiences were not seen as authentic, but subjective, while men's were seen as the basis for the production of 'true' knowledge. Consequently, sociological knowledge portrayed women through the eyes of men and male-made theories.

In this way, sociology, along with other disciplines such as biology and anthropology, was implicated in maintaining the subordination of women by providing a scientific justification for it. Mainstream sociological theories underpin and justify the subordination and exploitation of women by claiming to be factual. They have framed what is considered to be the subject matter of sociology – what should be studied, how studies should be undertaken, what questions it is important to seek answers to, what variables are significant and inform the conceptualisation and interpretation of the research findings. Feminist sociologists have argued therefore that what is necessary is to re-conceptualise sociology – not just to add women in, but to develop theories adequate for explaining the exploitation and subordination of women; ones that enable us to make sense of women's and men's positions in contemporary society.

Kuhn (1970) has argued that theories are not just rejected because they have been shown to be inadequate – not to explain everything. Theories are only replaced when more adequate theories have been developed, ones that can explain more adequately than the existing ones can. While feminists in the 1960s and 70s were concerned to demonstrate the inadequacies of existing sociological theories, to carry out empirical research in areas of interest to women, and to argue for the inclusion of gender as a variable in research, they also began to develop theories to explain gender divisions. There was not a single feminist theory, but a number of theories that challenged mainstream theoretical explanations for gender divisions and the exploitation and subordination of women.

Thus on the one hand, feminist sociologists were united in their rejection of mainstream theories, all being concerned with explaining how a male monopoly of knowledge and positions of power is exercised, how social relations are structured around gender and with how women can challenge man's privileged position. On the other hand, differences began to develop. The feminist theories developed in the 1960s and 70s had been 'totalising' theories that saw oppressive power as located in the structure of society – such as the capitalist economic system. However, there was a division between 'realist' feminists who argued that gender divisions had an existence in society beyond the lives of individuals who made them up, and those who argued from a 'social constructivist' position – that gender relations were bound up in our personal beliefs and how these were acted out in our day-to-day interactions with other people. The early feminist theories were mainly concerned with theorising gender divisions, but throughout the mid-1980s the need to recognise that race, class, age, disability and sexuality also structured the experiences of women has been increasingly acknowledged (Abbott and Wallace 1996: Chapters 1 and 12 this volume).

More recently, feminists accounts influenced by post-modernism and post-structuralism have been concerned to explain the operation of power through institutional arrangements and how social control is exercised through agencies that discipline the body. Post-modernism has been particularly problematic for feminists. On the one hand, feminist sociologists' critique of mainstream sociology has been seen as an important element of the development of post-modernism within sociology. However, the post-modernist claim that there is no valid (or verifiable) knowledge and the death of the subject (that knowledge is about control not liberation) is problematic for feminists who are concerned to uncover the systematic disadvantage of women and to produce the knowledge that will enable them to liberate themselves. While recognising that it is important to ask how we think about male power, it is also necessary to recognise the reality of the exercising of male power, which is a constant force within society, and its impacts on women's lives. Male power has a real existence outside of the 'discourse' of theoretical discussion, for example in rape, domestic violence, and sexual harassment.

Feminists are more ambivalent about the post-modernist claim that society and social relations are too complex to be understood through totalising theories. Some (for example Walby 1990) maintain that it is possible to have a theoretical explanation for the subordination and exploitation of women, whereas others argue that despite differences, there are shared commonalities in women's experiences (for example Doyal 1995). Others (for example Barrett and Phillips 1992) argue that it is no longer (if it ever was) possible to have universal theories and that the concern must be with explaining/understanding/theorising the local and the particular – the world as experienced by women and men in their everyday lives.

Gender and power

The key concept developed by feminists to describe male power was 'patriarchy'. This term, originally meaning 'rule of the fathers' was used in a specific sense in social anthropology to describe a kinship system in which males had dominant positions with respect to their female relatives. It was then adapted by feminists to mean any kind of male domination of women – at the level of society or within households. Although intended as an explanation of the multiple disadvantages experienced by women, patriarchy in this looser, second sense has not been an unproblematic term, because it is such an all-encompassing, general idea that it does not enable us to identify the causal elements that make up the patterns of gender divisions. Power relationships between men and women vary both historically and geographically, so to describe these just as 'patriarchy' is too universalistic and abstract. It also rules out the possibility of a society in which men and women are equal.

Furthermore, the term has been used in a variety of ways. The main difference is between 'realist' and 'social constructivist' explanations. The former sees patriarchy as embedded in economic structures (for example the labour market, the family), that is, the ideology of patriarchy justifies the inequalities rather than gives rise to them. For example, Hartman uses the term to refer to *male control of the female labour force*:

> The material base upon which patriarchy rests lies most fundamentally in men's control over women's labour power. Men maintain this control by excluding women from access to essential productive resources (in capitalist societies for example, jobs that pay living wages) and by restricting women's sexuality. (1981: 11)

However there are a variety of realist explanations: Firestone (1974) sees the material base of patriarchy as being men's *control of reproduction*, while Delphy (1984) places it in the *domestic mode of production* (that is, the ways in which the structure of the family means that women provide domestic services for husbands and children).

'Social constructivists', in contrast, see patriarchal control as emanating from men's aggression and use of sexual power in rape, domestic violence and sexual harassment, all of which are designed to keep women in their place. Men's super-ordinate position is maintained by an ideology that values men's 'natural' characteristics of aggression and competitiveness over those of women – cooperation and caring. Radical feminists see men as dominating and controlling women in their day-to-day *relationships*, whereas the realist feminists (Marxists, materialists and dual systems) see patriarchy as a *system* that dominates women.

The most developed analysis of patriarchy from a realist perspective is that of Walby who defines it as 'a system of social structures and practices in which men dominate, oppress and exploit women' (1990: 20). She indicates that it exists in six structures: paid work, domestic labour, sexuality, the state, violence and culture. She rejects the view of patriarchy as unchanging, and argues that the system articulates with that of capitalism and is dynamic. In particular, she points to the move from private patriarchy in the nineteenth century, when women were controlled within the private sphere, to public patriarchy in the twentieth century, where women are controlled within paid employment and by the state. However, many feminists argue that even this more dynamic version of patriarchy is inadequate to take account of the complex power relationships between men and women and between women and women.

Influenced by Foucault, post-modernist feminists have replaced the idea of patriarchy, that is, top-down power, with an interest in analysing gendered power and the way in which power is embedded in everyday practices and relationships at every level of society. This involves exploring how 'discourses' create particular forms of control and surveillance. 'Discourses' are groups of statements (which can change over time) that provide a language for talking about, and representing knowledge or 'truth' about, a topic. Discourses exist as dominant ways of framing what we believe, and men and women use them in their day-to-day lives every time they think or talk about each other. As a result, gender relationships are routinely re-affirmed and reconstructed in a way that enables male power to be perpetuated.

Discourses of masculinity and femininity powerfully control and regulate female behaviour, for example controlling the lives of young women as they try to avoid being seen as a 'slag', or 'easy lay' (Halson 1991; Lees 1993). Young men are similarly controlled as they strive to become seen as 'real men' (Mac an Gail 1994). The difficulty with this approach is that we are left with analysing local narratives of a particular context, such as young black women in school and the view that if discourses are changed then men's domination of women will cease. It is possible, however, to recognise the importance of the deconstruction of women and men as categories and develop more adequate understandings of how different men and different women are placed within the dynamics of gender inequalities.

Thus, Holland and her colleagues (1998) have argued that it is important to recognise that there are layers of power within which gender power is experienced, and to analyse each layer. They suggest that power is:

● Embedded in, and represented in language, ideas, beliefs, norms, values and so on; for instance, the belief that men are 'naturally better at science than girls'.

● Embedded in, and represented in agency and action; women's freedom to go out at night is curtailed by fear of rape and violent attack from men.

- Institutionalised and hierarchical.

- Embedded in 'embodied practices' – that is lived gender/how we do gender – also reproduces power relationships.

- Historically specific and subject to change.

Holland *et al.* argue that while individual men may lack power, Britain is still a male-dominated society but point out that this controls men as well as women:

> Individual men may reject, resist or ignore the demands and constraints of dominant masculinity. Yet in their first sexual relationship, they and their partners continue to be aware of, and subject to, the exercise of its surveillance power articulated through the male peer group and the efficacy of sexual reputation and both young men and young women live by these rules or take the personal and social consequences of social transgressions. (1998: 11)

Men, they suggest, have more access to power than women and are both oppressors and oppressed. Hegemonic masculinity controls men and there are powerful pressures on men to conform. Women do resist male power, both by challenging male dominance, by resistance and by celebrating rather than conforming to male expectations of behaviour, for example. However, their overall conclusion is summed up by the title of their book *The Male in the Head*. As Bartkey (1990) says, 'in contemporary patriarchal culture a panoptical male connoisseur resides within the consciousness of most women; they stand perpetually, before his gaze and under his judgement' (1990: 72).

Nevertheless, gender cannot be adequately represented solely as a single hierarchical division between men and women. As Lees (1993) points out, relationships between men and women and structured gender relationships are changing – they are not static, but gender remains as an important dimension of stratification. The structures of opportunities available to men and women remain unequal, but not fixed. Women do have 'agency' (self-determination and choice), but this agency is constrained by structures – unequal and controlled access to opportunities. There are also divisions between men and between women in their access to opportunity structures based on race, social class, age, sexuality and geographical location (as other chapters in this book show). I have referred above, and develop further in the next section, the ways in which young men negotiate their masculine identity in the face of changing labour market opportunities, which mean that 'real men's jobs' (Willis 1977) no longer exist for the 'lads'.

Gender and education

The educational process is central to an understanding of contemporary manifestations of gender. It is through the schooling process that identities are developed, and it is on the basis of educational outcomes that subsequent access to types of employment opportunities are determined. One might even argue that educational experience and qualifications are so important as to almost constitute a social division in their own right. Education therefore merits consideration in some detail.

Until recently, sociologists were mainly concerned with understanding why girls did not achieve as well as boys at school and in the education system more broadly. However, in the 1990s the question has been revised and the concern now is why young women are achieving *better* results than young, particularly working-class, men in public examinations. Indeed, there has been a widespread concern about the under-achieving boys which amounts to a 'moral panic'.

Chris Woodhead, Chief Inspector of Schools, is recently reported to have said that this is one of the most disturbing problems facing the education system. Media headlines and a BBC *Panorama* programme have all expressed concern about girls out-classing boys. At meetings that I have attended at one local education authority, continued concern has been expressed about the under-achievement of boys and how to develop strategies to reverse the increasing tendency for boys to become disaffected with schooling. However, while girls are outperforming boys, more boys than girls tend to score at the extremes, gaining either very good results, or very poor results in examinations. Sociologists are also aware that race (Chapter 4) and social class (Chapter 2) interact in complex ways with gender in terms of educational achievement.

The main changes that have taken place since the mid-1980s in the relative achievement of boys and girls come in the late secondary and post-compulsory school years. Girls out-performed boys in the primary and early secondary years in the 1960s, but boys then caught up with and out-performed girls in public examinations at 16+ and subsequently retained this advantage. Since the early 1980s, girls have caught up with, and overtaken boys so that girls now out-perform boys in GCSE examinations at 16+ and A-levels (and Highers) at 18+ (see Table 3.1). In the same period there has been a considerable improvement in the proportions of young men and young women gaining educational qualifications. In 1983, 26 per cent of boys gained five or more GCSEs at grades A–C. By 1996/97 this had risen to 41 per cent. In the same period, girl's performance improved from 27 per cent to 51 per cent.

Table 3.1   Examination results of pupils in UK schools by gender, 1996–97

Two or more A-levels		Five or more GCSEs grades A* to C		No graded GCSEs	
Males	Females	Males	Females	Males	Females
20	23	41	51	8	6

Notes:
Pupils aged 17–19 at end of school year in England, Wales and Northern Ireland as percentage of 18-year-old population. For Scotland figures relate to pupils in years S5/S6 gaining three or more SCE Higher passes as percentage of the 17-year-old population
Pupils aged 16 at end of school year as percentage of 15-year-old population at start of school year. Scottish pupils are in year S4

Source: ONS (1999), Table 3.18

Similarly, the proportions of young people passing A-levels has increased dramatically since the mid-1980s, with girls' performance improving at a faster rate than boys. In 1983/4, more boys than girls achieved three or more A-level passes; 11 per cent compared to 9.5 per cent. By 1995/6, 20 per cent of boys were gaining three or more passes, but 24 per cent of girls. However, the differences are less marked if we compare the populations of 19-year-olds who have achieved at least NVQ Level 2 or equivalent (equivalent to five passes at GCSE grades A–C) and 21-year-olds who have achieved at least NVQ Level 3 (equivalent to two passes at GCE A-level) (See Table 3.2).

Table 3.2   National targets 1996–98

	Males			Females		
	1996	1997	1998	1996	1997	1998
Percentage of 19-year-olds with at least NVQ Level 2 or equivalent	67	69	70	69	72	74
Percentage of 21-year-olds with at least NVQ Level 3 or equivalent	47	51	51	40	46	49

Source: ONS (1999) Table 3.21

There are also differences in the subjects that boys and girls choose to study after the age of 16. On the whole, boys out-perform girls in the higher status science subjects and girls out-perform boys in English and foreign languages. In the past, boys also out-performed girls in science and mathematics at 16+ examinations and it is only in the 1990s that girls have achieved the same level of performance as boys in these subjects (ONS 1999). Indeed, there is no marked difference in performance between boys and girls in the primary and early secondary stages, except for English where girls markedly out-perform boys (see Table 3.3).

Table 3.3   Pupils reaching or exceeding expected standards by key stages and gender, 1997

	Boys	Girls
Key stage 1		
Mathematics	82	85
Key stage 2		
English	57	70
Mathematics	63	61
Science	68	69
Key stage 3		
English	48	67
Mathematics	60	60
Science	61	60

Source: ONS (1999) Table 3.16

On the other hand, by A-levels there are marked differences. Here, boys out-perform girls in computer studies, mathematics, science and craft design and technology, while girls out-perform boys in humanities, arts, social studies and languages, as Table 3.4 shows. This broad pattern of girls specialising in arts subjects and boys in science and technology is even more marked in choice of higher education (Abbott and Wallace 1996).

At university, more men get first-class degrees than women and more men than women go on to study for higher degrees, but twice as many women as men study for a postgraduate teaching qualification. At degree level, there is gender stereotyping of subjects. Men are over-represented in engineering and technology, while women are over-represented in education and the humanities. In terms of degree classification, more women proportionately achieve degrees than men. Men achieve more thirds and pass degrees than women and more first-class honours degrees.

Further education and vocational training is also gendered. Young women tend to study social sciences, subjects aligned to medicine, or the creative arts. Women's subjects in further education are hairdressing, secretarial studies and health and social care. Men are more likely to study mathematics, agriculture, or engineering and technology.

Table 3.4   Girls' and boys' subjects

(Percentage of total entrants achieving grades A* to C in GCSE, grades A to E in A-level, 1995)

Girls' subjects	% A-level	% GCSE	Boys' subjects	% A-level	% GCSE	Not gendered
Social Studies	67	67	Craft/Design	81	52	Geography
Communication	64	54	& Technology			History
Studies			Computer Studies	84	61	Business Studies
Religious Studies	75	60	Mathmatics	65	51	
Music/Drama and Art	61	59	Physics/Chemistry	56	63	
Home Economics	90	89	and Biology			
Foreign Languages	60	89				
English and English Lit	69	51				

Source: Mitsos and Brown (1998)

The proportion of young women and young men participating in youth training is roughly the same. However, young men are more likely to be working towards a higher level qualification and to be paid a wage, young women are more likely to be on youth training because they could not find a job or gain a college course of their choice. Modern apprenticeships are also gendered, with nearly 100 per cent of apprenticeships in the motor industry, construction and electrical installation engineering going to young men. Young women predominate in hairdressing and business administration, while there is a rough gender balance in retailing and hotels and catering.

Given that the changes in the relative performance of boys and girls in the education system is recent, sociological explanations are only just beginning to be developed and empirical evidence is limited. Researchers have pointed to two key questions; why are boys under-achieving in the education system or why has the performance of girls improved so dramatically in the last 20 years? Those who focus on the former question tend to assume that boys are disadvantaged in the education system – that schools are failing boys. They argue that schools are not 'boy-friendly' and need to become so. In other words, that in meeting the earlier criticisms that schools have not been 'girl-friendly' in the past, the changes have gone too far and it is now boys who are disadvantaged. One example cited is the move towards course-work for public examinations, which is said to favour girls; another is the feminisation of teaching and the lack of role models for boys.

However, concern about the under-achievement of boys/young men at school is not new. Cohen (1998) traces commentary on the poor performance of boys back as far as worries expressed in John Locke's 1693 treatise *Some Thoughts Concerning Education*. The Taunton Commission (1868) also found that girls out-performed boys in reading, spelling, geography and history; in arithmetic, algebra and Euclid girls did better than boys when they had been prepared for the same examinations. Cohen also quotes a government report of 1923 that expressed concern about girls out-performing boys (*The Teaching of English*, Board of Education). She points out that boys' under-achievement is explained by factors external to them, for example the education system, whereas their success is seen to be intrinsic; high ability is seen as natural for boys. Conversely, girls' success is explained by extrinsic factors, or low status internal characteristics such as neatness and conformity. Failure in girls is seen as natural: girls are seen as 'naturally less able' than boys.

Those who focus on the second question, of why has girls' performance improved, tend to assume that in the past schools failed girls and that they under-achieved, while now girls' achievement is more in line with their potential. They point out that in the 1950s and 60s the pass grade for the 11+ was set higher for girls than for boys (to ensure more of the slower developing boys were able to pass) so that it was more difficult for girls to gain selective grammar school places. The move to comprehensive secondary schooling has removed this barrier. They see no evidence that schools themselves have become more girl-friendly. Indeed, they argue that while there has been some reduction in the bias against girls, girls are still at a disadvantage in schools. For example, in terms of teaching, 48 per cent of secondary school teachers are male and the majority of senior posts are held by men (ONS 1999: 50).

Indeed, some researchers have argued that schools in fact continue to be boy-friendly (Skelton 1993) in that boys continue to dominate the classroom and teachers do little to challenge this (Jackson and Salisbury 1996). Lees (1993) argues that mixed comprehensive education has increased sexism in schools and that teachers rarely challenge the sexual harassment that girls experience. There is evidence that teachers continue to believe, or at least to work on the assumption, that boys are more academically able than girls. Text books and other teaching material continue to divide men and women into sex-stereotyped roles. It follows that explanations for the rapid improvement in the educational performance of girls in public examinations, and the slower rate of boys, must be sought in factors outside of the school – for example, the decline in manual jobs for boys and the increasing labour market opportunities for women. In other words, we should ask why do girls do as well as they do in the education system, given that girls still under-estimate, and have less confidence in, their ability than boys, that they get less teacher time and have to tolerate the disruptive behaviour of boys in the classroom?

Among answers to this question are several based on notions of the masculine role. On the one hand, teaching staff are more tolerant of disruptive behaviour, poor performance and lack of effort by boys than girls. Because more boys are disruptive in the classroom than girls they lose more time and they are more likely than girls to be permanently excluded from school. On the other hand, parents control their sons less than their daughters, meaning that boys are less likely to do homework. Furthermore, boys think that they can 'muck around' in the early years in secondary school and catch up later – but they fail to do so. This is especially the case in their inability to catch up with and complete course-work for GCSE (Abbott and Wallace 1996).

It is also important to ask the question which boys under-achieve, and indeed, which girls do well. There is considerable overlap in the performance of boys and girls in school. While many boys under-achieve at school, many others do very well. Under-achievement of boys is a strongly classed and racial phenomena (see Table 2.7 above, and Chapter 4). For both young men and young women, social class is the major determinant of success (or otherwise) in school examinations. While there are differences between schools in their examination results, the best predictor of a state school's position in a league table is the LEA's position on the index of deprivation (DETR 1998). By no means all African-Caribbean boys do badly in school but on the whole they under-achieve at school and are more likely than other young people to be excluded from school (Gilborn and Gipps 1996).

The decline in masculine jobs, as contemporary society moves ever more to an economy based on the services sector, means that working-class young men, living in areas of high unemployment with no tradition of education, see few prospects for their future. This results in what is known as the 'new lad' culture, an alternative culture, in which 'lads' attempt to construct a positive self-image and draw attention to themselves by laddish behaviour and aggressive macho posturing. For many, the instrumental orientation to school, a limited compliance in order to get a job, no longer holds. In many deprived estates, especially in the north of England, the response to lack of opportunity has been a rejection of schooling.

Indeed, the concern about boys' under-achievement can be seen to be closely related to the concern about the high levels of unemployment among low-achieving males in areas of industrial decline. It is not that these young men are achieving less well at school than their fathers did, but that the unskilled and semi-skilled jobs that their fathers took upon leaving school no longer exist. To the extent that there are employment opportunities in these areas, they require credentials that these young men have failed to acquire. Rather than making the transition to 'adult man' in terms of full-time paid employment, marriage and fatherhood, they are said to become dependent on welfare benefits and 'fiddly' jobs (cash in hand employment taken while registered as unemployed). The restructuring of the labour market means that there are more jobs available for educationally low-achieving young women, who also have the 'option' of becoming lone mothers. When concern is expressed about teenage lone mothers, the pathway to this status is rarely directly related in public debates to under-achievement in education.

Given all the arguments for why boys under-achieve, it is important to remember that boys' performance has actually *improved* in recent years. After all, while *some* boys may be under-achieving, overall their levels of education and achievement have markedly improved in the last 15 years, even if girls have improved their performance at a faster rate than boys. It is this improvement in girls' performance that needs to be explained. One explanation is that the gap between the educational achievement of working-class and middle-class boys has widened, while the gap in performance between girls of different socio-economic backgrounds has not. The reason for this is that the women's movement has widened the aspirations of young women in general, so that the majority now expect to have paid work as well as being wives and mothers. There are more employment opportunities for girls than in the past, and girls are more controlled by their parents and consequently do homework and complete course-work.

Furthermore, it is important to recognise that not all girls conform to the demands of the school system or succeed in it. In the same ways that schooling is an important element in boys learning appropriate masculinity, so the majority of girls take on an appropriate feminine identity. School is centrally important to the process by which girls take on a complex identity that is feminised, racialised and located within a class system. Lees (1993) has suggested four strategies that girls adopt in secondary school:

- The pro-school academic orientation of white girls from middle-class backgrounds who aspire to academic success and an occupational career.

- The anti-school, pro-work orientation typical of some African-Caribbean girls who reject the racist attitudes of the school system, but are nevertheless committed to academic success and an occupational career.

- The pro-school anti-work orientation of some working-class girls who reject the discipline and academic elements of school, but see school as a place to have contact with friends.

- The anti-school, anti-work orientation of some working-class girls who want to leave school at the earliest opportunity and see their future major role as wife and mother.

Girls' orientations are crucially mediated by class and race, which inform their expectations for their future careers. While most young women expect to combine motherhood and marriage with paid employment, it is only academic girls, mainly from middle-class backgrounds, and some African-Caribbean girls, who expect careers. Mirza (1992) found that African-Caribbean girls anticipated a career, but that Irish girls saw their future as home-makers, child-carers and part-time workers. Working-class girls antici-pate having part-time employment that fits in with their domestic responsi-bility. As we shall see, school-girls' anticipations of 'work' are often misplaced.

Gender, 'work' and domestic labour

One of the major contributions of feminist sociology in the area of work was to re-define the term. In male stream sociology, work was used to mean paid employment, with priority given to full-time, life-long employment and the (male) bread-winner role. Feminists have challenged this, pointing to both the domestic labour and the emotional work that women undertake, and pointing out that this is real work. Glucksman has indicated that work refers to all 'activity necessary for the production and reproduction of economic and structures irrespective of how and when it is carried out' (1995: 68). By opening up the black box of the family, feminists have been able to demon-strate not only the persistence of gendered inequality of power in the private sphere, but also the long hours of unpaid work that women undertake in the home, doing the bulk of caring for the household, children and other dependent relatives, in addition to their paid employment; working the 'double shift'.

Seager (1997), in looking at gender and work globally, indicates that time diaries show that both men and women do more total work than conventional measures suggest, but that while most of men's work is paid, most of women's is not. Women and girls have the major responsibility for domestic labour. She concludes that not only do women work more than men, but they also perform a greater variety of tasks and have less rest. Similarly in Britain, women do more unpaid work than men, and while men do more paid work than women they also have more leisure time than women. In 1995, the monetary value of unpaid work in Britain was estimated to be between £341 and £739 billion. The lower value was more than the value of the UK manu-facturing sector, and the higher value equivalent to 120 per cent of the gross domestic product (Murgatroyd and Neuburger 1997).

When men become unemployed, some men take on more responsibility for domestic labour, but most tasks remained gendered – cooking the main meal and thorough cleaning remain exclusively female tasks, while washing the clothes and ironing are done predominantly by women, as is shopping and handling the household budget. The predominant male tasks are mowing the lawn, doing household repairs and taking out the rubbish. The British Social Attitude Survey (Jowell *et al.* 1992) found that the only domestic tasks not done mainly by women were shopping and washing up the dishes for the main meal, where the tasks were more likely to be shared. The only task that was done mainly by men in more than ten per cent of households was washing up the dishes, where 28 per cent of men were mainly responsible. As Delphy and Leonard (1992) point out, men do household work, but few are obliged to do family work.

Women continue to take the major responsibility for child care and looking after children, especially young children. Fathers do, however, take on some responsibility for child care. Half of the men interviewed in a survey in the United Kingdom in the early 1990s said that they would take on more responsibility for child care if they had the time. Clift and Fielding (1991) found that the nearer the wife's earnings were to a bread-winner's, the more equally domestic labour and child care were shared. Women expect, and are generally expected, to take time out of the labour market when they have children (or considerably to reduce the hours of paid work they undertake) and, as their children grow older, to take paid employment that fits in with child care responsibilities. In Sweden, where both part-time paid work and child care leave are equally available to wives and husbands, mothers are much more likely to take leave and/or part-time employment (Dryler 1998). Women are still seen primarily in their roles as wives and mothers and domestic responsibilities are expected to be given priority. A recent Eurobarometer survey (1997: Fig e) found that 60 per cent of women, but only 30 per cent of men, said that they were prepared to give up their job to look after children, and about 55 per cent of women (and 30 per cent of men) said that they would be prepared to give up paid employment to look after a dependent relative.

Despite married women's increased participation in employment there is little evidence that men have taken on significantly more responsibility for domestic labour and child care. The traditional domestic bargain – that women take on responsibility for child care and domestic labour and men the bread-winner role – is still the predominant ideal, even if not every family is able to live up to this. Women continue to be seen, not only as the main performers of domestic labour, but the ones mainly responsible for ensuring that it is carried out. This means that women are trapped in a cycle of dependency – they are not expected to be a bread-winner and are often not trained for an occupation that provides a bread-winner wage. Taking time out of the labour market to have children further reduces a woman's economic potential and her opportunities for career advancement and promotion. Women continue then, to be dependent on men for part of their livelihood. As Joshi notes:

> The traditional domestic bargain does not work to the advantage of all women. It involves loss of earnings, future earning potential and pension rights. It can involve social obligations, loss of autonomy and self and social esteem and, perhaps most importantly, loss of security. (1990: 52)

Gender and the labour market

Despite the 'traditional domestic bargain' there has been a steady increase in women's participation in the labour market in Britain especially since the Second World War. The most dramatic increase has been in married women in paid, especially part-time, employment outside the home. The majority of women (including married women) are in paid employment for the majority of years that they are of employment age. The time that married women take out of employment for child care has also reduced significantly. The employment pattern for women in Britain was, until the 1980s, an inverted M-shaped curve, rising as more women came onto the labour market in their late teens and then falling as the vast majority of married women took a break from paid employment while they had young children. The curve then rose again, as they returned to work when their children became more independent, before dipping again as women withdrew from the labour market as they neared 60 years. Now it is more of an 'inverted U', the same as for men, that is the majority of women, including those who have children do not take a break from paid employment (Abbott and Ackers 1997).

At the same time that the participation rate for women in the labour market (albeit mainly in part-time jobs; 27 per cent as compared with five per cent of men) has been going up, as it has been declining for men. This is partly a result of high male unemployment rates, especially in the North and also because of an increase in men, especially in their fifties and sixties, on long-term sick leave, taking early retirement or being made redundant and unable to gain further employment. In 1971, for example, just over half of women aged 25–44 years were economically active (in paid employment or seeking work); by 1997, over three-quarters of women in this age group were economically active. In comparison, 98 per cent of men aged 45–54 years were economically active in 1971, but by 1997, this had fallen to 91 per cent. It is predicted that the gender gap in economic activity will continue to narrow. The economic activity rate for women may indeed underestimate their rate because it does not take undeclared home work into account.

The reasons for non-employment also vary by gender. The main reason in 1998 for women being economically inactive was that they were engaged in non-remunerated work – 41 per cent looking after a family or home. The main reasons for men were that they had been made redundant (18 per cent), in full-time education or training (19 per cent), or that a temporary job had come to an end (19 per cent). Only four per cent of men were looking after a family or home (ONS 1999: Table 4.10). Non-employment is of course also connected to other factors, such as level of qualification, disability and ethnicity. However, even here, gender interacts with other social divisions. Thus differences in unemployment rates among women from different ethnic groups and women with different levels of educational qualifications are also marked (Chapter 4, below; Abbott and Tayler 1995; Iganski and Payne 1996; ONS 1999: Table 4.21).

The majority of married women, even those with young children, are economically active: in 1998 60 per cent of married/cohabiting women whose youngest child was under five years and 80 per cent of those whose youngest child was 11–15 years were in or seeking paid work. This compares with 77 per cent of married/cohabiting women who had no children (this latter group will include women in their 50s who have taken early retirement: ONS 1999: Table 4.4). However, the majority of employed married/cohabiting mothers work part-time – although the proportion working full-time increases as the youngest child gets older, from just over one-third for those whose youngest child was under five years old, to just under half for those whose youngest child is 11–15 years old. Married/cohabiting women with no children conversely are nearly twice as likely to be in full-time employment as part-time employment (49 per cent compared with 26 per cent).

Lone mothers are also more likely to be employed as their children grow older, 36 per cent of those with children under five are economically active, compared with 67 per cent of those whose youngest child is aged 11–15 years. The proportion working full-time also increases as children get older – from a third of those in employment with children under five years to the same proportion working full- or part-time for those whose youngest child is age 11–15 years. Single, divorced and widowed women with no children are much more likely to work full-time than part-time, 47 per cent compared with 20 per cent.

In contrast, being married, or having a child, has no impact whatsoever on men's labour market activity (Abbott and Ackers 1997).

Gender also affects the kinds of paid employment available, with women more likely than men to be in non-manual occupations. However, as Table 3.5 shows, men are more likely to be employed in the more 'desirable' (higher status/higher remuneration) occupations as managers and professionals and

Table 3.5   Population of working age by employment status and gender, 1986 and 1998. United Kingdom (percentage of working age[1])

Economically active	1986		1998	
	Males %	Females %	Males %	Females %
Full-time employees	62.8	32.3	60.4	35.7
Part-time employees	1.7	23.8	4.8	26.9
Self-employed	11.1	3.7	12.3	4.7
Others in employment[2]	1.6	0.6	0.5	0.6
All in employment	77.2	60.4	78.1	67.9
Unemployed[3]	10.0	7.3	5.9	4.1
All economically active	87.8	67.7	84.0	72.0
Economically inactive	12.2	32.3	16.0	28.0
Population of working age in millions	18.0	16.4	18.7	17.1

Notes:

1. Men aged 16–64 years, women aged 16–59 years
2. On government training scheme and, in 1998, unpaid family workers
3. Based on ILO definition, i.e. those 16 years and over who are without a job, or available to start work in the next two weeks, who have been seeking work in the last four weeks or are intending to start a job

Source: ONS (1999) Table 4.2

women are more likely to be in lower paid and less attractive routine, non-manual work and caring professions (Abbott and Wallace 1996). Similarly, within the manual category, men are much more likely to be categorised in skilled occupations than women. Despite over 20 years of equal opportunities legislation, there is still clear evidence that both the 'glass ceiling' (a barrier to women's upward mobility into the higher level positions) and the 'glass wall' (a barrier to women entering occupations defined as male) still act as barriers (Payne and Abbott 1990).

We have seen that the choices that young men and young women make, about which subjects to study in formal education (especially post-16 years), and the training schemes that they enter, remain gender stereotyped. Young men tend to choose science, technology and engineering and young women humanities, child care, floristry and hairdressing (*Daily Telegraph,* 9 April 1999: 4). Gender stereotypes still influence the job choices that are made on leaving formal education, despite the changes in the relative educational success of young men and young women.

Occupations are still heavily gendered, especially manual occupations in the declining industrial sectors of manufacturing. In 1998, 25 per cent of men were employed in manufacturing, compared with ten per cent of women; in construction, the figures were eight per cent of men, compared with one per cent of women. Women were mainly employed in 'other services' (40 per cent of all employed women compared with 19 per cent of employed men) and distribution, hotel, catering and repairs (26 per cent of all employed women, compared with 20 per cent of employed men).

The largest employment category for women remains clerical and secretarial work, although the percentage of women employed doing this kind of work has declined slightly from 29 per cent in 1991, to 26 per cent in 1998. The single biggest employment category for men remains craft and related occupations, although the percentage of men engaged in this category has fallen from 21 per cent in 1991 to 17 per cent in 1998 (and for women from four per cent to two per cent). Employers clearly have a view of what is appropriate work for women and women generally share this view (Chaney 1981; Yeandle 1984; Beechy and Perkins 1986). Many 'female' occupations are clearly regarded as using the 'natural abilities' women are seen as requiring in the private sphere: caring for young children, nursing, preparing and serving food, and in general securing the needs of others – 'emotional labour'. Thus, there is continuing evidence that women find it difficult to obtain employment in traditional male occupations and that men continue to be reluctant to move into traditional female ones.

There is also clear evidence that the glass ceiling remains, albeit that there may be some cracks beginning to appear. It is true that there are now more female head teachers, vice chancellors, women professors and managers, but they still remain in the minority. In 1990s Britain, less than five per cent of directorships are held by women and four out of five firms have no women directors. Only two per cent of the managers of National Westminster Bank, three per cent of the Midland Bank and four per cent of Barclays Bank are women (Giddens 1997). While 14 per cent of solicitors and barristers are women, only three per cent of High Court judges, all in the family division, are. In 1999, 17.8 per cent of senior, and 12.7 per cent of top, civil servants were female (Cabinet Office 1999).

The glass ceiling exists at a number of different levels, not just as a barrier to women entering top jobs. There is, for example, evidence that it is still virtually impossible for young women to get training places in the traditional male craft and related occupations, while those that do succeed then experience discrimination and sexual harassment. In terms of entry to middle management, women are less likely to be promoted than men, and those that are, are often promoted to positions that do not give them the necessary experiences to be seen as promotable to the next positions up. Examples include women police officers being promoted within the Domestic Violence Unit, women managers in the National Health Service running health centres, rather than to positions in the central administration, and female teachers promoted to pastoral posts, rather than the management of resources (Abbott and Wallace 1996). Savage (1992) found that female bank managers were generally employed in specialist units where they used specific expertise and were rarely promoted to managerial jobs involving the exercise of client control and/or authority. Devine (1992b) in her study of women engineers found that they were promoted to managerial positions where they managed women, rather than men. Women who are promoted to these middle level managerial posts are then often unable to gain the experiences seen as necessary for further promotion.

In addition, men are often seen to have the skills and competence necessary for senior managerial positions, whereas women are perceived to have the characteristics necessary for the caring roles. There is some evidence that women may choose these types of positions where specific expertise dominate because they enable them to cope with the conflicting demands of family life and 'organisation' woman. Crompton and Le Feuvre (1996) found female pharmacists in jobs in which expertise or professional technique were predominant, as this was more flexible than those in which the exercise of organisational power was the main function.

Organisations are dominated by masculinities, and femininities are subordinated. There is a denial of emotional life in organisations (Pringle 1988). Women often feel uncomfortable in the masculine environment and sexual harassment is one way in which men subordinate and control women in the workplace. It is one of the tactics used by men in restricting and resisting moves towards sexual equality in organisations (Cockburn 1990).

Despite the implementation of the 1970 Equal Pay Act, in 1975 women still earned less than men. There was some narrowing in the gap for a few years after 1975, but it has not narrowed subsequently. The gap between men and women's pay increases with age, and this is partly because men's average pay does not peak until they are in their 50s, whereas pay for women peaks in their 30s. Younger women are better qualified than older ones, which is part of the explanation for this. Differences in pay are partly accounted for by differences in labour market positions and partly by hours worked. In 1998, women earned 80 per cent of the hourly pay of men, but only 72 per cent of the weekly pay (mainly because women work for fewer hours a week in paid employment than men – the majority of women work less than 40 hours a week, whereas nearly two-thirds of men work over 40 hours a week: (ONS 1999: Table 4.12). Even when women are in full-time employment, they work, on average for fewer hours than men – 40.7 hours, compared with 45.8 hours a week. This is partly because men are more likely to work overtime than women, and partly because of differences in basic hours of work in predominantly male and female occupations.

There is, however, clear evidence that even when they are in similar jobs, women earn less than men, that there is a 'gender premium'. A comparison of the relative earning positions of men and women in 1978 and 1991 using data from the British Birth Cohort Studies found that women earned 60 per cent less than men in 1978 and about 40 per cent less in 1991. In 1991, men were paid on average about £1.50 for every £1.00 paid to the average employed women. Thus, despite formal access to employment in Britain for women since World War Two, the Equal Pay Act 1970 and the Equal Opportunities Act 1975, women have not achieved equality with men in the labour market.

The labour market remains vertically and horizontally segregated, with women occupying the lower strata, less-well remunerated levels within all strata, and concentrated in particular industrial sectors. Women are less likely to be promoted than men, and are concentrated in jobs that have fewer opportunities for career progression than men. Even in female professions such as social work, nursing and primary school teaching, men are proportionately more likely to be promoted than women. Routine non-manual, service and manual occupations are more clearly and specifically gendered than professional and managerial ones.

As with professional and managerial occupations, the movement of women into an area of employment tends to result in decline in its status and relative remuneration. This process is clearly evident in the history of clerical work. It is not self-evident, however, that any less skill is involved now than was the case in the past, even if those skills required may be different (this contrasts with the ways in which male printers have retained their high status and remuneration with the move from typesetting to computers – see Cockburn 1983).

It is evident that participation in the labour market remains highly gendered and the gendered role expectations of men and women influence this. Men are expected to be bread-winners and to support their dependants (women and children) financially. Women's main role continues to be seen as domestic worker and caring for her dependants albeit that the majority have paid employment in addition to the non-remunerated work they undertake in the domestic sphere. The ideology of separate spheres of man in the public sphere and woman in the private sphere influences both the expectations that employers have and the occupational opportunities available to men and women, as well as the way paid employment is organised. It continues to be assumed that women have a man's wage to support them (even if an increasing number of households depend on two wages, that not all women have a man and that in some cases, women are the bread-winners). Woman's orientation to work is clearly influenced by her role in the domestic sphere, as well as the labour market opportunities open to her. There is clear evidence, however, that the majority of women have paid employment because they wish to work and this is both for the economic independence that it brings and the social contacts and status rewards that emanate from paid employment (Martin and Roberts 1984).

Explanations of women's labour market participation

Feminist sociologists argue that the major factors explaining the segregated labour market are structural (Crompton and Le Feuvre 1996). However, Hakim in a series of articles (for example Hakim 1991, 1995) has argued that insufficient account has been taken of women's orientation to paid employment and work commitment, in exploring their patterns of labour market participation. She argues that there are three main groups of women:

- The home-centred (accounting for between 15 and 30 per cent of women) who prefer not to work and whose main priority is children and family.

- The adapters (accounting for between 40 and 80 per cent of women) who are a diverse group including women who want to combine work and family and those who want to have paid employment, but are not committed to a career.

- The work-centred (accounting for between ten and 30 per cent of women) who are mainly childless, and whose main priority is paid employment.

She suggests that there are also two extreme groups of women, those who are childless from choice and those who see motherhood and domesticity as their destiny. Professional managerial women are, she argues, a minority who cannot provide the basis for a general theory of women's employment choices. She develops what she calls 'preference theory', arguing that women can now choose whether to have an employment career or not. She argues that the majority of women who combine domesticity with employment ('the uncommitted') seek part-time work even when it is concentrated in the lower grades, and is less-well remunerated than other work. In contradiction to feminist sociologists who have argued that women's employment patterns are the outcome of structural factors and the exclusionary tactics used by men, she argues that women positively choose low paid, low status part-time work that fits in with their domestic and familial roles, which they themselves see as the priority. Tam (1997) found that female part-time employees are generally satisfied with their employment, although younger and well-qualified ones are less so.

However, Crompton and Le Feuvre (1996), arguing on the basis of their study of women in banking and pharmacy employment in both Britain and

France, conclude that there is little empirical evidence to support the view that there are different categories of women as far as work commitment is concerned. They suggest that there is no evidence, even when these professional women work part-time, to suggest that they are not committed to their paid employment. Martin and Roberts (1984) provided some information on women's attitude to work. They did find that social and domestic circumstances had a considerable influence on the way women thought about it. Some, for example, found it difficult to cope with paid work and domestic responsibilities. However, type of work and the employment situations also affected women's orientations to work. Contrary to popular opinions, they found that the majority of women, including married women were highly dependent financially on their wages from work and the majority of women were fully committed to work but this varied over the life cycle. The most highly committed were childless women older than 30 years.

Further support for this argument is provided by the findings from a study of 1182 part-time female workers in Australia (Walsh 1999). Walsh argues that female part-time workers are not homogeneous in terms of their characteristics or orientations and that there were a variety of reasons for women working part-time. While a majority of women in her sample were content with their current situations, a substantial majority wanted to return to full-time work in the future. She questions Hakim's view that a majority of female employees are not committed to a career and suggests that commitment to the labour market of female employees varied over the life course.

Feminist studies of women factory workers, for example Pollock and Nicholson (1981), Cavendish (1982) and Westwood (1984) suggest that women's orientation to work is primarily as housewives. Women on the shop floor have a shared culture of romance, marriage and family. However, studies such as the one by Martin and Roberts demonstrate that paid employment is central to the lives of many women employees. Women are expected, however, to cope with the 'double shift' and this influences their ability to demonstrate total loyalty to the job in the way which men can. They have to juggle their responsibilities to their families and their employers in ways that men rarely have to do. Furthermore, working in paid employment part-time does not prove a lack of commitment to that employment or to a career.

In order to understand women's position in the labour market, and their experiences of paid employment, we need to understand the ways in which patriarchy and capitalism articulate together to subordinate and exploit women. The essence of patriarchy is that women should be subordinated to and serve the needs of men, including their sexual needs, whereas capitalism as an economic system can only function with a flexible cheap labour force. It is in the interest of patriarchal relations to keep women in the domestic sphere and in capitalism's to employ them in the labour force. In terms of employment, this has meant a move from strategies designed to exclude women from paid employment to segregationalist and subordinating strategies. Women's participation in the labour force, and the way the labour market is segmented into jobs for women and jobs for men are not only driven by economic forces of demand for and supply of labour. They are also driven by family and sexual ideologies. The search for profit in the capitalist system of production is not incompatible with the power of men to exploit women and define skill (Phillips and Taylor 1980; Walby 1986).

The relationship between capitalism and patriarchy is a dynamic and changing one and it impacts differently on different groups of women. In the nineteenth century, it was mainly middle-class women who were excluded from paid employment, while in the late twentieth century, Afro-Caribbean women are most likely to experience public patriarchy and Muslim/British women private patriarchy (see also Chapter 4). Patriarchy and capitalism have competing interests but reach accommodation. Thus men (as husbands) clearly benefit from the additional income generated by their wives' paid employment – especially as research suggests that women retain the major responsibility for child care and domestic labour. Conversely, employers have been able to create jobs that use the assumed 'natural' skills of women, justifying the low wages that they are paid. Men benefit from the servicing and emotional labour that women provide in the public sphere as well as enjoying and controlling women's sexuality, where employers are able to sell goods and services by exploiting women's sexuality and potentially disruptive men are controlled by women's sexualised servicing, as, for example, in the case of the female flight attendant.

Finally, it is essential to remember that women choose to combine their commitments to both unremunerated (and often undervalued work) with paid employment. The choices they make, and their orientation to both, are the outcome of constructed choices and the socially constructed expectations of women's role and women's responsibilities. For example, highly qualified women in managerial and professional occupations can pay for quality child care and domestic help and avoid the criticisms often directed at working mothers/wives of neglecting their children/husbands.

Gender, poverty and the family

The (assumed) social and economic dependency of women on men means that women are more vulnerable to poverty than men. Pahl (1983) in her work on money management in marriage found that joint or male management of finances was the norm in households with average and above average incomes but in low income households, women were expected to manage the household's resources. Pahl (1985) and Graham (1987) found that household resources are not necessarily shared and that some women in households with average and above average incomes can have little or no access to these resources.

Indeed, in the last 20 years sociologists have pointed to the feminisation of poverty, although women have always been more vulnerable than men. Women usually bear the brunt of poverty when they live in poor households, being the ones 'to do without', and having to manage the scarce financial resources. Middleton and her colleagues (1997) have pointed to the sacrifices that many mothers make so that their children do not have to do without. A very large percentage of mothers often, or sometimes, go without clothes and shoes, holidays and entertainment in order to provide things for their children. Lone mothers on Income Support are more likely than other mothers to go without each item and to go without more of the items. These mothers are 14 times more likely to go without food than mothers in two-parent families not on Income Support. Glendinning and Miller have suggested that:

> women bear the burden of managing poverty on a day to day basis whether they live alone or with a partner, on benefits or low earnings, it is usually women who are responsible for making ends meet and for managing the debts which result when they don't... As more women and men lose their jobs, as benefits are cut or decline in value, women are increasingly caught in a daily struggle to feed and clothe their families... usually at considerable personal sacrifice. (1992: 60)

Women's vulnerability to poverty is the outcome of their restricted roles in the private sphere and the weak position they hold in the labour market (Payne *et al.* 1996). Women earn less than men (as we have seen above), have breaks in employment to care for children and elderly relatives and not only live on average longer than men, but also, given the tendency of women to marry men older themselves, outlive their partners. Women are especially vulnerable to experiencing poverty when they are caring for children and in old age. The groups of women most vulnerable to poverty are then: lone parent mothers, women caring for children and married to men in low paid jobs or who are unemployed and women in later life. In 1996/97, 20 per cent of the UK population lived in households in the bottom fifth of the income distribution; 16 per cent of men, 19 per cent of women and 29 per cent of children. Thirty-nine per cent of the population lived in households in the bottom two-fifths; 33 per cent of men, 39 per cent of women and 50 per cent of children. Of households comprising one adult and dependent children, 77 per cent are in the bottom two-fifths, and of households comprising single pensioners, 55 per cent are in the bottom two-fifths (ONS 1999: Tables 5.18 and 5.17).

Those households in the bottom two-fifths are heavily dependent on state benefits in cash and kind. Over the last 20 years, there has been a growing divide between 'work rich' households and 'work poor' households. In 1993 16 per cent of working age households had no-one in employment compared with 7 per cent in 1975. Married/cohabiting women in paid employment generally have a partner who is also in employment. The wives/partners of unemployed men rarely have paid employment because the benefits system is a disincentive to do so. There is then an increasing gulf between households in employment (and young pensioner households with occupational and/or personal pensions) and those dependent on welfare benefit. Furthermore, in a substantial proportion of two-earner households, women's earnings contribute to keeping the family out of poverty. In the 1990s, people in households with a male bread-winner and a female home-maker had between a four and six times higher risk of being in the bottom income quintile than those in households where both partners had paid employment.

Women who are lone parents are especially vulnerable to poverty. There has been a dramatic increase in lone parent families in the last 40 years. In 1961, two per cent of households comprised a lone parent with dependent child/children. By 1998, this had risen to seven per cent. This is mainly because of the increase in the divorce rate. The main route to lone parenthood is divorce – 72 per cent of lone parent families are headed by a divorcee, whereas only 18 per cent are the result of the birth of a child outside a relationship. Despite the introduction of the Child Support Agency to enforce the absent parent paying towards the cost of child support, the normal consequence of divorce is that the absent parent (generally the father) is financially better-off and mothers with custody are less well-off than before the separation.

Children are generally looked after by their mothers when parents divorce: the assumption that children should be cared for by their mother is deeply embedded in cultural and legal attitudes and values. In 1998, 19 per cent of children lived in a family headed by a female parent and two per cent in a household headed by a male parent. There are variations by ethnic groups: although only seven per cent of lone parents in Britain are African-Caribbean (NCOPE 1993), 55 per cent of African-Caribbean children lived in families headed by a lone parent, compared with 22 per cent of white children, 17 per cent of Pakistani/Bangladeshi children, nine per cent of Indian children and seven per cent of children from other ethnic groups (ONS 1999: Table 2.7).

The majority (around 70 per cent) of lone parent families with dependent children are dependent on state benefits and are the poorest of all types of

household in Britain. Lone parent mothers are less likely to be in paid employment than other women. Even when they are in paid employment, they often
earn low wages. In the period 1991–95, nearly half of lone parents in full-time
employment received family credit. Government policy to encourage lone
parents into paid employment is unlikely to improve their financial situation,
and challenges the government's emphasis on the important role of parenting.
Mothers in two-parent families are not encouraged to have paid employment.

Poverty and older women

Older women are especially vulnerable to poverty – and women are a majority
of those 65 years and over – and the proportion of older women to men
increases with age. Fifty-five per cent of women expect their husband/partner
will provide for them in retirement (*Sunday Times* 19 October 1997) but
women, as we have noted above, tend to outlive their partners on average by
about ten years. Two-thirds of all people aged 75 years and over are women,
and three-quarters of those 85 years and over. Older women are much more
likely to live in single person households than older men: 47 per cent of
women (35 per cent of these being widows) do so compared with 26 per cent
of men. Seventy-two per cent of those 75 years and over are women: 62 per
cent of these are widows, compared with 38 per cent of men who are
widowers (for further discussion, see also Chapter 6).

Retirement from paid employment for both men and women and the
households in which they live means reduced economic and other resources.
However, women are less likely than men to have an occupational private
pension. Two-thirds of men over 65 years have an occupational private
pension, compared with less than one-third of women. Even when women do
have an occupational pension, its final value will be considerably reduced by
the time they reach very old age. Men's occupational pensions often cease, or
their widows only receive a considerably reduced pension, when they die and
again, the 'real value' declines with increasing age.

Married/cohabiting women are also less likely than men to have a state
pension in their own right. Many older women did not have paid employment
in the past and therefore have no entitlement to a state pension, while others
chose to pay the married women's contributions (an option that was abol-
ished in 1976) and therefore also do not have a state pension in their own
right. Furthermore, many married/cohabiting women who have been in paid
employment will often have worked too few hours a week over extended
periods to pay National Insurance contributions and therefore have no entitlement to a pension, or have a reduced pension when they retire. Four-fifths

of the 2 million employees who have weekly earnings below the National Insurance lower earnings limit (McKnight *et al.* 1998) and 3.1 million of the 3.5 million pensioners who do not qualify for basic pension are women (Baroness Hollis of Higham's statement in the House of Commons: *The Times* 18 October 1997).

Although women are now entitled to have National Insurance contributions credited when they are not in work because they are caring for children under 16 years, and/or dependent relatives receiving disability living allowance, this does not protect the state pension entitlement for all women. Those who earn below the lower earnings limit are even more unlikely than other employees to have had access to an occupational pension. Increased divorce rates also affect women's income in old age: a divorced woman has no automatic access to her former husband's pension even though her decision not to have paid, or to have taken only part-time employment when she was married, was in order that she could look after the home, provide support for her husband and care for their children.

Women in old age, then, are much more likely than older men to be dependent on means tested state benefits, and much less likely than men to have an employer's or private pension and even when they do, because on average women earn less than men, it will be considerably smaller. For many women with a private or employer pension, it will also be further reduced because of periods when they have taken career breaks. Married/cohabiting (or formerly married/cohabiting) women are much less likely to have a state retirement pension in their own right, either because they have not had paid employment, or because they paid reduced women's contributions or worked too few hours to pay National Insurance contributions. Three-quarters of pensioners on income support are women (1.5 million women: *The Times* 18 October 1997) and many more women than men live on incomes just above the poverty line. Three in five older women are not married and must rely on their own meagre income.

While sociologists and others now frequently talk about the 'Third Age' – a period of relative affluence and good health after retirement enjoyed by pensioners in countries like Britain – this is not the case for all. Women are much less likely than men to enjoy this Third Age for a number of reasons. They are less likely than men to have the economic resources, they are more likely than men to have to care for dependent relatives (including their male partner), domestic labour does not cease on retirement and older women are more likely to have chronic health/disability problems. Furthermore, older women are more likely than men to live into the Fourth Age of increased dependence and to have to live on a low income – including those who may have lived in a relatively affluent household when their partners were alive.

Poverty and policy

Welfare policies in Britain have been mainly concerned with alleviating poverty, compensating the poor for its effects. Poverty is about more than income, it is about multiple deprivation (Townsend 1987). However, poverty is generally measured by reference to average male earnings, those in poverty being those who receive below a certain percentage of mean male income. Many commentators have used 40 per cent of mean income as a measure – a level above income maintenance benefits in the UK.

Poverty/being poor highly correlates with being dependent on the state for income maintenance benefits. Not only are these benefits means tested and stigmatising, but for women they in effect replace private patriarchy (control by men in the private sphere) with public patriarchy (control by the patriarchal state).

The Conservative government in office until May 1997 argued that it was necessary to reduce welfare (benefits dependency) by providing incentives for people to work. The incentives for the unemployed were mainly to reduce the real value of benefits and to increase the subsidies for those on low wages with children (Abbott and Wallace 1992). However, the consequence of these policies, combined with the restructuring of the economy (the decline of old heavy industries such as coal and steel), has been a polarisation of inequalities. While there is little evidence to support the existence of an 'underclass' – a permanently excluded group with anti-work values – there is evidence of a growing gap between those in employment and those without.

The Labour government that came to power in 1997 has made the tackling of poverty and inequality a major concern. They have, however, focused on social exclusion, on rising educational standards and getting people into employment as the major strategies – tackling the causes of poverty, rather than compensating people for its effects. The core approach recognises that poverty is part of wider social exclusion, a more inclusive term that takes in health, housing, employment, and so on. Whereas a sociological analysis of social exclusion is concerned with the dynamic processes by which individuals and communities come to be disadvantaged, and raises questions about the role of social institutions including the welfare state in generating these problems, New Labour terminology really signals an interdepartmental collaborative style of seeing social exclusion. Social exclusion creates a group of people who are 'non-citizens', who are excluded from exercising the rights enjoyed by other citizens. A 'Social Exclusion Unit' has been set up, charged with developing proposals for a range of policies designed to tackle social exclusion through enhancing individuals' economic capability and empowering them to take on responsibility for their own welfare. The policies introduced include 'employment action zones', 'health action zones', 'educational action zones' and 'new deals for communities'. All of these are based on the idea of developing partnerships and encouraging members of the community to be involved in both decision making and the delivery of services. The objective underlying all of these initiatives is to get people back into paid employment as well as encouraging active citizenship.

However, the policies are not based on consideration of the differences between men and women in terms of their role in the community or the family – they are gender blind. Single parents (mainly women) are encouraged to take paid employment with child care and wage subsidies provided to make this possible. This takes no account of the difficulties of being a lone parent mother and combining this with paid employment. In two-parent families, partners can share child care and domestic responsibilities. A lone parent has no such support.

Policies designed to encourage community participation take no account of the different ways in which men and women involve themselves in the community. While women tend to play a greater role, it is generally on an informal basis, helping neighbours and other members of the community. When men become involved in the community, it is normally in formal organisations. Agencies working with communities are more likely to work with organisations and therefore men are likely to be over-represented in consultation and empowerment exercises, thus marginalising women. Finally, these policies are likely to have little impact on the economic plight of older women as they are designed predominantly to help young people and those of working age.

Conclusions

In this chapter, I have examined gender divisions in modern Britain – the persistence of inequalities between men and women. Despite equal opportunities and equal pay at work legislation, there has been little improvement in the overall situation of women *vis à vis* men in paid employment. The majority of women continue to be dependent on men because legal changes do not change relationships between men and women in the private sphere, where women are expected to provide care for children and other dependent relatives. Nor do they provide help for women in carrying out the informal care for which they are seen as responsible. While the welfare state has challenged patriarchal power – for example, enabling women to leave men who beat them up – it has replaced private patriarchy with public patriarchy.

Gender then is a key aspect of social division and classification in modern industrial societies. It is not just that there are differences between men and women, but that there are inequalities that are built into the structures of society. Gender is a fundamental way in which every aspect of our lives is organised. It is the key category through which we make sense of our social and natural world and our experiences of that world. There are inequalities in the distribution of wealth, power and privilege between men and women. Gender inequalities are ordered and consistent in type – although in the longer term there are changes. Gendered relationships exist outside of the ways in which we categorise men and women – although the categories affect the ways in which gendered relationships evolve.

Nevertheless, gender as a concept is, at the same time, a social construct that is used to define, explain and justify inequalities, and as such is unstable and contestable. The structured inequalities and the socially constructed discourses of gender work together to perpetuate gender inequalities in hierarchies. Everyday struggles to change and resist the discourses of gender take place within the context of the pre-existing structural relationships within which men, on the whole, have more power, more ability to control, and more access to scarce resources than women. Historically, women have resisted men's power and fought to gain equality and men have resisted the attempts of women to improve their situation, *vis-à-vis* men.

Despite the gains of women over the last two centuries in terms of achievement of the right to vote, laws against rape, laws to protect women from domestic violence, equal opportunities and equal pay legislation, women on the whole continue to be subordinate to men within contemporary industrial societies. However, we should not lose sight of the fact of the fragmentary nature of social stratification and social divisions within contemporary societies. Men and women's experiences are structured not only by gender, but also by class, ethnicity, age, sexuality, and so on. At the same time, gender remains an important and fascinating element of social division in its own right.

FURTHER READING

Bradley, H. *Fractured Identities: Changing Patterns of Inequality*, Cambridge: Polity (1996) offers a comprehensive introduction to past and current theories of stratification and inequalities with a major focus on gender. A more specialist edited collection, dealing with gender inequalities and ageing, is Arber, S. and Ginn, J. (eds) *Connecting Gender and Ageing: A Sociological Approach*, Buckingham: Open University Press (1995). A selection of articles that considers and analyses the debates about the changing outcomes of education, as based on gender can be found in Epstein *et al.*, *Failing Boys? Issues in Gender and Achievement*, Buckingham: Open University Press (1998).

CHAPTER 4

Ethnicity

DAVID MASON

As we saw in Chapter 2, the analysis of class divisions has characteristically been concerned first to map and explain the causes of underlying material inequalities, and then to investigate their implications for people's conceptions of themselves and how this affects their relations with others. In other words, people's identities, and their relationship to others' identities, are usually second order questions in the study of class. Ethnicity, by contrast, presents us with a different problem. Ethnic differences are not constituted by material inequalities, even if they may frequently be marked by them. We cannot know people's ethnicity by seeking information about their occupations, income, wealth, or housing circumstances. Only in situations of extreme segregation will these kinds of information offer us good clues to people's ethnic status and, even then, few would argue that these characteristics represent the essence of their ethnicity in the way that is common in class analysis. Thus, if we are to understand the implications of ethnic differences for social divisions, we must ask some rather different questions.

Specifically, we must start by considering what constitutes ethnic difference. Then we need to map the patterning of that difference in the societies that we are studying. Only then can we proceed to ask what patterns of material inequalities are to be observed among the groups concerned. In other words, when we begin to consider ethnic differences we may find that these divisions are manifested in ways other than simple material inequality.

Some conceptual ground-clearing

Thus far we have spoken of ethnic differences as if the concept of ethnicity were unproblematic and uncontested. Unfortunately this is far from being the case. Before we can proceed, therefore, we need to consider what we mean by this term. As in the case of social class, we shall rapidly discover that 'ethnicity' is used in a variety of different ways and has been subject to a range of different theorisations. Moreover, the term is not one confined to sociological discourse but is widely used in lay debate and policy formulation in

91

ways that considerably complicate our task in this chapter. Not only that, but
the concept is related in complex ways to other commonly used terms such as
'race' and 'minority'. The term 'ethnic' is often found in combination with
'minority', while 'race' and 'ethnicity' are not infrequently used interchange-
ably (Mason 1996). I begin, then, by considering the origins and character of
the concept of ethnicity. In the process I touch on the related concept of
'race'. Mainly for reasons of space, however, I do not attempt a comprehensive treatment of the complex issues surrounding these concepts. Nor do I
treat systematically a range of other terminologies that the reader may
encounter. For an introduction to these issues, see Mason (1995).

The first thing to say about both the terms 'race' and 'ethnicity' is that they
are distinctively modern. By that I mean that they are products of what
Kumar (1978) has called 'The Great Transformation' of European societies
and particularly of the global expansion of European societies from the late
fifteenth century onwards. As they explored other parts of the world, Europeans came into contact with other human societies with unfamiliar patterns
of social organisation and which were populated by persons whose physical
appearance was noticeably different from their own. Europeans' encounters
with other societies rapidly turned to conquest and annexation, while they
adapted the ancient institution of slavery to the new requirements of colonial
expansion and capitalist production (Davis 1984). Against this background,
not only the striking differences between themselves and those whom they
met and conquered, but also apparent European superiority seemed to
require explanation. The result was the emergence of a distinctive way of
thinking about and explaining human variation – 'race'.

The modern concept of race emerged between the end of the eighteenth
and the middle of the nineteenth centuries (see the discussions in Banton
1967, 1977, 1987, 1988; Stepan 1982). By the middle of the nineteenth
century race science was characterising human diversity in terms of divisions
between fixed, separate and hierarchically ranked races, rooted in biological
difference and a product of divergent ancestries. The differences between
them were seen not merely as markers of current status but as determinants
of their past history and future potential. By the turn of the century this view,
expressed increasingly in terms of 'Social Darwinism', was being harnessed to
the justification of conquest and war as the age of high imperialism dawned
in wake of the 1885 Congress of Berlin (Mason 1995: 7).

By the end of the Second World War, as the horrors of the Holocaust were
revealed, race science was becoming discredited. At the same time, modern
genetics were undermining notions of biological fixity. The result was a
gradual disappearance of the concept of race from natural science debates
(Banton and Harwood 1975; Montague 1964, 1974). Nevertheless, biological

notions persisted in both political discourse and popular conceptions of human variation. As a result, even those such as sociologists who were convinced by the evidence that races in the biological sense did not exist, found themselves having to confront the persistence of the concept. However uneasily, sociologists found themselves continuing to use the concept on the basis that social actors treated it as real and organised their lives in terms of it (*cf.* van den Berghe 1967). Only relatively recently have writers such as Miles (1982, 1993) challenged this usage, arguing that it serves to legitimise an ideological category, naturalising divisions that are really the outcome of exploitation and oppression. One result of this challenge has been the tendency for recent sociological writing to substitute the problematic of 'racism' for that of 'race' (see, for example, Solomos and Back 1996). Readers wishing to pursue further the issues raised by this ongoing debate may find the fuller discussions in Mason (1994, 1995) a useful starting point.

In what follows, I shall not use the term 'race' except where this is unavoidable in referring to the work of others. Nevertheless, if we are to understand the status of the concept of ethnicity – the focus of this chapter – it is necessary to grasp the extent to which it has emerged, and continues to appear, in dialogue with that of race.

The concept of ethnicity entered sociological and policy discourse partly as a reaction to the perceived inadequacies of race. It is frequently seen as more legitimate because it avoids biological determinism and appeals, at least in part, to the self-definitions of members. Because of the range of theoretical traditions from which the issue can be approached, there is no universally accepted definition of ethnicity. It is probably true to say that, if pressed for a definition, most academics and policy makers would stress some sort of cultural distinctiveness as the mark of an ethnic grouping. For example, M. G. Smith has defined an ethnic unit as 'a population whose members believe that in some sense they share common descent and a common cultural heritage or tradition, and who are so regarded by others' (1986: 192).

Nevertheless there are among sociologists considerable differences of view about how negotiable ethnicity is. How much freedom do social actors have to define themselves and their relationships to others? To what extent can people chose their ethnicity? For some there is a primordial element to ethnicity that explains the fervour of commitments to particular cultural identities. For others, ethnicity is little more than a symbolic resource to be used instrumentally (Jenkins 1986a, 1997; Mason 1986; Yinger 1986: 26–31, 1994).

One influential approach argues that ethnicity is more a matter of the processes by which boundaries are created and maintained between ethnic groups than it is of the internal content of the ethnic categories (Barth 1969; Jenkins 1997: 16–24; Wallman 1986). Whether and how social boundaries are erected is an empirical question and not one that can be simply read off from the existence of cultural difference. Thus, Wallman argues that:

> two sets of people with common cultural origins placed in similar minority positions [will not] necessarily use the same elements of their traditional culture to mark themselves off from non-member 'others'. What they do use will depend on the resources they have, on what they hope to achieve (whether consciously or not) and on the range of options available to them at the time (1979: 5–6).

Ethnicity is then situational. People may have different ethnic identities in different situations. It is possible to be simultaneously English, British and European, stressing these identities more or less strongly in different aspects of daily life or at different times. Similarly, the same person might identify as Gujerati, Indian, Hindu, East African Asian, or British depending on situation, immediate objectives and the responses and behaviour of others.

Ethnicity is thus an explicitly relational concept entailing both categorisation and identity. It implies 'we' statements and 'they' statements. Nevertheless in much popular parlance, the term 'ethnic' is used to refer only to those who are thought of as different from some assumed indigenous norm of 'Britishness' (see Chapter 5). It is frequently used as a synonym for those thought of as culturally different. Talk of an ethnic 'look' in the world of fashion is only one, relatively trivial, example of the way white British people are apt to see ethnicity as an attribute only of others – something that distinguishes 'them' from 'us'. This is exemplified by the way in which in Britain the term 'ethnic' is usually qualified with the word 'minority'. We almost never hear mention of an ethnic *majority*.

Matters are, however, more complicated still. Not every group having a distinctive culture and constituting a minority in the British population is normally included in the designation. Instead, in order to qualify for designation as an ethnic minority, a category of people must exhibit a degree of 'difference' that is regarded as significant. In practice, a mixture of skin colour and distinctive culture is the criterion that is usually thought to mark off 'ethnic minorities' from the 'majority' population in Britain. At the same time, 'ethnic minorities' are frequently seen to have more in common with one another than with the 'majority'. The term thus often seems to de-emphasise *diversity among minority* ethnic groups while exaggerating *differences from* the white population. Even those who argue that 'ethnic minorities' are united by a common experience of racism, often fail to be sufficiently alert to the diverse ways in which racism may impact upon different communities or, within them, upon men and women (Field 1987; Modood 1988, 1990, 1992; Yuval-Davis and Anthias 1989; Anthias and Yuval-Davis 1992).

Ethnic differences in Britain: some problems of measurement

We have seen that the term 'ethnic minority' and, by extension 'ethnicity', has a particular resonance in Britain. Despite the fact that Britain's population is one forged from successive historical migrations, the term characteristically refers to people descended from the populations of the countries of the former British Empire – the so-called New Commonwealth. Indeed it is interesting to note that in popular parlance the term immigration is now automatically associated with the immigration to Britain of people whose origins lay in these countries.

A key reason for this lies in the rapid growth of this population in the years following the end of the Second World War. At the end of the war, the British Empire was still largely intact. It provided a ready source of potential labour until the period of immigration control was initiated with the passing of the Commonwealth Immigrants Act in 1962. (For a discussion of the history of immigration control to Britain see Layton-Henry 1992; Mason 1995.)

Due to a number of factors, a severe labour shortage developed in post-war Britain. Partly this was a result of the need to engage in post-war reconstruction. At the same time, British industry was becoming increasingly large scale and capital intensive, with a growing demand for skilled workers. In addition, new employment opportunities were opening up in the rapidly growing service industries, and in the public sector which was expanding as a result of the new welfare state established by the Labour government. Increasingly British workers, and in particular those of the first generation to receive secondary education, had access to avenues of upward social mobility as they moved into newly created and more desirable occupations. This process left a pool of hard-to-fill unskilled and routine semi-skilled jobs at the lower levels of the labour market. These were often dirty, poorly paid and involved unsocial hours like night shift working. Many were found in declining industries where cheap labour was an alternative to capital investment or collapse (see Fevre 1984; Duffield 1985.). Given Britain's labour shortage in a period when women had been encouraged to leave the labour market and raise young families, these vacancies could best be filled by substantial immigration.

From an early stage, then, Britain's new minority ethnic citizens found themselves differentiated from the rest of the population, first by socio-economic situation and later by immigration status. These characteristics established the conditions in which early attempts to measure the size and growth of the minority ethnic population were made. However, over time the sources of data about Britain's ethnic diversity have changed and developed in the light of changing policy concerns, changing political priorities (both within government and outside) and changing patterns of political struggle, including the demands of minority ethnic communities themselves. The same is true of the categories in terms of which members of different groups are categorised. One consequence of this is that tracking changes over time is extremely difficult.

Early discussions of Britain's growing ethnic diversity were framed within debates about immigration. As a result, until recently, most official estimates of the size of the minority ethnic population were based on the place of birth of those born outside the UK, in the 'New Commonwealth'. The term New Commonwealth is a euphemism for the countries of the former British Empire populated by people whose skin colour is not white. The New Commonwealth is thus distinguished from the Old Commonwealth of countries having predominantly white populations. The term 'New' was justified largely on the grounds that these countries attained independence after the Second World War, in contrast to Australia, Canada and New Zealand which had been granted effective self-government much earlier. The convolutions entailed in this usage are well illustrated by the fact that when Pakistan left the Commonwealth in 1972, it was necessary to revise the term to 'New Commonwealth and Pakistan'. This is often rendered as 'NCWP'.

Counting those born in the New Commonwealth made some statistical sense in the early days of immigration but it became increasingly unsatisfactory as a growing proportion of the New Commonwealth-descended population were actually being born in Britain. The initial solution was to count those living in households where the 'head of household' had been born in the New Commonwealth. Yet again, this could only ever be a temporary solution until the children of initial migrants began to establish their own households. Nevertheless, until data from the 1991 Census became available, estimates of this kind based on the Censuses of 1971 and 1981 were the main sources for both official and academic purposes.

The 1991 Census asked respondents for the first time to classify themselves in ethnic terms. The following schema was the one finally adopted:

White	Pakistani
Black – Caribbean	Indian
Black – African	Chinese
Black – Other (please specify)	Any other ethnic group
Bangladeshi	(please describe)

These categories have also been adopted by the Commission for Racial Equality as those that it recommends for ethnic monitoring purposes. This increasing standardisation offers the future benefits of comparability between data sources and over time. As we shall see, however, these features are not without their problems when faced with the realities of changing ethnic identities.

We should also note that, in addition to figures derived from the Census, there have been some other sources of data. The most important, and widely used, are the periodic surveys conducted by the Policy Studies Institute (formerly Political and Economic Planning; Smith 1974; Brown 1984; Modood *et al.* 1997), and the results of the annual Labour Force Survey conducted by the Office for National Statistics. Both have utilised self-classification measures of ethnicity. However, there are technical differences not only between one another but also between those used in the 1991 Census, so that comparisons are fraught with difficulty, particularly where they involve attempts to measure change over time. In the rest of this chapter much of the discussion will rely upon the data from the 1991 Census augmented by material from analyses of the Labour Force Survey (Jones 1993) and the Fourth PSI Survey (Modood *et al.* 1997). The discussion of the 1991 Census data is largely drawn from the analyses by Dr David Owen published as Census Statistical Papers by the Centre for Research in Ethnic Relations (Owen 1992, 1993). The data themselves are Crown copyright and are made available to the academic community through ESRC purchase.

Minority ethnic groups in Britain: evidence of inequality

Results from the 1991 Census indicate that there are now in more than 3 million people of minority ethnic origin resident in Great Britain. They constitute 5.5 per cent of the population of Great Britain, 5.9 per cent of the population of England and Wales, and 6.2 per cent of the population of England (Owen 1992: 1–2).

This population has an uneven geographical spread, concentrated as it is not just in England but also overwhelmingly resident in the most densely populated urban areas. Forty-five per cent of the minority ethnic population lives in London (which contains just over ten per cent of the white population) and 14 per cent in the West Midlands (by comparison with nine per cent of the white population: Owen 1992: 2–3). Other areas of high minority ethnic residence are West Yorkshire, Greater Manchester and parts of the East Midlands, as Table 4.2 shows.

There has been a tendency over a lengthy period, for the minority ethnic population to become more spatially concentrated (*cf.* Brown 1984: 59; Owen 1992: 9–10). It is important to note that within this overall pattern the distribution of individual ethnic groups varies widely. For at least some groups this

Table 4.1   **Ethnic group composition of the population in 1991 (%)**

Ethnic group	Great Britain	England and Wales	England
White	94.5	94.1	93.8
Ethnic minorities	5.5	5.9	6.2
Black	*1.6*	*1.8*	*1.9*
Black-Caribbean	0.9	1.0	1.1
Black-African	0.4	0.4	0.4
Black-Other	0.3	0.4	0.4
South Asian	*2.7*	*2.9*	*3.0*
Indian	1.5	1.7	1.8
Pakistani	0.9	0.9	1.0
Bangladeshi	0.3	0.3	0.3
Chinese and others	*1.2*	*1.2*	*1.3*
Chinese	0.3	0.3	0.3
Other-Asian	0.4	0.4	0.4
Other-Other	0.5	0.6	0.6
Total population (000s)	**54,888.8**	**49,890.3**	**47,055.2**

Source: Owen (1992)

concentration in areas of initial settlement has important implications for their economic and other opportunities (see Mason 1995: 36–7).

As we have seen, ethnic differences are not, in themselves, constituted by material inequalities. However, to the extent that ethnicity is a source of social division it would be surprising if ethnic differences were not associated with such inequalities. Indeed, access to economic resources is usually a key to people's ability to control other aspects of their lives and for most of Britain's citizens, income from employment represents the major economic resource for day-to-day living.

As a result, it is appropriate, in the next part of the discussion, to focus on labour market placement. Research from the 1960s through into the 1980s (Smith 1974; Brown 1984) consistently showed that people from minority ethnic groups were clustered in particular industries and occupations, over-represented in semi-skilled and unskilled jobs and frequently excluded altogether from the labour market. More recent evidence reveals both continuity and change from earlier periods. We should remember, however, that material inequalities have other dimensions (some, but not all, directly related to control of economic resources). They include housing status and access to health and health care. For an introduction to these issues see Mason (1995) and Modood *et al.* (1997).

Table 4.2 **Ethnic minorities in Great Britain by region, 1991**

Regions and metropolitan counties – GB	Total population (000s)	White			Ethnic minorities		
		(000s)	*(%)[1]*	*%[2]*	*(000s)*	*(%)[1]*	*%[2]*
South-East	17,208.3	15,512.9	90.1	29.9	1,695.4	9.9	56.2
Greater London	6,679.7	5,333.6	79.8	10.3	1,346.1	20.2	44.6
East Anglia	2,027.0	1,983.6	97.9	3.8	43.4	2.1	1.4
South-West	4,609.4	4,546.8	98.6	8.8	62.6	1.4	2.1
West Midlands	5,150.2	4,725.8	91.8	9.1	424.4	8.2	14.1
West Midlands MC	2,551.7	2,178.1	85.4	4.2	373.5	14.6	12.4
East Midlands	3,953.4	3,765.4	95.2	7.3	188.0	4.8	6.2
Yorks and Humberside	4,836.5	4,622.5	95.6	8.9	214.0	4.4	7.1
South Yorkshire	1,262.6	1,226.5	97.1	2.4	36.2	2.9	1.2
West Yorkshire	2,013.7	1,849.6	91.8	3.6	164.1	8.2	5.4
North-West	6,243.7	5,999.1	96.1	11.6	244.6	3.9	8.1
Greater Manchester	2,499.4	2,351.2	94.1	4.5	148.2	5.9	4.9
Merseyside	1,403.6	1,377.7	98.2	2.7	25.9	1.8	0.9
North	3,026.7	2,988.2	98.7	5.8	38.5	1.3	1.3
Tyne and Wear	1,095.2	1,075.3	98.2	2.1	19.9	1.8	0.7
Wales	2,835.1	2,793.5	98.5	5.4	41.6	1.5	1.4
Scotland	4,998.6	4,935.9	98.7	9.5	62.6	1.3	2.1
Great Britain	**54,888.8**	**51,873.8**	**94.5**	**100.0**	**3,015.1**	**5.5**	**100.0**

Notes:
1. % of region's population in given ethnic group
2. % of total ethnic population, living in given region

Source: Owen (1992)

Employment, unemployment and earnings

Successive studies (Smith 1974, 1981; Brown 1984; Jones 1993) have revealed that persons of ethnic minority origin are at a consistently higher risk of unemployment than are white people. There is evidence that unemployment among people from minority ethnic groups is 'hyper-cyclical' (Jones 1993: 112). In other words it rises faster than white unemployment in times of recession and falls more rapidly when the economy recovers. Over an extended period, however, we can say that the rate of unemployment among minority ethnic men has tended to be roughly double the rate for white men. This is confirmed by data from the 1991 Census (Table 4.3) which show the unemployment rate among people of ethnic minority descent once more running at twice the white rate among men, and around two and a half times the white rate among women (the higher rate being what one might expect from the arguments in Chapter 3).

We should also note, however, that there are marked variations in the experience of different groups and of men and women. Thus, for example, the female unemployment rate for Bangladeshis was nearly 35 per cent, five times higher than the overall female rate of 6.8 per cent. Even among those of Indian origin, a group often identified as experiencing upward occupational mobility, the unemployment rate was about 25 per cent higher than the white rate among men and twice as high among women (Owen 1993: 6). Among young people, who represent a relatively larger proportion of minority ethnic groups than of whites, there are similar variations as among the economically

Table 4.3   Unemployment rates by ethnic group, Great Britain, 1991

| Ethnic group | Unemployment rates | | |
	Persons (%)	Males (%)	Females (%)
White	8.8	10.7	6.3
Ethnic minorities	18.3	20.3	15.6
Black	*21.1*	*25.2*	*16.6*
Black-Caribbean	18.9	23.8	13.5
Black-African	27.0	28.9	24.7
Black-Other	22.2	25.5	18.3
South Asian	*18.2*	*19.2*	*16.5*
Indian	13.1	13.4	12.7
Pakistani	28.8	28.5	29.6
Bangladeshi	31.7	30.9	34.5
Chinese and others	*14.1*	*15.5*	*12.1*
Chinese	9.5	10.5	8.3
Other-Asian	13.4	14.2	12.3
Other-Other	17.7	19.7	14.8
Entire population	**9.3**	**11.2**	**6.8**

Source: Owen (1993)

active as a whole. Only among men of African Asian origin (Jones 1993: 113) and among Chinese men (Owen 1993: 7) are unemployment rates as low as those for white people (compare Modood *et al.* 1997: 88–93).

There are also regional variations in unemployment rates with a number of important areas of minority ethnic residence in the North and Midlands of England exhibiting high levels of unemployment. At the risk of oversimplifying, we can note that while levels of minority ethnic unemployment are consistently higher than the white rate, these differences are larger outside Greater London. In these areas, even groups such as African Asians are likely to experience higher unemployment than white people (Jones 1993: 113–14; Owen 1993; Modood 1997a: 88–93).

A long series of studies has shown that in general terms members of minority ethnic groups have been employed in less skilled jobs, at lower job levels and concentrated in particular industrial sectors (for example Smith 1974; Brown 1984). More recent data such as Jones's (1993) re-analysis of the Labour Force Survey for 1988, 1989 and 1990, and the fourth PSI survey (Modood *et al.* 1997) suggest that the position is becoming more complex as the experience of members of different groups has begun to diverge. Iganski and Payne (1996, 1999), who have argued that the disadvantaged occupational position of the minority ethnic groups has become progressively ameliorated, nonetheless stress the major differences between groups and between men and women.

The data presented in Table 4.4 suggest that male members of some minority ethnic groups are beginning to experience employment patterns that increasingly approximate those of white men.

This is true of African Asian, Chinese and, to a slightly lesser extent, Indian men where the proportions approximate or exceed the proportions of white workers in each of the top two categories. However, these figures conceal important variations since, although African Asian and Chinese men are more likely to be professional workers than white men, they are considerably less likely to be represented among senior managers in large enterprises. Among those of Afro-Caribbean, Bangladeshi and Pakistani descent, there is much less evidence of progress in the top category (although there is some convergence in the 'intermediate and junior non-manual category). Bangladeshi men in particular, 53 per cent of whom are in semi-skilled manual occupations, remain concentrated in the lower echelons of the labour market.

Table 4.5 presents comparable data for women. It shows that women of all groups are less likely than men to be in the top category and, for all groups, the largest concentrations are to be found in the 'intermediate' and 'junior' non-manual categories, followed by 'semi-skilled manual'.

This finding matches that of the 1982 Policy Studies Institute survey (Brown 1984) and Jones's (1993) re-analysis of Labour Force Survey data.

Table 4.4   Job levels of men (employees and self-employed)

Socio-economic group	White	Caribbean	Indian	African Asian	Pakistani	Bangladeshi	Chinese
	column percentages						
Prof./managers/employers	30	14	25	30	19	18	46
Employers and managers (large establishments)	11	5	5	3	3	0	6
Employers and managers (small establishments)	11	4	11	14	12	16	23
Professional workers	8	6	9	14	4	2	17
Intermediate and junior non-manual	18	19	20	24	13	19	17
Skilled manual & foremen	36	39	31	30	46	7	14
Semi-skilled manual	11	22	16	12	18	53	12
Unskilled manual	3	6	5	2	3	3	5
Armed forces or N/A	2	0	3	2	2	0	5
Non-manual	48	33	45	54	32	37	63
Manual	50	67	52	44	67	63	31

Source: Modood *et al.* (1997)

Despite detailed variations between groups, therefore, this suggests that 'gender divisions in the labour market may be stronger and more deeply rooted than differences due to race and ethnicity' (Iganski and Payne 1996; Modood 1997a: 104).

It is important to be clear that data about occupational placement may conceal important differences between groups in status, in the kinds of enterprise worked in or in working conditions. Of particular importance are earnings. Brown's (1984) study found that minority ethnic employees had significantly lower earnings than their white counterparts. A number of more recent studies (McCormick 1986; Pirani *et al.* 1992) have suggested that the pattern revealed by earlier studies continued into the late 1980s and 90s. This finding is further confirmed by the results of the fourth PSI survey (Modood *et al.* 1997). These reveal, however, marked differences between groups, with African Asians and Chinese men approximating white rates. Caribbean rates are slightly lower while Indians, Pakistanis and Bangladeshi earnings (in descending order) all fall significantly behind. Among women, there is much less variation with all groups except Bangladeshis outperforming whites. We must, however, note that these figures are affected by low rates of labour market participation among some groups and by patterns of full- and part-time employment. For a full discussion see Modood (1997a: 112–17).

Table 4.5   Job levels of women (employees and self-employed)

Socio-economic group	White	Caribbean	Indian	African Asian	Pakistani	Chinese
			column percentages			
Professional, managerial and employers	16	5	11	12	12	30
Intermediate non-manual	21	28	14	14	29	23
Junior non-manual	33	36	33	49	23	23
Skilled manual & foremen	7	4	11	7	9	13
Semi-skilled manual	18	20	27	16	22	9
Unskilled manual	4	6	4	1	4	2
Armed forces/inadequately described/not stated	0	1	1	1	0	0
Non-manual	70	69	58	75	64	76
Manual	29	30	42	24	35	24

Source: Modood et al. (1997)

It is important to note that, while part-time employment is dominated by women (accounting for nearly 90 per cent of such employees) a significantly higher proportion of white women work part-time than is the case among minority ethnic groups. The differences among women from different minority ethnic groups are, by comparison, quite small. Interestingly, part-time working is somewhat less strongly feminised among minority ethnic groups than among white people, the data revealing particularly high levels of part-time working among men of Bangladeshi, Pakistani and Black-African origin. Part-time working, of course, has implications for earning. It may also reflect differences in the representation of various groups in insecure and poorly paid jobs – a sector where the growth in part-time, as well as casualised, employment has been significant (Owen 1993: 3–4).

Discrimination

A variety of explanations for the disadvantage suffered by members of minority ethnic groups in the labour market have been reviewed by the various studies conducted under the auspices of the PSI (or its predecessor Political and Economic Planning; Daniel 1968; Smith 1974; Brown 1984; Jones 1993; Modood et al. 1997). All have shown that when matters such as language competence, skill levels and qualifications are controlled for, there remains a residue which is not explained by such factors. As a result, it is difficult to avoid the conclusion that discrimination on the part of employers plays a significant part in the labour market placement of minority ethnic groups.

In this context, it is interesting to note that the fourth PSI survey found that a large majority of all respondents believed that discrimination was widespread. Indeed white respondents were the most likely to hold such a belief (Modood 1997a: 129–35). This belief is consistent with the findings of an overwhelming body of research evidence which has demonstrated that direct, and apparently intentional, discrimination remains a feature of employment selection decisions (Daniel 1968; Hubbock and Carter 1980; National Association of Citizens Advice Bureaux 1984). A common method has been to submit job applications from candidates matched in every way except ethnic origin. Using this method Brown and Gay revealed continuing systematic discrimination, despite the many years of race relations legislation. They found that white applicants were more than 30 per cent more likely to be treated favourably than those of minority ethnic origin. Moreover, when compared with the results of earlier studies dating back to the early 1970s, the researchers found no evidence of a diminution in the level of racial discrimination and concluded that a major reason was the fact that employers were very unlikely to be caught in the act of discrimination (Brown and Gay 1985).

More recently Noon (1993), using similar methods, tested the responses to letters of inquiry, apparently from soon-to-qualify MBA students, sent to personnel managers at the top one hundred UK companies identified from the *Times 1000 Index*. The research compared both the frequency of responses sent to the two applicants and their quality in terms of the assistance and encouragement offered. It found that, overall, companies were more helpful and encouraging to white candidates. Moreover, the author concluded that, even in companies ostensibly sensitive to equal opportunities issues, direct discrimination was taking place on a routine basis.

Equally serious a problem is posed by indirect discrimination, where selection criteria are applied equally to everyone but where they are such that they disproportionately affect members of particular groups. A good example is where there are occupationally unnecessary dress requirements that members of some groups cannot comply with for religious or other reasons. Indirect discrimination may be deliberate but it may also frequently be unintentional and unrecognised. Jenkins (1986b) has argued that many selection decisions are based not on whether candidates have the right qualifications for the job but on whether they are thought to be likely to 'fit in' to the workplace without causing any trouble. Such judgements are applied equally to everyone but become discriminatory when they are consciously or unconsciously informed by managers' stereotypes of minority ethnic groups.

Jenkins's research and other studies (Jewson *et al.* 1990) have revealed that negative stereotypes were widespread among managers responsible for recruitment decisions. Even ostensibly positive stereotypes can be disadvantageous: Gray *et al.* (1993) found that employers' characterisations of Asian women workers as loyal, hardworking and uncomplaining could work against them in a situation where qualities demanded of employees were increasingly those of flexibility, ability to exercise initiative, and readiness to carry responsibility and acquire new skills. These examples reveal how easy it is for the taken-for-granted routines of everyday working life to disadvantage minority ethnic groups unintentionally. Of course they also make it easy to hide intentional discrimination as unplanned and accidental results of impersonal forces.

Self-employment

It is sometimes argued that self-employment represents an escape route from disadvantage and discrimination in employment and that this accounts for its prevalence among minority ethnic groups. The results both of the 1991 Census and the fourth PSI survey (Modood *et al.* 1997) show that self-employment is generally more common among minority ethnic groups than among the white population. This generalisation conceals some significant differences among minority ethnic groups. Thus among the 'black' groups, self-employment is markedly less common than among the white population. By contrast, among 'Asians' it is considerably more common. Once again, however, there are variations among Asian groups, Bangladeshis having a smaller propensity to be self-employed than other South Asians (Owen 1993: 4–6; Modood 1997a: 122–9). The pattern is similar for both male and female populations, although among African Asian women levels of self-employment are similar to white women, and in all groups a larger proportion of men are self-employed. Labour Force Survey data also indicate that, for all groups, self-employment is generally concentrated into a smaller range of activities than employment in general, with distribution, hotels, repairs and catering making up the largest sectors. Retail distribution is particularly prominent among the African Asian, Indian and Pakistani populations (Jones 1993: 65–6).

Data such as these, of course, appear to confirm a number of popular stereotypes of 'Asian' business – notably the thriving corner shop. It is important to note, therefore, that a number of studies have drawn attention to the difficulties faced by entrepreneurs from minority ethnic groups (Ward and Jenkins 1984). Ram (1992) has argued that the racism is often a key factor in pushing minority groups into self-employment. His research shows, however, that the effects of racism are difficult to overcome. Many ethnic minority entrepreneurs find it difficult to expand beyond an ethnically defined market and frequently have to use white intermediaries or agents in order to develop contacts and establish credibility with customers.

Other studies have shown that minority ethnic businesses are often under-capitalised, operate on the margins of profitability and remain over-dependent on a narrow ethnic market (Robinson 1989: 263). In addition, as Ram's analysis shows, the family often plays critical role is sustaining viability. This may have specific implications for women, whose critical contributions to the internal management of the enterprise go unacknowledged while they simultaneously retain responsibility for the domestic sphere.

Ethnic inequalities in Britain: some trends

The data reviewed above suggest a variety of experience, with widespread discrimination and disadvantage contrasting with significant upward mobility for some. Modood's analysis and Census data appear to show an increasing similarity of experience between white people and at least some minority ethnic groups (Owen 1993; Modood 1997a). The growth of a middle class of professional and managerial workers in some ethnic communities, and the entry of these groups into the service sector, has led some to suggest that there is underway a convergence in the class structures of minority ethnic groups towards that of the white population (Iganski and Payne 1996, 1999). However, the patterns are complex and need to be approached with caution. We should be wary of concluding, as have some on the political right, that the success of *some* members of *some* groups gives the lie to the claim that discrimination lies at the root of differences in achievement and opportunity between groups (Honeyford 1993).

The first point to note is that there are also significant differences between members of different ethnic groups. We have seen that those of Caribbean, Pakistani and Bangladeshi descent in particular tend to occupy the lowest positions in the labour market and also experience the highest levels of unemployment. Indeed patterns of exclusion altogether from the labour market must be taken into account when considering the successes of those in work. The same is true for the differences between the experiences of women and men.

We should also remember that upward mobility is not incompatible with continued occupational segregation, or with continuing discrimination. We know, for example, that there may be important differences of level *within* broad occupational categories, such as those between senior and middle management (compare the experience of women in this connection:

Cockburn 1991, and see Chapter 3). Members of all minority ethnic groups are under-represented among managers of large enterprises. The kinds of enterprises in which people work may also have significant implications for their opportunities and earnings. These may even be reinforced by the strides in self-employment made by some groups if their result is to increase opportunities for advancement by other members of the same groups. This suggests that there are significant patterns of ethnic segregation to be discerned in the labour market.

Finally we should reiterate the extent to which experience in the field of employment is in some ways the key to overall life chances. The labour market situation of minority ethnic groups has had knock-on effects in other fields, such as health and housing. There is, however, one further source of information about material inequalities that we must consider. This is the evidence on household incomes and standards of living.

The fourth PSI survey (Modood *et al.* 1997) attempts for the first time to produce an analysis of the *household* incomes of minority ethnic groups. This is important because the household is commonly used as the unit of analysis in studying living standards and economic well-being. We saw above that minority ethnic groups differed from one another and, with the exception of African Asians and Chinese, from whites in *individual* earnings. It is a plausible assumption that individual earnings differences would be likely to feed through into *household* differences but the manner in which this takes place is not clear. Among relevant factors influencing outcomes will be relative household size, the number of wage earners, the number of dependants and the availability of source of income other than earnings.

The analysis undertaken for the PSI reveals that the outcomes are complex and influenced by a range of factors. It also shows that, while some of the patterns revealed by analyses of employment continue to hold, there are other patterns that differ. Among key findings, we should note the extent of poverty (defined as incomes below half the national average) among Pakistani and Bangladeshi households. As Berthoud puts it:

Name any group whose poverty causes national concern – pensioners, disabled people, one-parent families, the unemployed – Pakistanis and Bangladeshis are poorer. (1997: 180)

The data also show that only Chinese households have incomes close to those of whites. Caribbean, Indian and African Asian household were all more likely than whites to experience poverty and less likely to have large family incomes. These results lead to an important qualification to the evidence on upward occupational mobility. When household incomes are taken into account,

African Asians and Indians fare less well than those of Chinese descent, while Caribbeans are much better placed than Pakistanis and Bangladeshis (Berthoud 1997: 180). These data thus provide further reasons to be cautious in assessing the significance of occupational mobility and the relative labour market placement of groups.

Social divisions, identities and change

In the preceding sections we have reviewed some of the evidence of material inequalities among Britain's varied ethnic communities. These material inequalities are changing in often complex and subtle ways such that any generalisations about the patterning of divisions based on those inequalities are fraught with difficulty. We have also noted that material inequalities, manifested primarily in labour market placement and incomes, are overlain by a complex of advantages and disadvantages in a variety of other aspects of social life. As Scott (Chapter 2) observes, it is not just the direct differences in income, wealth or power that define social class divisions. It is the location of people in class situations that shapes their life chances, even to the extent of setting the length of life and probable cause of death (Chapter 10). Shared social experiences generally follow from a structured sharing of material circumstances.

As we noted at the outset, however, the understanding of social divisions cannot rest simply with the mapping of material differences. In addition to the question of whether we can discern social categories on the basis of 'objective' structural characteristics there is also the question of whether the people so discerned *think* of themselves as constituting a group and *act* in terms of this perception. This brings us back to the question of identity, a concept, as we have seen, that is central to ethnicity.

Ethnicity is a matter both of self-identity ('we' statements) and of categorisation ('they' statements). Moreover, identity and categorisation do not proceed entirely independently of one another. In most societies some groups and individuals have a greater capacity than others to define the terms under which categorisations are made. As a consequence, self-identification takes place in contexts where others' categorisations to some extent constrain the choices that can realistically be made. In other words, if others do not accept one's identity choices it may, in practice, be difficult, if not impossible, to act out the implications of those choices.

These kinds of constraints may take the form of subtle social cues and messages that constrain behaviour. They may, however, take much more concrete forms. Two examples of some importance in modern Britain include the persistence of high levels of racial violence and the operation of immigration law.

The murder of Stephen Lawrence and the subsequent publication of the Macpherson report (Macpherson 1999) into the event and its investigation by the Metropolitan Police have raised the public profile of racially motivated violence in Britain. However, the Lawrence case represents only the most publicly known example of the extreme end of a continuum of harassment and violence which have been the daily experience of many of Britain's minority ethnic citizens. The phenomenon is not new, although it has come increasingly onto the public policy agenda since the 1980s. It is impossible to know with any precision what the overall size of the problem is. Moreover, there are clear differences between groups in the scale and nature of the varieties of harassment which they suffer. Nevertheless, on the basis of the results of the fourth PSI survey (Modood *et al.* 1997), Virdee has concluded that in a twelve month period, about 20,000 people are racially attacked, 40,000 are subject to racially motivated damage to property and 230,000 are racially abused or insulted (Virdee 1997).

A second source of difficulty has been immigration law. From the outset, the increasing restrictions on inward migration that followed the introduction of the 1962 Commonwealth Immigrants Act have targeted potential migrants whose skin colour was not white. Indeed the very term 'immigrant' has often been a synonym for 'person of minority ethnic descent'. A continuing source of grievance in many minority ethnic communities has been the way they, their relatives and often their legitimate visitors and business contexts, are more likely than their white counterparts to have the legitimacy of their residence questioned, or to experience difficulties at passport control when entering the country (Mason 1995: 109–10). Once again, the subtle message received by many of Britain's minority ethnic citizens is that they are second-class citizens. Such messages are only reinforced by the nature of press coverage of scares about illegal migration and allegedly bogus asylum seekers (Gabriel 1998: 97–128).

The message of these two kinds of experience is frequently that, notwithstanding their formal entitlement to full citizenship rights, many members of Britain's minority ethnic communities experience a sense of exclusion from the identity 'British'. Of course, there is a variety of different characteristics that go to make up the identity of all of us including, crucially, gender. Evidence from the fourth PSI survey shows that Britain's minority ethnic citizens call on a wide variety of cultural and other characteristics in defining their ethnic identities.

In order to explore this issue, the PSI survey adopted the strategy of asking respondents to rank in importance a range of characteristics in terms of which they might describe themselves to strangers. These included: nationality, skin colour, country of origin, age, job, education, height, colour of hair or eyes, level of income and father's job. In other words, they included a range of more or less visible personal characteristics and attributes only some of which are conventionally associated with ethnicity. In particular, characteristics often used in the measurement of social class, such as job and education, scored highly among all minority ethnic groups. In addition, religion was of great significance, especially among members of the Asian groups. Put another way, it is clear that in constructing their identities, the respondents in the PSI survey utilised a range of physical, positional and lifestyle characteristics in combinations which both varied between groups but which also exhibited considerable similarities (Modood 1997b: 290–338).

Nevertheless, there is also evidence that these identifications are made in the context of a recognition that others categorise them in a way that constrains the choices they themselves can make. A number of persons of Asian descent who responded to the PSI survey indicated that they were inclined to think of themselves as 'black' in situations where they were in contact with white people. Among the reasons given was the belief that this was how they were defined by whites – in other words, they felt their choices were constrained (Modood 1997b: 295–6). It is in this context that both subtle messages about what constitutes 'Britishness' and brutal acts of violence exercise exclusionary pressures that limit choice.

Having said this, it would equally be a mistake to believe that identities are static or that Britain's minority ethnic citizens are simply passive victims in the face of economic exclusion and racist attitudes and behaviour. There are myriad examples ranging from self-help community organisations, through various forms of political mobilisation, to the exemplary courage and persistence of the Lawrence family, of Britain's minority citizens challenging their exclusion. More subtly there is considerable evidence of a process of continuous change in the ways the identities of Britain's varied citizens are constructed and negotiated. Modood has attempted to capture the ways in which, for second and third generation members of minority ethnic groups in Britain, subtle and complex changes in patterns of ethnic identification have occurred. His analysis suggests that there is no straightforward relationship between 'the cultural content of an ethnicity and strategies of ethnic self-definition' (Modood 1997b: 337). The result is a shift from what Modood calls 'behavioural difference' to an emphasis on 'associational identity':

> for many the strength of their ethnic identity was owed to a group pride in response to perceptions of racial exclusion and ethnic stereotyping by the white majority. The consequent sense of rejection and insecurity was instrumental in assertions of ethnic identities, often in forms susceptible to forging new anti-racist solidarities (such as 'black') and hyphenated (such as British-Pakistani) or even multiple identities. (Modood 1997b: 337)

Modood is at pains to argue that the resultant identifications are not weaker than those of the first generation but differently constructed. They are much less taken-for-granted (based on shared cultural values) and more consciously chosen, publicly celebrated and debated, and part of a contested arena of identity politics. As a result, they are potentially fluid and may change with political and other circumstances. In the process, they may either revive old cultural practices or generate new ones (Modood 1997b: 337).

It is appropriate, at this point, to note that much recent work in sociology has argued that, in the modern world, *all* identities are more fluid, provisional and multifaceted than some more traditional characterisations of cultural difference would suggest. We may identify two broad bodies of literature from which these kinds of arguments have developed. The first is a feminist critique, and the second writing in the post-modern and post-structuralist school of thought.

One of the earliest challenges came from feminist scholars and activists who, from the early 1980s onwards began to challenge what were described as 'essentialised' conceptions of woman. In other words, they were critical of the implication that women constituted a single undifferentiated category sharing a common set of interests. Some of these criticisms came from black feminists who contested what they saw as the dominance of white middle-class perspectives and argued that patriarchal oppression was mediated by racism in ways that made the experience and opportunities of black and white women quite different. More recently, other writers in the feminist tradition have challenged the essentialisation of ethnic difference, arguing that ethnicity is gendered in ways that both differentiate the experience of men and women but which are also constitutive of ethnic difference. Anthias and Yuval-Davis have argued, for example, that women play a vital role not only in the physical and cultural reproduction of ethnicities but also in marking their symbolic boundaries (1992: 113–15).

A second source for the recognition of the provisionality and negotiability of identity is to be found in post-modernist and post-structuralist writing. According to this view, the pace of change in the (post-)modern world, together with an ever-expanding array of choices and possibilities, creates conditions in which individuals are increasingly free to make multiple identity choices that match the purposes (or even the whims) of the moment (Rattansi and Westwood 1994; Bradley 1999: 21–7). In other words, old-style, modernist explanations of the social world in terms of large-scale and relatively stable social categories do violence to the complexity of the everyday experiences of individuals in the post-modern world.

It will be apparent from what is said above about the relationship between choice and constraint that I am sceptical about the more extreme versions of this kind of perspective. Nevertheless, as we saw above, there is some evidence that Britain's young minority ethnic citizens do perceive a wider range of identity options than some of the more rigid characterisations of ethnic difference may suggest. A historical analysis of the changing patterning of identity among Britain's minority ethnic citizens can be found in Luthra's account (1997: 9–64).

Understanding social divisions, difference and diversity

It is difficult to deny the power of accounts that recognise the dynamism of ethnic identity in modern Britain. They are, after all, consistent with the conception of ethnicity (discussed above) that recognises the significance of the boundary process. Moreover they also challenge the simplistic victimology that has all too frequently characterised discussions of ethnic inequalities in Britain. On the other hand they also present a potential problem. When we take these insights together with the evidence reviewed above about increasing social mobility, it is all too easy to make the mistake of assuming that social divisions based on ethnicity are, if not a thing of the past, at least on the way to solution. As the evidence above demonstrates, however, measured by material inequalities and differences of treatment, this is far from yet being the case.

The difficulty arises not simply because of a debate about the meaning of the evidence, or even the pace of change. There is a more fundamental difficulty arising from the clash of modernist and post-modernist perspectives. As the example of traditional class analysis shows, concern with social divisions based on material inequalities is firmly located within a modernist world view. From whatever theoretical perspective it is approached, there is an implicit acceptance that social divisions are problematic. This may be because they are thought to undermine some minimum common standard – expressed in such notions as equality or human rights. Alternatively, it may be because they are perceived to threaten social cohesion either by undermining shared value systems (anomie) or by encouraging political dissent. Thus whether inequalities are to be challenged or justified, there is a common belief that solutions are available in the form of political and social action.

By contrast, for post-modernist writers the old meta-narratives underpinning these traditional approaches are no longer tenable in a world characterised by diversity, fluidity and fragmentation. Abandoning faith in such certainties, post-modernism is more likely to move to a celebration of difference rather than to detect in it signs of social decay. In its extreme forms, post-modernism represents a celebration of choice and the triumph of style. Even in its less triumphalist guise, however, it identifies in the diverse identity options open to individuals in the modern world, the opportunity to challenge the stereotyping and categorisation all too often characteristic of the behaviour of 'ethnic majorities' (Jenkins 1997: 29–30). It thus celebrates rather than problematises difference. At the same times it challenges the essentialisation of the ethnic categories that are central to the process of measuring and tracking social inequalities, conventionally defined.

The difficulty with this is that while it may be easy to agree that ethnic diversity in modern Britain should be viewed positively – as something contributing to the richness of the lives of all citizens – all too often difference has been seen as problematic. Indeed, as we have seen, even when it gives rise to positive assertions of identity, 'difference' has frequently been a product of exclusionary processes and practices. Is there a solution to this apparent impasse? Modood has suggested that the way forward lies with a conception of equality that recognises:

> the right to have one's 'difference' recognised and supported in both the public and the private spheres. (1997b: 358)

It implies, he argues, common rights and responsibilities and, in the end, a renewal of concepts of Britishness within which currently negative views of difference are framed. We need:

> to develop a more plural approach to racial disadvantage, and to formulate an explicit ideal of multicultural citizenship appropriate to Britain in the next decade and beyond. (1997b: 359)

But herein lies the dilemma. Without the capacity to measure the patterning of material inequalities and differences of treatment among Britain's minority ethnic groups, how will it be possible to know whether progress has been made in reducing disadvantage? Such measurement must, by definition, use some set of categories in terms of which data can be collected. However sensitive we seek to be to people's self-definitions, any category system runs the risk of failing to capture the richness and complexity of people's identity choices. There is a danger, then, that we may reproduce the very divisions we seek to problematise.

I have tried to show in this chapter that there are very real social divisions in modern Britain arising from ethnic difference. They are, however, neither static nor unchallenged. Moreover, they interact in complex ways with sources of social differentiation based on class and gender to the extent that not only are their effects difficult to disentangle but that they may be thought of as mutually constitutive.

FURTHER READING:

Mason, D. *Race and Ethnicity in Modern Britain*, 2nd edn, Oxford: Oxford University Press (2000) provides a comprehensive introduction to race and ethnicity in contemporary Britain, while Solomos, J. and Back, L. *Racism in Society*, Basingstoke: Macmillan (1996) is an accessible introduction to some of the key contemporary debates on racism. Modood, T. *et al. Ethnic Minorities in Britain*, London: Policy Studies Institute (1997) represents the most up to date and comprehensive source of data on the current situations of Britain's minority ethnic groups, as well as comparisons with earlier surveys. Luthra, M. *Britain's Black Population: Social Change, Public Policy and Agenda*, Aldershot: Arena, Ashgate (1997), (the third in a series with the same title) is another very useful source of evidence on ethnic inequality.

CHAPTER 5

National Identity

DAVID McCRONE

Who are you? If you are asked what nationality you are, what do you say? If you live in the archipelago of islands called the 'British Isles', think about it for a moment. Would you say you are British? English? Scottish? Welsh? Irish? None of these? How do you decide? You may say you are British because you are a citizen of the UK. But strictly speaking that terms refers to people who live on the British mainland. The state, after all, is the United Kingdom of Great Britain and Northern Ireland. So we are UK-people – 'Ukanians' in Tom Nairn's ironic term (1977), who live together in the same state but who have not bothered to find a proper name for ourselves. While virtually all modern states have problems defining who 'nationals' are, it is instructive to focus on people in these islands where such issues are especially problematic. By focusing on these, we can begin to understand just how complex and changing national identity is at the start of the new millennium.

Let us try another tack. What do you call the country you live in? The 'United Kingdom' sounds too stilted. Britain? Great Britain? England? Scotland? Wales? Ireland? Northern Ireland? Ulster? To many foreigners this is England (even to the English), but the Scots, Welsh, and Northern Irish know that it is not so. So who is right? Let us try some elementary algebra. Formally, the United Kingdom = Great Britain (the big island) + Northern Ireland, where Great Britain = England + Scotland + Wales. The problem with that (correct) formulation is that it does not correspond with sociological reality, that is, with how people see themselves. The non-English peoples – the Scots and Welsh in particular – define their nationality (their 'nation-ness') as Scottish and Welsh, while recognising that their citizenship – their state identity – is British. In Northern Ireland, on the other hand, being 'British' is a *political* statement that you *do* wish to belong to the UK, that you are a 'unionist'.

Indeed, Northern Ireland provides us with the starkest home-grown example of why national identity is such an important principle of social division. Hundreds of people who were ordinary 'citizens', living in a territory that, as an accident of history and constitutionality is part of the United Kingdom, have killed or been killed in an internal war over nationality, state and culture. Social divisions do not come much sharper than that (except in the scale and intensity of fighting elsewhere in Europe, as the Balkans have shown us). In Northern Ireland, when about two-thirds of Protestants say they are British, it is no casual observation, just as when the significant minority (about three in five Catholics: Curtice 1990) assert that they are Irish, they are expressing a powerful counter-identity. Catholics and Protestants do not just divide on national identity or religious grounds. They live in different areas, go to different schools, often work in separate organisations, and mix with 'their own people' who share similar experiences of good or poor housing, education, occupational opportunity or exclusion. Those who lead the most separate lives in this way are also the most likely to express a distinctive sense of nationalism (Breen 1998).

Although the sense of difference is not so extreme in Scotland, Scottish 'social arrangements' are not the same as in England, as many media correspondents seemed to discover for the first time in the run-up to elections for the Scottish Parliament in 1999. Scotland has its own legal system; a less selective and subject-specialist education service; unique churches; separate organisation of trade associations, banks, charities and political parties; and media production systems that ensure a diet of news coverage about Scotland that even Wales with its distinctive language, and certainly no mere regional service, can match. For some sociologists, Scotland is just as suitable a 'unit of analysis' as is the more conventional, mirror-image way of thinking about the size and geographical spread of what we research; namely the area usually defined as 'England and Wales' (Payne 1987b; McCrone 1992).

These nuances in parts of the UK are mostly lost on the majority people, the English, who make up 85 per cent of the UK state's population. This distinction between national identity and state identity in these islands is not one they usually make. Anthony Barnett who helped to found Charter 88, the pressure group for constitutional change, put it this way:

What is the difference between being English and being British? If you ask a Scot or a Welsh person about their Britishness, the question makes sense to them. They might say that they feel Scots first and British second. Or that they enjoy a dual identity as Welsh-British, with both parts being equal. Or they might say: 'I'm definitely British first.' What they have in common is an understanding that there is a space between their nation and Britain, and they can assess the relationship between the two. The English, however, are more often baffled when asked how they relate their Englishness and Britishness to each other. They often fail to understand how the two can be contrasted at all. It seems like one of those puzzles that others can undo but you can't: Englishness and Britishness seem inseparable. They might prefer to be called one thing rather than the other – and today young people increasingly prefer English to British – but, like two sides of a coin, neither term has an independent existence from the other. (Barnett 1997: 292–3)

Before analysing why people seem confused about their nationality, let us explore a little more how they define themselves. One way of doing this is to ask people on the British mainland how they relate their state identity (being British) to their national identity (being English, Scottish, or Welsh: the political-religious significance of identity in Northern Ireland makes this question inappropriate in the Province). For simplicity, we can imagine a five-point scale ranging from one extreme at which national identity (being English, Scottish, Welsh) is everything and state identity (British) is nothing, to the reverse of that, with dual identities in between.

What the data in Table 5.1 suggest is that people living in Scotland are about seven times more likely to give priority to being Scottish than to being British (points 1 or 2 on our scale – either 'Scottish not British', or 'more Scottish than British'). The Welsh are twice as likely to say they are Welsh than British. In England, the 'English' and the 'British' are about equal (at around 25 per cent each), with almost half saying they are equally English and British. Here, of course, Barnett's health warning applies: we can't be sure people in England make the distinction between England and Britain.

How, as sociologists, are we to make sense of this confusion? This is, we might say, a meaningful error. There is a puzzle about Britishness. In Cohen's helpful metaphor (1994), it is 'fuzzy', that is, blurred and opaque. (Cohen is making the analogy with 'fuzzy logic' in mathematics by which a solution is reached by way of eliminating the uncertain edges to a problem.) This fuzziness is a legacy of history and sociology in these islands, and at its heart is the confusion of nationality and citizenship.

Table 5.1 National identity by country

	Scotland	Wales	England
X not British	23	13	8
More X than British	38	29	16
Equally X and British	27	26	46
More British than X	4	10	15
British not X	4	15	9
None of these	4	7	6
Sample sizes	882	182	2551

Notes:
(X = Scottish/Welsh/English), percentage in columns

Source: Brown et al. (1998: 213)

At this point in our argument you may be asking yourself why any of this matters. After all, you may say, I do not actually think it matters much what nationality I am. Let me press you on this point. If you go abroad, do you feel yourself more or less 'national'? During the football world cup, or for that matter most international sporting occasions, which team do you support? Well, you may reply, I do feel patriotic, but not nationalistic. That is a fairly common answer. It implies that feeling pride in one's country is not the same as hating, even killing, other people. Indeed not, but can we be sure that this is a valid distinction we are making between patriotism and nationalism? Most of us in the UK today are too young to remember the Second World War – you would need to be over 65 to have been an adult in 1945 – but most people in those days had little difficulty going and fighting, and even dying, for what they felt was right. Perhaps the problem we have in thinking that we are not susceptible to feelings of patriotism and nationalism – because, in truth, they are the same thing – is that we have not been confronted by the need to do so. Those who are so confronted often feel they have no alternative. Let us take an example from the other end of Europe to make our point. Here is a comment by a Croat writer who found herself caught up in the national war fever of the Balkans war in the early 1990s:

> Being Croat has become my destiny... I am defined by my nationality, and by it alone ...Along with millions of other Croats, I was pinned to the wall of nationhood – not only by outside pressure from Serbia and the Federal Army but by national homogenization within Croatia itself. That is what the war is doing to us, reducing us to one dimension: the Nation... One doesn't have to succumb voluntarily to this ideology of the nation – one is sucked into it. So right now, in the new state of Croatia, no one is allowed not to be a Croat. (Drakulic, S. quoted in Brubaker 1996: 20)

What is perhaps surprising about this statement is that she felt resentful, because the powerful sense of belonging usually sweeps people up in a way that makes them wish to act willingly for the nation. If this did not happen, how, we might ask, do states manage to get anyone at all to fight for them?

Perhaps part of the issue here is that, as Barnett made clear above, for the most part English people are not very aware of their Englishness, compared, for example, with the Scots, the Welsh and the Irish, all of whom have historically looked to the English as the 'Other' against whom they define themselves. For English people, however, there is a more fundamental confusion with being British. Let us now explore that in some depth.

Making Britain

There are two historical parts to our puzzle: how the British state was created in the eighteenth century; and how modern citizenship evolved in the twentieth. The creation of Great Britain in the early eighteenth century before the wave of modernising states transformed our world is the key. The British state managed to contain within it quite distinct self-governing 'civil societies', which co-existed within its formal boundaries quite contentedly as long as a fairly high degree of limited autonomy was afforded them. By 'civil society' we mean that social sphere between the individual and the state; the domestic world, economic relations, cultural activities, and even legal institutions which are organised by private or voluntary arrangements and largely outside the control of the state. We can now see with hindsight that by the middle of the twentieth century the relationship between the state and these civil societies had been radically altered in such a way that peaceful co-existence is no longer logically possible. Above all, the generic shift between the boundaries of the state and civil society in the modern world created particular difficulties for relations between the British state and its constituent civil societies.

The central relationship is the one between England and Scotland because that was the basis of the creation of the new state of Great Britain in 1707, and is and always has been the most problematic and intriguing one. Of course, other civil societies existed within the state – notably those in Wales and (after 1801 when the state became the United Kingdom) Ireland, as well as local and regional ones within England itself. However, their relationships to the political centre were different. On the one hand, the national societies of Wales and Ireland had been the subject of successful conquest by England from the thirteenth century, and had elements of colonial status attached to their civil and political institutions. On the other hand, regional autonomy within England did not have to contend with competing national identities and institutional residues of historical statehood like those north of the English border.

How did Scottish (or Welsh) civil society develop in the context of the unitary British state since 1707? Given that all formal political power resided in Westminster, how much (or little) autonomy did these nations continue to have? There was a consensus of political opposites on this issue. For nationalists, Scotland had ceased to exist in 1707 when it was incorporated into greater England. Their project was and is that Scotland should rise and be a nation again (in the sense of being an independent state). For unionists, on the other hand, a new, integrated society was born called Britain (or the UK), and they argue that it would be disastrous if the whole was unscrambled into its weaker constituent parts. The problem with these two stark representations is that they play fast and loose with history as well as sociology.

At this point it is useful to clarify some of our terms. The 'state' refers to the institutions of governance, and includes not simply parliament, but the legal system and the civil service. It is in essential terms a 'political' concept. The 'nation' on the other hand refers to the 'cultural' realm, to what people see as their shared characteristics, most usually language, religion and/or common history. In Anderson's useful term (1996), a nation is an 'imagined community' of people who believe themselves to belong to the same cultural group, and which has the right of self-determination. The important aspect to grasp here is that 'state' and 'nation' belong to different spheres, even though they are frequently treated as the same, and linked together as in the term 'nation-state'. As we shall see later in this chapter, there is nothing inevitable about linking the two together, and it is becoming increasingly problematic to do so in the modern world. How does this apply to the United Kingdom?

What is nearer the truth is that Scotland, while ceasing to be an independent state, did not stop being a nation or a civil society in 1707, nor was it incorporated into greater England. The Treaty of Union in 1707 did create something new. Greater England it was not. Instead, Scots took full advantage of the opportunity that England and the Empire provided. As Colley has pointed out, a genuine sense of Britishness was 'forged' with reference to two related aspects: war with France, and Protestantism. Britishness was invented in the long period of virtual or actual warfare with France from 1707 until 1837. These wars were religious wars, and perceived as such on both sides. The overthrow of the Catholic Stuarts in 1689 and their replacement with the Protestant William of Orange reinforced the political-religious nature of the settlement. Britain, she says,

> was an invention forged above all by war. Time and time again, war with France brought Britons, whether they hailed from Wales or Scotland or England, into confrontation with an obvious hostile Other and encouraged them to define themselves collectively against it. They defined themselves as Protestants struggling for survival against the world's foremost Catholic power. They defined themselves against the French as they imagined them to be, superstitious, militarist, decadent and unfree. (1992: 5)

This struggle against the French may seem like an integrating mechanism, a forging of a new national identity, but Colley argues that 'Britishness was superimposed over an array of internal differences in response to contact with the Other, and above all in response to conflict with the Other' (*ibid.*: 6). It worked with rather than against the grain of older national identities that were to persist, and out-last the later British one. Britishness sat lightly on top of the constituent nations as a kind of state-identity. This is the key to understanding state–society relations in the UK. The British state was quite unlike later state formations that sought to integrate political, cultural and economic structures in the classical 'nation-state' outlined above. These formations demanded the lining up of state, nation, society, economy and culture in such a way that 'national identity' ran through all of these institutions. Being a citizen in these nineteenth-century modern states demanded allegiance, and in return the state was made accountable, and its sovereignty limited, often by means of the doctrine of popular, rather than Crown/Parliamentary, sovereignty as in Britain.

The British state, on the other hand, as a 'nightwatchman state' was content to concern itself with matters of defence, foreign policy and maintaining a stable currency. It was a state externally oriented to managing its dependent territories and arranging their defence. Above all, it left civil society to its own devices, and only intervened where it perceived a threat to social and political order. This it did most notoriously after the Jacobite Rising of 1745, and only at the behest of, and largely by the hands of, lowland Protestant Scots.

The point here is that the British state sat lightly upon civil society, whereas continental European states were thoroughly interwoven with theirs. The unreformed quality of the British state has been commented upon by many writers. Marquand, for example, has called the UK an 'unprincipled' society because its state structures are fundamentally deficient. He observed:

> Thanks to the upheavals of the 17th century – thanks in particular to the victory of the English landed classes over the Stuart kings – one cannot speak of a 'British state' in the way that one speaks of a 'French state' or in modern times of a 'German state'. The UK is not a state in the continental sense. It is a bundle of islands (including such exotica as the Channel Islands and the Isle of Man which are not even represented at Westminster), acquired at different times by the English crown, and governed in different ways.
>
> Its inhabitants are not citizens of a state, with defined rights of citizenship. They are subjects of a monarch, enjoying 'liberties' which their ancestors won from previous monarchs. (1988: 152)

Marquand's point is not that the British state suffers from a form of arrested political development. It was a minimal state with a small bureaucracy that was clearly suited to market-driven adjustment in the eighteenth century, but which failed to make the transition to full modernity in the late nineteenth century. At its root lies an ethos of market liberalism, which has survived long after the doctrine that created it has been abandoned.

A similar point is made by Colley who points out that for a time the British state (at the turn of the nineteenth century) was one of the most modernised and democratic in Europe. Its Protestant 'ethic' gave it a commitment to civil and economic liberalism that helped to make it the premier power until the late nineteenth century. The problem was, she comments, that whereas the reforms of 1832 established a high degree of civil and democratic rights, by 1865 it had been overtaken by most continental powers. Its political development had been arrested, possibly because its route to modernisation was much more conservative than is usually made out, that a thoroughgoing reform of political and constitutional structures with, for example, a written constitution and bill of rights, did not take place.

You may by now have noticed an important omission in describing who the British are. What, you may ask, about the Irish? Was Ireland not incorporated into the United Kingdom of Great Britain and Ireland in 1801? Constitutionally speaking, this is correct. However, if we take Colley's point that Protestantism was a prime shaper of Britishness, then as Catholics, most of the people on the island of Ireland could not, and indeed, were not allowed to be British in this sense. To be British was to be a Protestant which in turn made one loyal to the British crown. That is the origin of the term 'loyalist', and the reason why in Ireland over the last two centuries religion is less a matter of theology, and more a matter of constitutional politics.

In Northern Ireland today, issues of national identity are framed by this nexus between politics and religion, in so many ways, one being a proxy for the other. Hence, 60 per cent of Catholics in the Province give their nationality as 'Irish', and two-thirds of Protestants say they are 'British' (Curtice 1990). Intriguingly, however, a sizeable minority in both communities say they are 'Northern Irish' – 25 per cent of Catholics, and 16 per cent of Protestants – perhaps implying that over the 70-plus years since the Partition of the island of Ireland into two unequal parts, a territorial, regional identity has been forged in the Province, in spite of two powerfully competing national identities.

Making British citizens

The second piece of our puzzle about British nationality and citizenship is to be found in the second half of the twentieth century: how modern citizenship in these islands was made. The inhabitants of the UK attained formal citizenship by a legislative sleight of hand under the 1948 Nationality Act as 'citizens of the UK and the colonies'. Prior to that date the inhabitants of the British Isles and the British Empire were formally 'subjects' of the Crown. Hitherto,

Britain was not so much a geographical entity; it was perceived in terms of those who owed allegiance to the Crown, and included those who inhabited the far-flung territories of the Empire. In other words, there was something unusual about the relationship between the British state and its inhabitants.

In essence, Britishness had grown up as an imperial identity, although a fuzzy one, defined more by an allegiance to the Crown than residence in these islands. Britain, in other words, exists (or existed) as an imperial state – with colonies and dominions that came to embody its identity. It took a New Zealander, P. A. Pocock (1975) to define 'British' history as something quite different from English, Scottish, Welsh and Irish history, and also something that belonged to those living beyond these shores. Whatever else it was, Britain was not England. It evoked an imperial identity, much as in the Roman empire. '*Civis Britannicus Sum*' was the nineteenth-century equivalent of '*Civis Romanus Sum*'.

The post-1945 crisis arose because former parts of the Empire such as Canada and India wished to redefine citizenship for immigration purposes, and so a separate status was necessary for the remaining inhabitants of the UK. The preferred position of the British government was that people in Commonwealth countries were subjects of the British crown first, and citizens of individual states second, but it quickly became obvious that newly independent countries balked at this constraint on their sovereignty. The British political parties reflected the confusion. In the post-imperial age the Labour party sought to encourage a 'traditional' that is, non-ethnic definition of 'Britishness' to encompass the Commonwealth while supporting colonial peoples in their liberation struggles (Goulbourne 1991). The Conservative party for its part developed an 'ethnic' definition ('those groups which consider themselves to be British, and also the indigenous and/or white population' (Goulbourne 1991: 245). This was reflected in the 1962 Commonwealth Immigration Act, the 1971 Immigration Act, and the 1981 Nationality Act, and an ethnic definition was reinforced ideologically under the influence of right-wing politicians like Enoch Powell and Margaret Thatcher (see above, Chapter 4). The politicisation of ethnic identity has helped to highlight the racial context of the debate over the last 30 years. By the 1981 Act, patriality – the right to settle in the UK if one had at least one grandparent born here – drew on the law of blood (*ius sanguinis*) rather than the law of territory (*ius soli*), so that ethnic definitions of Britishness are at least as important as civic ones. We will return to this important distinction between 'blood' and 'soil' later.

This brief overview of how 'Britishness' has come to be redefined in the post-colonial age provides a context for important shifts in national identities within the United Kingdom itself. If British identity is externally fuzzy, so too is its meaning within these islands. Until Ireland became a republic in 1948, its citizens remained formally 'subjects' of the British Crown (reinforced by the new republic leaving the Commonwealth a year later, largely to break finally with this colonial legacy). A number of other key confusions remained, notably that between 'Britain' and 'England', a distinction that was rarely made in the UK's largest country as well as overseas. It was the norm to describe the UK as a 'nation-state', an extension of England. Although the Scots and the Welsh worked within a more logical model whereby their national identities were nested in the broader British state identity, the unitary nature of that state with a single, sovereign parliament, seemed to reinforce the equation of Britain and England, and the tendency to see the UK as 'greater England'.

We have, then, in these islands a complex set of national political identities. Following Cohen's idea of 'fuzzy frontiers', we can identify the following:

- that between the English, the largest nationality, and the Scots – who were jointly responsible for founding the 'Great Britain' in 1707;

- the relationship between the English/Scots and the other Celtic peoples – the Welsh on the one hand, and the Irish on the other (most of whom are citizens of an independent republic, but with voting and residence rights in the UK – and leaving aside the complications in Northern Ireland);

- the (white) Commonwealth or former 'Dominions' such as Australia, New Zealand and Canada – which are politically independent, but genealogically, culturally and legally linked (via 'patriality' rights of settlement);

- the (black) Commonwealth, with the history of post-war settlement (defining 'ethnicity' in the UK);

- European links (via but not exclusively with) the European Union, which also implies rights of settlement and residence to 'non-British' people;

- Anglophones (especially via cultural and historical links with the United States of America).

The result, in Cohen's words is that:

British identity shows a general pattern of fragmentation. Multiple axes of identification have meant that Irish, Scots, Welsh and English people, those from the white, black and brown Commonwealth, Americans, English-speakers, Europeans and even 'aliens' have had their lives intersect one with another in overlapping and complex circles of identity-construction and rejection. The shape and edges of British identity are thus historically changing, often vague and, to a degree, malleable – an aspect of the British identity I have called 'a fuzzy frontier'. (1994: 35)

The issues of ethnicity and nationality, then, in the UK are especially 'fuzzy'. Britishness is a political identity, roughly equated with citizenship, but growing out of a pre-modern prior definition of people as 'subjects' of the Crown, and even applying to those who do not live in these islands. As this older sense of Britishness declines (after all, those entering pensionable age in 1998 were not even in their early teens when the Second World War ended), it is tempting to predict its demise.

Citizens and the nation-state

Let us, however, take a broader and comparative view of the making of modern states. It is part of our vocabulary to talk of 'nation-states'. Why does the term nation-state have such strong currency in the western world? The answer lies in the fact that the term was captured by the process of state-building, which has shaped western Europe over the last two centuries. If states were not actually 'nations' too, then they could be imagined as such either now or in the future. Essentially, the state is a political concept, whereas the nation is a cultural one. So successful is this alignment between state and nation that it is part of our common sense, our taken-for-granted political and cultural world (McCrone 1998). Does it matter that we align state and nation, the political and the cultural? Most certainly, because it gives a fundamental legitimacy to the modern state without which it could not function. After all, the modern state derives its legitimacy from its claim to speak on behalf of 'the people'.

In his study of citizenship and nationhood in France and Germany, Brubaker (1992) argues that definitions of citizenship in these states result from the fact that whereas in France the unitary state was established before the concept of nation took hold there, in Germany it was the other way round; the 'nation' preceded the 'state'. In France, the monarchy held sway over a fairly defined and gradually expanding territory, and promoted the concept of citizenship based on *ius soli*, the law of soil or territorial jurisdiction, in such a way that whatever their ethnic or geographical origins, all residents on French soil could in principle be subjects, later citizens, of the French state. Peasants had, of course, in Eugene Weber's phrase, to be made into Frenchmen, but this formulation expresses nicely the prior existence of the state over the sense of nation, at least in popular terms.

In Germany, by contrast, the unitary state did not arrive until 1871, and the nation had to be defined differently. Since members of the German nation might be subjects of different kings – Bavaria, Saxony, Prussia, even Austria and Russia – national identity was based on *ius sanguinis*, the law of blood, so that anyone with German blood was German, and thus after 1871 eligible to be a citizen of Germany whether or not they actually lived on German soil.

As a result of these different routes to 'nation-statehood', the interpretation of nationality differs. In France, according to Brubaker, it is state-centred and assimilationist, so that anyone living within the territory of the French state became a French citizen. In Germany, on the other hand, it is nation-centred and differentialist. Anyone who could prove German ethnicity was counted as 'German', but the definition differentiated among those living within Germany itself so that some were counted as ethnically German and others, such as people of Turkish origin, were not, until the law was changed as late as 1998. Brubaker comments:

> The state-centred assimilationist understanding of nationhood in France is embodied and expressed in an expansive definition of citizenship, one that automatically transforms second-generation immigrants into citizens, assimilating them – legally – to other French men and women. The ethnocultural, differentialist understanding of nationhood in Germany is embodied and expressed in a definition of citizenship that is remarkably open to ethnic German immigrants from Eastern Europe and the Soviet Union, but remarkably closed to non-German immigrants. (1992: 3)

Further, as Cobban points out: 'during the early modern period... the word nation changed its significance: it lost its linguistic and acquired an almost wholly exclusively political meaning' (1994: 245). In general, there has been a progressive down-playing of the cultural component in modern definitions of the state. Held comments:

> All modern states are nation-states – political apparatuses, distinct from both rulers and ruled, with supreme jurisdiction over a demarcated territorial area, backed by a claim to a monopoly of coercive power, and enjoying a minimum level of support or loyalty from their citizens. (1992: 87)

We might be surprised that the cultural component is downplayed and operates merely as a loyalty device for the state, but this view of the 'nation-state' is the dominant one. In like manner, Giddens virtually reproduces this definition, but without any cultural component being mentioned. The nation-state, he comments, is 'a set of institutional forms of governance maintaining an administrative monopoly over a territory with demarcated boundaries, its rule being sanctioned by law and direct control of the means of internal and external violence' (1981: 190). Giddens sees the 'nation' as a 'bordered power-container', which can exist only 'when a state has a unified administrative reach over the territory over which its sovereignty is claimed' (1985: 120). Max Weber well understood the distinction between state and nation, and defined the key characteristics of the modern state as follows: territoriality – having fixed and defensible borders; control of the means of violence – both internally and externally; an impersonal structure of power – the idea of a sovereign and impersonal political order; and legitimacy – requiring the loyalty of its citizens (Held 1992).

Does this reduction of the nation to the state matter? My argument is that it does, because the concepts actually operate on different planes, and lead us to imagine that modern states have captured political and cultural power. This is problematic because the ideal-typical process had always a much more messy reality lying behind it.

Particularly in the late twentieth century, the concepts are coming apart. The (con)fusion of nation and state is a common one, and requires to be taken seriously rather than as an unfortunate error. What it signifies is that so closely allied have the cultural and the political become in the modern state that we usually treat their outcomes – nation and state – as synonyms. In its conventional expression – the nation-state – it is expected that the 'people' who are governed by the institutions of the state are by and large culturally homogeneous in having a strong and common linguistic, religious and symbolic identity. We see more clearly than most, the 'impending crisis of the hyphen' (Anderson 1996:8). Some scholars have pointed out that very few so-called nation-states are actually such. Connor (1994) claims less than ten per cent in 1971, and historical sociologists like Tilly distinguish between 'nation-states' and 'national states' that are governed by common political and institutional structures. He comments that very few European states have ever qualified as nation-states (possibly Sweden and Ireland), and that 'Great Britain, Germany and France – quintessential national states – certainly have never met the test' (1992: 3).

Why should the use of 'national' and 'nation-state' matter? In large part because it frames the world as it is meant to be, not how it is. Strictly speaking, 'nation-state' implies that all self-governing political units – states – correspond with culturally distinctive units – nations, so that the world appears as a giant jigsaw of such entities. Of course, the pieces do not fit. Not only are most states not culturally and ethnically homogeneous, but many, even most, nations are in formal terms stateless, such as Scotland, and even England.

We might, then, ask why it is that the term nation-state has such strong currency in the West. It is one thing to fret about the inexactness of the term, a more interesting one to ask why it has such hegemony in describing the contemporary world. The root of the answer lies in the process of state-building, which also shaped western Europe over the last two centuries. If states were not actually 'nations' too, then they could be imagined as such or at least aspired to. So successful has this alignment between state and nation been that it is part of our sociological 'common sense', our taken-for-granted political and cultural world. Does it matter? – most certainly, because it gives a fundamental legitimacy to the modern state without which it could not function.

The problem with this formulation is that, on the one hand, the covert influence of nation-state building in the nineteenth and twentieth centuries dominates politics, sociology and history alike. On the other hand, societies bounded in geographical and social space are less and less likely to be unified totalities in the late twentieth century when economic, political and cultural forces have eroded the homogeneity of states.

The key changes that impact on the relationships between state, society and nation in the twentieth century can be characterised as follows. On the one hand, and contrary to expectations, nationalism has waxed rather than waned in importance as this century has progressed. Nationalisms have arisen in regions or territories that wish to break away from existing states. When we think of nationalism in the West, we think of its rise in Scotland, Wales, Catalonia and Quebec and other formally 'stateless' nations (McCrone 1992). Nationalism has become an active basis for social divisions within states.

We need to recognise, however, that in the post-war period there has also been a core form of nationalism that is frequently implicit. As the modern state became the appropriate instrument for guaranteeing the life chances of its citizens, and ironing out social inequalities, governments became major actors in economic competition between states in the quest for economic growth 'in the national interest'. This is 'state nationalism' expressed in economic and political competition. Nationalism, in this form, became more, not less, common in this process of post-war international competition. This nationalism of the 'core', that is, existing states such as the UK, Spain and Belgium, developed alongside counter-nationalisms on the periphery among stateless nations within core states (such as Scotland, Catalonia and Flanders), which sought to redraw the limits and responsibilities of central state power, and in many cases secede from it.

And yet, just as nationalism was growing in importance, so the 'nation-state' appeared to be losing its powers. The growing interest in nationalism coincides with the apparent decline in the powers of the state. This is one aspect of a wider process known as 'globalisation', whereby economic, cultural and political influences increasingly operate at a world or global level. After all, we live in a world of global economic markets, with its cultural products like Coca-Cola, and supra-state institutions such as the European Union, the International Monetary Fund and the World Bank. All of these forces would seem to have eroded the power of the independent state. Why then has there been an increase in national movements wanting a state of their own? How is it possible to explain this apparent contradiction? One possibility is that the sovereignty of the nation-state was always a trick of the eye. In the words of one writer:

> The era of the homogeneous and viable nation-states is over (or rather the era of the illusion that homogeneous and viable nation-states are possible is over, since such states never existed) and the national vision must be redefined. (Tamir 1993: 3)

Nowhere is this more obvious than in these islands where, as we have seen, nationality and citizenship have evolved in an idiosyncratic way. The British are not at all like the French in that their civic republican tradition defines (possibly over-defines) who is to be French, and how one is to behave as French. The British, we might say, are under-defined. There is no common football team, no rugby team (and the British Lions includes all the Irish, most of whom quit this state over 70 years ago). Sport is a good indicator of nationality. After all, you are a 'national' if you play for the national side. In the 1980s, the Conservative politician Norman Tebbit provoked controversy when he talked about his 'cricket test'. How could people of Caribbean and Asian origins be considered English, he implied, if they opted to cheer for the West Indies, India or Pakistan against England? What he failed to notice was the 'fuzzy' nature of national identity (and that England was not Britain). In recent years an important debate has started in England about whether or not black people can be 'English' rather than simply 'British'. In many ways this is a debate about ethnic (being English by lineage or 'blood') versus civic defi- nitions (being British by residence and citizenship). Black footballers and brown cricketers playing for England help to highlight the issue.

There is a related matter that is worth exploring at this point in our argu- ment, and that is the issue of regional identity. When English people are asked to describe their nationality, it is not uncommon for many to echo the views of the person who replied: 'I'm not English. I'm from Yorkshire.' In strict terms, of course, being from Yorkshire (or Lancashire and so on) is a regional not a national identity. However, the speaker is possibly reacting what could be perceived to be the 'capture' of Englishness by a southern 'home counties' version. (In passing, it is interesting to note the revealing terminology of English geography. The cultural core is 'the home counties' (not the Midlands), and the peripheries are described as 'the North' and 'the West'.)

It would be difficult to argue, however, that with very few exceptions any English region has the cultural wherewithal – language, history, institutions – to turn regionalism into nationalism. Perhaps the only one that has these is Cornwall, where there is an embryonic 'national' movement based on precisely these cultural markers.

Being British today

What, then, does it mean to be British? We know that being British was 'forged' in Colley's apt word in the eighteenth century as a result of war with France, and relatedly being Protestant in contradistinction to Europe's greatest Catholic power (Colley 1992). 'Forgery' of course implies not simply something beaten into shape on the blacksmith's anvil, but a counterfeit, a subterfuge. It was nevertheless a very convincing one because it created Britons (who were also Scots, English, Welsh – but only rarely Irish, most of whom were too Catholic to be British). We can measure the success of this creation by the number of so many Britons who died for their country. *Dulce et decorum est pro patria mori.* The 'patria' in question was undoubtedly British, and it even encompassed others in the far-flung empire as a visit to any war-graveyard will show.

What makes people British these days? By and large the same criteria that are used by other states: where you are born, your legal citizenship, being resident in the country, speaking the language, respecting the country's political institutions and the law, and generally feeling a national citizen. In these respects, they are no different from other west Europeans (McCrone and Surridge 1998). The British appear to have above-average levels of national pride. In the ISSP survey, they scored more highly on national pride than other comparable countries such as Germany, Spain, and Sweden when asked a battery of questions on national pride. What marked the British from citizens of these other countries was the disproportionate pride they took in their history and the armed forces, compared with the Germans, for example, who had much higher scores on pride in economic achievements and the social security system.

These findings are broadly in line with those of the late 1980s when the British cited the monarchy as the national institution they took most pride in, compared with the West Germans (as they were then) who were most proud of their system of Basic Law (Topf *et al.* 1989). Again, Northern Ireland is more complex (Dowds and Young 1996). Those who define themselves as 'British' are broadly in line with their mainland counterparts in terms of pride in British culture and heritage, whereas those who say they are 'Irish' have very low levels of pride in being British.

There are, of course, also important social differences in these matters. Older people, and those with the minimum levels of education are most likely to rank highly on national pride, whereas younger people and those with a university education score significantly lower. There appear to be little significant gender differences. On the other hand, pride in the monarchy in the 1989 survey was highest among older women with basic education who were members of the Church of England. Scots, Catholics and university-educated younger people were those least likely to claim pride in the monarchy as a national emblem.

What we are able to identify in such surveys is evidence for a proto-English nationalism. Englishness differs from Scottishness, Welshness and Irishness in so far as it does not look to these 'Celtic' identities to provide the necessary 'Other'. Instead, we would have to look to continental Europe – to France and to Germany in particular, and possibly 'Europe' as a whole – for that alter-ego against which being English can be constructed. We can see this most easily in right-of-centre opinion that is hostile to the European Union, what is commonly – and revealingly – referred to as 'Little Englanders' (not, of course, 'little Britishers', for there is perhaps more of a 'greater England' perspective on these matters in right-wing circles). Such opinion also tends to be hostile to devolution for Scotland and Wales, and we might speculate that opposition to Europe as well as to constitutional change in these islands provides a solid platform upon which a right-wing version of English nationalism might emerge in the early decades of the twenty-first century.

That, however, is to look too far ahead. Instead, we might ask: how significant is national identity as a source of social division and differentiation in modern Britain? There is a strong case for saying that there is no single 'national' identity in these islands, and that, if anything, it is likely to get even weaker than it currently appears to be. The United Kingdom is a *de facto* (but as yet not *de jure*) multinational state, which is likely to grow more diverse in constitutional terms as the different nations acquire their own parliaments and assemblies. What is the prognosis for Britishness? One scenario would be that the political, religious and cultural conditions that created and sustained it – war, empire, religion, and the welfare state – no longer operate to hold the British together. An alternative scenario is to say that the loose, umbrella-like identity of being British is best suited to adapt to the multicultural – ethnic as well as national – conditions that now exist in these islands. The last 50 years have seen the growing importance of nation and ethnicity as markers of social identity. The next 50 years are likely to see an expanding sense of European-ness with greater political and economic integration. One key task for sociology is to make sense of the new identity-politics that this new era will bring.

FURTHER READING

McCrone, D. *The Sociology of Nationalism*, London: Routledge (1998) reviews the various contemporary manifestations of nationalism, while Colley, L. *Britons: Forging the Nation*, New Haven: CT: Yale University Press (1992) is the key text on how 'being British' was manufactured from the eighteenth century. A useful analysis of ethnic and national identities in the United Kingdom can be found in Cohen, R. *Frontiers of Identity*, Harlow: Longman (1994). Brubaker, R. *Citizenship and Nationhood in France and Germany*, Cambridge, MA: Harvard University Press (1992) is an elegant review of the different nationalisms of the two countries.

CHAPTER 6

Age and Old Age

JOHN A. VINCENT

Age has been used in all societies as a way of differentiating people. Anthropological studies suggest that age is one of the few genuinely universal social criteria, forming a significant part of the social structures by which collective life is ordered. However, this fact in itself, although directing us to look towards issues of age, does not take us very far. Understanding age as social division requires us to understand the wide variations in:

- the degree to which age is used as a mechanism for social differentiation;
- which age criteria are used;
- the significance attached to these criteria.

All three of these factors are extremely varied. Societies range from those in which age is not particularly important, to those in which it is the key structural principle, and from those in which old age is highly valued, to those in which it is of very low status. Further, what is thought to constitute 'old age' varies not only cross-culturally but even within our own society. Our first step needs to be an exploration of the idea of age divisions, and how age has been 'used' in organising human society.

In more egalitarian types of society, the social categories of age and gender do not take on the rigidity and determining quality that these criteria do in many other societies. For example, the Mbuti, as described by Turnball (1984) illustrate the highly flexible character of small-scale societies that live by foraging, and that have low social differentiation. Many accounts of foraging societies characterise them as living opportunistic lives in the natural environment, gathering and hunting a wide-ranging diet (Lee and De Vore 1968). These people live together in small bands in which, although differences between men and women and old and young are acknowledged, all voices make some contribution to communal decision making.

On the other hand, in societies in which access to inherited property is crucial for economic well-being, age and gender criteria are frequently quite rigid and strongly sanctioned (Vincent 1995). The idea of the patriarchal extended family, as found for example in parts of rural India, contains the idea of patriarchy as not only the domination by male members of the household over the females (see Chapter 3) but also of the older (particularly the senior generation) over the younger. All household structures have potential for problems or conflicts. Thus the power and authority of the older over the younger and the duty and obedience owed by younger to older may create frustrations in some circumstances. Waiting for the old man to retire so that the younger generation can take control of the land and make their mark on the world is observed in literature (Hardy 1902, 1975; Synge 1911; Naipul 1964) and ethnography (Arensberg and Kimbell 1940, on rural Ireland). From the opposite point of view, the older generation may feel a lack of filial piety on the part of children who have left to work in distant towns.

These frustrations of rural family farmers have parallels in modern Britain, in the emotions of elderly people and their families when making decisions about continued independent living in the face of increasing frailty. What are the right amounts of duty owed and reasonable expectations anticipated from one generation to another? Society's general norms can seldom be applied unambiguously to the complexities of individual circumstance.

The aspect of age that is significant to a society may be the accumulation of years, but in many societies without formal or bureaucratic recording of age people do not know their chronological age in a precise way. People may measure the passing of the years by reference to personal, social and historical events – when they had their first child, when the pogrom took place, or when the great flood happened. In these ways people know who is older or younger and may be differentiated into age strata even without an exact counting of the years.

People's ages are usually described in terms of calendar age – the numbers of years that have lapsed since birth. So one is described as aged 'twenty-one' between 7665 days and 8030 days (give or take the odd leap year) after one's birth. This is because we use the Gregorian calendar, which has become a world-wide standard. But there are other ways of measuring dates and times – the Jewish and the Islamic to mention but two. Age can be both a verb (to age; to grow older) and a noun (how old one is; the age of consent). Ageing is a process that is continuous. Thus, strictly, age as an attribute requires an additional set of criteria to demarcate people into groups. Society recognises that a group of people, defined by chronological age or through collectively reaching a certain stage in their lives, should occupy certain social roles and be entitled to certain privileges or duties.

In many societies the transitions from one 'age' to another are marked by ritual; ceremonies such as initiation rites, which publicly mark the change from one social role to another. Some age categories may be given or obtain a special significance. In modern society many legal rights are defined by age. For example, the age at which you can *legitimately* buy alcohol or tobacco, drive a car, have sex, leave home, marry, join the army, vote, serve as a juror or be expected to retire as a judge, are legally defined. Hence the association of 'old age' with those 65 years and over, as historically this has been the pensionable age for men in the UK. Similarly, in the UK centenarians are regarded as special and were acknowledged by the nation with a telegram from the monarch.

It is important to note that the boundaries of age categories are not fixed by any objective criteria, they are social constructions. The age categories thought up by demographers or legislators for their own convenience, are just as much social constructions as any reported sense of common identity among teenagers, pensioners, or 'the over-forties'. Because of historical social change, the age at which individuals born at different times acquired these age-based rights and duties, may have been different. The experience of a generation, or the common experience of those born at a particular time, can form part of developing age-based social structures. People will move in and out of age strata as they add years to their life.

Age and stratification: age groups, chronological age, age classes

Given the wide variation in the way in which age is used as a social criterion it is important to be clear about the conceptual basis of the categories with which we describe age-based divisions in society. We may first talk of 'age strata' or 'age classes', that is *groups of people of the same age who, by virtue of this characteristic, have distinct sets of life chances and similar social rights and duties*, much like but not identical to social classes (see Chapter 2). The roles and norms society allocates to age groups create barriers and opportunities. This can be seen to give people of similar age common interests as against those of people of other chronological ages. A weak view of 'age stratum' would be that the people in each stratum simply happened to be in the same chronological age band; a strong view would be that they are people who have conflictual common interests over and against other age strata (see for example the discussion of childhood in Chapter 7).

The idea of age strata is sometimes mixed up with 'generation' and 'cohort'. *'Generation' refers to the fact of reproduction* and that each family experiences a sequence of people passing through in life. Thus today's children will be tomorrow's parents and will subsequently take their turn as grandparents. The idea of 'generation' can rather more usefully be used to refer to position within the family. Confusion between this and age is easily made when the image of the nation or the society as a family is used, such that those over 60 can be referred to as the 'older generation'. Generation and age are not synonymous – grandparenthood and retirement do not occur together, nephews and nieces may be older than their aunts or uncles. Similarly, 'the sixties generation' refers to people who were young during a particular period of history, that is, a 'cohort'.

Cohorts (or 'age-sets') are groupings of people born at the same time. Their members therefore age simultaneously and consequently have many historical experiences in common. Rapid change in society means that people with similar dates of birth may well have distinct sets of experience. The experience of military service is something that differentiates cohorts in Britain and also provides contrasting experiences in different European and North American societies. Those who did National Service in Britain or were drafted in the USA carried the mark of this experience through life. The experiences of the cohort of 'immigrant' minority ethnic groups is quite different from that of the cohort made up of their children (Chapter 4). Common experience may even give rise to a label, such as 'baby-boomers' or 'Thatcher's children'.

Cohorts may also be socially recognised in a more structured way, as when a set of people are given a common identity early in their lives and carry that common identity through the rest of their days. These groups may be 'age sets', for example all those initiated at a certain time forming a group that earns a reputation and feels a common sense of solidarity throughout the lives of its members. There may even be a special name given to each age set. In contemporary society, and in particular in the USA, a good example would be class groups at school or college ('the class of 47') who keep in touch and hold reunions. Just as age since birth is a continuous variable, so dates of birth can be allocated into cohort categories only by the use of culturally constructed systems of classification. Societies structured around age sets have a static set of age grades into which successive age sets or cohorts pass (Bernadi 1985).

That is to say, cohorts whose formative years have given them common attitudes, values or perceptions may thus form an identifiable group (*cf.* Mannheim 1927). These common experiences may lead to a common *sense* of identity and even common interests. So, people in Britain who are now in their eighties were children in the First World War, were starting families in the Great Depression of the 1930s, went through the Second World War in prime middle age, and reached retirement when the long post-war economic boom was coming to an end. Similarly, it has been argued that the cohort born in the post-war baby boom, who experienced the changes in social conventions of the 1960s, and the collective sense of liberation at that time, has consequently a degree of common identity. One social repercussion of this differing cohort experience is sometimes misleadingly referred to as a 'generation gap'. However, these cohort differences are not merely cultural. Demographic considerations and other changes in family structure will mean that the experience of parenthood, and other inter-generational social relations, will change. The current life course will now, much more typically, include the experience of being grandparents in middle age and a great-grandparent in later life (Bengston 1996).

The 'life cycle' is a common-sense term used to describe the typical sequence of age categories in a society. It is most frequently understood in terms of the sequence of generations; a continually turning wheel. Thus, all members of society are thought to age by following typical sequences of roles, for example, from child, to adolescent, spouse, parent, grandparent, then ancestor. Sociologists, however, prefer the term 'life-course' because whereas 'life cycle' is a static image of an unchanging society, 'life-course' is an image of a *process* that reflects the flow of time and the sequencing of cohorts as well as generations. Life-courses happen to people in historical time and in particular places, so they reflect the fact that 'life cycles' change over time and place. Life-courses vary not only between different social groups, for example across genders or ethnic groups, but significantly they also vary historically.

The life-courses of different cohorts also interact in a complex and dynamic pattern. The current cohort who are now 70 to 80 years old and were born in the years 1920 to 1930, have had opportunities achieved by the struggles, often through trade unions and the Liberal and Labour parties, of the preceding generation who started the movement down the road to universal retirement pensions. The success of those struggles enabled them to retire with greater security than their parents. Subsequently they have been affected by the increasing proclivity of their children to separate and divorce. Thus they may be obstructed in meeting some of their previously held expectations of grandparent/grandchild relationships. In other words the experiences of that cohort have been in part determined by the action of the immediately preceding and succeeding cohorts.

Age strata and cohorts are two separate bases on which social life is patterned. There are difficult methodological problems when trying to study old age and inequality in working out which phenomena are the result of becoming a certain age and which result from being a member of a particular cohort (Hardy 1997). Thus for any particular moment in time, those who are old appear to have certain characteristics. However, these characteristics when viewed critically may not be due to advancing years *per se* but to cultural conventions that define differences between age strata, or to cohort experiences of specific historical circumstances. As will be seen in Chapter 10, explaining the health of older people is not just a question of their current physiological condition, but may well involve looking at particular dietary, housing or occupational experiences earlier in their lives.

The changing historical pattern of life-courses

In the centuries leading up to radical social changes of the eighteenth century, life-courses in Europe and America were structured around certain basic social realities. The most important of these were uncertainties about longevity. Demographic characteristics of the time included very high rates of infant mortality, death in childbirth, and epidemics of fatal infectious diseases. On the whole, living standards and nutritional levels militated against living in a healthy condition to a ripe old age. There was not the close association between death and old age that exists in contemporary society; death could, and did, strike at any time. The agrarian basis of much of society, and the relatively lower levels of geographical and social mobility meant that life-course transitions could be marked by public rituals in the local community, not strictly tied to a bureaucratised, national, legal framework. Baptism, confirmation, marriage, funerals of parents or spouse and the birth of one's children, were ritualised transitions that placed people appropriately and publicly into their life-course positions. Old age was not identified with a particular chronological age but implicit in relationships *vis-à-vis* children and other relatives, control of property and an independent livelihood (Grillis 1987; Cole 1992).

We need to be careful not to romanticise the position of respect and care provided for elderly people in these earlier extended families. The demographic patterns were different; people did not live for so long. Not only were many families larger than today but there were also more celibate/never-married people and childless couples. Historical research has suggested that extended families may well have been an adaptation to urban poverty as much as an inherited rural tradition (Laslett 1968; Laslett and Wall 1972).

Three major changes since the eighteenth century have been industrialisation, urbanisation and the development of the nation-state, and along with these have come characteristic ways of thinking and behaving. Kohli's (1986) threefold life-course pattern identified pre-work, characterised by education and training and other forms of socialisation; work, as the dominant life-course stage; and post-work, usually characterised by loss of income and status. The key life-stage in 'modern' society was that of work. It was through employment that people gained their principal income and achieved status. The pre-work and post-work stages were, as a corollary, of less status and income. In Britain, old people feared the degradation of the 'workhouse', the repository of those who could not maintain themselves, and disliked the loss of status felt when having to accept charity (Townsend 1957, 1979; Phillipson and Walker 1986). These attitudes are still widespread among older British people, many of whom do not claim welfare benefits to which they are entitled, in some cases associating residential care with the workhouse (indeed in many towns there are buildings which have a direct historical continuity from one function to the other).

Only with the development of a well-established urban industrial working class did retirement become an established stage of life, following a long and hard labouring life. Large-scale industrial employment organised and controlled a labour force into set patterns of timekeeping – shift work; the six-day/50-hour week; 'Wakes Week' for holiday – which dominated the lives of the vast majority of people. Set patterns of apprenticeship for craft skills, the introduction of compulsory education, and a minimum school leaving age also set a lifetime schedule for work. Following on from 'work', old age in the twentieth century became a recognised part of 'Fordist' mass-production society.

Pensions were previously the prerogatives of military, professional and administrative classes. In the late nineteenth and early twentieth centuries came the experience of a common mass of retired working people. Although an improvement on a situation where people had either to work or depend on charity or endure the rigours of the workhouse, this retired population generally had a lower standard of living than the working population. Almost universally a person's rights to a pension still derive from their work history.

The framework of governance for urbanisation and industrialisation was the emerging nation-state (see Chapter 5). In the new nation-states, people were increasingly governed by universalistic criteria that treated all citizens as being equal, rather than on the basis of personal favour or privilege. The development of modern political thought in the eighteenth century elaborated the ideas of constitutions, citizenship and equality before the law. Paradoxically, the achievement of new individual rights was dependent on greater regulation: national systems for birth and death registration were required to administer duties, such as conscription and taxation, and rights such as child benefit and pensions. Legal-rational authority was the basis of bureaucratic allocation of rights and duties by age.

Kohli (1991) argues that the concept of age-specific rights runs against many of the modern state's universalistic, liberal democratic tenets, for example that all individuals should be equal before the law. In practice, of course, some people are not equal because of their age. He cites struggles in America over compulsory retirement ages, which were seen as conflicting with anti-discriminatory legislation. The issues surrounding the Children Act in Britain, which granted children rights independent of, and potentially in conflict with, those of their parents, are a parallel example of the conflict between universal and age- (or generation-) based rights.

The interconnection of age and social change

Over the past 200 years life-course patterns in the West do appear to be more determined by age than in the past, but certain writers have started to suggest this age-determined life-course is now starting to break down (Grillis 1987; Hareven 1994). Elderly people are now able to choose from a wide diversity of lifestyles. Featherstone and Hepworth (1989), writing from a post-modernist perspective, suggest that the life-course is becoming de-structured. Common social patterns determined by chronological age are becoming less critical to people's life experience. In many parts of today's world, political instability and forced migration have added to the unpredictability of the life-course. Mass expulsions and genocide may be as old as state society but modern society has an unparalleled technical and organisational ability with which to execute them.

Two key areas where this apparent breakdown of established life-course patterns, and therefore a weakening of the social division of age, has been particularly remarked upon are in the fields of employment and the family. With regard to the first of these, the former three-fold pattern of school, work and retirement that framed employment has been undermined. There have been significant changes in retirement; early retirement has dramatically expanded, depriving the age of 65 (for men) of its watershed character (Kohli *et al.* 1992). In the last two decades retirement age has dropped and Guillemard (1989, 1990) suggests that not only is the age of retirement declining, but that there is a whole loosening of the life-course grid. Early retirement is more popular these days with firms, workers and the state, but this can also be seen as a response to the particular condition of the labour market and the growth in unemployment. At the other end of the age range, education has been extended and a comparatively small section of the population leave school at 16 while fewer still start their work careers from such a young age (Chapters 3 and 7).

Decreasing labour market stability and rapidly changing employment patterns introduce increased uncertainty and decreased standardisation of the work career components of the life-course. Patterns of migration, employment and early retirement interact, as do periods of unemployment, retraining, and extended periods of education, to create complex life careers. Current welfare structures across Europe (Giarchi, 1996) depend substantially on insurance contributions and a work record. High levels of unemployment and disrupted careers will have lasting effects into old age for young, casualised, entrants to the labour market (Laczko and Phillipson 1991; Walker 1993; Hugman 1994). Already in the 1990s we are experiencing the growth of a fragmented society in which some have been able to use market position (earnings-related pensions and property-related windfalls) to secure good (that is, not much reduced) material conditions while others have missed out. Those who miss out are those with poor market opportunities.

The second area of life-course modification lies in the family. Patterns of married life and cohabitation are changing. This is often portrayed as consisting of more living together instead of marriage, and more divorce among those who do marry. It is true that the family of orientation (the family in which we were born) is no longer automatically followed by a single, formalised family of procreation (the family we set up on marriage and in which we raise our own children).

However, whereas it is clear that divorce rates have increased substantially, it would be simplistic to look on this as the sole cause of family dissolution and changes in the form of the family. Many policy initiatives and much research are actually oriented towards 'strengthening the family', while the dissolution of family units and kinship networks comes from several causes, such as greater geographical mobility, and changing life expectancy. Rural-urban migration and the ageing of the countryside are worldwide phenomena (Sen 1994: 10). The social barriers erected by cultural assimilation of migrants also disrupts intergenerational expectations of old age and the final part of the life-course (Askham *et al.* 1993; Blakemore and Boneham 1994; this volume Chapter 4).

Further, changing patterns of longevity mean that spouses live together longer and the majority of married life is no longer spent rearing children. One of the successes of modern society has been to improve the health and increase the life expectancy of people. Thus in contrast to what 'post-modernist' writers have seen as a decline in stability of family work and lifestyle patterns, a certain demographic standardisation has taken place. People are now much more likely to live a full span and die in their eighties. The age of death and length of life is becoming more standard; although more people are living to older ages, the maximum life span does not seem to have increased. Further, medical advance means that there are fewer childless couples. This phenomenon combined with a desire and ability to limit family size has meant that family size is standardising on two children, most typically born to parents in their twenties (Jackson 1998).

These complex changes mean that for older people the development of new grandparental roles on the positive side, and new forms of social isolation on the negative side, are associated with changing patterns of family life at the end of the twentieth century. What we think of as old age reflects employment and family patterns, which in turn are modified by an interconnecting set of other factors. The separation of old from young is thus not fixed for all time: the form that age as a social division takes draws of a set of wider processes that are themselves evolving.

The social conditions of older people

Societal ageing has been going on in Europe for a considerable time and is still largely identified as a European issue (Czechoslovak Demographic Society 1989). In fact, other world populations are also ageing and indeed ageing faster than Europe, but these changes have not yet reached the proportions of those currently experienced in the West.

The most obvious change listed in Table 6.1 is the increase in people over 75, because this marks a prolongation of life in old age. The extent to which there is a consequent period of physical frailty, greater dependency, and need for new services, is controversial (Victor 1991). It is in the interests of certain sections of society, such as the financial elites seeking to expand their profit-making potential in the fields of pensions and insurance, or the professional groups whose members provide care for the elderly, that such concerns become widespread (Vincent 1996). What is clear is that the issue has been taken up as a threatening 'social problem', to the extent of warranting a royal commission of enquiry (Royal Commission 1999). How will care for these very old people be delivered and how can a society, with relatively fewer of its members being of working age, afford to pay for it?

This reaction has the character of a 'moral panic' where a small-scale issue is amplified by the media and the 'chattering classes' into appearing to be a much bigger problem than it really should be. This is not to deny that there are real problems to do with the social conditions in which many older people live, and the way society needs to provide for them. However, no country with

Table 6.1   Demographic characteristics of UK, 1974–95

Population	1974	1984	1994	1995
United Kingdom population (millions)	56.2	56.5	58.4	58.6
Percentage of population aged under 16	25.2	21.0	20.7	20.7
Percentage of population between 16 and retirement age 59/64 inclusive	57.9	61.0	61.1	61.2
Percentage of population over retirement age 60/65+	16.9	17.9	18.2	18.2
Percentage of population aged 75 years+	4.9	6.3	6.8	7.0

economic growth, progressively being produced by an economy that requires a smaller and smaller labour force, with time to adapt and plan, is facing a crisis of elder care. Nor is it true to represent 'older people' as being 'a problem', as if they were a single homogeneous category.

Demographically, economically and culturally, old age is experienced differently by different people. An obvious difference is between men and women; the well-known gender difference in life expectancy. Current British life expectancy at birth is approximately 74 years for men and 80 years for women. The life expectancy difference is somewhat less at age 60, when men can anticipate a further 18 years to age 78, while women can typically expect to have a further 22 years of life to age 82. This difference in life expectancy means that old age is most typically a feminine stage of life and is becoming increasingly feminine.

In England and Wales 16 per cent of the population is over 65, with a sex ratio of 1.5 women to each man. For older age groups, seven per cent of the population is over 75 years, with a sex ratio of nearly two women to each man, while for the over-85 year olds who make up just under two per cent of the population, there are three women to every man. Widowhood has become normal and feminised. Women will experience an average of nine years widowhood. Male widowers on the other hand are much more likely to remarry. There is a higher proportion of women than men in residential care (about twice as many). In the 85 and over age-group 15 per cent of men and 27 per cent of women are in residential care (Arber and Ginn 1991, 1995; Ginn and Arber 1996).

For those in the labour market, exit from employment is typically at 61 for men and 57 for women. This means that men average 17 years, and women 25 years of life after leaving paid employment. Women are more likely to work part-time and tend not to have the same benefits from occupational pensions as men. Only 24 per cent of all women aged 40–59 belong to an occupational pension scheme. Small occupational pensions tend to bring women only up to the income support level so that many do not really gain benefit from paying into such schemes.

Material deprivation in all areas of society is structured by gender, class, and ethnicity, but these differences become exaggerated in later life. This is related in particular to the structure of the labour market. As incomes in later life tend to be dependent on pension rights achieved through contributions from salary and from saving and investments made from income during working life, those who received the best material rewards in their working lives do best in old age. Those who found difficulty entering the labour market at all and who achieved poor rewards from their labour tend also in their old age to be among the most materially deprived section of the British population.

Material deprivation in old age is then of central importance. Age helps to explain the distribution of 'poverty', and lack of income is the means by which social divisions can be seen to open up. Poverty in old age interacts with former social class and gender: the interplay of social divisions is striking. We therefore need to discuss income and pensions as indicators of poverty, and the way these have changed in recent decades.

In practice, making such comparisons is not straightforward, because we need to know who are dependent on pensions, and whether we are to count people or households. The Office for National Statistics in its *Family Spending* 1996–97 reports that the average weekly expenditure per person in the UK was £126 per week, while for one-person households of people not retired (that is, mainly young people in employment) the average weekly expenditure was over £191. In contrast, the typical one-person household consisting of a retired adult mainly dependent on *state* pensions, the equivalent figure was £83.34 (that is, only two-thirds of the national average). Of course, not all pensioners are poor: expenditure for households with one retired adult *not* mainly dependent on the *state* pension averaged £146. A similar pattern of reduced expenditure is found for two-person households (consisting of a male and a female adult) – £147 for those retired and mainly dependent on state pensions, £269 for those retired but not mainly dependent on state pensions and £376 for couples not retired. Undergraduates coping with low incomes will recognise the real constraints such sums of money indicate, but of course, pensioners are on low incomes for the rest of their lives.

Another way of looking at this is to compare average national gross weekly expenditure for retired and employed people, regardless of household. In 1996–97 the figures were £145 for the employed and £111 for the retired (with an overall national average of £126). To put it another way, the retired spent only 77 per cent of that spent by the employed. A decade earlier, in 1987, the equivalent figure was £82 for the employed, and £69 for the retired. That is, the retired were able to spend 85 per cent of that spent by the employed (DoE 1988, 1998). Not only is there a lower comparative expenditure, but the difference between retired and employed people has actually been *increasing*.

If we go back another decade, in 1979 the average income of the bottom 20 per cent of pensioners was £56 per week, compared with £170 for the top 20 per cent. By the mid-1990s, 16 years later, the average weekly income of the bottom 20 per cent had risen by almost £15 but the average income of the top 20 per cent had risen by over *£100* (DSS 1997). The history of this period, coincident with the Conservative government, is of worsening emiseration of those old people dependent on state pensions.

Table 6.2   Comparison of those on low incomes (under £88 per week) and high incomes (£145 or more per week), 1991

Item	Total sample (per cent)	Low income (per cent)	High income (per cent)
Enjoying life more than used to	27	18	38
Good thing about growing old: none	29	36	20
Activities: taking exercise/going for a walk	70	66	80
Find need extra care/attention	50	56	37
No planning of retirement	22	38	4
Often/occasionally lonely	32	45	18
Wish for more social contact	25	33	18
Regular use of car	50	32	74
In receipt of private pension	22	18	42
Sometimes struggle to pay bills	31	53	8
Concern about paying bills	24	39	8
Often/occasionally cut back on basics	28	44	12
Never cut back on basics	72	56	89
No money left after basics paid for	11	19	3
Often/occasional problems with winter warmth	19	30	7
Home with central heating	81	79	90
Council tenancy	24	42	5
Owner occupation	60	37	87
Married	57	35	73
Preferred name: Senior citizens	36	40	26
Preferred name: Retired	36	26	45

Source: adapted from Midwinter (1991: 31)

A British Gas survey of a sample of retired people, aged of 55 or over, found 33 per cent had incomes of less than £88 per week; 41 per cent had incomes of £88–£144 per week; while 26 per cent of the sample had incomes of over £145 per week (Midwinter 1991). A comparison of the rich and poorer sections of the sample concluded 'the survey demonstrates that, if money doesn't buy happiness, then, at least, a lack of it edges one toward misery' (Midwinter 1991: 31). Some of the implications of this can be seen in Table 6.2.

These figures document a growing material inequality (and by implication social division) between older people and the general population and a growing differentiation among older people themselves. However, elderly people's subjective feeling about their standard of living is influenced by a range of things over and above simply how much they can afford to spend. They have, for example, a variety of reference groups against which to compare their own living standards.

Elderly people's memory of the past includes memories of the conditions in which older people lived in the early part of this century. They are also aware of the former standard of living they were able to achieve before retirement. They may also compare themselves favourably, or otherwise, with other retirees, as well as with those enjoying the current general living conditions of society as a whole. Thus just as there is no clear single common experience of material deprivation among contemporary older people, so there is also no common interpretative framework by which older people feel a collective sense of their standard of living.

Social policy issues: everybody needs pensions

The position of older people is not simply a matter of academic analysis: it is a concrete, lived experience, directly affected by social policy enactments. The reason for the growing objective inequality between old people lies largely with what has happened to the pensions and benefit system. The two key political developments that affect today's British pensioners were the introduction of State Earnings Related Pensions (SERPS) by the Labour government in 1978, which superseded the graduated pension scheme 1961–75 (Arber and Ginn 1991: 86), and the removal by the Conservatives in 1980 of the 'Rooker-Wise amendment', which linked pensions to both earnings and prices (Atkinson 1989: 233). This change by the Thatcher government in 1979 was one of a series of measures designed to restrict the long-term cost of benefits to the Exchequer; once the link with earnings was broken, pensioners on the basic state pension fell steadily further and further behind the general standard of living of the country. On the other hand those who have retired after long periods of steady employment paying earnings-related contributions into SERPS are now receiving substantial top-up pensions. These pensions are smaller than in most other EU countries, but they represent a very substantial improvement on what might have been expected a generation previously.

Pensions have become an important political issue in that they form a key point in the debate on the role of the state in redistribution of wealth, in the provision of welfare and managing a framework for economic activity. Should the state provide pensions for all? Should it merely look after the most vulnerable, whether economically and through infirmity? Should the state administer pensions schemes or should that be left to the private sector?

Despite much media comment, the UK does not face a serious long-term problem of pension (social security) payments. The present value of net public pension liabilities is estimated at five per cent of Gross Domestic Product, compared with over 100 per cent in Japan, Germany and France. The reason for this is a failure to increase the basic state pension in real terms since 1980. It is currently about 15 per cent of average earnings. If this policy is continued it is calculated that future reductions in contribution rates will be possible. Further, only 17 per cent of employees belong to SERPS, which provides earnings-related additional pensions. Most employees belong to funded private occupational schemes (Budd and Cambell 1998).

What is at stake here can be called 'generational equity'. It has been argued that the younger age groups are being disadvantaged by paying for the pensions of the current generation of older people, but because of demographic changes, they cannot themselves necessarily expect to receive an equivalent pension from the succeeding generation (Johnson *et al.* 1989; Johnson 1995). Despite the way it is frequently presented, this problem is not merely, or at all, a demographic issue. The issue is in essence one of redistribution and the role of the state in evening out unacceptable inequalities of wealth and power. In other words, it is a question of how government deals with the factors that generate a significant part of the social division based on age. If we take a wider view of redistribution than who pays and who benefits from various forms of taxation, we can also take into account issues associated with exploitation and non-financial contributions to society's well-being.

In these terms, the debate centres on rights and claims to a share of society's *current* economic output. After all, nursing care cannot be stored, or saved up to bring out when it is needed later in life. 'Care' exists only at a single moment, so that if there is currently not enough to go round it has to be rationed (allocated) through some mechanism, whether this happens through a market to the highest bidder, by allocation to the most needy, offered first to those who fought to defend their country or some other process. We need to see age as a division in a wider context, but a balanced one. Why do we hear more about the cost of state pensions than, for example, the long-term cost to future generations of disposing of nuclear waste? The 1990s recipients of building society windfalls, who were cashing in their elders' prudence and reducing successive generations' opportunities for cheap housing loans, seldom considered generational equity and how attitudes between old and young might be affected.

The extent to which there will be an economic difficulty in meeting the need for satisfactory pensions in the future must be related to the future productivity of the workforce and to the extent to which declining rates of economic participation among elderly people continue. The assumption is frequently made that the elderly population is economically unproductive. Patterns of work and the reasons for non-participation in the labour market have varied considerably over time, but elderly people have not always withdrawn from work. In Britain in 1881, according to Johnson (1985), 73 per cent of the male population of 65 and over were in employment, but by 1981 the percentage had shrunk to less than 11 per cent. This major change in the distribution of work is not because the population has become physically less able and therefore less employable. Non-employed does not mean non-productive; it may mean productive potential is being lost, or that useful work is not recorded or recognised as such.

Ageism and the cultural construction of old age

Older people not only suffer from increased chances of a materially deprived lifestyle but they are also subject to the experience of 'ageism'. They tend to be culturally devalued; getting older is regarded by most people as a kind of inevitable tragedy.

> Ageism is about acting on stereotypes about chronological age which prevent (older) people from having control over their lives and participating fully and purposefully in society. (Age Equality Action Group, LBH 1991, quoted in Meade 1995)

Ageism, like racism or sexism, refers to both prejudice and discrimination; the first being an attitude, the second a behaviour. Comfort (1977, quoted in Meade 1995) suggests that ageism is based on fear, folklore and hang-ups, and that ageism, like racism, needs to be met by information, contradiction and, when necessary, confrontation.

Negative stereotypes of people based on their age may refer to different age groups; both young and old can be stereotyped. The negative image of old age is extremely prevalent and indeed, getting older seems often to carry no positive connotations at all. A quick browse through any shop selling birthday cards will indicate the disgust with which ageing is widely held.

Discrimination on age grounds is not illegal in the same way as sexism or racism, although the practice of age discrimination with regard to employment is likely to change under pressure, including that from EU equal opportunities regulations. It is common both for young job applicants to find themselves passed over for older, supposedly more mature applicants and vice versa, for older people looking for work to find younger, supposedly more lively, people preferred. It may be feared that training older workers will not be cost-effective, or that they will be more prone to illness and absence. Reverse discrimination also takes place whereby older workers are offered dead-end jobs in which employers assume that younger people looking to further themselves would not stay.

Bytheway (1995: 1–18) suggests that simple definitions of ageism are inadequate for two reasons. First, they should not be based on parallels with sexism and racism because each is a unique phenomenon. Second, he points out that it should not be presumed that old people exist as a group (older people are as varied as the rest of the population) and that labelling them with this single category is itself part of the problem. Separating out older people for special consideration (even for special study as in the field of social gerontology, or in this chapter) implies a 'them' and 'us' situation. It presumes a situation in which the old are 'them', different from 'us' who are defining the meaning of the situation and who are not old. It is to take the social division of age as given.

We might observe that much of the care provided for the very elderly comes not from the social services, but from old people who are younger than those for whom they care. We can treat this as a differentiation within the category of 'older people': the social division into young and old in real life is more complicated than the 'us' and 'them'. Alternately, the care provision patterns could be read as a marker of how the elderly meet with and support each other, thus creating a separate social identity. In rural areas, the sparsity of the population may reduce this interaction, just as physical distance from centres providing services tends to reduce knowledge of, and access to, services (Giarchi 1990). Such rural/urban differences are another reason to eschew the us/them dichotomy.

Bytheway asks us to consider different approaches implied in the following formulations. He takes a quotation by way of illustration: 'ageism is discrimination against people because they are old'. He suggests that in using the phrase the author is creating the same distinction: between a kind of ageless 'we' (ageless in the sense that our age is considered irrelevant) and 'them' who are old. He offers the alternative:

Ageism can be seen as a process of systematic stereotyping of and discrimination against us when we are considered old (italics in original)

He points out that this second formulation implies a concern with ourselves and our future selves, rather than with older people currently suffering the consequence of ageism (Bytheway 1995: 128). He concludes by arguing that it is a fundamental mistake to equate an anti-ageist stance with thinking positively, but adds that this is not to say that we should resist being positive. Scepticism that playing with vocabulary and framing language around idealised scenarios and unreal beliefs is misplaced. Rather than claim that:

> Most elderly people are really nice, absolutely fascinating once you get to know them... The things they say!... Working with them is really interesting... Some of them are real characters!

he argues that it is far less patronising, self-righteous and ageist to say that:

> The people I work with are pretty ordinary. They have lived long lives and survived many experiences. I like working with them because there are things I can do to make life more satisfactory for them They tell me what they think and I listen to them *and* sometimes *argue*. You can learn a lot from ordinary people. I enjoy the work; it is worth doing.

Age as a social division

Age is a distinctive social division if for no other reason than we anticipate moving from one side of the division(s) to the other, thus ultimately having direct experience of it in more than one form as we follow our life-courses. As we have seen, life-courses are social because they have general and observable patterns, shaped by norms and values (for example those associated with the life cycle), which are part of the structure of society. They are also given characteristic forms by historical patterns of social change. This means that while the life-course is the normatively expected transition of stages in the process of social ageing, those of us currently at different ages will not experience the life-course in the same way. The life-course is both an individual and a social process of ageing.

Life is periodicised through age strata sequences; the teenagers of today will become the pensioners of tomorrow. It is structured by the sequence of generations; today's children are tomorrow's great-grandparents. It is further structured by history, in that the life-course of each succeeding cohort takes its form from the historical events through which it lives. The idea of the life-course, in addition to these social and historical aspects, has a psychological dimension in that individuals will develop and change personality in response to life experience.

Therefore when we seek to understand social inequality and stratification we must consider the life-course as a social process, rather than as a static social divide between generation or cohort. The systematic differences in material circumstances and life chances of people of different age do not arise because when people's hair gets greyer, they slip into a prepared social box labelled 'old, poor and useless'. Rather, in the struggle for a decent standard of living and a modicum of social esteem, the life-courses of some people offer them greater chance of success than others. Some kinds of people collectively reach old age in times and circumstances in which their personal history and changing social circumstances lead to a relative lack of social and economic power; it is this that constitutes the real basis of social division.

RECOMMENDED FURTHER READING

A good overview of current ways of understanding old age is Phillipson, C. *Reconstructing Old Age*, London: Sage (1998), while an introduction to the conflicts, struggles and issues that structure older people's lives in the modern world can be found in Vincent, J. *Power, Politics and Old Age*, Buckingham, Open University Press (1999). An excellent anthropology of the cultural process of ageing, which looks at both children and older people, is Hockey, J. and James, A. *Growing Up and Growing Old*, London: Sage (1993), while for a thorough empirical examination of the relationship between the two social divisions of age and gender, Arber, S. and Ginn, J. (eds) *Connecting Gender and Ageing*, Buckingham: Open University Press (1995), is a valuable source. Blaikie, A., *Ageing and Popular Culture*, Cambridge, Cambridge University Press (1999) is a recent welcome addition to the literature.

CHAPTER 7

Childhood

STEVI JACKSON AND SUE SCOTT

Childhood is the only form of social subordination that is still romanticised as a state of freedom. This may seem a startling assertion given that this is not the way in which childhood is usually thought about in everyday life. Generally childhood is seen as a natural state, as a stage of biological immaturity during which children are both prepared for and protected from the 'real' adult world. It is supposed to be a carefree time, a time for play rather than work, a time without the burdens of adult worries and responsibilities. Yet childhood is also, and perhaps self-evidently, a social status, one of subordination to adults. Childhood is defined, in part, by exclusion from adult rights of citizenship and also by dependence on adults. Children spend most of their lives either within families or within institutions catering for their supposed 'needs'. In all these settings they live under adult authority.

Traditionally social scientists have conceptualised childhood primarily within the socialisation paradigm, in which children were seen as adults-in-waiting, whose experiences were only worth investigating in so far as they shaped adult attributes or life chances (Thorne 1987). Recent sociological work has challenged such adult-centred approaches (Thorne 1987, 1993; James and Prout 1990; Leonard 1990; Waskler 1991; Mayall 1994), but developmental perspectives remain prominent in everyday thinking and in professional and public discourse. It is still taken for granted that the process of maturing from child to adolescent to adult unfolds as a series of naturally occurring stages, that there is a 'right age' at which children should develop certain competencies and acquire particular freedoms and responsibilities. These assumptions are so pervasive that it is difficult to think outside them, so widely accepted that they have become unquestioned 'truths'. Childhood is thought of as a linear trajectory towards the future and children as themselves representing the future. It is not only the future of society as a whole that is the issue but the propensity of parents to live vicariously through their children, to treat them as carriers of their own hopes and dreams (Beck and Beck-Gernsheim 1995).

New sociological approaches to childhood suggest that rather than viewing children as future adults in the making we should focus upon children's own lives and activities. This entails a shift away from the idea of a child as 'becoming' an adult to the 'being child', conceptualised as an active social agent (James *et al.* 1998). While these new perspectives are essential in challenging adult-centred views, we should not forget that children's lives are largely bounded by adult surveillance. There is no free and autonomous realm of childhood outside the social relations in which childhood in general, and particular individual childhoods, are forged. In this chapter we are concerned with the construction and maintenance of the social division between children and adults and therefore treat childhood and adulthood as social constructs rather than natural, pre-given stages of life.

The lives of children are, of course, shaped by divisions of gender, class, ethnicity, (dis)ability and so on. Since these divisions are discussed in detail in other chapters, here we are concerned with the division between children and adults as a fundamental social division in its own right. We begin by discussing the social construction of childhood, drawing attention to its cultural and historical variability and identifying specific features of late modern childhood. Two issues are explored in some detail: relations of power and dependence between adults and children, and the risk anxiety associated with childhood and children. We conclude by drawing attention to differences among children, locating childhood within wider social divisions.

Childhood as socially constructed

In arguing that childhood is socially constructed rather than being intrinsic to the state of being a child, we suggest that the construction of childhood needs to be understood at a number of different levels: the structural, the discursive and the situated. Childhood is institutionalised through family, education and the state, resulting in dependence on adults and exclusion from full participation in adult society. At the level of discourse, childhood has been constituted as an object of the scientific gaze through such disciplines as psychology, social work and education, which have claimed expertise in monitoring, categorising and managing childhood and children. These expert knowledges have in turn shaped common sense thinking, so that we are all assumed to 'know' what a child is, to be able to comment on what constitutes a 'proper' childhood. The meaning of childhood is also negotiated through everyday situated interaction, where children themselves enter into the picture as active social agents. However, children's participation in constructing their own everyday world takes place within the constraints set by their subordinate location in relation to adults.

Anthropological and historical evidence suggests that current ideas of childhood and practices of child-rearing are culturally and historically specific. Childhood is not the same the world over. There are vast differences between the cosseted and protected lives of many children in wealthy (post) industrial nations and the harsh realities facing street children in, say, India or Brazil. Yet 'western' ideas about childhood profoundly affect the ways in which children in poorer countries are represented in the global media. They are almost universally depicted as helpless victims deserving of our sympathy and patronage – an image exploited in charity fund-raising campaigns. The autonomy and resilience of these children, their ability to look after themselves, is rarely acknowledged, or where it is noted, it is seen as either a tragedy or a threat, evidence of children deprived of the childhood they should have had. This is not to deny the harsh reality of such children's lives, nor the exploitation and suffering they experience, but rather to point out that our ideas of a 'proper childhood' may be entirely inappropriate to the social, cultural and economic contexts in which such children live (Punch 1998). Some anthropologists have argued that modern western societies are unusual in the sharp distinction they make between childhood and adulthood and in the degree to which children are excluded from adult concerns and activities (Benedict 1938). In societies based on subsistence technologies children are more fully integrated into adult life, whether or not they play an active part in the economy, and generally develop adult competencies earlier than is common in the modern West (Turnbull 1966; Fortes 1970; Draper 1976; Punch 1998 – but see also Chapter 6).

In European societies ideas about children and childhood have changed markedly over the centuries. In drawing attention to these changes, the historian Ariès (1962) suggested that there was no concept of childhood in medieval Europe, that once past infancy children were treated simply as miniature adults. They were dressed like adults, took an active part in adult work and recreation and were held fully responsible for their actions. Ariès, however, overstated his case. While children in medieval times were treated far more like adults than they are today, it is clear that they were not regarded as exactly the same as adults. In particular, Ariès' own evidence indicates that children were seen as social subordinates within a patriarchal and feudal social order, that they were very much under the authority of the head of the household in which they lived and worked. Moreover childhood was regarded as a stage that prepared the young for later responsibilities, a period of moral and practical training for later life (Shahar 1990). Yet medieval childhood was not childhood as we know it today. Archard (1993) suggests that while there has probably always been a *concept* of childhood, the current *conception* of childhood is a modern invention. The way childhood is actually lived has also changed over time.

In medieval and early modern times (up to the early eighteenth century), infancy, childhood and youth were socially recognised as stages of life preceding adulthood, but these stages did not have the same meaning as they have today (Gillis 1974). Infancy was the period before a child attained the 'age of reason', which for most medieval thinkers was at the age of seven, the age at which they could be betrothed, or, in the case of boys, begin training for the priesthood (Shahar 1990). Even before they reached this age, however, children were expected to work, to make a contribution to household subsistence. Although children could be tried and sometimes executed for crimes, from age seven, the age of full criminal responsibility corresponded with the beginning of youth, at 12 for girls and 14 for boys. These were also the ages at which is was legally permissible to marry, although early marriage was in fact very rare. During youth it was common for children of all classes to leave the parental home to enter service or apprenticeships in another household, thus becoming more independent of their parents but remaining under the authority of their employer or patron. The end of youth and the beginning of adulthood was ill-defined, but was usually taken to occur on marriage and the establishment of an independent marital household – which for women, who could not hold property once married, meant becoming dependent on their husbands.

In general children were far more integrated into adult working and social life than they are today. For those privileged enough to receive any formal education, there was no notion of age-grading or of reading material tailored to children's needs. Boys (and only boys) could go to university at age 11 or 12 and only in the seventeenth century was the age of university entrance raised to 15. By this time it had become less common for the sons of the bourgeois and landed classes to be sent into service and more usual for them to be formally educated – trends that affected girls of these classes a century later (Pinchbeck and Hewitt 1969). Age-grading in schools was gradually being introduced, books to educate and entertain children began to be published and children began to be dressed differently from adults.

The inception of modern childhood was, however, apparent only among the privileged classes. The bourgeoisie, in particular, became concerned for the moral welfare of children. It has been argued that the dominant image of the child at this time was that of the 'demonic child' tainted by original sin (Skolnick 1973), whose spiritual well-being was best safeguarded by breaking his or her will. The idea of the innocent child did not appear until the end of the eighteenth century and did not gain wide credence until its Victorian sentimentalisation in the nineteenth century. By this time, modern ideas of childhood were beginning to affect working-class children.

Once industrialisation separated the worlds of work and home, working children became more visible – and increasingly offensive to the bourgeois ideal of childhood. As the nineteenth century wore on children's work was gradually limited while their lives came under more surveillance from philanthropists, educators and legislators. As older family or craft-based forms of training became obsolete, schools came to be seen as the most efficient context in which to impart knowledge. As children were excluded from work, it was seen as necessary to keep them occupied and contained. Elementary education became compulsory in 1870. Moral welfare, especially that of girls, also became a major issue and the age of heterosexual consent for girls was raised to 16 in 1882. Childhood was thus prolonged and increasingly seen as a stage of life requiring particular forms of regulation, protection and guidance.

> The modern child has become the focus of innumerable projects that purport to safeguard it from physical, sexual and moral danger, to ensure its 'normal development', to actively promote certain capacities or attributes such as intelligence, educability and emotional stability. (Rose 1989: 121)

This trend has continued and is particularly evident in the developmental paradigm and its institutionalisation in school age-grading. The result is that children are held to be incapable of doing what, in fact, they are not permitted to do (Thorne 1987). This learnt incapacity in turn justifies their exclusion from the adult world.

The late modern conception of childhood entails an imputation of 'specialness' to children (as particularly cherished beings) and childhood (as a cherished state of being). There is a strong cultural emphasis on marking the boundary between childhood and adulthood (Jackson 1982), on maintaining childhood as a protected state and children as a protected species. Childhood is now frequently being constructed as a precious realm under siege from those who would rob children of their childhoods, and as being subverted from within by children who refuse to remain child-like. Anything which threatens to destabilise the boundary between childhood and adulthood provokes anxiety about childhood itself.

> To have to stand and wait as the charm, malleability, innocence and curiosity of children are degraded and then transmogrified into the lesser features of pseudo-adulthood is painful and embarrassing and, above all, sad. (Postman 1994: xiii)

Here Postman is expressing a widely aired concern that children are growing up too quickly without experiencing childhood to the full. Childhood is seen as being at risk from pressures towards early maturity, conspicuous consumption and precocious sexuality, highlighting a fundamental contradiction in discourses around children and childhood: childhood is regarded as a natural state and yet also as perpetually at risk. This contradiction and the constant vigilance required in order to protect, preserve and manage childhood should lead us to question whether childhood is as natural as it seems.

The boundaries we construct between childhood and adulthood are clearly products of history and change over time. Modern legal systems institutionalise childhood by setting an age of majority at which a person becomes a legal subject responsible for their own affairs and able to exercise citizenship rights. The United Nations Convention on the Rights of the Child defines a child as anyone under the age of 18 unless, under the laws of his or her country, the age of majority comes sooner. Even with such legalistic dividing lines there are still areas of ambiguity. Within any one country there may be various markers of adult status, so that one ceases to be a child for some purposes while remaining one for others. For example, the right to vote and the right to marry without parental consent may be acquired at different times. In both the USA and the UK a young person can hold a driving licence, marry and fight for his or her country while still being below voting age – in the words of the Barry McGuire song from 1966 'old enough to kill but not for voting'. Indeed in some states of the USA it would be possible to marry (with parental consent) up to nine years before being able legally to purchase alcohol. In the UK, at the time of writing, the age of heterosexual consent is 16 – two years below that for homosexual men (there is still no legislation pertaining to lesbian sex: see Chapter 8).

Despite our cultural emphasis on the distinction between childhood and adulthood, we lack a clear rite of passage marking the boundary. The prolongation of childhood and uncertainty about where it ends has created adolescence as a peculiarly problematic liminal stage of life. Young people in their teens are excluded from many adult activities while being expected to behave like adults in other respects. However, when they do behave like adults, for example in relation to sexual activity, it can cause an outcry in defence of the need for the retention of childhood innocence. It is hardly surprising that young people are often confused and resentful. Adolescence itself, along with many of the problems associated with it, is a product of a specific, modern, Western construction of childhood.

Power and dependence

As we have noted, children in western societies have historically lost their role as economic actors. For children to work is now seen as intrinsically problematic, as antithetical to being a child. Children's exclusion from work has been seen as a mark of social progress, what differentiates us from the exploitative past in which children laboured in mines and factories and from Third World nations in which child labour is still common. Yet 'freeing' children from economic exploitation has rendered them economically powerless, increasing their dependence on adults, specifically their parents. Economic dependence is now a defining feature of childhood, one that marks children as subordinates in a society where the capacity to earn – and thus to spend and consume – is central to the construction of identity.

Economic dependence has long been a marker of subordinate social status and power. For women, gaining economic independence, the right to earn and the right to control their own income was seen as a key step towards emancipation (Chapter 3). Yet as women have gained financial independence, children have lost it (and, ironically, mothers' extra earnings often go into maintaining children's dependence). The gradual raising of the minimum school leaving age from 12 to 14, to 15 and finally to 16 has prolonged economic dependence. Only a generation ago, most 15-year-olds left school to enter the labour force, and it is only just over half a century since most 14-year-olds did so.

More recently, changes in the benefit structure have meant that those who leave school early have no entitlement until they reach 18. For the more privileged who go on to higher education, the erosion of the value of student grants and their replacement by loans has lengthened the period of dependence on parental support until young people reach their early 20s. At the same time, a higher proportion of young people have been entering higher education. Hence although the legal age of majority was reduced from 21 to 18 in 1971, for many young people the period of dependency has since increased.

Paradoxically, as economic dependence has increased so children have come to be targeted as consumers. Indeed the pressure to consume is often seen as a pressure towards precocious maturity (Postman 1994). While the emphasis on the child as consumer has no doubt intensified in recent years, there has long been a trend in this direction. Indeed as soon as children became singled out as a special category of being, this created a market niche for products designed specifically for them, for toys, games, books and clothes; for wallpaper and furniture for their rooms. Children's very separateness from the adult world thus serves to include them into the adult economy as consumers.

Children do not, however, consume in quite the same way as adults: children's consumption is dependent, adult-mediated consumption (Leonard 1990). Children have things bought for them and exercise consumer choice only if their parents permit it. Gifts of money and pocket money are given at adults' discretion and adults may seek to influence how these sums are spent. Young children in particular are constrained to consume only what their parents buy for them. They can wheedle, cajole, shout and scream to get what they want, and they may sometimes succeed, but ultimately it is adults who hold the purse strings. Older children may be permitted more latitude in disposing of their own pocket money but only if, in their parents' eyes, they exercise this discretion responsibly.

Ability to earn their own money through paper rounds, weekend or holiday jobs can be attractive to children in enabling them to have an income which is not dependent on the good will of adults (Morrow 1994). Children may also work, paid or unpaid, in the home (Brannen 1995) or in a family business (Song 1996). However, whether or not children are allowed to undertake any paid work or receive payment for tasks in the home will depend on whether parents view this positively as preparation for economic independence. Parents may on the other hand see such economic activity as a slur on their ability to provide adequately for their offspring, or as interfering with more legitimate childhood activities, such as schoolwork or recreation. Giving and witholding money, and indeed permission to earn outside the home, is one means by which parents seek to control their children.

Parents do not only exercise power over children through controlling them, but also seek to mould and shape their children. This is a facet of the responsibility placed upon parents to raise children 'properly'. This responsibility extends beyond caring and providing for children, because parents are also held responsible for their children's well-being and conduct (see Chapters 2 and 11). Not only are parents expected to govern and regulate their children's current lives, but their futures as well. Child-rearing can thus be seen as a reflexive project:

> A child can no longer be accepted as it is, with physical idiosyncracies, perhaps even flaws. Rather it becomes the target of a diversity of efforts. All possible flaws must be corrected... all possible talents must be stimulated... Countless guides to education and upbringing appear on the book and magazine market. As different as each one is, at bottom they all have a similar message: the success of the child is defined as the private duty of the parents/the mother. And the duty reads the same everywhere: the parents must do everything to give the child 'the best start in life'. (Beck-Gernsheim 1996: 143)

Of course, the resources available to parents for this project vary according to not only the income (Chapter 2) but also the knowledge and social networks (what Bourdieu (1984) has termed 'cultural capital') available to them. The ways the project is executed will reflect parents' own priorities for their children, their ideas about what is appropriate according to their children's gender, the neighbourhood in which they live and the cultural milieu they inhabit. Nonetheless, the assumption that children are what their parents make them is widespread. Modern families are often described as child-centred and certainly children's needs may be given a high priority, but these needs are defined for them by adults. Children's own autonomous desires frequently take second place to their parents' view of what is best for them.

It has been suggested that parental power is no longer as absolute as it once was, that child-rearing is now 'policed' by a host of experts and state agencies (Donzalot 1978). 'Expert' advice not only informs parents' practices, but bureaucratises child-rearing and increases anxieties about 'doing it properly'. While this constrains parents it does not necessarily increase children's autonomy within families. Children are neither citizens nor full legal subjects and thus live, in a very real sense, under their parents' jurisdiction. Any other agencies that deal with them, from schools and clubs to care facilities, are seen as acting '*in loco parentis*'. Parents themselves retain a great deal of latitude to rear their children as they wish, to set acceptable standards of behaviour and to decide how they should be educated and disciplined. Think, for example, of the ways in which debate about choice of schooling for children are framed in terms of parents' rights rather than children's rights. If others interfere with parents' practices or choices it is seen as an infringement of their rights and an assault on family privacy. Public regulation is seen as justifiable only where parents are deemed to have abused their power or not exercised it effectively enough – where children are 'at risk' or 'out of control'.

Holding property in one's bodily person is a fundamental aspect of citizen's rights in modern democratic societies; however this right is not extended to children. Adults, and parents in particular, exercise an exceptional degree of control over the bodies of children (Hood-Williams 1990). Children's bodies are routinely regulated through adult decisions about what and when they should eat, what clothes they can wear on what occasions, by admonitions about bodily movement and deportment, by restrictions on their mobility – all of which would only be experienced by adults under extreme conditions of institutionalisation, in prisons, residential care or the military (Goffman 1961). It is quite acceptable for known adults to pat children's heads; tickle them; throw them in the air; tidy their hair and clothing and even pick them up and move them bodily – behaviour that would only be acceptable between adults in the most intimate of rela-tionships – and then only with consent. It is interesting that one of the greatest anxieties surrounding children today is that they might be molested, that they are taught, in order to protect themselves, that their bodies are sacrosanct, yet those same bodies are routinely interfered with and contained in the name of hygiene, tidiness and discipline, and also, ironi-cally, to ensure their safety.

Children are not always willing to be bounded either by definitions of them as dependent and lacking in adult competencies or by attempts to curtail their activities. Moreover, the powerlessness of children does not go unchallenged by the wider, adult society. At the same time as we have seen increasing surveillance of children in the name of protection or control, we have also witnessed a growth in the movement for children's rights enshrined in such documents as the UN Convention on the Rights of the Child. At first sight this would seem to signal a shift towards recognising children as autonomous beings, but this is not always the case. Some of the rights conferred by the UN convention include children into basic interna-tionally recognised human rights such as freedom of association, freedom of expression and the right to privacy. Other provisions of the convention exclude children from adult activities or responsibilities such as work and armed conflict. Still other rights are specific to children such as the right to education and freedom from abuse and neglect. On the other hand, the rights conferred on parents by the Convention can, in practice, undermine all of these rights.

The confusion evident in the different forms of rights enshrined in the UN Convention derives from a widespread ambivalence about the forms of rights children should be granted. Children's rights can be framed from two opposing perspectives: in terms of rights to autonomy, control over their own lives and independent status as citizens or in terms of rights to protection and freedom from adult risks and responsibilities. The former conceptualisation of rights challenges the subordinate status of children, the latter rarely does. The UN Convention attempts to balance these opposing views, to expand chil-dren's autonomy without undermining adult authority. Hence children's continued exclusion from citizenship is tacitly reinforced.

However, even rights that offer protection rather than independence can improve children's lives and potentially temper the near absolute authority parents wield over them. Within the UN Convention parental rights are not absolute and legislation within Britain and elsewhere can override parental authority in the interests of the child. For example, state agencies can now intervene to protect children against parents who abuse or neglect them. In such cases a higher – adult – authority is called upon to decide what is in 'the best interests of the child' (the guiding principle behind the Convention).

Risk, risk anxiety and the construction of childhood

The tension between protecting children from harm and fostering their autonomy also underpins many of the anxieties expressed about children and childhood in late modern society. Social theorists such as Giddens (1990, 1991) and Beck (1992) have recently suggested that today we live in a climate of heightened risk awareness engendered by an increasing lack of trust in both the project of modernity and expert knowledges. While anxieties about children and childhood – a product of the modern idea of the child as an innocent in need of protection – date back to the nineteenth century, the conditions of late modernity may have exacerbated them. The anxieties specific to childhood are part of a general sense that the social world itself is becoming less stable and predictable, coupled with a nostalgia for an imagined past in which children played safely throughout a carefree innocent childhood.

Risk anxiety helps to construct childhood and maintain its boundaries – the specific risks from which children must be protected serve to define the characteristics of childhood and the 'nature' of children themselves. Threats to children's well-being are seen as coming from all pervasive, global social 'ills' such as the 'pernicious' consequences of sex and violence in the media and also from the unforeseen (but constantly anticipated) danger from a specific 'monstrous' individual – the shadowy figure of the paedophile that haunts the popular imagination. For example, the new film version of *Lolita*, released in 1998, was read as symptomatic of a generalised moral depravity and as a potential incitement to individual paedophiles.

One of the major theorists of the 'risk society', Beck (1992, 1998), associates risk anxiety with the individualisation and de-traditionalisation characteristic of modernity. Individualisation entails the almost constant reflexive monitoring of risk that pervades our sense of how to manage ourselves and the world. Risks may be produced by social conditions, but we are expected to assess and manage them as individuals. De-traditionalisation has produced a less predictable world in which we are faced with many options and no easy solutions (Beck 1998). Where childhood is concerned, de-traditionalisation engenders anxieties about the loss of stable families embedded within secure communities (Chapter 11). The everyday world of childhood thus no longer seems so safe and predictable. At the same time, individualisation renders each parent uniquely responsible for their children and encourages them to invest in their children's childhood as part of their own life project (Beck and Beck-Gernsheim 1995; Beck-Gernsheim 1996). Parents must not only guard against immediate threats to their children's well-being but must also plan for any event that might disrupt their development towards physically and psychologically healthy adulthood. Hence the developmental paradigm, so central to modern constructions of childhood, may heighten risk anxiety.

It is these individualised parental hopes and fears for their children that are mobilised in wider, publicly aired concerns about children and childhood. Increasing anxiety about risk has been superimposed upon an older 'protective discourse' (Thomson and Scott 1991) within which children are located as vulnerable innocents to be shielded from the dangers of the wider social (implicitly adult) world. The fusion of risk anxiety with protectiveness engenders a preoccupation with prevention (Scott and Freeman 1995; Green 1997), a need for constant vigilance in order to anticipate and guard against potential threats to children's well-being. Concern for children's safety is of a different order from concerns about adult safety. Risks to children are represented as inherently more grave than risks to adults. This is most marked in extreme circumstances, as in the media reaction to the shooting of 16 children in the Scottish city of Dunblane in March 1996.

Children most often come under public scrutiny when they are perceived as being in danger (as victims of adult abuse or neglect) or as a danger to others (as delinquents and vandals) (Thorne 1987). Often such concerns can be seen to reflect risk anxiety as much as actual danger – for example, the recent heightened awareness of sexual and fatal risk from strangers in the UK, despite the lack of evidence that risk to children comes primarily from this quarter. While there has been an increase in recorded crimes of violence against children, three-quarters of the perpetrators are parents and other relatives. The children most at risk of being murdered are infants under the age of one: hardly those most exposed to 'stranger danger'; children aged 5–15 are, of all members of society, the least likely to be victims of homicide. It is not until children reach the age of 15 or 16 that danger from strangers becomes more significant than that from intimates (CSO 1994, 1995). Up to February 1996 (prior to the killings in Dunblane) fewer than six children under 14 had been killed by strangers each year since 1984 in the UK. This can be contrasted with approximately 600 per year who die in accidents (CSO 1994). Yet a recent British study found that fear of attack by strangers was seen as the single most significant risk to children when they ventured outside the home, and in the case of girls this was identified as a specifically sexual risk (Hood *et al.* 1996).

It would, however, be unwise to interpret this apparent gap between parental worries and statistical probabilities as indicative of ignorance or stupidity. We cannot assume, in the absence of reliable research, that parents fail to assess risks 'realistically'. Parents may know the statistical probability of their child being sexually assaulted or murdered by a stranger to be slight, but the fact that it happens at all might be enough to make them fear for their own. This point has been born out in our own recent research (Jackson *et al.* 2000).

Risk anxiety has material effects. Parental fears can limit children's lives and experiences in a range of ways, thus increasing their dependence on adults. For example, whereas 80 per cent of seven- and eight-year-olds in the UK went to school on their own in 1971, only nine per cent were doing so in 1990 (Hillman *et al.* 1990). While there are undoubtedly other factors that contribute to this trend, such as increased car ownership, this statistic is nevertheless indicative of decreasing opportunities for children to develop autonomy and self-reliance. This in turn produces yet another set of publicly aired risk anxieties relating to children's health and life experience (see, for example, *Guardian* 10 March 1999). These concerns, initially focused on fears about unfit overweight children, are increasingly giving way to anxieties about the longer-term consequences of over-protecting children. For example, an article in the *Scottish Daily Mail* (20 January 1998) accused parents of 'raising a generation of mollycoddled children who will be incapable of taking responsible decisions as they grow up'. This, we were told, came as a warning from 'experts'.

It is hardly surprising, given the tensions between protecting children and permitting their autonomy, that parents should look to 'experts' for a set of rules which, having external authority, may lend a sense of certainty to the decisions parents take. In Britain the National Society for the Prevention of Cruelty to Children offers guidelines on the age at which children are competent to do certain things. For example, eight-year-olds are too young to go to school alone and seven-year-olds are too young for unaccompanied visits to the shops. Such guidelines tend to bureaucratise decisions in relation to children, producing standardised responses without regard to the social context or life experience of individual children. They are couched within a developmental linear model that serves to delineate the boundaries of children's lives, thus creating a self-fulfilling prophecy – children cannot be competent to do things which they have never been allowed to do (Thorne 1987). Thus keeping children 'safe' can entail keeping them childlike and dependent.

The degree of anxiety generated by risks to children is associated with a particular construction of childhood as an age of innocence and vulnerability.

Yet the idea of the innocent child has never entirely subsumed an alternative, older view of the child as sinful and unruly (Skolnick 1980; Jackson 1990). Children are often characterised in everyday talk as little devils in one breath and little angels in the next. However, it is common for parents to see their own children primarily as innocent and vulnerable as opposed to other children who are potentially threatening (Valentine 1996). Whereas the dead children of Dunblane, as innocent angels, symbolically became all our children (Scott and Watson-Brown 1997), those children whose actions belie the notion of innocence are characterised as truly demonic. When in 1993 the British toddler James Bulger was murdered by two older boys, idealised images of childhood were de-stabilised (Jenks 1996): hence the efforts made to distance the boy killers from 'normal' children through depictions of them as evil beyond comprehension. Similarly a spate of killings at schools in the USA in the late 1990s received global media coverage. One of these involved 15-year-old Kip Kinkel who murdered his parents and two school mates. Kinkel was described as a '"schizoid" kid from a good home'. As in most cases of this kind it emerges (in retrospect of course) that he was 'dangerously disturbed' but that adults aware of this did nothing about it (*Guardian* 23 May 1998).

The demonisation of child killers parallels the media representation of women such as Myra Hindley and Rosemary West; women and children who kill are deemed monstrous, doubly transgressive – in having murdered they have also acted against feminine or childlike 'nature'. In May 1998 considerable controversy was generated in the UK by the publication of a book about Mary Bell who, over 30 years earlier when she was 13, had killed two small children. Bell was retrospectively re-demonised as both a child who killed and a woman profiting from her crime by accepting payment for her story. Her depiction as monstrous was highly gendered. 'Her extraordinarily pretty, heart-shaped face looked out beneath headlines, as it looks out again now: a beautiful icon of evil' (*Observer* 3 May 1998, p. 3).

Here our attention was drawn to the appearance of feminine, childish innocence and the 'truth' of the evil beneath the surface. We were reminded of the lack of remorse shown by Mary Bell at her trial (and by implication since) in contrast with her co-accused who was acquitted and was described as 'normal' in her tearful appearance in court, as 'just a little girl'. Mary Bell, however, was clearly not a proper 'little girl'. Throughout the trial she was 'tearless and defiant, bandying words with the prosecution' (*ibid.*: 3). Her cleverness, her refusal to be cowed by the full weight of adult power represented by the court underline her exclusion from normal childhood and her status as a monstrosity.

Differences among children

Since our primary focus has been on the institution of childhood and the social division between childhood and adulthood, we have made only passing references to differences of class, gender, ethnicity and age (Chapters 2, 3, 4 and 6). Clearly children are not socially homogeneous. One aspect of the social construction of childhood and the distinctions drawn between children and adults is that 'the child' becomes an abstraction representing a universal and often idealised childhood. It is this universal child that figures in media representations of tragedies affecting children, such as the Dunblane shooting, and which, as a symbolic representation of all our children, evokes an emotional response (Scott and Watson Brown 1997). In other contexts this universalising of childhood serves to conceal or pathologise social divisions among children. If children's differing experiences of childhood are noticed at all it is within a developmental paradigm that assumes a fixed set of stages that all children pass through, or within a discourse that marks out 'deviant', 'problem' or 'deprived' children from the ideal, 'normal' child. This normal child is, unsurprisingly, defined from a white middle-class perspective that even in its most liberal, caring variants has the effect of branding working-class or black children as 'other' (Lawler 1999). It is these children who are likely to be seen as not proper children, cast either in the mould of the demonic child or the child deprived of a childhood.

This is not to deny that middle-class children enjoy all manner of privileges that working-class children lack. The point is that setting up middle-class childhood as the norm results in it being viewed uncritically as a more positive version of childhood. It also tends to represent the difference of working-class childhoods as the product of cultural deficit or lack, so diverting attention away from the material inequalities that underpin both working-class and middle-class childhoods. Where ethnic differences are concerned, taking white middle-class childhood as the norm too easily gives rise to racist stereotypes of dysfunctional black families and neighbourhoods, or to a glib multi-culturalism that celebrates diversity while denying racism.

Arguably the greatest social division affecting children is poverty, both between rich and poor areas of the world and within relatively affluent countries such as the UK. It is important to point out, however, that children are poor because adults are poor and children are, as we have shown, highly dependent on adults economically (Chapter 10). Children are extremely vulnerable to the effects of poverty – malnutrition, disease and so on. Adults with children are generally worse off than equivalent adults without children, because there are economic costs entailed in having children. Children are dependent on parental altruism and while the evidence suggests that mothers generally display such altruism (see the discussion of poverty in Chapters 3 and 10), fathers frequently do not and thus poor households may be financially better off without men (Graham 1987). However, because children are considered to be the personal responsibility, or even the property, of their parents there is rarely adequate social support for children.

Thus the issue of poverty can be taken as an illustration of children's dependence. While, as a result of their dependence, children are particularly vulnerable to poverty, the ways in which concerns about this are expressed clearly illustrate and reinforce the issues that we have raised in the course of this chapter. More concern is expressed about child poverty than about the situation of women in general or elderly people (Chapters 3 and 6) – both groups in which poverty levels are high globally. This is, we suggest, because images of 'innocents' are more appealing – quite literally in the context of charity campaigns. Poor children are the antithesis of idealised images of childhood and can be easily appropriated into a story that constructs them as deprived of a 'proper' childhood and thus of particular concern and interest (Lawler 1999).

The central argument of this chapter is that the division between childhood and adulthood, despite not having received as much sociological attention as divisions like class, gender and so on should, nevertheless be seen as one of the key lines of stratification along which societies are organised. It follows from this that, for children as for adults, the actualities of their everyday lives are shaped by their location in relation to all of the other divisions discussed in this book. It is important therefore that the adult/child division is not simply reproduced by a reading of the other chapters as if they pertained only to adults.

FURTHER READING:

Jenks, C. *Childhood* Routledge: London (1996) in the Key Ideas series offers an introduction to sociological ways of thinking about childhood from a social constructionist perspective, while the collection edited by James, A. and Prout, A. (eds) *Constructing and Reconstructing Childhood*, Basingstoke: Falmer Press (1990) also provides a very useful introduction with an emphasis on cultural and historical differences. For a collection that explores the social status of children in a range of social settings, see Mayall, B. (ed.) *Children's Childhoods Observed and Experienced*, London: Falmer Press (1994); this book also includes chapters that deal with children's rights. A short account of how knowledge of children is deeply adult-centred can be found in Thorne, B. 'Re-Visioning Women and Social Change: Where are the Children?' *Gender and Society*, 1: 85–109, (1987).

CHAPTER 8

Sexuality

SUE SCOTT AND STEVI JACKSON

The social ordering of sexuality gives rise to two forms of social division and inequality. On the one hand, within modern Western societies, heterosexuality is institutionalised as the 'normal' form of human sexuality and this is reflected at many levels of society from the legal regulation of marriage and the provisions of the social security system to the content of popular culture and everyday social practices. This privileging of heterosexuality serves to marginalise lesbian and gay sexualities, gives rise to both formal and informal discrimination against lesbians and gay men, and sometimes to more brutal forms of oppression. On the other hand heterosexuality is, by definition, itself differentiated by gender. Being heterosexual does not have the same consequences for men and women – indeed historically it has evolved as an institution that is closely bound up with the perpetuation of male dominance and female subordination, as was argued in Chapter 3.

While there are apparently two distinct forms of inequality here – that between heterosexuals and non-heterosexuals and that between men and women – they are interrelated. A sociological understanding of both forms of inequality requires that we pay critical attention to the taken-for-granted character of the heterosexual norm. This chapter will therefore draw upon sociological analysis of heterosexuality as institution and practice. We will begin by introducing some basic concepts, defining key terms such as gender, sexuality and institutionalised heterosexuality. We will then explore sociological challenges to biological determinism, explaining why sociologists see sexuality as socially constructed and how we might conceptualise the sexual as fully social, rather than 'natural' or individual. Having explained the concepts and theories underpinning sociological approaches to sexuality, we will examine some of the research that has accumulated on both heterosexual relations and the forms of social exclusion experienced by lesbians and gay men. We will argue that, despite changes in sexual mores toward less restrictive and more egalitarian ideals, inequalities associated with sexuality persist.

Sexuality, gender and institutionalised heterosexuality

Sexuality cannot be understood without consistently paying attention to its intersection with gender. The concepts of gender and sexuality both take 'sex', a highly ambiguous term, as a point of reference. In the English language the word 'sex' can denote either the distinction between male and female (as 'two sexes') or sex as an erotic activity (to 'have sex'). Similarly 'sexual' can refer to the different activities or attributes of men and women, as in such phrases as 'the sexual division of labour', or it can refer to the erotic sphere of life, for example, to 'sexual fantasies'. Moreover the term 'sex' can be used – more commonly in French, but sometimes in English – to name sexual organs which are simultaneously erogenous zones and body parts that distinguish male from female.

This linguistic confusion is not a mere accident, but tells us something about the male dominated and heterosexist culture in which we live (Wilton 1996). It is commonly assumed that being born with a particular set of genitals (sex organs) defines one as of a particular sex (female or male), which means that one will normally become 'properly' feminine or masculine (the appropriate gender) and will desire and engage in erotic activity with 'the other sex', with someone possessing a different set of sex organs from one's own. This circular and deterministic reasoning has served to justify women's subordination as a 'natural' outcome of sex differences and to define heterosexuality as the only fully 'natural' and legitimate form of sexuality. As sociologists we should challenge the taken-for-granted assumptions underlying this way of thinking.

A first step is to separate out the three terms 'sex', 'gender' and 'sexuality'. Sociologists and feminists usually do distinguish between them, but there is by no means a consensus on how each of these three terms should be used. Hence we need to define the sense in which they are being used in this chapter. The term 'gender' was originally adopted by feminist sociologists to emphasise the social shaping of femininity and masculinity, to challenge the idea that relations between women and men were ordained by nature. In the past it was common to make a distinction between 'sex' as the biological differences between male and female and 'gender' as the cultural distinction between femininity and masculinity along with the social division between women and men (Oakley 1972). This is no longer acceptable, because it has become increasingly apparent that our understanding of the anatomically sexed body is itself socially constructed, that scientific understandings of sex difference have been shaped by cultural ideas about gender and that the everyday recognition of others as men and women is a social act requiring us to decode cultural signifiers of gender (see, for example, Butler 1990; Delphy

1993). This realisation also helps to resolve the ambiguity of the word 'sex', which is still often used – even by some sociologists – to denote both the male–female distinction and intimate erotic activity.

Here we will use the term 'gender' to cover all aspects of what it means to be a woman or a man and to refer to the social division and cultural distinction between women and men. The word 'sex' is then reserved to describe erotic activity. The term 'sexuality' is generally broader in meaning, encompassing erotic desires and identities, as well as practices. In this sense the concept of 'sexuality' remains somewhat fluid, in part because what is deemed erotic, and hence sexual in this sense, is not fixed. What is erotic to one person might be disgusting to a second and immoral to a third. In using this rather slippery term, we wish to convey the idea that sexuality is not limited to 'sex acts', but involves our sexual feelings and relationships, the ways in which we are, or are not, defined as sexual by others, as well as the ways in which we define ourselves.

While gender and sexuality are analytically distinct, they are empirically interrelated. When we label ourselves and others as heterosexual, lesbian, gay or bisexual, we define sexuality by the gender of those we desire. Masculinity and femininity are validated, in part, through conventional heterosexuality, hence the idea that lesbians are not 'real women' and gay men are not 'real men'; conversely, those who flout conventions of femininity and masculinity are often assumed to be lesbian or gay. Sexual desires and practices are also gendered and heterosexual relationships, in particular, are governed by all manner of gendered expectations from the double standard of morality to the sequences of acts that occur within any given sexual encounter. The normative status of heterosexuality is pivotal to the social ordering of both gender and sexuality.

The term 'institutionalised heterosexuality' refers to all social practices and forms of social regulation through which 'normal' sexuality is equated with heterosexuality. Heterosexuality *is* a social institution; it is definitive of another key social institution – marriage – and is the norm against which other forms of sexuality are judged and policed. Not only does it entail the outlawing of dissident sexualities, but it governs social expectations about relations between women and men in both the private and public spheres of life. Heterosexuality *is* so taken for granted, even by sociologists, that we often overlook its importance; we think within what has been called 'the heterosexual imaginary', which masks the operation of heterosexuality as an institution (Ingraham 1996: 169). Moreover, heterosexuality is legitimated by the concealment of its social character, through its definition as simply 'natural'. This brings us to the most important contribution that sociology has made to the study of sexuality: the demystification of its apparent naturalness.

The critique of essentialism

Since the 1970s sociologists and feminists have challenged 'essentialist' modes of thinking that view sexuality as an essential, innate, universal fact of human nature. Within western culture there has been a long history of religiously based essentialism within which some sexual practices were defined as natural in the sense of god-given and others as 'against nature' and hence a transgression of God's law. In modern societies, however, it is biological essentialism that predominates, although the moral categorisation deriving from its older, religious form has by no means disappeared. It is now common to find human sexuality reduced to hormones, genes and the urge to pass on our genetic inheritance to the next generation. This perspective remains popular in lay and scientific circles even though sexual activity is now increasingly thought of as recreation rather than procreation.

Sociologists have identified a number of problems with essentialism. In the first place, it rests on something unknowable, a hypothesised 'natural' sexuality somehow uncontaminated by cultural influences. Human beings do not exist outside society and culture; we each become sexual within specific social contexts. The forms of sexuality we are familiar with today are the product of a particular society at a particular point in its history. Even within our own society, experiences of both gender and sexuality are highly variable. Since gender and sexuality intersect with other social divisions, such as those based on class, ethnicity, age and community (Chapters 2, 4, 6 and 10), we each live our sexuality from different locations within society and our individual biographies affect our sexual preferences and practices in complex ways. When we turn to historical and anthropological evidence we find even greater diversity.

Erotic conventions change over time and vary from one society to another. We know, for example, that in medieval western Europe women were regarded as beings possessed by insatiable carnal lust while in the Victorian era they were seen as almost asexual. This might be explained by differing degrees of repression of some innate female sexuality, but this is not a very satisfactory explanation. The idea of differential repression cannot account for the complexity and variety found in different cultures. In our own society the 'missionary position' (man on top and woman supine) has, until recently, been considered the most 'normal' and 'natural' way to engage in heterosexual intercourse. Yet people in other societies did not always agree (hence the term 'missionary position'). According to the anthropologist, Malinowski, the Trobriand Islanders 'despise the European position and consider it unpractical and improper' (1929: 284) – mainly because it restricts women's movements and deprives them of pleasure. Early anthropologists documented a wide variety of sexual practices within different cultures, demonstrating that what counts as erotic varies from one society to another (Ford and Beach 1952). More recent anthropological work has questioned the very definition of the sexual, suggesting that what is sexual is by no means self-evident. Consider, for example, a young man sucking an older man's penis. Is this a sexual act? Is it, more specifically, a homosexual act? In some Highland New Guinea societies this act is ritualised as part of the passage to manhood; ingesting the semen of an adult man is essential if a boy is to become a man. In this context it is an act with more immediate significance for gender than sexuality, although it also prepares the initiate for heterosexual adulthood (Herdt 1981; Meigs 1990).

Given that there is no natural, universal human sexuality, we cannot simply peel back the layers of social and cultural influences and find some core, 'natural' sexuality. The idea that there is some essential human sexuality that is then moulded modified and repressed runs counter to anthropological and historical evidence. It also misleads us into thinking of the social regulation of sexuality as a negative force and hence does not allow for the social *construction* of sexuality. The social and cultural shaping of sexuality happens not simply through prohibiting, restricting or repressing sexual practices, but more tellingly through permitting, promoting and organising particular forms of eroticism. In other words we learn not only what not to do, but what we should be doing sexually, how we should do it and in what order we should perform the actions which make up a sexual encounter. This is why there are so many cross-cultural variations in what is seen as erotic and in the range and form of acts deemed 'normally' sexual.

The essentialist paradigm does not address the social divisions arising from sexuality. It cannot account for differences in masculine and feminine sexuality except in terms of 'natural' differences or differential repression. Either women and men are innately different and nothing can change this, or women's sexuality is seen as more repressed than that of men. This latter view takes current definitions of male sexuality as the bench-mark of unrepressed sexuality, in other words what sexuality should be like, and does not allow for any other possibilities for either women or men. It also equates normality with heterosexuality. Since the essentialist paradigm ultimately reduces sexuality to reproduction, only heterosexual sex can be fully 'natural'. Hence its implications are heterosexist as well as sexist.

The social construction of sexuality

In countering essentialism sociologists have suggested that sexuality is socially constructed. Social constructionism is not a single unified perspective, however, and has been informed by three main strands of theory: psycho-analysis, interactionism, and forms of post-structuralist and post-modernist thinking influenced by the work of Foucault (1981) especially, in recent times, 'queer theory' (see Seidman 1996).

Psychoanalysis originated with the work of Freud in the early twentieth century. Freud saw the human psyche as being shaped by the repression of the libido – an inborn sexual energy. According to Freud infants are born bisexual (neither male nor female, heterosexual nor homosexual), with their sexual desires focused on their mothers. It is only through castration anxiety that, as small children, they become differentiated as boys and girls. The real-isation that girls lack a penis leads the boy to fear that his father will castrate him for daring to desire his mother; he represses that desire through identifi-cation with his father, but remains sexually oriented to women. The girl, seeing herself as already castrated, blames her mother for this fate, despises her for sharing it and turns her attention to her father. She abandons active clitoral sexuality and later adapts herself to passive, vaginal sexuality directed, in adulthood, towards a father-substitute (see Freud 1977). Read literally, this account remains essentialist in that it presupposes an innate sexuality and assumes that anatomy is destiny, even if that destiny is mediated through familial relationships. More recent readings of Freud, influenced by the work of Lacan (1977) suggest that it is through entry into language and culture that we become sexed subjects and that it is the symbolic phallus, rather than the 'real' penis through which this is ordered. Yet the problematic phallocentricity of Freud persists, as does the assumption of an infantile sexuality later repressed by cultural forces.

The interactionist approach, deriving from the work of Gagnon and Simon (1974), is fundamentally opposed to psychoanalysis. Gagnon and Simon argue that there is no such thing as an innate sexuality that can be repressed. What is sexual depends on what is defined as such. It is through learning 'sexual scripts' (the sexual meanings and conventions circulating through social interaction) that we are able to make sense of acts, emotions and sensa-tions as sexual and to locate ourselves within potentially sexual scenarios. Since children in Western cultures are denied access to adult sexual knowl-edge, they acquire a gendered identity before they see themselves as sexual actors. Gender then becomes the lens through which they later make sense of sexual knowledge and practices and construct a sense of themselves as sexual. Here differences between male and female sexuality have nothing to do with genitals and everything to do with the social construction of gender and the scripting of sexuality in gendered terms (for example, assumptions about active male sexuality and passive female sexuality). From this perspective, one's sexuality is not something fixed in childhood but evolves through interaction with others in social settings. Sexual scripts themselves are modified through interaction and subject to historical change (see Simon 1996).

Foucault (1981) also challenges the notion of repression, in this case through historical analysis of shifting sexual discourses – discourses being the language and frameworks of understanding through which we categorise, order and explain the world around us. He contests the idea that the Victorian era was one of repression, arguing that it produced a 'discursive explosion' around sexuality. It was in this period that 'sexuality' as we understand it was brought into being, constituted as an object of discourse, in which diverse sexualities were classified, catalogued and elaborated. These discourses made it possible to distinguish between normal and perverse sexualities, to think of sexuality as an attribute of our inner selves. Acts once considered as carnal sins (to which all were susceptible) came to define the essential character of those who engaged in them. For example, where committing an act of sodomy was once a crime, but one which any sinful man might commit, that act was now seen as definitive of a particular sort of person: it became possible to *be* a homosexual.

Feminist sociologists have also made major contributions to the study of sexuality. Feminism is not a single theoretical perspective and feminists have drawn on and contributed to all three of the theoretical traditions outlined above. What feminism has added is a concern with the intersection between sexuality and gender divisions, with the ways in which the current ordering of sexual relations, especially heterosexual relations, is implicated in the maintenance of male domination see (Jackson 1996, 1999). Radical gay and lesbian and, more recently, 'queer' theorists have shared feminists' interest in social constructionism. Queer theory, which has been influential in recent years, sometimes utilises psychoanalytic concepts but is more centrally preoccupied with developing Foucault's ideas on the historical contingency of sexual identities and the cultural construction of the binary distinction between heterosexuality and homosexuality (see Halperin 1995; Seidman 1996, 1997).

These perspectives offer differing ideas about how sexuality is socially constructed and also about what is being socially constructed, whether it be our individual desires, the cultural meanings of the erotic, the distinctions between normative and perverse sexualities or male dominated sexual practices. Existing theories often concentrate on only some aspects of the social construction of sexuality while ignoring or down-playing others. We would argue that in order to understand sexuality as fully social we need to understand how it is constituted at four levels (see Jackson 1999):

- At the level of social structure and social institutions, through the institutionalisation of heterosexuality and through gender hierarchy.

- At the level of everyday social and sexual practices.

- At the level of meaning, through the discourses circulating within our culture as well as the meanings emerging from, and negotiated within, everyday interaction.

- At the level of our individual subjectivities, through the social shaping of our sexual desires, responses and emotions.

A sexualised culture?

Part of the problem we have in thinking about sexuality is the way in which it is singled out as a 'special' area of life, as uniquely personal and private yet frequently provoking heated and disproportionate public controversy (Hawkes 1996): think for example, of the number of politicians whose careers have been threatened by sexual indiscretions that had little or no bearing on their capacity to perform their public functions. The American sex-radical feminist, Rubin, has called this 'the fallacy of misplaced scale' whereby sexual acts have come to be 'burdened with an excess of significance' (1984: 278–9). Rubin associates this with 'sex negativity', with a culture that has long regarded sexuality as a dangerous, socially disruptive force. Certainly its sex-negative manifestations are dramatic, when we realise that a single act of anal sex carried the death penalty in England until 1861, and that men could be imprisoned simply for being homosexual until 1967, and that in many states of the USA sodomy (whether heterosexual or homosexual) still carries a prison sentence.

Yet the fallacy of misplaced scale is not only evident among moral puritans but also among those espousing the cause of sexual liberation. Sex is not only uniquely tabooed, but also uniquely valorised as a route to personal fulfillment and even social revolution. The writings of sexual radicals popular in the 1960s, saw sexual repression as fundamental to the bourgeois social order (Reich 1951; Marcuse 1964, 1972). Hence free sexual expression came to be seen as a means of undermining capitalism. Later libertarian writers do not make such grand claims for the disruptive power of sexuality, but still argue that transgressive sexual practices destabalise the status quo (see Rubin 1984; Halperin 1995). More generally, sexuality is marketed as a means to personal fulfillment in what Stephen Heath calls 'the sexual fix', which, far from being a form of liberation, represents 'a new mode of conformity' (Heath 1982: 3). For example, numerous sex manuals and magazines now tell us that sexual fulfillment is virtually a precondition for a full and happy life (see also Jackson and Scott 1997).

Sexual mores at the turn of the millennium are confused, contradictory and contested. We inhabit a culture saturated with representations of sexuality yet who may talk about it where and with whom is still circumscribed. Sexuality has become an ingredient of most forms of entertainment and is used to sell everything from cars to chocolate, yet it is rarely treated simply as a routine aspect of everyday life. Its very specialness as an area of human experience makes sexuality a problematic public issue and a troublesome aspect of our personal relationships. Young people today grow up in a culture in which they are constantly exposed to sexual imagery and innuendo, yet recent research tells us that they still find it difficult to access appropriate information and to articulate their sexual wants and desires within intimate relationships (Holland *et al.* 1998).

That sexuality is still regarded as problematic in many western societies, including Britain, is illustrated by the issue of sex education. Here the idea of sex as a 'special' area of life meets the conceptualisation of children as a special category of people, so that anything which links childhood and sexuality is potentially highly controversial. Sex education has been a topic of public debate for decades. What is at issue is its form, content and timing: when young people should receive it, what they should be allowed to know and how this knowledge should be imparted. It is not, however, simply access to knowledge that causes concern, but what young people do with that knowledge: whether or not it promotes 'promiscuity', whether it might 'cause' or 'prevent' teenage pregnancy (Thomson 1994). The debate is framed by a tension between public health (the desire to promote 'safer' sex and prevent early pregnancy) and public morality (the concern to maintain 'family' values). In this context there is little concern with sexual pleasure; at best sexual activity is an inevitability whose ill-effects should be ameliorated. In practice, school sex education remains didactic, focused on the imparting of biological and practical information with little emphasis on the complexities of young people's sexual lives (Thomson and Scott 1991; Wight *et al.* 1998).

The form and content of sex education is one of the means through which male-defined heterosexuality is institutionalised as the only 'normal' form of sexuality. Priority is given to reproductive sexuality, in that the most important 'facts' to be imparted concern the link between sex and conception. In this context relationships are an issue; rights (to say 'no') and responsibilities may be included along with the emotional entanglements of sexual relationships. Yet the sex that happens in these relationships is skirted round and skipped over. Sexual pleasure, and in particular women's pleasure, is rarely discussed. Heterosexual penetrative sex is, in the main, taken for granted as defining *what sex is*, so that activities designed to '*turn women on*' – if discussed at all – are defined as foreplay. Where gay or lesbian sex is addressed, it is at best treated with liberal tolerance. Discussions of issues of sexual pleasure and alternative sexualities are hedged around with all manner of anxieties, in particular teachers' worries about imputations of corruption, causing offence to more conservative parents or provoking a media furore. Teachers and pupils also lack a common language with which to talk openly about sexuality. The constraints on those entrusted with imparting sex education result in what has been called 'defensive teaching' (Trudell 1993), with teachers staying on safe ground as far as possible and seeking to control the agenda, to guard against pupils who might raise difficult issues (Scott, Wight and Buston 1997). By default, if not by design, heterosexuality dominates the sex-education curriculum, the underlying assumption being that young people will grow up to be heterosexuals. While it may be possible, in a classroom context, to challenge the most coercive aspects of heterosexuality, it is rarely possible to challenge the conventional sexual script in which foreplay leads on the 'real sex' (vaginal penetration) which ends when *he* 'comes'.

Heterosexuality as a gendered sexual practice

The prioritisation of male sexual needs has long been challenged by feminist writers. Feminists seized on the sexological work of Masters and Johnson, which demonstrated that all female orgasms, however produced, are clitorally centred, in order to demystify the 'myth of the vaginal orgasm'. This created the possibility of de-centring so called 'sexual intercourse', of treating it as one sexual act among many possibilities rather than the predictable end point of a sexual encounter. Information on women's sexual response is now widespread in women's magazines and such writings tend to assume that women possess active sexual desires and have a right to sexual pleasure. If one drew on these magazines as the only source of data, it would appear that equality in sexual relations had been achieved. However, sociological research reveals a different picture. The National Survey of Sexual Attitudes and Lifestyles (Wellings *et al.* 1994) found that vaginal intercourse is still far more common than any other form of sexual activity and that non-penetrative sex which did not culminate in intercourse was in the main found among the young, who were avoiding 'going all the way'. The consequences of the double standard are also evident in the data, with 24.4 per cent of men reporting 10 or more sexual partners in total, compared with 6.8 per cent of women.

The most extensive qualitative study of young people's sexuality so far conducted in Britain is the Women Risk and AIDS Project (Holland *et al.*

1990, 1991, 1998; Thomson and Scott 1991). The research revealed that young heterosexual women found sexual pleasure both difficult to discuss and hard to attain, and that many of them felt pressurised, by men, into having sex. Almost all the young women and men in the study accepted the conventional equation between sex and penetration. They disciplined their own bodies and pleasures to suit men in ways their partners were unlikely even to be aware of. In so doing they conceded to men's definitions of what was pleasurable and acceptable, finding 'fulfillment primarily in the relationship, in giving pleasure' (Holland *et. al.* 1994: 31). The ethic of service to men is, of course, not confined to erotic encounters and underlines the importance of placing heterosexual sex in the wider context of gender relations. This is not to say that young women simply passively accede to unpleasureable sex. Many do develop strategies of resistance, but their success is constrained both by the assumptions of the majority of their sexual partners and by the generally unquestioned norms of heterosexuality.

There is no comparable data on older heterosexuals, but what does emerge from the few studies that have addressed this issue suggest that these patterns are not confined to the young and inexperienced. Research seems to suggest that sex is experienced positively in the early stages of a relationship, that when couples are 'in love' desire masks any lack of care or competence. In longer-term relationships women begin to feel uncared for and experience men's sexual demands as unwelcome, objectifying and coercive (Duncombe and Marsden 1996; Langford 1999). Duncombe and Marsden found that women in long-term heterosexual relationships complained of being pressured into sex that was mechanical and preceded by only perfunctory foreplay. Men in this study were more likely to complain about their partner's lack of interest in sex and of therefore being deprived of their conjugal rights. As one man said:

> It would be no skin off her nose... Sometimes I just want her to let me put it in and do it... She's broken the contract. Sex is part of marriage. (Duncombe and Marsden 1996: 230)

Langford also found that women in long-term relationships expressed deep dissatisfaction with routinised sex in which emotional intimacy was lacking. For some sex appeared to have become simply a chore that was no more enjoyable than housework and in which they had become objects for men's use. As one woman put it:

> I am not really sure it's me he is having sex with any more, not inside his head. Yes, I feel I am just a useful vehicle. (Langford 1999: 123)

Underpinning these accounts is the widespread belief that men are driven by unstoppable sexual urges that must be satisfied – an idea that is also used to explain rape. These data support the feminist claim that sexual violence is an extension of 'normal' heterosexual sexual practice (Kelly 1988), that our culture supports coercive sex and sexual violence. All the evidence available suggests that there is nothing particularly unusual about the rapist – he is a very average man. Scully (1990), in a US study of convicted rapists, characterises rape as a high reward, low risk crime, in that men gain a great deal of pleasure from it and run a very low risk of being convicted for it. In the UK, despite some improvements in the ways in which the police treat rape victims, there has been a dramatic fall in the proportion of rapists brought to justice in recent years (Gregory and Lees 1999). Since an alleged rapist (like any other defendant) is presumed innocent until proven guilty, the courts effectively treat the victim as guilty (of having 'provoked' rape or 'consented' to it) until proven otherwise. Although there has been legislation limiting intrusive questioning of rape victims, British courts still scrutinise their sexual histories and reputations; defence lawyers still use any evidence of autonomous female sexuality to discredit a woman's testimony, still routinely imply that if she is less than completely chaste she must have deserved it (see Brown *et al.* 1993; Lees 1997). We live in a society that constructs a form of male sexuality which can readily turn predatory and then fails to call the predator to account. This is why feminists have argued that rape is a product and expression of male domination (Jackson 1999). It is the starkest possible illustration of the inequality and oppression scripted into heterosexual practices.

Heterosexuality as institution

The lynch-pin of institutionalised heterosexuality is marriage – or at least heterosexual coupledom. Some sociologists, notably Giddens (1992), argue that this emphasis is declining, that we are living in the era of the 'pure relationship', which is freely chosen and conditional for its continuation on both partners defining it as successful. While marriages may be less stable and enduring than was once the case, there is little evidence of the population abandoning the ideal of heterosexual monogamy – even if the reality is now more commonly serial monogamy. The vast majority of the population still marry, at least once.

As an institution heterosexuality is not just about sex; it is as much about who washes the sheets as what goes on between them (Van Every 1996). As we have seen, women are still expected to service their husbands sexually, and this is bound up with the other services they provide such as housework and child care. Historically men acquired rights in women's bodies, property and labour through marriage. This is why, until 1990, a man could not be accused of raping his wife: if he did so, he was simply exercising his conjugal rights. It was and is sex (the act of consummation) that confirms the existence of marriage. Women still lack some very basic rights in relation to their own bodies; for example, a married woman cannot be sterilised without her husband's consent, but the converse is not the case.

The assumption that everyone is or should be living in a heterosexual union with a male bread-winner has also underpinned the welfare state and structured the labour market. While many of the resultant gender inequalities are slowly being eroded (Chapter 3), the presumption of heterosexuality itself remains firmly in place. Not only is marriage itself by definition heterosexual, but rights to welfare benefits and pensions for dependants are premised on the normality of heterosexuality (Liberty 1994). Those who are not heterosexual are frequently implicitly or explicitly excluded from entitlements granted to heterosexuals, such as access to reproductive technologies, rights to adopt or rights in relation to children they have co-parented but to whom they are not biologically related (Liberty 1994; Jackson 1997). Lesbian and gay sexualities have often been seen as 'threats to family values', the best example of which is the infamous clause 28 of the Local Government Act 1988, which barred local authorities from 'promoting' homosexuality and led to the presentation of homosexuality as a 'pretended family relationship' being outlawed in schools (Weeks 1991; Cooper 1995).

The lesbian feminist writer Rich first coined the term 'compulsory heterosexuality' to emphasise that heterosexuality is imposed on us rather than freely chosen (Rich 1980). Rich was concerned to explain the ways in which women are kept within the boundaries of heterosexuality and kept down within it (Jackson 1999). Some of her arguments apply only to women, for example the idea that lesbianism is a form of resistance to patriarchal domination. In other respects however, the concept of compulsory heterosexuality can be applied to the ways in which both lesbianism and male homosexuality are socially and culturally marginalised. One of the most pervasive forms this takes is through the everyday assumption that everyone is heterosexual unless we know otherwise. Heterosexuals are rarely named and identified as such. While key aspects of their identity may be related to their heterosexuality (for example as a wife or husband), they rarely adopt the identity 'heterosexual' for themselves. Lesbian and gay sexualities, on the other hand are routinely named and made visible as 'other'.

While heterosexuality entails a great deal more than sex, homosexuality is always and everywhere sexualised, and lesbians and gays reduced to their sexualities. For example, the rationale behind the exclusion (until the year

2000) of lesbians and gays from the British armed forces was that their sexuality was in some sense threatening to others, somehow ever-present and predatory, threatening to undermine morale. Until the recent change in the law, lesbians and gays serving in the British military were, if discovered, immediately discharged even if they had exemplary records in all other respects: the only thing that counted was their sexuality. Elsewhere, there are signs of greater tolerance even a certain fashionability associated with sexual dissidence, with lesbian and gay characters and images increasingly visible in the media. Yet lesbians and gays are still represented as the exception to the heterosexual norm.

The binary divide between heterosexuality and homosexuality has been deconstructed by what has become known as queer theory, a perspective developed by lesbian and gay writers influenced by post-modern theory. The main aim of queer theory is to expose the hetero/homo binary divide as a cultural artifice rather than a natural division in such a way as to reveal its arbitrariness and instability. Hence queer challenges the idea that there is such a thing as a fixed homosexual identity, rather queerness is constituted by its marginal location in relation to the heterosexual norm (Halperin 1995; Seidman 1997). Conversely, the normativity of heterosexuality depends on the identification of lesbians and gays as 'outsiders'; yet in shoring itself up in relation to its 'outside' it admits of a destabilising potential, the possibility that lesbian and gay sexualities might disrupt its claims to be the only legitimate form of sexuality (Fuss 1991). Thus queer theorists tend to focus on the points at which heterosexual normativity can be disrupted. However, while heterosexual normativity might be unstable in theory, in everyday life it is sustained through a range of oppressive and coercive practices.

Physical violence and verbal abuse are still common experiences among lesbians and gay men; young gay men are routinely raped by heterosexual men in prisons. The HIV epidemic provoked widespread concern only when it was seen to be spreading from gay men to the 'general public' – the terminology used illustrates the exclusion of gay men from the 'normal' population (Watney 1987). This exclusion is underpinned by the law. While homosexual behaviour has been decriminalised since 1967, it is legal only within limited circumstances – in private (that is, indoors with no other person present in the house) and between 'consenting adults' – and at present the age of consent remains at 18, two years later than the age applying to heterosexual women. Sexual consent is a highly gendered concept. Applied to gay sex only after decriminalisation, it arose in a heterosexual context and rests on a construction of sex as something that men do and women consent to (McIntosh 1993; Waites 1998). This is why there has never been an age of consent for lesbians – and indeed why lesbianism has never been legally prohibited. Since the definition of the sexual act has been enshrined in law as the penetration of a vagina by a penis, premised on the assumption of active male and passive female, women can neither initiate sex with each other nor consent to it. This absurd illogicality, while it might make lesbians safer from prosecution, effectively erases lesbian sexuality, stigmatising it as so 'unnatural' as to be beyond definition. Where lesbianism does come into view it can provoke punitive responses. For example, lesbian mothers have sometimes lost custody of their children solely on the grounds of their sexuality (Harne 1984).

Conclusion: sexual inequality and commodity culture

Hennessy has drawn attention to the contradictions of a society in which claiming a non-heterosexual identity is, on the one hand, 'a potentially lethal transgression' and, on the other a sign of radical 'cool' (1998: 1). She cites the case of a young gay man, brutally beaten to death in the USA in October 1998, a far from isolated victim of bigotry in a nation where, according to the FBI, lesbians and gays are twice as likely to be physically assaulted as African Americans. Yet at the same time lesbians and gays are being marketed as icons of style in advertising, fashion and film. The continued stigmatisation of lesbian and gay sexualities persists in a society in which those same sexualities are increasingly visible, and apparently acceptable, in the cultural mainstream. This is not merely a case of bigotry and tolerance existing side by side, but tells us something about the limits of tolerance and the place of sexuality within the commodity culture of late modernity – a culture in which consumerism is increasingly associated with the maintenance of identity.

'Tolerance' is not, of course the same thing as equality and even where valorised as 'cool', the radical chic that lesbians and gays embody depends on their marginal location in relation to the straight world. They are still singled out as 'other', whether damned as the perverse other or celebrated as the exciting, exotic other, and still serve to confirm the heterosexual norm in relation to which their 'otherness' is established. Lesbians and gays have made real gains in terms of rights, but their marginality creates a barrier to further progress. As Sinfield puts it: 'The trick is to have us here *but* disgraceful' (1994: 189, Sinfield's emphasis). Non-heterosexual lifestyles can be tolerated, even admired, as long as gays and lesbians know their place and do not attempt to challenge heterosexual privilege. Evans (1993) suggests that the only capacity in which lesbians and gays are regarded as full citizens is as consumers and that this may have become a substitute for, and a deterrent to pursuing, more fundamental rights. The visibility of gays and lesbians within our society and culture is in part a result of their political struggles, but it is also a result of late capitalism's relentless search for innovative advertising images and new markets. Here it should be noted that the purchasing power of the 'pink pound' is concentrated in male hands, since lesbians share with all women a disadvantaged position in the labour market relative to men.

The commodification of gay sex is also part of a wider aestheticisation of daily life, evident in the preoccupation with 'lifestyle' in the commercial sense (Hennessy 1995). In this context, it is not only gay sexuality that has been commodified, but also heterosexual sex. 'Good sex' is itself increasingly associated with other indices of taste and style such as wearing the right jeans or drinking the right coffee (see Jackson and Scott 1997). The concern with sexual proficiency sustains and is sustained by a huge market in books and magazines devoted to sexual self-improvement. Meanwhile, the sociological evidence we have cited suggests that the lived reality of everyday heterosexuality is a long way from the glossy advertising – and even the apparently endless 'consumer choice' offered by the new sex manuals entails little more than variations on the conventional sequence of heterosexual sex.

Of course commercial sex itself is nothing new. Women's sexuality, in particular has long been commodified through prostitution and pornography. Even when it is male sexuality on sale it is marketed largely for male consumers. Many feminists have seen pornography and prostitution as an instance of the sexual exploitation, enslavement and objectification of women (see, for example Jeffreys 1997). Others, however, see 'sex work' as just another occupation. Here the issue is the economic exploitation of workers and the exacerbation of that exploitation by their social exclusion (Alexander 1988). Libertarian feminist and queer thinkers tend to see prostitution and pornography as issues of sexual freedom in which sex workers are ranked alongside other sexual dissidents resisting the repressive policing of dissident sexualities (Rubin 1984) We would argue that we need to keep both gender and sexual hierarchies in view when considering these issues. That it is largely men who provide the demand for this sort of sexual service should make us think critically about the construction of male sexual desires and ask why it is the prostitutes rather than their clients who are stigmatised. That commercial sex is today being transacted within a society that increasingly commodifies sex itself should also cause us to consider whether the marketing of sex opens up new possibilities for self-realisation, or imposes new constraints upon us.

The idea that we are all free consumers able to make whatever 'lifestyle choices' we choose is clearly sociological nonsense in a world still characterised by gross economic inequalities. In the sexual realm access to choice in our sexual practices is limited by institutionalised heterosexuality and gender hierarchy. The concern with style and aesthetics also diverts attention away from the labour entailed in producing the objects we consume – and where heterosexual sex is concerned this includes sexual services performed by women for men. The commodification of sexuality glamorises and mystifies sexuality, concealing the inequality, oppression and human suffering associated with the gender inequalities and heterosexual privilege underlying everyday sexual relations and practices.

FURTHER READING

The chapters in Richardson, D. (ed.) *Theorising Heterosexuality: Telling it Straight*, Buckingham: Open University Press (1996) address aspects of contemporary feminist debates on heterosexuality. Two historical accounts are Weeks, J. *Sex, Politics and Society*, Harlow: Longman (1989), which has a useful introductory chapter on theories of sexuality, and deals with social regulation up to and including the so-called 'permissive' era; and Hawkes, G. *A Sociology of Sex and Sexuality*, Buckingham: Open University Press (1996), which links sexuality to modernity. Seidman, S. *Queer Theory/Sociology*, Oxford: Blackwell (1996) includes some of the classic pioneering articles on the sociology of sexuality, as well as more recent work. A collection of reading covering feminist debates on sexuality since the 1960s can be found in Jackson, S. and Scott, S. (eds) *Feminism and Sexuality: A Reader*, Edinburgh: Edinburgh University Press (1996).

CHAPTER 9

Disability

MARK HYDE

Without wishing to underestimate the dimensions of inequality reviewed in other parts of this book, and which of course are also relevant to the social disadvantage of disabled people, they do not account for the unique and intense forms of deprivation that the disabled experience. Disabled people – nearly 4 million of the working age population – are largely excluded from satisfactory employment opportunities, experience considerably higher levels of poverty and are often dependent on state social services and benefits. Mainstream sociological approaches to the analysis of social divisions therefore provide a necessary but an insufficient basis for understanding disability. Disabled people are disadvantaged because they belong to a social group that is the object of pervasive institutionalised discrimination. Thus disability engenders distinct forms of social inequality and, like gender, age and social class, should be regarded as an organising principle of social inequality in its own right. Disabled people are socially divided from the rest of society.

Disability in modern industrial society needs to be understood as a series of social restrictions that prevent disabled people from taking part in mainstream taken-for-granted activities, leading to profound social disadvantage. Although there is a substantial body of work on the significance of disability in contemporary society, it has largely developed outside of mainstream sociology in the specialist field of disability studies. It follows that the starting point for our analysis is to look at the concepts and perspectives used to (mis)understand disability, not least the recent ideas and arguments developed in official studies of disability, and the pioneering work of disabled writers (Union of Physically Impaired Against Segregation 1976; Barnes 1990; Oliver 1990).

Competing definitions

Debates about the meaning of disability in the social science literature typically centre on two definitions. 'Official' or 'medical' definitions tend to focus on the *functional limitations* of people with impairments, whereas the disabled people's movement has defined disability as the *social restrictions* faced by disabled people in their daily lives.

Official and medical definitions of disability are usefully summarised by the International Classification of Impairment, Disability and Handicap (ICIDH) developed for the World Health Organisation in 1981 (see Berthoud *et al.* 1993). The ICIDH distinguishes and links four concepts in a causal sequence; a *complaint* such as a spinal injury may lead to an *impairment* where a person is unable to control his or her legs; this may lead to a *disability* such as the inability to walk resulting in a *handicap* where the individual is unable to take part in normal day-to-day activities. This approach is often referred to as the 'medical model' because of its primary focus on impairment and functional limitation. Ultimately, it treats disability as a property of individuals who, because they are physically or mentally incompetent, are unable to take advantage of the opportunities enjoyed by those without impairments.

The influence of this individualistic medical model (see also Chapter 10) on official policy and government-sponsored research into disability is suggested by the nature of the questions in Table 9.1 taken from one of a series of OPCS surveys of disabled people in the UK (see Martin *et al.* 1988). The questions clearly suggest that the inability of the individual to take part in social activities can be explained in terms of an underlying impairment. Instead of promoting social rights and opportunities, the welfare state has attempted to compensate disabled people for the limitations allegedly imposed by their impairments either by segregating them in specialist institutions or by exposing them to *rehabilitation* programmes.

In spite of its influence, the medical model has been criticised on a number of grounds. First, it takes the notion of *normality* for granted and therefore as fixed, when what is and is not normal is socially and culturally relative. For example, the once widespread view of heterosexuality as the norm, backed by the law and sanctioned in mainstream arts, literature and

**Table 9.1   Selected questions from the 1985
OPCS survey of disabled adults**

1. Can you tell me what is wrong with you?
2. What complaint causes your difficulty in holding, gripping or turning things?
3. Does your health problem/disability mean that you need to live with relatives or someone else who can help look after you?
4. Does your health problem/disability make it difficult for you to travel by bus?
5. Does your health problem/disability affect your work in any way at present?

Source: adapted from Oliver (1990)

especially popular culture (Chapter 8), is arguably now beginning to give way to a greater acceptance of diverse and legitimate sexual preferences. Second, the medical model fails to recognise the *social constraints* that prevent social participation and therefore offers only a partial explanation of social disadvantage. For example, while a focus on impairment may highlight some of the difficulties experienced by disabled people at work, it ignores discriminatory barriers such as prejudice among employers that impede their progress in the labour market. Third and following on from this, the medical model endorses policies that at best are likely to be *ineffective in promoting social participation* and at worst reinforce disadvantage and social exclusion. Employment policy has focused on *individual rehabilitation*, when an emphasis on the removal of discriminatory barriers may have been more successful (see Hyde 1996 for a fuller discussion).

Recognising these inadequacies, academics associated with the disabled people's movement have proposed a simpler classification scheme, which distinguishes two concepts, *impairment* and *disability*.

> we define impairment as lacking all or part of a limb, or having a defective limb, organ or mechanism of the body; and disability as the disadvantage or restriction of activity caused by a contemporary social organisation which takes no or little account of people with physical impairments and thus excludes them from participation in the mainstream of social activities (Union of Physically Impaired Against Segregation 1976: 14).

Frequently referred to as the 'social model', this approach to defining disability also makes causal assumptions about the factors underlying social disadvantage. It argues that people with impairments are excluded by a social environment that is inaccessible and discriminatory. For example, disabled people are often prevented from travelling to work, not by their inability to use the buses, but because public transport has been designed for the exclusive use of people without impairments. If the social model of defining disability had been used to frame the OPCS disability survey questions, they could have been reformulated to resemble those in Table 9.2. Clearly, these questions suggest that inability to take part in social activities can be explained primarily if not exclusively in terms of a discriminatory and inaccessible social environment.

Although the social model provides a definition that may be preferable to many disabled people, it is weakened by its apparent lack of reference to the role of impairment in restricting social participation. It is possible to imagine circumstances in which impairment is a considerable influence on a person's inability to perform social activities; for example, people with profoundly

Table 9.2   Survey questions informed by the 'social model'

1. Can you tell me what is wrong with society?

2. What defects in the design of everyday equipment like jars, bottles and tins cause you difficulty in holding, gripping or turning them?

3. Are community services so poor that you need to rely on relatives or someone else to provide you with the right level of personal assistance?

4. Do poorly designed buses make it difficult for someone with your health problem/disability to use them?

5. Do you have problems at work because of the physical environment or the attitudes of others?

Source: adapted from Oliver (1990)

debilitating mental impairments may find it difficult to take part in social activities irrespective of how these activities are defined and organised. Although the limiting effects of impairment are not always this clear-cut, they should not be dismissed lightly.

The two definitions reviewed here provide radically different interpretations of disability, each of which is endorsed by particular social constituencies. The view of disability as the inability of the individual to perform normal social activities is not only widely held by the public but has been the main influence on government-sponsored disability research and policy. In contrast, the definition of disability as social restriction is endorsed by the disabled people's movement, by definition a much smaller and less influential minority group. Both definitions have distinct implications for the nature of social policies for disabled people.

The social construction of disability

Although impairment and the social environment both play a role in preventing disabled people from participating in mainstream social activities, the influence of the latter far outweighs that of the former. In western societies from Greek civilisation to the present day, disabled people have been socially marginalised, discriminated against and oppressed. However, social disadvantage among disabled people takes a distinct form in western capitalist societies, involving exclusion from economic activity and dependence on statutory social services.

In a significant contribution, Oliver (1990) relates the experiences of disabled people in contemporary society to the distinctiveness of capitalist economic relations. Before the industrial revolution, many disabled people were able to take part in economic activities that were largely based in scattered rural communities involving agriculture and small-scale industry. The development of industrial economic organisation during the eighteenth century had profound implications for disabled people.

> The speed of factory work, the enforced discipline, the time-keeping and production norms – all these were a highly unfavourable change from the slower, more self-determined and flexible methods of work into which many handicapped people had been integrated. (Ryan and Thomas 1980: 101)

The subsequent development of heavy industry based on coal, iron and shipping in the nineteenth century reinforced the exclusion of disabled people from employment. Moreover, the worth of individuals came to be assessed according to their economic value, particularly the extent and nature of their participation in paid employment. Thus the prevailing ideology of industrial capitalism, competitive individualism, ensured that those among the working class who were not in employment were assigned an inferior social status.

This economic marginality was reinforced by the distinct form taken by many state welfare interventions during the nineteenth century. With the rise of capitalism, the total institution was adopted as the main official response to the needs of the non-working poor. At first, people with impairments were treated less harshly than able-bodied paupers but official concern about work incentives led in practice to many being incarcerated in the workhouse. In distinguishing between able-bodied paupers and the long-term sick, the 1834 Poor Law represented a significant milestone in the treatment of disabled people. From the early 1800s onwards, disabled people were increasingly admitted to long-stay hospitals and asylums, indicating a shift in official responsibility away from the Poor Law authorities to the expanding medical profession (Abbott and Sapsford 1988). Medical practitioners assumed growing responsibility for the assessment, treatment and care of people with impairments – a legacy that continues to this day.

Institutionalisation continued to be the main official response to the needs of people with impairments up to the 1930s. Since then, there has been a significant shift in the location of care back to the community, but disabled people continue to experience isolation, social disadvantage and dependence. Oliver describes how these problems are constructed around three organising principles. First, disabled people continue to be excluded from employment resulting in higher levels of deprivation and social exclusion.

> Work is central to industrial societies not simply because it produces the goods to sustain life but also because it creates particular forms of social relations. Thus anyone unable to work for whatever reason is likely to experience diffi-

culties both in acquiring the necessities to sustain life physically, and also in establishing a set of satisfactory social relationships. (Oliver 1990: 85)

Second, disabled people are largely excluded from the formal political process, meaning that they are unable to take part in official discussions about the development of rights, provisions and services to meet their needs. Policy for disabled people is framed by able-bodied public servants who are more likely to have a poor understanding of the needs and aspirations of disabled people, resulting in the provision of inappropriate services. Third, services for disabled people are largely delivered by able-bodied professionals who often fail to take account of the felt-needs and preferences of those who use them. Taken together, these experiences result in profound levels of social disadvantage among disabled people in Britain today.

Experiencing disability: economic disadvantage

The most striking levels of social disadvantage are experienced by disabled people of working age. Work is central to personal welfare and life-chances in industrial society, but disabled people are largely excluded from satisfactory employment opportunities. This can be illustrated by the findings of three main studies. The first is the Labour Force Survey (LFS), which provides, *inter alia*, data on the labour market circumstances of disabled people in the UK (see Sly 1996). Second is a study of data combined from other UK official surveys, an OPCS survey of disabled people and the Family Expenditure Survey, both conducted in 1985 (Berthoud *et al.* 1993). Although the data in this study are becoming slightly dated, it continues to be the most detailed quantitative analysis of labour market disadvantage among disabled people in the UK. Our third source is the 1994 European Community Household Panel (ECHP) survey, which provides the best source of comparable data on the labour market circumstances of disabled people in the member states of the European Union (European Commission 1998).

Perhaps the most significant form of labour market disadvantage among disabled people is that they experience higher unemployment. Disabled people have an unemployment rate of 20 per cent compared to only 7.5 per cent for non-disabled people (see Table 9.3).

Disabled people are 2.6 times more likely to be unemployed but this official figure underestimates the full scale of the problem because it excludes those who have been classified as 'economically inactive', that is, not in paid employment nor actively seeking it at that point; 61.5 per cent of disabled people were economically inactive compared to only 17 per cent of non-

Table 9.3   The employment circumstances of people of working age in the UK, winter 1995 (not seasonally adjusted)

	Disabled		Not-disabled	
	Millions	*Per cent*	*Millions*	*Per cent*
Population of working age	3.9	100	30.6	100
Official unemployment				
Economically inactive	2.4	61.5	5.1	17
Unemployed	0.3	20	1.9	7.5
Non-employment	2.7	69	7.0	23
Hidden unemployment				
Economically inactive but wants work	0.7	46.6	1.4	5.5
True unemployment				
Adjusted economically inactive[1]	1.7	43.6	3.7	12.1
Adjusted unemployed[2]	1.0	45	3.3	12.3

Notes:
1. Official economically inactive minus the hidden unemployed
2. Official unemployment plus the hidden unemployed

Source: Labour Force Survey (CSU 1995, Winter)

disabled people. The LFS study also provides an estimate of the proportion of those who are economically inactive who would nonetheless like to work; 46.6 per cent for disabled people and 5.5 per cent for non-disabled people. For convenience, this group can be referred to as the 'hidden unemployed'. Table 9.3 shows that when the hidden unemployed are taken into account, the true unemployment rate for disabled people is 45 per cent compared to 12.3 per cent for non-disabled people. In other words, in 1995 disabled people were actually 3.6 times more likely to be unemployed, rather than the official figure of 2.6. This pattern of exclusion from work is evident in all EU member states although unemployment levels among disabled people vary according to overall levels of unemployment. Thus in countries where general unemployment is higher, unemployment among disabled people is more significant; in countries where general unemployment is lower, unemployment among disabled people is less significant.

A second area of labour market disadvantage is suggested by the number of hours worked by disabled people in paid employment. Again, it is widely acknowledged that part-time work is not as highly regarded or rewarded as full-time work; part-time workers tend to be concentrated in low-status occupations, they have lower hourly earnings, they have fewer employment rights and they have little job security. On average, disabled workers are more likely to be found in part-time jobs. According to the LFS, 29 per cent of disabled workers are in part-time work compared to only 23 per cent of non-disabled workers. The ECHP study suggests that disabled workers are more likely to be in part-time employment in all member states of the European Union.

Disabled workers are also more likely to be employed in low status occupations. The LFS study shows that 50 per cent of disabled workers are in manual jobs compared to only 40 per cent of non-disabled workers. This finding is reinforced by the OPCS/FES study, which shows that in 1985, 18 per cent of disabled male workers had professional or managerial jobs compared to 46 per cent of men in general; 28 per cent of disabled women in full-time paid employment were in higher or intermediate non-manual jobs compared to 39 per cent of women in general. The ECHP survey confirms that disabled people are disproportionately employed in low status occupations throughout the member states of the EU.

The social division of age (Chapter 6) also interacts with disability in the employment field. Reflecting the 'ageist' values of the wider society (see Fennell *et al.* 1988), disabled workers tend to experience higher levels of labour market disadvantage when they reach 'middle age'. Berthoud *et al.* (1993) show that the chances of finding employment for disabled workers aged 45 and over are considerably less than for younger disabled workers. For the former, 'disability' and 'age' foster significant disadvantage in employment, resulting in higher levels of poverty. However, economic disadvantage is *less* significant among disabled pensioners who, as a group, are less likely than non-pensioners to be living on incomes that are below the state benefit poverty threshold. The overall impact of chronological age on the welfare of disabled people is therefore ambivalent.

Evidence on the income of disabled people from employment is not as extensive as the areas that have been looked at so far, but it suggests that disabled workers are particularly disadvantaged in terms of their earnings. According to the 1985 data in the OPCS/FES study, disabled men earned on average £1.50 per hour less than non-disabled men. Similar earnings differentials are found elsewhere in the EU (European Commission 1998).

Labour market disadvantage has implications not just for the welfare of disabled people of working age but also for disabled people in retirement. Because their employment circumstances are unfavourable, disabled people are in a weaker position to accumulate savings and adequate pension entitlements (see Chapter 6). Their economic and social well-being is thus reduced throughout the life-course.

In view of these experiences, it is hardly surprising that disabled people have a higher risk of poverty. The OPCS/FES study estimates that 45 per cent of disabled adults are living in poverty, while only 13 per cent could be classified as 'prosperous'. The poverty standard used is the long-term rate of means-tested social assistance, combined with an estimate of the additional costs that are often incurred by disabled people. Prosperity is defined as an income that is at least 200 per cent of this standard. Not surprisingly, poverty rates are higher among those not in employment (59 per cent), the long-term unemployed (42 per cent) and those on unemployment benefits (33 per cent). Prosperity rates are higher among those in employment (48 per cent) and those on a War Pension or Industrial Injuries Benefit (36 per cent). Overall, the weight of evidence suggests that disabled people in the UK today experience profound economic disadvantage.

Experiencing disability: discriminatory social barriers

Social disadvantage among disabled people in modern industrial society reflects their experiences of discriminatory social barriers. This section explores the nature of some of these barriers drawing upon the findings of the most comprehensive audit of discrimination against disabled people in the UK. The Disability Research Unit at the University of Leeds and the Policy Studies Institute are currently working on a joint study of discrimination but at the time of writing, Barnes' (1990) work is the most recently published. The analysis below focuses on three areas of social policy; community care, education and employment practices.

While they represent a vast improvement on the institutional provision of previous decades, current arrangements for delivering community care are often unsatisfactory (see also Chapter 11). Although ostensibly designed to move away from a reliance on specialist institutions, institutional care continues to be a significant component of state support for disabled people. A large proportion of health and local authority spending on community care is directed towards residential and hospital-based services and many disabled people are confined to segregated residential homes.

The response of health and local authorities to the needs of disabled people who are living in the community at large is also widely regarded as being unsatisfactory (Chapter 10). For example, although local authorities are required by the 1986 Disabled Persons Act to provide disabled people with information that is relevant to their needs, few do so. According to OPCS surveys, many disabled people fail to receive the technical aids and equipment that they need; this limits their participation in mainstream social and economic activities and reinforces their dependence on others. Where assistance from local authorities is provided, it is largely directed towards informal carers rather than disabled people. Because they fail to receive the support they require to live independently, 'disabled people are denied the right to organise their daily lives in the same way as the rest of the population' (Barnes 1990: 144).

It is widely acknowledged that there is a strong association between educational attainment and employment outcomes (see Chapter 3), but disabled
people are particularly disadvantaged in the education system. In principle,
education policy in the UK has endorsed 'integrated' provision but in practice, a large number of children and young people with impairments continue
to be educated in segregated special schools. If the perpetuation of special
schools is the most obvious form of discrimination in the education system,
children with impairments are also disadvantaged in mainstream schools.
Many receive their education in separate Special Educational Needs (SEN)
classes while others are placed in classes with younger non-disabled children,
even though their impairments may be physical. The low priority assigned to
SEN within mainstream schools often leads to inadequate provision for children and young people with impairments. Not surprisingly, this results in
lower levels of educational attainment.

Disabled people also experience considerable discrimination in tertiary
education. Increasingly, young people with impairments are taking up places
in further education, but the nature of the opportunities provided reflects
those that are available in compulsory education and is therefore subject to
the same criticisms. Disabled students are frequently segregated in special
programmes in which they are invited to study courses in 'life-skills' rather
than academic or vocational areas. This further education experience does
little to compensate for the lower levels of educational attainment from
secondary education. Not surprisingly, very few disabled people become
qualified for higher education. Because the education system is failing to
enable disabled people to acquire the qualifications and credentials required
for access to satisfactory employment, it is directly contributing to subsequent economic disadvantage among the disabled when they go on to seek
paid employment.

However, the primary responsibility for the unsatisfactory employment
circumstances of disabled people lies with employers; disabled applicants for
jobs are six times more likely to be refused an interview than non-disabled
applicants, even when they have suitable skills and qualifications. Employers
are reluctant to adapt premises and equipment to the needs of disabled
workers. Statutory employment policy and provision, despite any intention to
counteract this, have in fact also played an important role in reinforcing
labour market disadvantage among disabled people. The 1944 Disabled
Persons (Employment) Act introduced the Quota Scheme, a measure which
required employers to hire a three per cent quota of disabled workers.
However, there were only ten prosecutions over a 50-year period for a failure
to comply, even though a majority of employers have been 'under quota'. In
1996, the Quota Scheme was replaced by the employment provisions of the

Disability Discrimination Act providing disabled people with a right not to be discriminated against, but this legislation applies only to a minority of employers, namely those with 15 or more employees.

In practice, the government continues to rely on a policy of voluntary compliance and persuasion, even though a considerable volume of research has shown that a large majority of employers are prejudiced against, and in some cases actually hostile to, disabled people. The failure of the voluntary approach has resulted in many disabled people taking jobs in segregated sheltered workshops or subsidised placements in mainstream industry. For these reasons, employment policy has failed to provide an adequate response to the vocational needs of disabled people.

Given what is happening in other social institutions, perhaps it is not surprising that employment policy has been such a failure. Barnes (1990) shows that discriminatory practices also pervade the political process, social security, transport systems, the mass media and the leisure industry. Many disabled people are therefore excluded from taking part in mainstream social activities. In a variety of ways, disabled people experience pervasive discrimination resulting in profound social disadvantage.

Structure, identity and action

If the experience of disadvantage and discrimination is a certainty for many disabled people, their responses to these problems is variable. A number of sociological studies of social divisions in contemporary society have posited a causal relationship between *structure, identity* and *action* (for example Crompton 1998); the assumption is that social conditions such as structured economic inequalities are strongly associated with individual psychology and behaviour and even group identity (see Chapter 1 this volume). In the context of disability, 'structure' can be defined in terms of the discrimination and social disadvantage reported in the previous section; 'identity' is defined as the psychological responses of disabled people to these experiences, particularly the persona that they adopt in relation to the social world; 'action' refers to their behavioural response to social marginality and in particular, to patterns of acquiescence and resistance.

In addition to the forms of discrimination and social disadvantage already discussed in this chapter, disabled people are frequently the object of negative stereotypes in popular media such as books, movies, theatre, magazines and national and local newspapers. In a recent review of research on popular disability imagery, Reiser (1995) identifies a number of negative stereotypes that are perpetuated by the mass media. One powerful image is that disabled people are pitiable and pathetic. This stereotype is particularly evident in the publicity campaigns of the disability charities which aim to maximise income from public donations.

An alternative common stereotype is that disabled people are sinister and evil. For example, people with mental health problems are often presented as frightening and dangerous when in reality, they are likely to be confused and withdrawn. A third stereotype is that disabled people are incapable of taking part in everyday life. This is mainly perpetuated by the *absence* of images of disabled people as members of the workforce, schools and families. Other negative media stereotypes about disabled people are that they are self-pitying and non-sexual. In the absence of positive images, it is hardly surprising that the general public regards disabled people in a negative light. The preponderance of these images perpetuates and compounds economic and social disadvantage.

Oliver and Barnes (1998) identify four mechanisms through which disabled people internalise these negative experiences and images. The first concerns those who are born with impairments who grow up as members of communities in which there are few disabled people to provide *positive role-models*. Because they experience a range of discriminatory barriers from day one, children in this situation are socialised into an early acceptance of an inferior social status. We can contrast this position of early acceptance with the experiences of those with congenital impairments who are shielded from the wider community until they reach adolescence. Children in this category may not be fully aware of the existence of discriminatory barriers until they attempt to access mainstream social activities such as leisure and work. The acquisition of a negative personal identity for this group tends to occur during their late teenage years and early twenties.

A third mechanism of internalisation of negative experience concerns those who are forced to reconsider their personal identity as a result of acquiring an impairment. The sudden realisation that disability implies discrimination and exclusion often leads to negative feelings of hopelessness and despair. Oliver and Barnes' fourth mechanism relates the experiences of those who refuse to accept their impairment and attempt to pass off as 'normal'. This is easier for those with a hidden disability such as diabetes but still requires diligence at managing information and social interaction. For those with an obvious impairment, denial is perpetually self-defeating. Many disabled people respond to their circumstances by adopting a negative self-image and ulti-mately, a passive acceptance of discrimination and social marginality.

This suggests that the link between structure, identity and action is one-directional for a majority of disabled people. In spite of this, a growing number of disabled people have challenged conventional negative stereotyping, a process that has developed in the context of political self-organisation. The disabled people's movement provides a collective framework in which a minority of disabled people have been able to re-evaluate their negative experiences in the light of the social model, developing what might be described as a 'positive disabled identity'.

The disabled people's movement can best be defined by distinguishing between organisations *for* and organisations *of* disabled people. Organisations *for* disabled people are concerned with disability issues but are largely staffed by able-bodied people, working in partnership with national and local government agencies. Examples of such organisations include SCOPE, the Royal National Institute for the Blind (RNIB) and the Royal Association for Disability and Rehabilitation (RADAR). Organisations *for* disabled people have been criticised for adopting conventional official and medical approaches to the needs of disabled people. In contrast, organisations *of* disabled people are run exclusively by and on behalf of people with impairments and are informed by the social model.

Oliver (1990) develops a three-fold typology of these organisations. 'Consumerist/self-help' organisations are those that provide services to meet the self-defined needs of members. A good example is the Centres for Independent Living, which aim to provide appropriate support for disabled people living in the community. 'Populist/activist' organisations typically focus on consciousness raising and political action. During the 1970s, the Union of Physically Impaired Against Segregation (UPIAS) was established to promote political organisation among disabled people living in residential institutions. More recently, the Direct Action Network (DAN) has achieved national publicity through its involvement in a campaign of civil disobedience. 'Umbrella/co-ordinating' organisations are those with a membership of disabled people's groups. In 1981, the British Council of Organisations of Disabled People was established to provide a national focus for the activities of its constituent organisations. Now the British Council of Disabled People (BCODP), this organisation has been at the forefront of the campaign against discrimination in the UK. The BCODP is itself a member of another umbrella organisation, the Disabled People's International (DPI). In addition to the three types of organisation, 'disability arts' has emerged as a form of cultural self-expression for disabled people.

The existence of these collective political and cultural activities may have a considerable impact on the psychological responses of disabled people to discrimination. The active propagation of the social model provides an alternative framework through which they are able to reinterpret their negative experiences, one that focuses on discriminatory barriers rather than personal inadequacies. The disabled people's movement also provides a focus for disabled people to become actively involved in challenging dominant negative stereotyping and discriminatory practices, an experience that can be profoundly empowering.

> Direct action is in your face. Disabled people are supposed to be invisible; they are not supposed to go out and be seen. Direct action has changed this. We are noticed! (Liz Carr, disabled activist, cited in Varo-Watson 1998: 13)

Significantly, collective organisation among disabled people can have a broader positive impact on society, as suggested by shifts towards minority programming on British television. Arguably, the Disability Discrimination Act 1995 was introduced in response to the growing public profile of discrimination, engendered by the activities of the disabled people's movement. If collective self-organisation provides an ideological and experiential framework within which disabled people develop a positive identity, it also has the potential to transform official responses to their needs, suggesting a multi-directional link between structure, identity and action.

Although the achievements of the disabled people's movement appear to be significant, it has recently been criticised by dissenting voices from within its ranks. It has been suggested for example that the movement is not representative of disabled people as a whole. A recent study by Barnes *et al.* (1999) observes that people with physical and sensory impairments are disproportionately involved in disability politics. While this seems to sit comfortably with popular stereotypes of disabled people, it may exclude a substantial number of people such as those with 'intellectual' impairments. Table 9.4 shows that 33 per cent of those who are defined as disabled by the Disability Discrimination Act have 'learning and understanding' related impairments. Similarly, Shakespeare *et al.* (1996) argue that disabled women, gays and lesbians are not adequately represented at an executive level within the disabled people's movement. This suggests that the 'positive disabled identity' associated with collective political action is a privilege that is enjoyed disproportionately by heterosexual disabled men with physical and sensory impairments.

Taking a different approach, Finkelstein, a leading UK disability activist, identifies two recent developments which he believes have reduced the effectiveness of the disabled people's movement (Finkelstein 1996). First, he notes that there has been a shift away from 'grass roots' activity to parliamentary lobbying, resulting in fewer disabled people being actively involved in disability politics. Second, and perhaps more contentiously, he argues that the disabled people's movement has been 'hijacked' by disabled academics who have replaced the 'active' vision of disability rights as polit-

Table 9.4   Type of reported functional problem by sex (per cent)

Reported functional problem	Men	Women	All
Lifting and carrying	50	68	60
Mobility	52	50	51
Physical co-ordination	51	47	48
Learning and understanding	40	28	33
Seeing and hearing	26	17	21
Manual dexterity	21	19	20
Continence	15	13	14
Perceptions of risk	7	5	6
Unweighted base	(500)	(763)	(1263)

Notes:
Base: All people covered by the Disability Discrimination Act
Columns total more than 100 per cent as people could report having more than one functional problem

Source: adapted from Whitefield (1997)

ical action with the 'passive abstraction' of intellectual enquiry. For these reasons, Finkelstein believes the disabled people's movement has 'run out of steam'.

Disability and social divisions

These accounts of contemporary disability incidentally show how much of the source material has been only marginally 'sociological'. The basic framework for the analysis has, however, been sociological. The core idea has been a society characterised by social divisions, suggesting that social exclusion may have a variety of causes that need to be seen in terms of social processes shared with other social divisions. Nonetheless, it remains true that while in the late 1990s sociology has begun to provide some welcome descriptions of the social processes of disablement, it has largely failed to develop explicit and systematic theories to account for the unique and particularly intense deprivation experiences among disabled people.

Payne *et al.* (1996) provide a useful summary of three mainstream sociological approaches to understanding the relationship between social divisions and deprivation. Drawing on the work of Max Weber, one approach sees deprivation as resulting from people's (in)capacity to sell their labour to employers. A person's life-chances including their income, health and housing are strongly associated with their type of employment, manifested in social divisions based on occupational status or class (see Chapter 2). In this view, deprivation is a consequence of sharply constrained ability to sell one's labour in a socially defined market, leading to unemployment or low occupational status. This approach has particular relevance for the circumstances of disabled people who, as reported above, experience considerable difficulties in selling their labour to employers. It identifies the interaction in the labour market between the sellers (both abled and disabled) and the buyers (employers). However, it does not entirely explain the processes that produce the disproportionate representation of disabled people among the ranks of the semi-skilled and the unemployed, suggesting the need for a more specific and clearly defined focus on disability.

Perhaps a more fruitful approach within the Weberian sociological tradition is provided by 'consumption sector' theory, which argues that social divisions need to be understood in terms of differential access to public and private welfare. Encouraged by privatisation policies during the 1980s and 90s, growing numbers of working-class households have opted out of the welfare state, leaving behind a minority who are entirely dependent on public sector provision, providing the basis for a new social division based on consumption sector. However, although disabled people are disproportionately dependent on the state, their consumption experiences are not identical to those of other groups of the poor. As reported previously, many disabled people are excluded from areas of state welfare provision such as local authority housing and mainstream education and instead, are segregated in special disability programmes. While it seems to articulate the exclusion of disabled people from private welfare, consumption sector theory fails to specify their unique experiences of state welfare.

The focus of Marxism on the 'non-working poor' seems to be particularly relevant to understanding the experiences of disabled people in industrial society. For Wright (1993), the key to understanding this 'underclass' lies in the exclusion of the poor from satisfactory education and training leading to long-term unemployment. Paradoxically, although the non-working poor are largely surplus to the requirements of the industrial system, they are sometimes deployed as a 'reserve army' to accommodate fluctuations in the demand for labour.

Using this approach, Hyde (1996, 1998) describes how disabled people were actively encouraged to take up paid employment during the Second World War to substitute for able-bodied men who had been conscripted into the armed forces; after the war, they were promptly expelled from the labour market and segregated into special employment programmes. During the 1980s, out-of-work disability benefits were expanded, and the disabled were reclassified as being entitled to non-work related benefits as part of the Conservative government's massaging of the official unemployment count. As we move beyond the second millennium, disabled people of working age are, once again, being encouraged to enter the labour market, 'assisted' by the provisions of the Welfare Reform and Pensions Bill 1999 (see Hyde *et al.* 2000 for a fuller discussion). The 'New Labour' government wishes to reverse Conservative policies, believing that a combination of vocational training and reductions in eligibility for welfare benefits will encourage disabled people to take up employment opportunities in the flexible labour market. While a focus on labour market regulation seems to account for changes in employment policy for disabled people, it fails fully to explain the disproportionate representation of the disabled among the ranks of the non-working poor, which, as we have seen, has much more to it than state policies alone.

The three approaches reviewed so far have little to say about the particular experiences of disabled women even though they often have higher levels of social disadvantage than disabled men. For example, the OPCS/FES study reported earlier shows that the higher incidence of low-paid, low-status and part-time work among disabled women mirrors similar trends among non-disabled women, highlighting the importance of underlying gender inequalities. While feminist theories have been instrumental in promoting a growing profile for gender divisions in sociology (Chapter 3), they have neglected deprivation experiences that are specific to disabled women. For example, the latter's failure to conform to popular cultural body images leads many physically disabled women to be stereotyped as unattractive and non-sexual. Thus in addition to the discrimination and disadvantage they experience because of their gender, disabled women are often prevented from taking up traditional female roles such as those of wife and mother.

It has also been argued that 'ethnicity' is a powerful source of social division among disabled people, although there is much less published empirical evidence on this. For Vernon (1998), black disabled people experience the 'double disadvantage' of racial discrimination (Chapter 4) and discrimination on the grounds of disability. When combined, both result in qualitatively distinct and intense forms of social disadvantage.

The interplay that we have seen between disability and other social divisions – ethnicity, gender, age and occupational class – means that there is a general framework of analysis with which to explore the isolation of disabled people. However, contemporary sociology on its own can provide a necessary but as yet insufficient basis for understanding disability in present-day society. Disabled people have unique and particularly intense experiences of deprivation, suggesting that there is something distinctive about their circumstances. It has been argued throughout this chapter that disabled people:

- experience profound levels of economic disadvantage, resulting in intense deprivation and ultimately, a poor quality of life;
- are particularly dependent on state social services and benefits, which means they are frequently regarded as objects of charity;
- are often segregated by state welfare programmes, reinforcing the belief that they are unable to take part in mainstream social activities;
- experience a significant level of state regulation, a problem that may undermine individual freedom and autonomy;
- experience considerable discrimination throughout society resulting in exclusion from a range of mainstream social activities;
- are the object of negative stereotyping in popular media. Negative attitudes towards disabled people are deeply entrenched in popular culture.

The distinctiveness of these experiences suggests that disabled people are divided and separated from the able-bodied in the rest of society: disability provides the foundation for a social division in its own right. Like other disadvantaged groups in society, disabled people experience pervasive institutionalised discrimination. At the same time, their experiences of disadvantage may also be shaped by broader social divisions based on social class, consumption and gender. Ultimately, a flexible approach is required that recognises the specificity of disability as distinct from other social divisions but which is sufficiently sensitive to recognise differences between disabled people.

FURTHER READING

Barnes, C. *et al. Exploring Disability*, Cambridge: Polity (1999) provides an up-to-date and comprehensive introduction to disability, while a 'classic' statement of the social model can be found in Oliver, M. *The Politics of Disablement*, London: Macmillan (1990). Barton, L. (ed.) *Disability and Society: Emerging Issues and Insights*, Harlow: Longman (1996) is a collection of articles from the journal *Disability & Society*, which looks particularly at how sociological theories may be applied to disability research and to the experiences of disabled people. The findings of the first comprehensive audit of discriminatory social barriers in the UK, Barnes, C. *Disabled People in Britain and Discrimination*, London: Hurst Calgary (1990), still contain many relevant insights.

CHAPTER 10

Health

JUDY PAYNE AND GEOFF PAYNE

Health is a different kind of social division from the ones that we have so far considered. In some of its manifestations, it does not even fully meet all of the defining criteria as set out in the Introduction or the start of Chapter 12. For example, people can often move quickly from one side of the divide to the other, from the category of being healthy to that of being ill (and indeed back again). Health is also the only social division in which one category, being 'well', is universally seen as desirable, whereas its opposite, being 'ill', has its own major institutions – like Britain's National Health Service – dedicated to its eradication.

Despite these peculiarities, there is still a strong case for treating health and illness as a social division. At its most basic, the sense of difference that comes from even small losses of health (minor changes that would otherwise hardly warrant calling a social division) is arguably among the more intense of all divisions. The misery and social isolation caused by catching the common cold, let alone being disabled (Chapter 9) or having a serious illness, can feel overwhelming, while in turn serious illness can lead to death, arguably the most absolute of all 'social divisions'. But whereas we all must come in the end to death, the risks of an early death or of being ill are not the same for everybody in society. These variations in health, illness and death are strongly related to other social divisions, so health cannot be treated separately from them.

It follows that we need to approach health in a somewhat different way from that used in the earlier chapters in this book. These each took *one* social division and explored its meaning and significance in contemporary life, analytically separate from all the others. While we shall look at the categories of 'healthy' and 'ill' as comprising a division, this chapter (like the next one on community) will also reflect on the ways other social divisions can be seen to interact with and indeed, produce this particular one. Health can be thought of as an 'arena' in which various social divisions compete to influence a particular outcome. Gender and age are self-evidently related to certain kinds of physical conditions, and therefore the ways that age and gender are *socially* constructed (Chapters 2 and 6) are relevant to the social construction of what we think of as being 'healthy' or 'ill'. Class and ethnicity have also routinely been shown to have statistical associations with variations in health. It follows that in incorporating the divisions that have already been discussed, and in emphasising social construction rather than a 'bio-medical model' (challenged in each of the earlier chapters on childhood, sexuality and disability) this chapter is a natural development of our original approach.

Although the *consequences* of lack of health are fundamental to our feelings and opportunities to lead a full life, and to our sense of identity, this chapter is more concerned with the social *explanations* of health and illness. This focus involves an exploration of how a range of social divisions interconnect to produce health (or interact more generally, as we shall see in the next chapter, in the context of producing a sense of community). The starting point for this is to consider what is really meant by the terms 'health', and 'illness'.

Defining health and illness

'Health', 'illness', 'well', 'unwell', 'fit' and 'unfit' are all terms that we use to describe our perceptions of bodily states. Because contemporary society is characterised, *inter alia*, by having specialist medical services and personnel operating in permanent organisations, there is an administrative system to measure and record *illness*, but no comparable social apparatus to record *health* systematically. The existence of social institutions to combat illness – being 'ill' is an undesirable problem whereas being 'fit' is not – means there is a strong normative tendency to talk more about illness, leaving health to be a residual category implicitly defined as a lack of illness. One notable exception is the positive view of health as well-being, which was central to the definition put forward in the Constitution of the World Health Organisation in 1946, and still prominent on their web pages. Here, health is defined as 'a state of complete physical, mental and social well being and not merely the absence of disease or infirmity' (WHO 1999). In contrast, medical definitions are primarily based on the process of diagnosis of the bio-medical pathology that constitutes 'disease' (or its absence).

But even a disease-based approach can lead to quite different ways of identifying ill health. What counts as disease is not a given biological fact, but in part socially constructed. When does mental illness become, or cease to be, an illness? Do the symptoms and medical treatment of pregnancy render it an illness? When we say someone is ill, that categorisation arises out of a social process, in which human beings decide what is going to be called sickness or health. A detailed study of the social construction of these medical definitions by clinicians is reported by Brown (1995).

Social construction means not only that our general perceptions of what is health arise out of social processes, but also that some things are *counted* as lack of health while others are not, and this in turn feeds back into our perceptions. To take the most obvious example, we could define 'illness' as cases recorded by General Practitioners and hospitals. Such *morbidity* records are used to describe social and geographical variations in health within and between countries. Morbidity data (together with death rates) have played an important part in influencing the development of welfare policies. Information about rates of illnesses has been collected in most countries as they industrialised – and so encountered the need for welfare programmes to deal with the public health problems of overcrowding and lack of sanitation (Strong, 1990). However, morbidity measures depend first on what people *report* as 'illnesses' to doctors, and how that comes about (Dingwall 1976; Blaxter and Paterson 1982); then on how doctors and paramedical professions perceive, process and *medically diagnose* them; and finally on how administrators *register* them as cases of particular diseases in the population.

Thus on the one hand there are apparent 'facts' about illness, such as cancer registrations, outbreaks of communicable diseases (for example various types of food poisoning, measles, hepatitis, tuberculosis and meningitis) and cases of congenital malformations such as spina bifida and Down's syndrome. Similarly, the medical process produces data on low birth weight, teenage pregnancies and the number of permanently sick or disabled, which then become the 'truths' around which public policy is debated. On the other hand, even in the examples of serious illness, 'cases' only occur if first the 'patients' see themselves as sufficiently 'ill' to consult a doctor, and second, when doctors decide on *medical* diagnoses. As we shall see below, attendance at surgeries and self-descriptions of being ill, vary between men and women, old and young, and middle and working classes. The ways doctors react to and treat their patients are similarly socially patterned and socially produced (Cartwright and O'Brien 1976; Doyal 1994, 1995; Bloor 1976). This suggests that the 'facts' about illness are more dependent on processes of social construction than is commonly recognised.

A clearer and less disputable measurement is death (certification of deaths is one of the more complete administrative records), but *mortality rates* imply a somewhat extreme level of illness, shifting the focus from the living to the dead. Despite this, the *Black Report* – 'which remains one of the most influential documents on health inequalities' (Bury 1997: 48; Townsend *et al.* 1992) – chose mortality rates and causes of death as its key measurements.

These convey the powerful notion of life chances, fairness of expectations and the penalty some groups pay through early death. Death rates also are well documented over a long period, and do not suffer from short-term fluctuations, so that comparisons between periods, locations and groups is relatively secure.

It has been long recognised that rates of death vary: for example, higher mortality rates are found among older age groups and, within this, men tend to die at an earlier age than women. Obviously then, populations with high proportions of older people (and men) would be expected to have higher mortality rates than those with lower proportions. To control for this, mortality rates can be statistically standardised to allow for variations in age and gender distributions between sub-populations. The most widely used standardised mortality measure is known as the *Standard Mortality Ratio* (*SMR*). However, even when age and gender distributions between specific populations are controlled for, differences in mortality still remain. Other commonly used mortality rates include infant mortality rates and deaths from specific causes (for example different types of cancers, heart disease, asthma and suicide).

These individual rates have normally been used as separate variables. However, they can also be combined to produce composite indices of health status, such as that developed by Townsend *et al.* (1986) to study the relationship between health and poverty. Administrative health data for census wards, consisting of premature SMRs (deaths below the age of 65), long-term sick and disabled persons (aged over 16 years) and low birth weight rates (under 2500 grams) were used to calculate a single health status score for each ward. The rationale for choosing these particular variables was that they reflected different aspects of health status: past health experience (premature deaths); future child development and past maternal health (low birth weight); and past and current health status (long-term sick and disabled).These index scores were then used with other variables and indices to investigate the association between health status and other socio-economic factors. High correlations were found between poor health status and material deprivation in *urban* areas, but less clearly so in rural areas.

The example of mortality rates shows that, while medical records and official statistics need to be treated with caution because they are socially constructed, they should not be dismissed out of hand. Often they are the only available data, and as the Black and Townsend studies demonstrate, can still be used effectively to explore social aspects of health. If anything, there is too much data on specific illnesses, so that researchers have to select which items to explore, so opening the door to further confusion.

Asking the 'patient'

The only realistic alternative to starting from the use of medical records, collected for purposes other than social research, is to ask ordinary people directly how well they feel, and how they define health. This approach has been forcibly advocated as a corrective to the medical standpoint, and a way of increasing information about health among sub-populations such as ethnic minorities and local communities (Williams and Popay 1994; Popay *et al.* 1998; Payne 1999). Studies that have examined such *lay definitions* have found that people think about health in several different ways, according to who they are. One of the most influential of these studies identified three different elements of health: health as *absence* of illness or *vacuum*; health as *reserve* or *capital* (for example a 'strong constitution' that is resistant to illness); and health as *equilibrium* or *well-being* (Herzlich 1973). Despite differences in the terminology used, later studies found similar distinctions (Blaxter and Paterson 1982; Pill and Stott 1982; Williams 1983; d'Houtard and Field 1984; Calnan 1987; Blaxter 1990). A fourth element, *functional capacity* (the ability to do things) is also identified by Blaxter.

These elements are not discrete, and individual accounts are often found to contain aspects of each. This is clear from our comments added to the following extract:

> I feel alert [*well-being*] and can always think of lots of things to do. No aches and pains – nothing wrong with me – [*absence of illness*] and I can go out and jog [*functional capacity*]. I suppose I have more energy [*reserve*], I can get up and do such a lot. (Blaxter 1990: 19)

Although the different elements are found in combination, accounts are socially patterned. Many studies have found that 'health as well-being' was more likely to be expressed by the middle class or those with higher levels of education, with working-class respondents and those with lower educational levels expressing health as 'absence of illness' (for example d'Houtard and Field 1984). However, this pattern was not repeated in the *Health and Lifestyles Survey* (Blaxter 1990). Here the greatest distinction was found between those of different age groups, with the young more likely to see health as well-being and older respondents drawing on ideas of functional capacity. Gender differences were found among the younger age group: young men often expressing ideas of physical fitness while young women emphasised health as vitality. Howlett *et al.* (1992) also report differences in health beliefs between ethnic groups.

Health status questionnaires have also been designed to quantify health in general populations, those with specific diseases and disabilities, and to measure 'quality of life'. These questionnaires attempt to measure the multidimensional aspects (social, psychological and physical) of health and illness through self-rating scales. Thus, the Nottingham Health Profile (Hunt *et al.* 1986) includes the following 'yes/no' statements, to which we have added comments:

> I'm in pain when I walk [*physical*]
> I lose my temper easily these days [*psychological*]
> I feel there is nobody I am close to [*social*]

The widely-used Short Forms-36 and -12 (Ware 1993) concentrate on the self-assessment of physical and psychological health alone, while others focus on behavioural/lifestyle factors (for example Berkman and Breslow 1983; Pill *et al.* 1993). Although not often employed by sociologists, these approaches have been important in health policy, such as the 'Health of the Nation' programmes. A full discussion of these and other health status scaling techniques can be found in Bowling (1997).

Explaining patterns of health

The previous section showed that the study of health variations involves dealing with a complex phenomenon. They can be studied from the perspectives of several disciplines, not least sociology, social policy and epidemiology (the branch of medicine concerned with the distribution of disease in human populations), and indeed, from alternative positions within disciplines. Differences between these approaches are made all the more acute by the political nature of health policies: each particular conception of health and illness implies that one kind of intervention would be more effective than others.

In other words, there are variations both in how health is defined and in the kinds of explanation that are sought for them; of course, definitions also imply certain types of explanation. If ill health is thought of mainly as symptoms, viruses or genetics, this points towards solutions in medical technology, whereas if ill health is defined in terms of loss of well-being, then intervention might mean tackling pollution, poverty, unemployment, loneliness or institutionalised racism. Those accounts that have drawn on lay definitions and focused on health status have been associated mainly with identifying *inequalities* in health, and have sought explanations of them based in social processes. But even here there are disagreements about what are the most important causes of differences in health. These disagreement have sometimes been intense (Macintyre 1997).

Dahlgren and Whitehead (1991) have suggested that the complex picture of factors affecting inequalities in health can be mapped into five related clusters. Their starting point is the cluster of studies using physical or straightforward biological models of illness. These take age, sex, genetic inheritance and *in utero* (pre-birth) experiences that predispose to being at risk of certain illnesses later in life, as producing differences in health. Individuals have no control over these factors.

In contrast, a second cluster of factors are sometimes seen (not least by health educators, moralisers and right-wing politicians) as things that people can and *should* control as matters of personal responsibility. These are the individual 'lifestyles' of diet; consumption of alcohol, nicotine and other drugs; and exercise, that differentially predispose to health. The 1999 White Paper's 'Popular Summary' (DoH 1999), with its '10 Tips for Healthy Living', is a good example of this kind of well-intentioned advice.

Any objection that unhealthy lifestyles are mainly associated with people living in poverty, and therefore that intervention should be addressed to the alleviation of poverty, found little favour with government in the 1980s and early 1990s. The 'official line' was reflected in the Conservative Minister of Health's 1986 observations about the connection between health and poverty:

> I honestly don't think that it has anything to do with poverty. The problem very often for many people is just ignorance... and failing to realise that they do have some control over their own lives. (quoted in Bury 1997: 64)

Dahlgren and Whitehead's next two clusters are more sociological: 'social and community influences', and 'living and working conditions'. Although these might be considered by some as individual features, in practice most refer to life experiences that no single person can control. For instance, social circumstances involving a lack of supportive personal relationships, community processes such as risk of crime, and the occupational experiences of stress or accidents at work, are not simply there for individuals to experience or avoid at will.

In this sense, the distinction between the two categories, social/community and living/working, is not particularly helpful, nor should they be regarded as equally important: for example, the 'Whitehall studies' have demonstrated how working conditions have a major impact on health (see below). There is also overlap with Dahlgren and Whitehead's final category, 'general socio-economic, cultural and environmental conditions', which is meant to identify factors even more susceptible to international market forces, and therefore even less within individual control. In practice this category is similar to the previous two – are poor housing, low income, and unemployment 'general socio-economic' or 'living and working' conditions?

While the Dahlgren and Whitehead typology is less than perfect (Syme 1996; Shy 1997), it has been widely adopted: if nothing else it offers a way of identifying where particular research contributions stand. Developments of the model have been influential in the Acheson Report (DoH 1998a) and the subsequent Public Health Green and White Papers (DoH 1998b, 1999). These government documents all place greater emphasis on the social nature and interactions of the clusters, and the need for improvements in access to services.

It would be wrong to think that this change in government policy reflects unanimity among those who have studied health inequalities. A number of writers have identified four major points of disagreement about the explanations of inequalities (see Armstrong 1994; Benzeval *et al.* 1995; Bury 1997; Macintyre 1997; Scambler 1997; Taylor and Field 1997; and, with a more medical emphasis, BMA 1995). On the one hand, there are two arguments why health inequalities are *not* a product of socio-economic processes, and in particular, social class. The first of these argues that it is poor health that leads to social disadvantage, rather than the other way round, thus standing the conventional sociological wisdom on its head. The second view proposes that the apparent connection does not even actually exist, being no more than an artificial product of unreliable statistics and incorrect reasoning. Against these two positions are those who do argue that there are health/deprivation connections, but this camp is split into two. One group attributes unequal health outcomes to socially structured differences in people's financial and resource circumstances, while the other sees the key issue as being what people know, believe and think (their 'culture') and how this makes them act. Each of these four positions is given fuller consideration in the next section.

Health inequalities and their explanations

The last-mentioned of these schools of thought – 'cultural' or 'behavioural' theory – is the basis for the 'lifestyle' approach already discussed, in terms of the Dahlgren/Whitehead typology and Conservative reactions to the Black Report. It focuses on what people believe, suggesting that because groups perceive health and its causes in different ways, their health-related behaviours are going to vary. As well as being specifically concerned with 'good practice' in healthy living behaviour, this approach also takes account of basic orientations to life. For instance, compared with less advantaged groups, well-educated people in jobs where they have personal autonomy, and can control others, are more likely to be knowledgeable about good health practice, to have higher expectations of the effectiveness of taking action against illness, and to expect faster and better medical treatment to protect their health. This cultural 'mind-set' can be seen as contributing to their lower levels of illness, translating any *material* advantage into attitudes conducive to good health: it is not the material resources available to them *per se* that counts but the way they think and act.

As well as offering this general mode of explanation, the cultural perspective has particular resonance in respect of ethnic group variations in health. While it is true that variation *within* each ethnic group tends to be greater than *between* groups (Nazroo 1997: 240), there are substantial differences in folk-ways and traditional remedies, ideas about health, religious beliefs, and morally and socially acceptable ways of life. For example, Howlett *et al.* (1992) report that Indians tend to see health as a matter of luck, and regard smoking and alcohol as major causes of illness, whereas the white group see ill health as the 'fault of the individual' and more often caused by stress. Thorogood's description of the home remedies used by women of Caribbean origin raises the question of when and why Afro-Caribbean families use medical services and so become part of medical statistics (1990). American research has suggested that psychiatric mis-diagnosis of Afro-Caribbeans may be attributable to cultural misunderstandings, such as the way language is used and social behaviour is sanctioned. These cultural and behavioural factors are not easily reducible to the material circumstances of class or employment.

Critics of this view argue that mind-sets come from social locations such as class position, and that rather than intervening to try to change ideas, it is the structural systems that must first be tackled. Among the poor, unsatisfactory housing, physical environments, working conditions and income constrain the freedom of choice which is otherwise open to the better-off. This argument from a 'materialist perspective', the second of the four points of contention (and exemplified by the discussion of class differences in Chapter 2) tends to treat cultural variations as a product of social class or wider socio-economic systems. Emphasis may be placed either on the constraints and workings of the economic system, or on the actual poverty that it produces.

The *Black Report* and Townsend's work on deprivation were key contributions to this latter position, arguing that poverty was more common in contemporary Britain than realised, and so a significant cause of ill health. While there is no single agreed measurement of poverty (Townsend 1987), most commentators agree that both absolute and relative poverty in Britain increased during the 1980s and early 1990s (Hills 1995a, 1995b):

Whichever poverty line is used, around a quarter of our society was living in poverty in the UK in 1992. The poverty encountered by children is even greater than for society as a whole – around a third of children in the UK were living in poverty in 1992/3. Well over 4 million people were living below the 'safety net' of income support. (Oppenheim and Harker 1996: 44)

Living in poverty brings direct problems, as well as the stress of dealing with them. In a 1991 survey of low income families, a fifth of parents and a tenth of children had gone without food at least once in the previous month (National Children's Home 1991). Morris and Ritchie (1994) report that at the lowest resource levels there are couples who regularly go without food and have difficulty clothing their children. As low income interviewees told the researchers in the *Hard Times* survey, they had to do without proper food and heating:

> I don't cut down, as I say, with the kids. I try to make sure they get, but like I cook a meal and as long as there's enough for them, I make do with a piece of toast... Many a Sunday afternoon our electric has gone. We've just waited 'til Monday. (Kempson *et al.* 1994)

It is hardly surprising if people exposed to these low levels of living tend to suffer ill health. Among families living on income support, over two-thirds report ill health, with asthma, bronchitis and eczema the commonest complaints (Cohen *et al.* 1992). They had no 'spare' money to meet the extra costs of illness or to pay for the heating needed to relieve symptoms. Not only do poor housing conditions contribute to poor child health, but their parents suffer from depression and stress-related disorders as a result of their financial difficulties (Morris and Ritchie 1994).

However, this view of health inequalities as the product of deprivation is rejected by the third of our four schools of thought. While not denying an association between ill health and disadvantaged economic positions in society, it has been claimed that people are 'socially selected' by their health to occupy distinctive social locations (Illsley 1955, 1986; Klein 1988). The healthy get better jobs, the unhealthy descend into unemployment or low paid jobs. Illness causes their poverty, rather than the other way round.

While at the margins (extreme physical or mental disability) bodily conditions may limit occupational achievement (although the research base to support this is limited), extensive social mobility research has shown that by far the biggest factors in movements up and down the class scale have been the changing availability of types of occupation, and class differences in access to qualifications and desirable jobs (Payne 1987a). Those advocating 'social selection' have not properly understood the dynamics of social mobility.

Nor is their underlying logic clear. If we take the case of infant mortality rates (deaths within one year of birth, per 1000 live births: Table 10.1), we

Table 10.1　Infant mortality[1] by social class.[2] UK

Registrar-General's Social Class	1981	1991	1994
I	7.8	5.0	4.5
II	8.2	5.3	4.5
IIIN	9.0	6.3	5.1
IIIM	10.5	6.3	5.5
IV	12.7	7.1	6.4
V	15.7	8.2	6.8
Other	15.7	12.4	8.8
All Classes	10.4	6.4	5.4

Notes:
1. Deaths within one year of birth per 1000 live births
2. Classified by occupation of father – births 'inside marriage'

Source: Office for National Statistics (1997)

need to explain why very young children die, and why infant mortality rates are worse the lower down the class scale one goes – a pattern that holds even as rates improve over the years.

This child health problem, coming *after* the parents became members of a lower class, could not directly have *caused* the parents' social class location. The social selection argument actually implies *either* a three-part logical chain: parents' previous poor health leads to low social class, which leads to poor infant health (that is, class *does* have a direct effect in the middle of the chain) *or* that parents' previous poor health directly causes poor infant health (which misses out the class element, but then does not explain the observed class differentials). Similarly if we examine class differentials in the use of dental services we see sharp contrasts, as in Table 10.2. Propensity to take up medical services, or prevalence of tooth decay, is an implausible explanation of why people are in their particular occupations or classes, whereas class differences (either as knowledge and good health practice or as having the resources to gain access to treatment) are a more convincing explanation of propensity to visit the dentist.

The last of the four arguments, that class and health are not actually connected in the way the *Black Report* suggests, is largely based on the argument that 'class' is not a real phenomenon, but rather an intellectual construct. Two things follow from this: first, 'class', because it is only an idea represented by categories of occupations, cannot *cause* poor 'health', and second, the way in which class is constructed becomes crucial. In connection with health inequalities, Illsley (1986, 1990), Klein (1988) and Carr-Hill (1990) have

Table 10.2   **Adults who visit dentists for regular
check-ups. UK, 1995–96 (percentages)**

Socio-economic Group	Males	Females
Professional	59	71
Employers and managers	55	70
Intermediate and junior non-manual	51	62
Skilled manual	40	57
Semi-skilled manual and personal service	37	49
Unskilled manual	38	52
All SEGs	46	61

Source: adapted from Office for National Statistics (1998a)

argued that classes have changed in definition and size (see Chapter 2) so that comparison over time is invalid. As they are large aggregates of people in a range of occupations, there must also inevitably be a range of variation *within* each class (not least because social mobility moves people between classes). A parallel debate in mainstream sociology has been stimulated by Pahl's doubts about using occupation to define class categories (Pahl 1993).

The case that class is an artefact, and that its association with health is 'artefactual', is in part correct. It is absolutely true that definitions and classification schemes have evolved over time, while the classes they identify have shown major changes – the manual classes decreasing, the middle classes expanding (Chapter 2). This does make time-based comparisons more difficult, and the replacement of the old Registrar-General's Social Class schema (very extensively used in medical records) for the 2001 Census is a long overdue recognition of the need to change. It is also the case that the present members of a class may well have been mobile into it, and so bring previous health-related characteristics from their former class.

However, some of the difficulties that Illsley identifies are due precisely to the limitations of the Registrar-General's classification; other schema offer more flexible alternatives. If there is 'excessive' variation within classes, the answer lies in devising better representations of the class structure, not in abandoning class as a variable. It is insufficient to claim that the nature of social classes has changed, or that people are socially mobile: that does not render *all* association between class and health irrelevant.

However, the main problem with the artefactual critique is that it misrepresents what research based on social class is actually trying to do. The purpose of a class schema is to provide a framework for analysis, not a complete answer. As Chapter 2 showed, class is the connection between the fundamental economic and power structures of society, and the lives people lead. Except for a few, unrepresentative purists, most researchers implicitly assume that class is not *directly* associated with *every* outcome, but works through a complex of other 'intervening variables' to shape the social patterns under investigation. Class is associated, for instance, with work conditions, education, income, housing, and beliefs; each of these factors interacts, and is in turn associated with health and illness. Class is only the starting point for the construction of a 'narrative' that explores how the end-point of health or illness can be traced back to the deep structures of the social order. To complain that any one class schema does not explain everything perfectly is to miss the point entirely. Tables 10.1 and 10.2 (above) showed clear 'class gradients' in two aspects of health: the challenge is how to explain them, not to try to explain them away.

Health inequalities and other social divisions

Infant mortality and visits to the dentist are only two examples from a strikingly large range of class/health associations. Figure 10.1 from the 1999 White Paper offers another illustration, comparing the death rate of professional male workers with those in the other classes. For the unskilled, the rate is nearly three times greater.

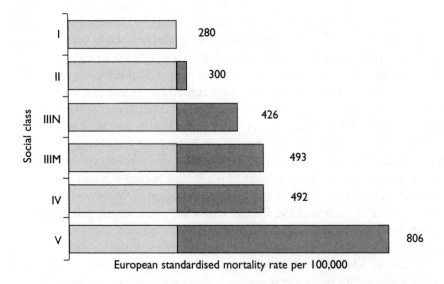

Figure 10.1   European Standardised Mortality Rate per 100,000 population for men aged 20 to 64. England and Wales, 1991–93

Source: adapted from Department of Health (1999). Figure 4.1

Health

Table 10.3 GP consultations[1] for age, gender and occupational group.[2] GB, 1996 (percentages)

	Male				Female			
	16–44	*45–64*	*65 and over*	*Total*	*16–44*	*45–64*	*65 and over*	*Total*
Non-manual	9	13	21	13	19	17	21	17
Manual	11	17	20	14	20	22	24	20
Unemployed	8	10	NA	9	21	15	NA	20
All	10	15	20	13	20	19	22	20

Notes:
1. Consultations in previous 14 days
2. Based on occupation of household head

Source: adapted from Office for National Statistics (1998b). Tables 8.24, 8.25

The same source also shows that this differential, far from decreasing, was not only very much smaller in the early 1930s than it is today, but seems to be currently growing at a faster rate (DoH 1999: Figure 4.2). Rather than seeing this as an artefact or social selection at work, the differential can be linked to the 'Whitehall studies' which show how civil servants at different grades, carefully studied over a number of years, developed illnesses in a pattern that reflected their hierarchical positions in employment. Those in controlling positions systematically enjoyed better health and survival rates than those with little control over their working lives (see for example Marmot *et al.* 1984, 1991; Bosma *et al.* 1997). The 'narrative' linking class to health seems to indicate work conditions and stress levels as key intervening variables.

It would be possible to present a series of class-based tables here, but this would be to misrepresent what researchers actually do (it could also create the impression that class is the only important social division). A more typical product is Table 10.3, which shows visits to GPs surgeries by gender (here, strictly-speaking, 'sex') and age, as well as household-head's class (and the unemployed). GP consultations are important, because as we saw earlier, cases of 'illness' cannot become part of the health record without them.

Inevitably, this table is a little harder to read because it includes three social divisions, but it is clear that the figures across the non-manual row tend to be lower than those across the manual row. Given the prior argument that non-manual workers have better cultural mind-sets about health – and so would not be slow to identify early symptoms and visit their doctors – these data strongly suggest that the manual working-class experiences show more illness. This is true for all but one of the age groups. The difference holds true for both men and women, but is slightly greater for women.

Table 10.4   Incidence of self-reported acute and chronic illness for gender, age and occupational groups. GB, 1996 (percentages)

	0–15		16–44		45–64		65 and over		Total	
	Chr	Acu	Chr	Acu	Chr	Acu	Chr	Acu	Chr	Acu
Male										
Non-manual	7	11	12	13	23	15	43	20	17	14
Manual	6	10	16	13	37	22	48	22	24	16
Unemployed	NA	NA	16	12	24	15	NA	NA	18	13
Total	7	11	14	13	31	18	45	21	21	15
Female										
Non-manual	6	9	15	16	28	19	43	20	20	16
Manual	8	9	17	14	36	24	48	26	25	18
Unemployed	NA	NA	17	17	28	18	NA	NA	19	17
Total	7	9	16	15	32	22	46	23	23	17

Notes:
Chr: limiting longstanding illness as indicator of chronic illness; Acu: acute illness in previous 14 days

Source: adapted from Office for National Statistics (1998b). Tables 8.3, 8.4, 8.6, 8.7

A broadly similar picture emerges if we take self-reported illness rather than GP consultations. The first two rows across in each panel of Table 10.4 show that people in manual households generally report worse health than non-manual households, and this tends to be greater for people later in their working careers (see particularly the columns for 45–64-year-olds). The class difference is found among men as well as women, but is greater for men with chronic illness. Tables 10.3 and 10.4 suggest that each of the three social divisions – class, age and gender – have *independent* effects on health. Before leaving this table, it is interesting to note that those classified as

Table 10.5   Selected causes of death for age and gender groups. UK, 1996 (percentages)

	15–24		55–64		75 and over		All ages	
	Male	Female	Male	Female	Male	Female	Male	Female
Circulatory disease	4	7	43	29	45	47	42	43
Cancers	7	17	37	48	22	15	27	23
Respiratory disease	4	5	7	9	20	19	15	16
Injuries and poisoning	63	43	3	2	1	1	4	2
Infections	2	4	1	1	–	–	1	1
Other	19	24	9	12	11	16	11	15
Base (thousands) (100%)	2.8	1.1	35.1	21.5	155.9	232.3	306.5	332.4

Source: adapted from Office for National Statistics (1998a)

unemployed have *better* health than the others: readers may like to speculate on what 'narrative' might account for this?

Although age and gender can be seen as separate social divisions, they also interact: for example women live longer, and young men are more prone to accidental death, as Table 10.5 shows. This table also shows that men are more liable to die of circulatory disease in late working life, and of cancer in old age. The gender differences (the 'all ages totals' columns) alone do not bring this out: it requires the inclusion of age to obtain a fuller picture. Attitudes towards illness, in terms of propensity to say in interview that one has health problems, are also gendered. Table 10.6, which cannot be directly compared with the previous table, shows that men are less likely to define themselves as having health problems, again most notably among the very old.

As Chapter 6 showed, these data are likely to be subject to change, as 'early old age' is progressively socially redefined as a life stage of greater activity and vitality, and 'late old age' expands with more people living longer.

The differences between men and women in these health data are particularly interesting in light of debates about gender. Feminist writers have drawn attention to the distinctive features of women's health (for example Arber 1990; Doyal 1995). On the one hand, medical records indicate that women suffer more from acute and chronic illnesses, are more likely to be treated for mental illness, and obviously have distinctive health needs concerning pregnancy and childbirth. On the other hand, they are less likely to work in hazardous occupations, or to engage in 'high risk' macho lifestyle behaviour such as excessive consumption of alcohol, dangerous sports, or violence. Women are more likely to consult their doctors and admit to illness, although their willingness to adopt the 'sick role' seems to be related in a complex way to child care and their continuing role in domestic labour (Chapter 3). The prevalence of male doctors (and female nurses) is seen as gendering health

Table 10.6   EuroQol[1] assessment for age and gender groups. GB, 1996 (percentages)

	16–44		45–64		65–74		75 and over		Total	
	M	F	M	F	M	F	M	F	M	F
No problems	74	70	54	50	38	38	30	21	60	55
Mild problems	15	16	18	20	23	19	19	19	17	18
Moderate problems	5	6	9	11	16	16	21	16	9	10
Substantial problems	6	8	18	18	23	27	30	44	14	17

Notes:
1. A self-assessed health status questionnaire

Source: Office for National Statistics (1998b). Table 8.38

care. The modern tendency to define social issues as medical problems has resulted in a 'medicalisation' of women's bodies.

This perspective has more recently been questioned in two ways. Cameron and Bernardes have argued that it is time to consider 'men's health for a change' (1998: 115). Men die younger, do not use health services properly and engage in more life-threatening activities. These basic social facts will not be properly investigated if women are seen as the only category having 'interesting' health research problems. Second, work by Macintyre and her associates has questioned whether women actually are more ill than men (for example Macintyre *et al.* 1996). In a study in which men and women were carefully matched for the grade of their jobs and perceived working conditions, there were no gender differences in health. Overall, women reported more colds, eye strain, aches, nerves and sleeping problems, but no more than men in the equivalent jobs. The higher female totals were a product of their concentration into certain jobs. Men as well as women were also found to encounter difficulties balancing domestic and employment commitments. These findings suggest that the relationship between gender, health and other social divisions is a more complex one than hitherto recognised.

The complexity of interacting factors can also be seen in health and illness patterns among ethnic groups. While overall there are relatively few health differences between ethnic groups, some do exist (see Table 10.7): For example, Afro-Caribbeans tend to be more prone to strokes, as well as the more commonly mentioned sickle cell disease. The several Asian groups suffer more from eye problems, high blood pressure and diabetes.

As well as cultural variations (language difficulties are a particular barrier to communicating about illness), ethnic groups also differ in the kinds of occupations they pursue, the proportions of men and women in paid employment, and their demographic profiles (see Chapter 4). Although health data including these factors are not readily available, it is reasonable to suggest that gender and age, in addition to class, play a part in explaining the inequalities

Table 10.7   Self-reported 'fair' or 'poor' health among different ethnic groups and work status (percentage rounded)

Ethnic group	No full-time worker	Manual	Non-manual
Caribbean	38	29	25
Indian and African Asians	35	28	20
Pakistani and Bangaladeshi	44	36	30
All ethnic minority groups	38	31	24
White	37	22	21

Source: adapted from Modood *et al.* (1997: 245)

Table 10.8   Standard Mortality Ratio (SMR) by social class and country of birth, men aged 20–64, all causes. England and Wales, 1991–93

Registrar General's Social Class	All countries	Caribbean	Indian sub-continent	Scotland	Ireland (all parts)
I/II	71	83	96	82	95
IIIN	100	84	112	121	127
IIIM	117	105	120	169	166
IV/V	135	99	158	186	173
Non-manual	77	83	100	89	102
Manual	124	102	140	176	169
Adjusted for class	100	82	117[1]	132	129

Notes:
1. India, 114; Pakistan, 110; Bangaladesh, 159

Source: Drever and Whitehead (1997). Tables 9.4, 9.5

in Table 10.7. Thus, in Table 10.8, differences between ethnic groups in standard mortality rates persist even after taking social class into account. Even greater specific group variation exists within the categories used here, as the footnote to this table shows.

Class, gender and age by no means constitute a complete list of explanatory factors in ethnic health inequalities. The range of factors and competing explanations discussed earlier in this chapter should not be forgotten. If we consider the psycho-social *stress* of being subjected to racism, the fact that some illnesses such as sickle cell anaemia have a *genetic* component, and that many ethnic groups live in inner city locations with poorer *health services*, we must not only anticipate ethnic health differences but expect to use a variety of explanations for this (see Senior and Viveash 1998: 158–86).

Table 10.8 also includes data for people born in Scotland and Ireland but now living in England and Wales. Particularly among the manual classes, these

Table 10.9   Standard Mortality Ratios (SMR) for UK constituent countries and gender, 1996

Country	Male SMR	Female SMR	Region SMR
England	98	98	98
Wales	102	102	102
Scotland	118	115	116
Northern Ireland	109	107	107

Source: StatBase (1999)

**Table 10.10   Self-reported health status indicators for
the ONS classification of English areas, 1994–96
(average percentage standardized for age)**

Area	Health: poor – bad	Longstanding illness	Acute sickness	Prescribed medication
England	22.6	39.6	15.0	40.3
Mining & industrial	28.0	42.7	16.7	42.7
Inner London	27.9	42.2	18.2	40.7
Urban	25.7	40.3	15.4	40.0
Rural	21.6	38.5	14.4	39.7
Mature	21.5	39.7	14.7	40.2
Prosperous	18.7	38.2	14.2	39.6

Source: adapted from Social and Community Planning Research (1999)

white migrants share higher SMRs. When we put those data alongside national figures, as in Table 10.9, further differences emerge.

England has the lowest SMRs, and the difference between nations is greater than between men and women. Scotland in particular has poorer health, which, taken together with the political and cultural characteristics discussed in Chapter 5, might suggest that a characteristic way of life exists north of the Anglo-Scottish border. Some caution is, however, needed in making statements about large aggregates of data like countries: this chapter's earlier analysis suggests a number of social divisions that could be explored in order to account for national patterns. There are nonetheless substantial geographical differences in health, as Table 10.10 shows.

The demographics, occupational opportunities, physical environment and health services of Inner London, and areas marked by the run-down of heavy industry, are clearly reflected in these figures. Residents of mature areas (long-established towns) are relatively advantaged, while prosperous areas – dormitory suburbs for the prosperous middle classes, mainly in the South East – show quite different health patterns from those in urban or rural areas (and indeed in other aspects of social life, as we shall see in the next chapter on communities). Rural areas contain a wider range of lifestyles, and a distinctive problem of service delivery for remote locations.

Conclusions

We would want to balance two broad views of health. Despite advocating here a sociological rather than an individual or biological approach, we would wish to maintain that no single perspective offers a complete answer. Indeed, while it is easy to show that health is *associated* with social divisions, there is much more work to be done on *why* there are such associations. What precisely are the causal connections between social factors and health?

We therefore welcome more recent developments that recognise how the various elements (not least the major social divisions) interact, such as Macintyre's speculation that the combined processes operating at the top of the social scale are not just the mirror image of what is happening at the bottom (1997: 740). Similarly, there seems much promise in new work based on three perspectives: a life-course approach (Chapter 6) that looks at the cumulation of effects and risks (for example Power *et al.* 1996); the connections being explored between social environment – low income and employment context – and psycho-social factors like stress (for example Marmot and Wilkinson 1999); and the recognition that broad-brush analyses that work for some purposes can also be elaborated into finer-grained and more sophisticated models based on explanations from several levels (for example Popay *et al.* 1998).

On the other hand, that does not mean that we should not actively pursue an understanding of the social dynamics of health. Health, however defined, does have a social as well as a physical basis. Risk of illness and premature death are socially patterned: health inequalities divide people in a range of ways. Consideration of social divisions – in particular class, gender, ethnicity and age – help at one level of analysis to explain health inequalities. Other social divisions, like national differences, childhood, sexuality, disability and community life, are all affected by questions of health and access to health services. Health and illness are not only social, but they are part and parcel of social divisions.

FURTHER READING

A rather introductory but very clear account of this field can be found in Senior, M. and Viveash, B. *Health and Illness*, London: Macmillan (1998). Among a number of very good textbooks, Bury, M. *Health and Illness in a Changing Society*, London: Routledge (1997) is particularly well written, while Taylor, S. and Field, D. *Sociology of Health and Health Care*, 2nd edn, Oxford: Blackwell (1997) gives systematic coverage. Townsend, P., Davidson, N. and Whitehead, M. (eds) *Inequalities in Health: The Black Report and The Health Divide*, rev. edn, Harmondsworth: Penguin (1992) remains a classic on health and poverty.

CHAPTER 11

Community

GRAHAM CROW AND CATHERINE MACLEAN

The inclusion of a chapter on 'community' in a book about social divisions is not as odd as it might appear at first sight. There is nothing automatic about people coming together as communities, even though the most effective community bonds may be those that members believe to be 'natural'. The unity of any community is always vulnerable to disputes among the individuals, and the social groups who make it up, and the achievement of community solidarity requires members to be mindful of the collective good alongside their own more immediate agendas. Communities frequently encompass divisive social identities: in many villages, for example, a distinction is made between those who 'belong' and those viewed as 'outsiders'. In addition, community is often the arena in which the social divisions discussed in preceding chapters are played out. It is here that the various dimensions of social division manifest themselves and come together in making up people's everyday lives, rather than existing as separate ideas, principles or variables in the realm of sociological 'macro' analysis.

Sociological interest in community matters has revived in recent years. In both theoretical and methodological terms, sociologists working in the field have become more sophisticated than earlier generations of researchers whose work frequently suffered from uncritical conceptions of 'community' and unreflexive techniques of investigation. This chapter examines the nature of 'community' and the ways in which social divisions figure in community life. In so doing, it raises the issue of social cohesion: if we are all so divided from one another, how do we collaborate in social life? In particular it discusses the various bases of community, the factors influencing the ease with which an individual can join or leave a community, and the question of the desirability of community as an ideal. The analysis first outlines the development of sociological analysis in this field, then considers recent conceptual trends.

223

The nature of community

Communities place a requirement on members to limit their individualism and to acknowledge their dependence on a wider network of relationships. The same sort of point can be made about community solidarity as Durkheim (1893/1984) famously made about social solidarity more generally, namely that people who have only narrow self-interest to motivate them constitute an insufficient basis for sustainable social relationships. Just as sociologists from Durkheim onwards have sought to answer the fundamental question of what makes 'society' possible, so too has the issue of the basis of 'community' been the subject of extensive discussion. If communities are defined as groups of people who have something in common, then the thing that they share may be identified as geographical location; position in the wider social structure; or sense of identity. On this basis Willmott (1986) makes the analytical distinction between 'place community', 'interest community' and 'community of attachment', although he is careful to note that in practice particular communities probably will have more than one of these elements in common.

The fact that they are constructed around members having something in common makes it appropriate to treat communities as phenomena of social cohesion rather than social division. However, even if potential social divisions between community members can be overcome, communities will still have associations with rivalry and conflict, because communities are exclusive as well as inclusive. People who do not share the common characteristic(s) by which a community is defined are necessarily 'outsiders'. Individuals who do not 'belong' to a community pose a threat because affiliations to other places, interests and/or identities make them potential rivals for the scarce material resources and social status to which communities lay claim. The sense of solidarity among community members may even be strengthened where divisions between 'insiders' and 'outsiders' are highlighted. Often it turns out to be harder to specify who we *are* than who we are *not*, and in this way a strong and positive sense of 'us' will be enhanced by a clear and correspondingly negative sense of 'them', the 'other' against which we define ourselves (Bauman 1990).

This is perhaps most obvious in 'place communities', but also applies to 'imagined communities' (see Chapters 5 and 8). In Chapter 1, the discussion of separateness and identity stressed that being *different* is not just an isolated state of distinctive existence but involves beliefs, feelings and attitudes to others. What appears to be a sense of community is often a way of expressing other underlying social divisions, which are perceived to mark off *our community* from the rest of the world, and *our part* of the community from their part of the community. The distinction between us and them that arises from this is an important one.

A common way this has been expressed has been through concerns about respectability. Traditional working-class communities frequently operated with a distinction between 'respectable' and 'rough' groupings (see Chapter 2), the difference being defined in terms of standards of appearance, type of employment, patterns of money management, religious observance, leisure activities and sexual behaviour. According to Meacham, a family would achieve 'respectability' in such circumstances only if its members avoided 'swearing, except at work; drinking, in excess of an occasional weekend pint or two; gambling; persistent rowing; sexual promiscuity on the part of mother or daughters' (1977: 27). Such ideas often had extremely localised expression, with not only neighbourhood but even parts of individual streets having distinct reputations. The judgmental language in which the respectable/rough distinction is framed could be contested by the alternative portrayal of people as either 'stuck up' or 'ordinary', but the underlying social division could not be denied. Similar distinctions operate in contemporary communities, as the continued use of vocabulary such as 'good neighbourhoods' and 'rough areas' demonstrates. Friction and rivalry between parts of communities identified in this way have also persisted, so that community in as far as it is a social division could be said to operate in a fragmented, localised way. Nonetheless, it is one that is nationally replicated, and which has been well-established over a long period of time (Chapter 12).

On the other hand, the dynamic nature of relations within communities and the competitive nature of links between communities mean that people's sense of the communities to which they belong is not fixed. Despite the appeal of the common sense notion that communities have enduring qualities, with a fixed character that is so desirable that we should all aspire to attain it, change is inherent in communities because of the inevitability that community membership is altered with the passage of time. Geographical mobility, social mobility and individuals' progression through the life-course all necessitate adjustment in community relationships (see Chapter 6). In consequence, the continuity of community phenomena is just as difficult to explain sociologically as is the process of change in community attachments.

The preponderant focus of sociological writing on community has been on change. From Tönnies' classic *Community and Association* (1887/1955) onwards, a powerful body of literature has argued that the Industrial Revolution and the development of capitalism, and more generally of 'modernity' bring with them the loss of community. Although it remains influential, this conclusion can be challenged. Many writers have identified important continuities in community relationships, thereby casting doubt on the claim that community is a declining phenomenon (Crow and Allan 1994; Payne 1996). Others have argued that vigorous new forms of community are emerging in response to major social trends such as globalisation and the rise of internet communities (Castells 1997). Globalisation may have the effect of generating new solidarities, some of which are constructed defensively around places or values that are felt to be threatened, while others involve people taking advantage of opportunities to communicate in the different ways that developments in information technology have made possible. Both perspectives suggest that the significance of community relationships in societies like contemporary Britain extends well beyond bemoaning the passing of how things used to be.

It has been noted already that communities are diverse phenomena that may be based on people having place, interests and/or identities in common. The association of community with place is an established tradition within the sociology of community, epitomised by community studies being given place names as their titles (sometimes substituting pseudonyms in order to protect anonymity). *Childerley* (Bell 1994), *Whalsay* (Cohen 1987), *Smalltown* (Dempsey 1990) and *Westrigg* (Littlejohn 1963) are examples of how easily community can be read into place. However, community is not just a sense of division between 'us in this locality' and the rest of the world.

People who share common interests are less readily identified in everyday language as 'communities'. One of the more common examples is people with the same employer, who may constitute 'occupational communities'. Most studies of occupational communities have been of male-dominated heavy industries, such as Hill's (1976) *The Dockers*, Roberts's (1993) study of shipbuilders, Tunstall's (1962) *The Fishermen* and Warwick and Littlejohn's (1992) study of coal-miners, but other groups of workers besides these (such as police officers) are also usefully regarded as occupational communities (Salaman 1986). Of course, where occupational communities live in a single, physically identifiable location, the two senses of community reinforce each other, giving an even stronger sense of separate identity.

Communities of the third type, 'communities of attachment' that are built around common identities, are more free-floating than either place or interest communities, because they are not tightly bounded by geography or social structural features such as social class. People in these communities come together through their shared culture, uniting around symbols that emphasise (for instance) common ethnicity (Baumann 1996; this volume Chapter 4), shared difference from able-bodied norms (Gregory and Hartley 1991; this volume Chapter 9), shared political visions (Lichterman 1996), or aspects of lifestyle like taste in music (Finnegan 1989).

Willmott's point that, in practice, communities do not always fall neatly into one of the three analytical types that he distinguishes is evident in the above examples. The people of Cohen's (1987) *Whalsay* are less a place community than a community of attachment in which place is drawn upon in the symbolic construction of boundaries around 'insiders' and 'outsiders'. Likewise, Roberts (1993) notes that the occupational community of Wearside shipbuilders has been weakened by their dispersal through patterns of residential migration, while Baumann's (1996) analysis of ethnic communities in Southall locates them in relation to common interests as well as shared cultural affinities.

As several of the other chapters in this book show, particular social divisions can be demonstrated to operate across society as a whole, that is, at the 'macro' level. In practice, where individuals find that they share a position with other people on the same side of a social divide, those others are likely in the first place to be found close to hand. If we can see and talk to others 'in the same boat' as ourselves in respect of social divisions, namely those who live and work nearby, our interaction has the potential to grow into a sense of shared social identity with regard to that division. Where residential areas are largely homogeneous, for example in terms of the social class or ethnicity of the residents, the social divisions discussed earlier in the book take on a sharp new focus (Rex and Moore 1967). Propinquity (closeness of location) does not necessarily entail common identity but it helps to explain why community of place can overlap with community of interest. While the less concrete community of attachment also depends on mechanisms for sharing symbolic meanings, a cultural sharing, such non-located attachments cut across the simplistic idea of homogeneous, unified 'communities' without social divisions.

Communities and change

It is also important to consider the temporal dimension of community relationships (Crow and Allan 1995). By constantly moving into and out of communities, people's arrival or departure highlights the fundamental question of what it is that community members share. Place communities may be constructed to include former residents who have migrated elsewhere but who retain some attachment to the location (so-called 'diaspora communities') while excluding those local residents whose recent arrival or temporary residence disqualifies them from being considered 'real locals' (Cohen 1982). Mewett has reported how people who have left the Scottish island of Lewis are referred to as 'exiles', a term which implies that 'though physically absent, the migrant retains a social presence' (1982: 230). Conversely, physical presence does not grant a person 'local' status, although the distinction between 'old incomers' and 'new incomers' that Phillips (1986) found in a Yorkshire parish indicates that the exclusion of the in-migrants can cease over time. Similarly, new recruits are frequently accepted as full members of interest communities and attachment communities only once they have been appropriately socialised and established the trust of existing members by demonstrating their loyalty to the group (Salaman 1986).

The question of how community relationships are affected by changing membership has particular significance in contemporary societies that are characterised by high rates of geographical and social mobility. In-migrants have to start from scratch when they enter a new community: their learning process and initial absence or lower levels of personal relationship will be complicated if the incomers are socially different, for example in class or attitudes to the locality (Payne 1973). Inward geographical mobility can be disruptive of existing arrangements where newcomers enter into competition with established community members for scarce resources such as housing. It is certainly the case that conflicts have been associated with much geographical relocation, including the migration of ethnic minority populations into inner-city areas (Rex and Moore 1967) and that of middle-class ex-urbanites into the countryside (Newby 1980).

In the latter case, there are well-known problems associated with the arrival of more affluent newcomers. These new middle classes (with their easier access to mortgages and loans) can afford to pay much larger sums for the kinds of small houses local (often working-class) young couples would otherwise rent, buy or inherit (see Table 2.2). This process prices existing local people out of the local housing market, producing social antagonisms far removed from the rural idyll that attracted the newcomers in the first place.

In more extreme cases, the new middle-class residents commute away to the city during the day, or spend only weekends or holidays in the locality. They therefore have little need of a local school, shop, library, public transport or other welfare or commercial services. Such part-time presence does not offer much to community life. Having contributed to the displacement of the next generation by buying up the available houses, their lack of involvement tends to weakens what is left. Even in localities in which this tendency is less pronounced, the potential for conflict between incomers' ways and those of the locals, often expressed through competition for control of policy in clubs, committees and council, remains high (Frankenberg 1957; Macleod 1990).

However, there is no simple causal connection between in-migration and conflict, since many of these patterns of in-migration were preceded by population exoduses. In such cases, as one local resident put it:

> You can't blame them (incomers) for wanting their own place to live. If they get a house then it's our own fault for selling it to them or letting them build it in the first place. Once they're in there's nothing you can do about it, so there's no point complaining. (Macleod 1992: 198)

Rural areas often have a history of migration to the towns that long pre-dates the more recent pattern of middle-class settlement (which is connected to the expansion of the middle classes (Chapter 2)), and a similar point can be made about 'white flight' from inner-urban areas preceding the settlement there of much of Britain's black population. Inner-city areas have been losing population for most of the twentieth century, and it was only once this process was underway that they became major centres for settlement by ethnic minorities who are better understood as a 'replacement population' (Sarre 1989:139) than as a group whose arrival displaced others.

Migration, then, affects social divisions in two contradictory ways. It may weaken the common sense of identity among the 'original' members of a category, by the loss of some of their number who gain new identities through migration. Alternatively, migration may strengthen division through new encounters with non-members across categories, and the conflicts that frequently arise as a result between locals and incomers.

The conventional view of in-migration as a cause of social problems has had to be modified further in the light of the recognition that newcomers may well generate additional resources for the benefit of established residents, not least by stimulating economic activity. In Gilligan's (1990) study of Padstow, for example, local people were often dependent on newcomers for employment, making it difficult to analyse conflicts there as straightforward contests between 'insiders' and 'outsiders'. Without the development of new industries to replace declining ones that had previously been major employers (such as the development of tourism to replace fishing in the case of Padstow) communities are likely to shrink as people move elsewhere in search of work. Despite extravagant claims by its proponents, individual 'teleworkers' can contribute little to shore-up collapsing local economies. This story is currently being played out in the former coal-mining areas of Britain. Even in the context of economic decline, however, Wight's (1993) study of the Scottish village of 'Cauldmoss' found people reluctant to move away permanently, and those who did move were careful to keep open the possibility of return migration.

Less research has been undertaken into the impact of out-migration and return migration than has been conducted into the effects of in-migration, but what studies there are tend to emphasise the loss of community vitality (and ultimately viability) that follows from people moving elsewhere. Out-migration can result in residual communities being highly unbalanced in terms of several of the social divisions dealt with in earlier chapters – age, gender, ethnicity and social class. Out-migrants tend to be younger, more affluent and better linked into non-local networks than are their less mobile counterparts. In the extreme, sustained out-migration can lead to the 'death' of communities (Porteus 1989), but it is more common for migration patterns to be made up of a mixture of out-migration, in-migration and return migration.

The common assumption that the dynamism of contemporary communities contrasts with static communities in the past does not bear closer examination, as Maclean (1997) found in her research into the changing population composition of the parish of 'Beulach' in the Scottish Highlands. The recent trend for people from the south of Scotland and beyond to make their homes in 'Beulach' is merely one more twist in a long and complicated story in which population losses and gains have contributed to a situation of constant flux. Maclean found that many of the elderly 'real locals' had forebears from outside the parish. Macleod and Payne (1994) similarly found that of 105 locally born residents, only 60 had one locally born parent, and less than one in ten could boast both parents had been locally born.

The dynamics of community living

People's sense of 'belonging' is indisputably important to understanding the attachment that underlies their reluctance to leave and desire to return to place communities. It would be wrong to attach too much significance to place in this context, however, since the attraction is to the social networks of kin and friends that are centred on these places as well as to the familiar geographical location. The association of community with social support reflects the repeated finding that many people live in close proximity to relatives (beyond those in their immediate household). The 'traditional' working-class communities that have entered folklore for their mutual supportiveness frequently revolved around extensive kinship networks.

While this type of arrangement has generally been superseded by decades of social change, the geographical link with kin has not disappeared. Rather it is the case that people's migration strategies often maintain closeness to relatives because of the social support that they provide. Kin ties had been re-established to a significant degree even among the affluent workers of Luton when they were re-studied by Devine (1992a) some two decades after Goldthorpe and his colleagues (1969) had identified them as pioneers of more 'privatised' lifestyles.

In communities characterised by geographical immobility, kinship can be a particularly prominent feature, as Wight (1993) reports regarding 'Cauldmoss' where as many as two-thirds of the population were linked together by kin networks and strong kinship loyalties persisted. However, it should also be acknowledged that the other side of the coin of a kinship system linking people together is that it also defines who are *not* kin, and thereby divided off from the category of people who are entitled to support. An offence against one person becomes a potential offence against all other members of the kin group. In some cultures this is institutionalised into the inter-group conflict involving prolonged 'settling of scores', namely the 'feud'. Kinship in Britain is, for many people, a much weaker principle of division and attachment, which is why it has not been treated as a full-scale social division in this book. Nonetheless, identity with both immediate family and the wider kinship group is not uniform across the country, having significant social class, gender, age and ethnic variations, as earlier chapters have shown.

The reinforcement of people's attachment to communities by ties of kinship is supplemented by other associations such as those with neighbours, friends and co-workers. Of course, kin, friends and colleagues are not limited to persons living in close proximity, and social network analysts like Wellman, Carrington and Hall (1988) argue that 'personal communities' have the capacity to develop well beyond the confines of an individual's neighbour-hood. The extent to which communities have been 'de-territorialised' has been a topic of considerable interest in recent years since, on the face of it, powerful social trends have given individuals greater freedom of choice over those with whom they interact socially. Improvements in transport and communications technology allow people to be more mobile geographically and to maintain contact with others over an expanded area. Rising living standards make it possible to take up opportunities to socialise beyond the locality and also make unnecessary the interdependence with neighbours that was forced upon members of traditional working-class communities by their shared poverty. In the extreme, Beck (1992) sees participation in community relationships as increasingly a matter of individual choice. Post-modern theorists have argued that personal identities can now be changed and manipulated, because they are no longer class-based. While there is undoubtedly more individual choice in contemporary society (and this must weaken *place* community identity), place communities can still exert strong influences, and choosing a 'new' social identity may in fact be only to exchange membership of a local commu-nity for membership of an 'imagined community'.

It is, of course, important not to exaggerate the impact of broad trends towards geographical mobility and rising affluence. In societies characterised by widening inequalities, the easy mobility enjoyed by those in more advan-taged situations is closed off to marginal groups (such as lone parents) whose poverty and social exclusion effectively deny them the same opportunities to overcome the constraints of place (Duncan and Edwards 1997). In a society increasingly dependent on the car as *the* means of transport that gives access to all aspects of life outside the home, we should also recognise who, in conventional two-parent families, is actually trusted to drive the car, and more important, who has regular first call on its use: it is seldom either the mother or the children, who are thereby more closely tied to place communities (see Chapter 7).

Additionally, it is necessary to keep in mind the peculiar character of face-to-face interaction to which theorists such as Goffman (1972) have drawn our attention. Communities are not confined to people who have face-to-face contact, as the extensive usage of Anderson's (1991) concept of 'imagined communities' demonstrates, but at some level community relationships need to be sustained by people coming together to reaffirm their shared member-ship (Weeks 1995). Family gatherings, conferences, political meetings and local carnivals all serve to bring people together in one place periodically for face-to-face interaction, which revitalises their sense of community in a way that impersonal contacts maintained at a distance cannot. On the more mundane level of everyday life, the significance of routine encounters and conversations for reproducing social solidarity among community members also deserves to be acknowledged. These processes help to forge the strength of category membership on either side of any social division.

Researchers in this area have examined the ways in which gossip operated in traditional working-class communities not just to reinforce what by today's standards appear to be highly restrictive and oppressive codes of behaviour but also to promote social support (Tebbutt 1995). The information passed on through gossip networks was often vital to securing the well-being of poor households where it concerned financial and employment opportunities, and cases of similar information channels have been identified in contemporary Britain (Allatt and Yeandle 1992). A modified version of gossip's role in policing community members' adherence to codes of 'respectability' in domestic, sexual and other matters has also survived the transition from the traditional working-class communities in which the majority of the population used to live. Before it became common for women to take paid employment outside the home (Chapter 3), their presence in the locality made them visible 'carriers' of gossip. Policing of behaviour in order to maintain or enhance reputations is particularly powerful within the kinship networks that continue to be an important feature of community life, as we have noted.

While people now are generally less constrained financially and socially than their ancestors were, gossip networks continue to thrive and to be effective in a variety of settings (Dempsey 1990; Maclean 1997). Analyses framed in terms of economic necessity are clearly inadequate to account for people's acquiescence to such social control, so explanations of gossip's continuing effectiveness within communities have to be sought elsewhere. What accounts of gossip emphasise

Graham Crow and Catherine Maclean 233

is the role it plays in maintaining people's sense of place in and belonging to communities alongside the influence over the behaviour of others that it gives.

One feature of community life that the analysis of gossip highlights is the persistently unequal nature of community relationships. Patterns of gossip reveal that established community members, affluent groups and men are more powerful than newcomers, poorer people and women and children. What is revealed, in other words, is that while gossip may serve to reinforce existing norms of behaviour by negative assessments of acts that transgress those norms, it also reinforces hierarchies and divisions whose existence is written into the heart of community arrangements. The very language in which everyday conversations are conducted reproduces the marginality of certain groups, such as when in-migrants are referred to pejoratively as 'emmets', 'blow-ins', 'bongleys', 'white settlers', 'outsiders' and 'foreigners', or when poorer people are labelled 'rough' and 'no-hopers'. In addition, the exchange of information that is a vital part of gossip is conducted selectively within communities, and exclusion from such exchanges reinforces the powerlessness of groups which are negatively labelled.

Against this background it is unsurprising to find that 'leadership' of communities is generally monopolised by more 'respectable' figures, although the processes determining precisely who becomes a community leader are often convoluted. Baumann's (1996) Southall study and Eade's (1989) study of Tower Hamlets both found political processes underlain by competition between the different ethnic groups living in the two areas of London. Among these groups there were widely divergent views about which individuals would be best placed to represent the community within formal political structures that define 'community' in territorial terms as the local ward or constituency population. Disputes over who should act as leaders to represent communities in turn reveal the contested nature of community definition.

Baumann (1996) and Eade (1989) both show that notions of place community sit uneasily alongside conceptions of ethnic community rooted in the common culture of a religious or linguistic group (Chapters 4 and 5), and the same could be said about tensions existing with conceptions of 'community' that are constructed around common interests. Competing community leaders operate with different understandings of community, with boundaries drawn more or less inclusively or exclusively, and with different conceptions of how actively community members can be mobilised. When faced with powerful challenges, such as the redevelopment of the Isle of Dogs into parts of 'Docklands', the competition between leaders, local council organisations and between the two, can incapacitate local involvement or resistance to change even among strongly based communities (Foster 1999).

In the context of the long-term decline in allegiance to traditional (class-based) party politics and the growing heterogeneity of the population (not least in terms of changing class structures (Chapter 2), community politics has increased dramatically in recent decades. The growth of community action is one of the most striking features of the contemporary political scene, and legitimation through appeals to 'community' has become a vital part of mainstream political discourses. This is partly a reflection of the flexibility with which such appeals can be deployed, although this flexibility is double-edged. The proliferation of phenomena treated as communities carries with it the danger that the effectiveness of appeals to community will be undermined by the meaning of the concept becoming ever more imprecise and contested. There are signs that 'community' is no longer automatically assumed to have only positive connotations. For some critics of discourses built around community, the problem is that they serve to mask particular sectional interests, while others detect in them the agenda of state agencies attempting to withdraw from publicly funded service provision (Craig and Mayo 1995). One result of these unfolding debates is that the meaning of 'community' is becoming further politicised.

Recent conceptual developments and trends

The general tendency to associate community with supportiveness and social cohesion has been widely noted, but the word community may be used negatively as well as positively. Recognition has grown that community relationships have the potential to constrain individuals as well as to empower them, and to be exclusive as well as inclusive. Social divisions are as much based on *unifying* the membership of each particular category as in mutual *opposition* across social divides. This reassessment has been prompted by policy initiatives in which community has figured prominently (such as policies of 'community care') as well as being the outcome of more theoretically and methodologically informed analyses. The assumptions made by policy-makers about the caring capacities of communities have been confronted by some fairly harsh realities. Numerous research projects have shown that there are very definite limits to the extent to which community members are able and willing to provide informal care for dependent people, and that the bulk of the caring that is provided informally is performed by female relatives (Dalley 1996).

The dangers of operating with idealised conceptions of 'community' have also been revealed in other areas of social policy such as housing. Manipulation of the 'built environment' with the aim of creating 'balanced communities' in the New Towns experiment was a notably ambitious venture in this respect (Crow and Allan 1994). Its history reveals the disjunction that exists between the image of communities as social phenomena that supposedly have a natural capacity to unite diverse individuals and the tendency in prac- tice for communities to be less than universally inclusive. The persistence of community exclusivity is a common theme in the literature on geographical segregation. A principal lesson of the New Towns experiment is that consider- able resistance exists to plans that mix people from different social classes in the same residential area.

The expectation that people from different ethnic backgrounds would become progressively less spatially segregated with the passage of time (Chapter 4) has also not been fulfilled in practice, and there is evidence of spatial segregation along other lines of social cleavage such as those of age and occupation (Crow and Allan 1994; this volume Chapters 2 and 6). Of course, there are limits to how far residential areas can be monopolised by particular groups, but the emergence of the phenomenon of 'gated communities' with definite boundaries and restricted access is a sign of the times in which we live. Understood alternatively as 'fortress communities', such settlements illustrate the general point that the boundaries of communities will be jealously guarded by members who feel themselves to be under threat from outsiders. Sometimes these boundaries will have the physical expression of fences, walls, 'keep out' notices or surveillance cameras, as in the early example of the Cutteslowe Walls built between two housing estates reported by Collison (1963). On the other hand, exclusion of outsiders can be effected by more informal social means, for example by requiring that members express their commitment or loyalty to some symbol of the community (Cohen 1985).

Such exclusion or residential segregation necessarily limits the opportuni- ties that people have to gain direct experience of 'how the other half lives'. Indeed, this may be one important reason why there is not more enthusiasm for the 'mixed communities' that planners aspire to create. One of the ways that we can tolerate differences in other people's lives – the ways of people on the opposite side of social divisions – is that we may not have to mix with them. If we do not meet, if they remain invisible, we can ignore them: we need not feel upset by encountering their differences. How can we feel human concern for other people's poverty, loneliness, or disadvantage if we never engage with them except in the most superficial ways?

This is not to say that if we somehow all lived in neat communities, every- thing would be fine. The assumptions embodied in inherited notions of community have led to extensive theoretical reflection about the desirability of community. Feminists have been prominent among those who have questioned the meaning of community, prompted in part by the need to re-examine the gender orders written into traditional conceptions of community relationships. As has been noted already, policy-makers' views about the caring capacity of communities turn out to assume women's availability and preparedness to undertake care work, and such ideas reflect broader, male-dominated, taken-for-granted understandings of the allotted places of men and women in public and private spheres (Chapter 3). It is for these reasons that feminists and others have been wary of the communitarian agenda, developed by writers like Etzioni (1993), in which the value of community is promoted as an alternative to both unbridled individualism and excessive state involvement in welfare provision. Young (1986), for example, regards as problematic the way in which community is constructed to deny scope for difference and heterogeneity. In like fashion, Dalley (1996) has challenged the way in which the language of community is used as a cover for policies that shift the responsibility for care from state agencies to families (and, within families, to women).

The pursuit of community is open to criticism for introducing a conservative bias into the political agenda, because of its associations with idealised social arrangements in which people of different classes, genders and ages come together in pre-set, traditional ways where everyone 'knows their place'. In addition, critics point to the parochialism of community's negative evaluation not only of change but of all things different, captured in a mistrust of 'strangers' or 'outsiders'. It is undoubtedly true that there are established sociological understandings of community which are conservative, in that they look backwards to supposedly golden ages of authentic communal relationships that have subsequently been lost (Nisbet 1970). Arensberg and Kimball's (1940) classic account of rural Ireland, with its overtones of permanence, integration, cosy neighbouring and the slow turn of the seasons, contrasts sharply with Brody's (1973) later inclusion of famine, poverty, social dysfunction and clinical depression in what is still an elegiac vision of life in 'Inishkillane'.

As was remarked above, however, the notion of a loss of community perspective does not stand up to scrutiny once it is recognised that various forms of community relationships are present in contemporary societies, some of which are modified versions of what went before while others are more innovative. Put another way, the concept of community is most useful sociologically when it is treated as having the potential to capture the essence of a variety of different social arrangements rather than being tied to one particular type, such as village communities of the pre-industrial era (Crow and Allan 1995). There is no compelling theoretical reason to restrict the definition of community to people who have place in common, a point established in Hillery's celebrated review of the many sociological definitions of the term 'community' (Bell and Newby 1971). Once this is acknowledged then the charge that the concept of community has a built-in conservative bias loses much of its force.

Broadening out the definition of community to include groups of people who have something other than place in common is important if many of the more innovative forms of collective endeavour are to be acknowledged. New social movements such as the groups of environmentalists that have grown in prominence in recent decades may be understood as radical and alternative communities, built as they are around cultural ideas at odds with the dominant ideology of consumer capitalism. A similar point can be made about the emergence of community identities among groups whose shared disability, sexual orientation or ethnicity (Chapters 9, 8 and 4, respectively) marks them as distinct from the 'normal' culture of the majority population (Weeks 1995). At the same time it should be noted that place continues to figure in the operation of many such alternative communities, even if their members are held together principally by common political, religious or other cultural values. As Castells (1997) notes, most of these new community movements are essentially defensive in character, forged in the attempt to limit the impact of global forces on their lives. The defence of place is a powerful element in the construction of what he calls the 'communal havens' that offer to provide anchor points for an individual's identity in an uncertain world.

The 'threat' to place community life of the new uncertainty of a global economy can take several forms. Communities based on single occupations – or more precisely, on a few employers – are potentially vulnerable to the effects of international competition. Agriculture, fishing, coal mining, ship-building, dock-work and metal manufacture, industries that tended to have specific, relatively isolated, geographical locations in Britain, have already experienced major decline with the growth of alternative suppliers in other parts of the world. Decisions about people's lives become even more removed from their own hands.

Similarly, the rise of international media, largely funded through advertising, has increased knowledge of alternative ways of life beyond local boundaries. However this new 'awareness' is less significant than the associated promotion through advertising and its spin-offs of certain modes of consumer behaviour, not least the 'Americanisation' of youth culture and the individualisation of identity. To the extent that a sense of local community is dependent of a sense of *valued* collective difference, the new culture can be seen as undermining traditional ways of life and producing a more homogeneous mass society.

Nevertheless, it would be wrong to place too much emphasis on these broad statements of general tendencies. In practice, life 'on the ground' is far more complex, with people and organisations engaging in a variety of strategies to sustain and change their social and physical environments. Even an account of major social innovation that stresses the power of external and global forces to change the local community, notes that connecting macro-economics

with the alarming predictions about globalization, and an individual development programme and its impact on local residents is very problematic. (Foster 1999: 344)

The growth of different sorts of communities is understandable as the expression of people's dissatisfaction with individualism and their consequent desire to feel part of a collectivity. Where conventional community organisations are exclusive of newcomers and other 'outsider' groups, alternative communities provide rival bases for community identities, quite possibly within the same spatial reference points. P. Wright's (1985) study of how Stoke Newington is home to middle-class, white working-class and various ethnic minority communities provides an excellent illustration of competing claims to place among groups who live alongside each other but do not constitute an integrated whole. Ethnic minority in-migrants and middle-class gentrifiers occupy the same space as the members of the white working class who have lived there for longer, but they live in different social worlds, leading Wright to conclude that they constitute more than one community. There is no necessary contradiction in noting how the definition of community has been broadened while at the same time recognising that place continues to matter to how interest communities and communities of attachment are constructed.

The need to broaden the definition of community beyond people having place in common has been highlighted by the debate over the difference between 'community' and 'locality'. According to Day and Murdoch (1993), the latter term fails to capture the subjective dimension of how place is experienced, and people's frequent use of the language of community to convey their sense of identity, belonging and common endeavour indicates that what is being referred to here is more than just locality. Yet if a broad definition of community has the potential to capture a wider spectrum of social phenomena than do more restrictive definitions, at the same time it compounds the methodological difficulties of studying communities empirically. The problem confronting researchers of how to gain access to a study population is obviously easier if people's location is known than it is when the people being investigated are 'hidden' by their not being fixed to particular places, as was the case with Finnegan's (1989) amateur musicians.

Of course, even place communities are not straightforwardly open to inspection. Frankenberg (1957) famously found himself physically present in the village in which his research was being conducted but excluded from many aspects of the social life of the place until he found his point of entry through involvement in the football team. The problem of research findings being influenced by the researcher's point of access to the social phenomena being studied is by no means unique to investigations of community relationships, but nor is it an exception. Indeed, Payne (1996) has suggested that selectivity in terms of the community members consulted by researchers has led to a systematic distortion in which communities are typically represented as being full of nice people and devoid of undesirable characters. When combined with romanticised notions of 'community', research methods that screen out people with whom the researcher has little sympathy produce community studies that are seriously one-sided and incomplete. Recognition of the fact that having something in common does not entail community members being alike in all respects has sharpened awareness that research in the field of community needs to be methodologically sound if it is to be credible.

Conclusion

The unity of 'community' cannot be taken for granted once the contested nature of communities is recognised (Hoggett 1997). Central importance is now attached to studying the processes by which unity is created and maintained over time. Equally important is the analysis of how community conflicts are generated and work themselves out. Sociologists of community have shown how appeals to community have the potential to transcend particular social divisions along lines of gender, social class and ethnicity, through (for example) community relationships being likened to family relationships. An illustration of this point is provided by Dempsey's Australian 'Smalltown' study in which he records how the community is represented by many of its members as 'one big happy family' (1990: Chapter 4). Such appeals are effective in securing the unity of community members to the extent that ensuing loyalty to the wider group overrides narrower sectional interests and perspectives. We can contrast this with the social situation in Northern Ireland (see this volume, Chapter 5).

Where identification with and loyalties to a community are secondary to narrower and more particular interests and perspectives, community solidarity will be correspondingly unstable. Just as contemporary societies are subject to disunity as the power of dominant groups is challenged from a range of other positions, so too are contemporary communities vulnerable to fragmentation. The challenge mounted by women to their subordination within conventional understandings of community has already been mentioned. Neutral-sounding social policies constructed around notions of community can in practice have gender-biased outcomes, and feminists have been prominent among those asking of community discourses, 'who is this "we"?' (Godway and Finn 1994).

In the same way that challenges to conventional conceptions of 'community' have problematised women's allocation to inferior positions, so too has the place of other subordinate groups been problematised by developments in community politics. Parry, Moyser and Wagstaffe's (1987) research in inner-city Manchester found extensive consciousness of ethnic minority groups constituting a black community distinct from the white population, and also subject to division into various 'sub-communities'. Taylor, Evans and Fraser's (1996) comparison of Manchester and Sheffield identifies further cleavages besides gender and ethnicity, along lines of social class, sexuality and age, which also problematise speaking of local people as if they constitute a community in the singular.

The conventional understanding of community as a sphere of harmonious social relationships does not stand up to scrutiny, and in many ways it is more appropriate to regard community as an 'arena' in which social divisions are given expression. Social divisions are encountered and expressed in specific concrete social situations: the place community in particular acts as a locus for personal life experiences. 'Community' is often in fact an expression of one or more social divisions of the kind explored in this book. This is not to say that the idea of community is reducible to one or more of the other social divisions. The appeal to community is a very powerful rhetorical device by which groups can seek to reinforce their solidarity, although as we have seen, this is often achievable only by the exclusion of others. It follows that the more 'community' is interpreted differently according to people's social class, gender, ethnicity, sexuality, age and health status, the greater is the potential for it to be the scene of social conflicts.

Paraphrasing Marx's formulation in the 1859 Preface, community can be treated as one of the ideological battlegrounds onto which people, who have become conscious of conflicts of interest, venture in order to 'fight it out' (Marx and Engels 1859/1969: 504). This ties in with Barnes's (1995) point that people are often motivated to act as members of communities rather than as members of more abstract entities such as social classes. Especially in place communities, there can be real and often visible splits, not least between newcomers and longer-term residents, as we have seen earlier in this chapter. These patterns are repeated up and down the country, each conflict independent and localised, but echoing those going on elsewhere. Thus while the idea of community identity may not offer the same purchase on social division as, say, class or ethnicity – that is, as a macro principle of categorisation – it does however show how such things may appear 'on the ground'. The interconnection between social divisions means that we cannot think of any one division in isolation: it is only seemingly a paradox that bonds of attachment are part of social division. Attachments to more than one category blur our perception of the sharpness of social divisions.

Currently fashionable analytical moves to deconstruct communities into their various component parts correspond to broader post-modernist concerns in sociology. People's consciousness of being members of communities is of growing significance in the context of the rise of identity politics, which has seen the rejection of over-arching theories of what it is that determines who we are and an emphasis instead on the multifaceted nature of individuals and the communities of which they are a part. Yet the operation of forces that fragment communities is only part of the story, since alongside them there are opposite forces that bring people together. Homans (1951) refers to these as centrifugal and centripetal forces, and this idea of social forces pushing people either to the margins or to the centre of community relationships has been employed by Warwick and Littlejohn (1992) in their analysis of change in Yorkshire mining villages.

The notion is interesting for several reasons. First of all, it suggests that people may be thrown together or pushed apart despite their personal wishes; a person's position within a community is governed by more than simply individual choice. Second, the notion of centrifugal and centripetal forces directs our attention to the dynamic nature of community relationships and the importance of 'community time' (Crow and Allan 1995).

Third, the imagery focuses attention on the question of what constitutes the 'centre' of 'community'. Shared place, shared interests and shared identities are all possible answers to this question, as is some combination of these. Whether such communities can come together on a larger scale as coherent and united societies, in the face of so many powerful social divisions, is one of the most pressing issues of our time.

FURTHER READING

A useful introduction to the sociology of British communities is Crow, G. and Allan G. *Community Life*, London: Harvester Wheatsheaf (1994). The potential of community studies to capture the complexity of local social life is well illustrated by Foster, J. *Docklands*, London: UCL Press (1999). Methodological issues relating to community research are considered thoughtfully in Payne, G. 'Imagining the Community' in Lyon, E.S. and. Busfield, J. (eds) *Methodological Imaginations*, London: Macmillan (1996), while an interesting collection of papers on the policy-relevance of community research can be found in Hoggett, P. (ed.) *Contested Communities*, London: Policy Press (1997). For a rural community in an Australian setting, see Dempsey, K. *Smalltown*, Oxford: Oxford University Press (1990).

CHAPTER 12

Social Divisions and Social Cohesion

GEOFF PAYNE

Up to this point, the chapters in this book have deliberately 'defined' social divisions indirectly, by talking about key examples. This gives a good 'feel' of what social division is all about, portraying what we mean through an exploration of details and cases. An alternative approach would have been to start with a formal definition expressed as a set of abstract principles. For completeness, of course, a proper definition needs both examples and a precise statement of principles. This will also enable us to reflect on what social divisions in the plural might mean as a way of 'seeing' society.

Thus at the core of the definition is the idea that, while division can result in two, three, or more categories, these form an inter-related whole that includes all members of a society: paradoxically the *distinction* between the categories expresses the logical *connection* between them. These distinctions are marked by clear-cut – rather than minimal – differences in material circumstances or cultural advantages (it is of course recognised that 'clear-cut' and 'minimal' are terms which at the margin involve subjective judgements). The differences between categories are maintained by a normative order that supports those who accept the division and constrains those who seek to alter it.

A 'social division' of the kind explored in the preceding chapters conforms to nine core characteristics.

- A social division is a principle of social organisation resulting in a society-wide distinction between two or more logically interrelated categories of people, which are socially sanctioned as substantially different from one another in material and cultural ways.

- Although not permanently established in a given form, a social division tends to be long-lasting and is sustained by dominant cultural beliefs, the organisation of social institutions, and the situational interaction of individuals.

242

- A social division is socially constructed, in the sense that it is not a simple manifestation of 'natural' or 'inevitable' laws of existence, but this does not mean that it can be ignored or revised by the moment-to-moment social interactions, interpretations, decisions or social acts of individuals.

- Membership of a category in a social division confers unequal opportunities of access to desirable 'resources' of all kinds – and therefore different life chances and life styles – from membership of other categories.

- The extent of differentiation between categories varies from social division to social division, but movement across a divide is either rare, or relatively slow to be achieved.

- Being socially divided tends to produce shared social identities for people in the same category, often expressed by reference to their perceived difference from those in an alternative category of the same division.

- Each social division encompasses all members of society in one or other of its categories, but individuals seldom have matching profiles of category membership across the range of social divisions.

- An examination of life chances and life styles is an empirical method of identifying social divisions and categories.

- However much *specific* social divisions are opposed by those disadvantaged by them, the *principle* of social divisions is a universal systematic feature of human society.

As we saw in Chapter 1, the idea of social division entails both extensive differences, and a continuity of existence over time, which stems from its integration in the social order through values, institutions and day-by-day interactions. On the one hand there is a sense, if not of permanence, then massive inertia: it is not easy to challenge and change the boundaries. On the other hand, all of the contributors have shown how things *have* changed over time, and stressed that social divisions are not immutable. The key to understanding this is the embedded nature of the social practices that sustain each division. It follows that, while not 'natural' laws, divisions are typically encountered as constraining (particularly so for those in the less advantaged categories) or sustaining (more so for the advantaged).

It might be tempting – and indeed not unfair – to read this emphasis on constraint, disadvantage, and differential life chances as meaning that to some extent each of the contributors perceives social division as inherently undesirable. Some commentators, like Marsland and Saunders, have commented on the general tendency of sociologists to side with the underdog, or indeed to be ideologically biased. While it will be apparent from the style and content of the chapters that the authors have varying degrees of personal commitment to their topics, they are also all concerned with its sociological *analysis*. The fact that the divisions can reasonably be identified as social injustice, a potential source of unhappiness and even civil strife should lend purpose, rather than bias, to the analysis. All social arrangements entail settlements that bring relative advantage: those who gain most from present circumstances are likely to wish them to continue, not to have them challenged, and to present the current outcome as a consensus supported by all parties, rather than one that yields advantages for some, to the disadvantage of others. One task of sociology is to question things that would otherwise be taken for granted, even if there are those who would rather not have such questions raised.

Because a social analyst happens to be unhappy with the current patterns of a particular social division does not then lead either to bias or to a simplistic belief that all social divisions can somehow be removed. One may take comfort that this division or that takes a different *form* in some society described by anthropologists or historians, but there is no evidence of societies – even the simplest hunting and gathering societies – operating without divisions. However, the universality of division is no justification for the continuation of all divisions in exactly their current form, nor of extremes of differentiation.

Nonetheless, it is a feature of social divisions that they persist. As has been seen, one class system may give way to another, or the role of women may be enhanced through emancipation or entry into the workplace, but the core division survives. It may be possible to be socially mobile between classes, or for cracks in the glass ceiling to be exploited, but these are opportunities for individuals who need to devote many years of their lives to achieving the transition from one category to the other, or moving the boundaries. Divisions are not absolute or invariable, but they do a pretty good job of seeming so to be.

In part, this appearance of substance comes from the nature of the categories. These are 'oppositional' both in the sense of opposing interests of different categories (advantaged/disadvantaged), but also in terms of defining one category in terms of another, as its mirror image. Although it is possible to make more of these notions of difference and comparison (for example see Hetherington and Munro 1997) there is little to be gained from straying into the arcane world of much post-structuralism and post-modernism. Contrary to any impression given by the often wordy elaborations of such writings, the core issue is fairly straightforward. Identity is not only shared with others, but expressed as not sharing or belonging with others. The identification of a more advantaged group, to which the disadvantaged do not belong and which is socially demarcated, makes the probability of change seem less likely. The characteristic life styles and life chances that go with category membership and identity mark off the boundaries between them, helping the sociologist to locate social division but reinforcing the maintenance of the differences.

This methodological point also relates to the observation that individuals hold dual (or multi-) memberships in a range of social divisions. As the Introduction stressed, people take their identities from a mixture of categories, and therefore have some choice of identity. The 'profile of membership' differs from person to person, and is one of the reasons why simple explanations of social behaviour being 'caused' by membership of a single category do not work. All social life is not determined by social class, whatever may have seemed to be the case with sociological analysis in former times.

Definitions as differentiation

The advantage of formalising and elaborating a definition in this way is that it provides a means of marking off a boundary between social divisions and other similar, but significantly different, ideas. As a start, not all 'divisions' of people into opposing categories are of a scale to merit inclusion. For example, the many 'rages' and 'hells' popular in media presentations in the late 1990s ('road rage', 'trolley rage'; 'neighbours from hell', holidays from hell', and so on) may involve disagreements and conflicts, but they hardly constitute a social division. They certainly are not society-wide, not all-inclusive divisions, not permanent, nor socially sanctioned as 'natural'. To be counted as a social division requires that all of the criteria just outlined must be in place. This latter requirement also helps to distinguish between the idea of a social division and other concepts such as social inequality and social differentiation.

Thus 'social inequality' is a condition of disproportionate access to 'resources' – that is, not just financial resources but any human or cultural resources. Statements about social inequalities tend to deal, at their most simple, with 'facts'. Thus one can talk about specific social inequalities in, say, housing, educational qualifications, risk of being a victim of crime, or access to political influence. It is certainly interesting to learn that seven per cent of the population own 84 per cent of the land in Scotland, that one per cent of adults own over 40 per cent of personal net capital in England and Wales, or that the worst-off one-fifth of our society have incomes lower than half the national average. But what is 'interesting' lies in discovering why and how such patterns of inequality come about and are maintained, which means searching for explanatory factors such as the social divisions discussed above.

Patterns of inequality may *result* from social divisions, or be the visible markers of divisions, and are closely associated with divisions. However, the idea of social divisions is a more extensive one, which brings greater meaning and structure to the simple patterns of differences. It attempts to include the way in which some core features cover the whole population, contributing to their various senses of identity, and working as an inter-related set, without prioritising one division above all others. The discussion of health (Chapter 10) illustrates this point very clearly.

'Social differentiation', on the other hand, is a more specific term often used to deal with a key difference between 'simple' tribal or agrarian societies and more complex, industrial and contemporary societies. In the latter societies with their more complex social division of labour, the greater specialisation and range of tasks, in particular around production and occupations, demarcates people from each other, and groups from other groups. This formulation, drawing on Durkheim's concerns with social cohesion and his ideas of mechanical and organic solidarity, was particularly attractive among those sociologists who were attempting to deal with evident and extensive social inequalities without recourse to class analysis, for example in a US context where 'class' carries the politically charged association of Marxism and anti-American ways. Social divisions may differentiate, but as noted above, they also carry with them the critical notion that divisions entail a sense of social injustice.

Social divisions and social cohesion

The account of social life presented in this volume is on the one hand characterised by division, disadvantage, hierarchy, inequality and resistance, and on the other by group or category identity as the basic unit, shaped by a sense of difference from others. The question this poses, and which was noted in passing in the Introduction, is that if social life is so fragmented, does it make much sense to think in terms of such a vast conglomeration as 'society', or even the extensive divisions like class, gender or ethnicity that create the categories on which identity is based. If people lead their lives in terms of divisions and categories, each remarkably different from the next, how is collective life possible? Why does everything not fly apart and collapse in chaos? On the whole, despite divisions, things do hold together (as the discussion of community in Chapter 11 showed). The simple answer to understanding this lies in seeing how social divisions interconnect, and institutional processes constrain.

In the first place, while human behaviour is not totally constrained by structures of relationships and normative assumptions, individuals conduct their unique lives within frameworks of accepted actions. Social divisions are 'sustained by dominant cultural beliefs', so that they are carried in our heads. Social divisions also operate through complex, powerful and extensive institutions, that is, through systems of ways of acting in recognised, appropriate ways backed by positive and negative social sanctions.

Our capacity to modify this through situational interactions is constrained not just by what is in our heads, or the promise/threat of sanctions, but the willingness of *others* to engage on their part in that modification. If they are members of the same category, they are also part of a constraining system that encourages group identification and solidarity, not non-conformity. If they are members of an oppositional category, they have a vested interest in preventing the individual from modifying a relationship that gives them an advantage. Thus the scope for adapting meanings and beliefs, innovatory action and creating change is limited by the willingness of other actors to tolerate and support non-conforming behaviour.

In that sense, social structuration is essentially a *social* process, and one that never starts with a clean sheet of uncommitted other actors. The normative order that is inherited and recreated is certainly not monolithic or uniform, but its component elements and segments are indeed powerful. It is usually *easier* to go on doing the same thing, easier not to 'make waves' or 'rock the boat'; acceptance of one's lot in a given category is usually the easiest solution – (social) 'life goes on'.

This does not however provide a complete answer, because if people are all in fragmented categories, how do the culture/institution/interactional processes hold the disparate *categories* together? Social cohesion is more common than social disorder or disintegration, and indeed, lower level conflicts of interest are largely kept within bounds, mainly because individuals have multiple memberships of categories. It follows that unless memberships (or boundary lines) coincide, social divisions do not reinforce one another. Being working class may offer one source of identity and motivation for action, but the members of the working class are also variously black or white, male or female, fit or ill, old or young. These other identities fragment the class identity, and in turn are fragmented *by* class and all of the others.

If we think only of the eight main divisions in this book (Chapters 2–9), and treat each of them as consisting only of a dichotomy, then that alone offers 16 categories to which individuals could belong. Those categories can logically be combined, in the sense of a profile that some individual might manifest as a result of her or his eight memberships, in over 250 different profiles. Of course, some profiles may be unlikely: to a considerable extent, disadvantage on one division tends to be associated with disadvantage on others, as Anthias argues with reference to gender, ethnicity and class (1998: 531). However, this is numerically balanced by the fact that most of the social divisions exist with more than two categories in each (see for example the number of classes in Chapter 2).

Complex multiple memberships blur differences in two ways. First, their complexity intervenes to reduce the chances of a 'single issue' identity or cause for action emerging. Even when individuals consciously define themselves in specific terms – feminist, black, class warrior, grey panther – their own other memberships still have a part to play. The same is true of those who attempt a dual identity, for example black feminist. The multiplicity of memberships of people in a group mitigates against them all 'moving in the same direction' at once; whatever the individual may intend, the views of the others have to be taken into account, and their membership-based agendas contribute to a confusion of perspectives. Complex profiles disguise the underlying divisions.

The second way multiple memberships inhibit disintegration is by linking individuals in one social context who are disparate in other contexts. Employees may define themselves in class terms, but share national identity with their employers. Conversely they may use gender or ethnicity as grounds for not acting in class terms, by seeking to exclude or discriminate against women or the minority ethnic groups despite their shared membership of the working class. Employers and managers are then able to exploit such differences for their own ends. Only when social divisions coincide are major 'fault lines' in society likely to develop.

These 'overlapping ties' were sharply demonstrated in Gluckman's classic account of feuding between clans among the Nuer and other African peoples (1960). Drawing on several anthropological studies, he shows first that even in open conflict, what today we would call 'rules of engagement' apply. Fighting with sticks was allowed among close kin, but not with spears or knives. The ultimate weapon of burning the granaries and killing the livestock of other tribes was acceptable, but never practised within one's own people. By extension, the capacity for society to fall apart is always reduced by constraints on how conflict is to be managed, constraints that protect social cohesion by virtue of still recognising other shared memberships even when relationships concerning one division do break down.

Second, Gluckman argues that in practice, this is not a simple matter of cultural norms but an outcome of situational processes. Because people belong to several groups, they have a vested interest in constraining and resolving conflict in any one group. In a simple society based largely on kinship, marriage partners may be chosen from outside the immediate kin group: clans intermarry. If there is a feud between two clans, both those who have 'married in', and their immediate marriage partners, have a strong interest in achieving a resolution. This is worked out, in part, in the relationships between partners, and by the interpersonal pressures that can be brought into play. In this sense the multiple memberships bind. Individuals become the glue that helps to hold the institutions together, rather than the untidy and unco-operative components that threaten to break them apart.

This, of course, is not to say that conflict is always contained. At one level, societies collapse into open warfare: Northern Ireland and the Balkans are painful reminders of what happens when the urge to compromise is weaker that the pressure to dispute. At a second level, institutional frameworks, such as citizens' rights in law, can offer a means of limiting the full impact of division, exploitation and discrimination. Even the process of challenging division is in itself a means of releasing tensions. A number of other safety valves (humour, symbolic public events, role-reversal festivals, and so on) operate to promote accommodation.

Social divisions as a distinctive perspective

In the Introduction, it was suggested that a social divisions approach represents a distinctive perspective on society. In part this is evident in its systematic concern with division, inequality and social injustice. However, to appreciate the extent to which this does constitute a particular perspective, it is necessary to reflect briefly on alternative theoretical stances.

Without wishing to engage in a detailed analysis, it can be claimed that sociological theories operate with underlying domain assumptions about the nature of the social world. This point can be illustrated by contrasting the core metaphors that seem to operate in three well-known theoretical perspectives. In the first, that of structural-functionalism (and in particular in the earlier work of Parsons), the image of society is one of coherence, order and integration: humans operate willingly within institutions, whose forms follow naturally from the socially sustaining functions fulfilled by those institutions. Any apparent inequalities or divisions (for example occupational classes or gender) are seen as positively contributing in some way to social cohesion and maintenance. Only those who are psychologically disturbed will disrupt this precise system. The metaphor is Newtonian clockwork, its cog-wheels accurately machined and neatly interlocking: a place for each part, and each part in its place in a tidy, integrated system.

In contrast, the conception advocated by Marx and Marxian accounts of society presents conflict as endemic, periodically breaking out as revolutionary change. The parts of the system are held in place by the power of the ruling classes, who are able to enforce their wishes on the working class by virtue of their ownership of the means of production, and by promoting their own ideological interpretations to create false consciousness among the other classes. The routine experience is exploitation, and the 'social' is essentially the 'economic'. Social order, indeed all social forms, can be derived from the economic 'base' of production, and in that sense are a superficial 'superstructure'. The one essential social division of class renders other social divisions mere superstructural irrelevancies. The image that can stand for this view of society is a heavy weight, balanced precariously on a coiled spring, or of two animals fighting inside a large but frail paper bag. Both images convey the idea of two forces in mutual opposition.

We can contrast the clock and the struggling bag with the view from the wilder shores of post-modernism. Here the emphasis is individuals, reflectively selecting a personal identity from a host of possible choices, and reconstituting the world through the thoughts and words used to apprehend experience. The idea of large-scale social processes or structures is an illusion, a product of social science's fevered imagination, of no more value than any other person's *opinion*. There is no need for 'logical consistency' or 'evidence', since these, too, are artificial constructions. Our social image might either be taken from a New Wave film, with the self-absorbed inmates of an up-market asylum drifting past each other on a sunlit lawn, or alternatively, of particles of dust floating in a beam of light.

A social divisions perspective does not start from the assumption that society depends on neatly integrated and accepted social practices. It rather seeks to *question* the assumptions and normative beliefs that veil division, in contrast to structural-functionalism's acceptance of the status quo. 'Social divisions' emphasise the *multiplicity* of social divisions, in contrast to the narrow Marxian focus on class. In displaying *systematic* undesirable social inequalities and injustices, the constraining power of institutions and the ordered way identities are *socially* created, social division rejects the hyper-individualism and relativism of post-structuralism and post-modernism.

One advantage of this perspective is that the components (or subsystems of division) of 'society' do not need to be neatly or tightly connected, or held in some specific relationship to each other. Social order is achieved through the operation of one or more social divisions, rather than through all of them, all of the time, in a fixed relationship to each other (called 'society'). This fluidity is one reason for not adopting the otherwise helpful metaphor of the 'vertical mosaic' so tellingly employed in Porter's (1965) analysis of Canadian society. In taking a more fluid or flexible view of society, the point is that flexibility operates through divisions rather than just individuals, and makes up a *series* of constraining practices that do not apply equally or consistently in every context. Not all aspects of multiple divisions impinge directly on our day-to-day interactions at the same time. Social division as the social injustice suffered by others is easier to accept when much of its multifaceted visibility is largely hidden from us. The metaphor might be a young child's very inexpert attempt to construct a complex multicoloured assemblage of Lego blocks.

Furthermore, as the chapters show, there is a tension within each division between its capacity to constrain social action, and the mutability of its assumptions and forms. In terms of how institutions operate at any given point, their constituent roles are not rigid blueprints that precisely, minutely and exactly define social action, but rather rough sketches, that can be altered. There is a great deal of 'play', in an engineering sense, in role play. In social situations, we exploit the room to manoeuvre that this 'play' allows us. There is also further room to adjust, because the divisions are not all neatly integrated. It is *normal* for there to be a conflict of expectations between them that will apply in typical social situations. Social divisions, however well-defined each may seem to be at one level, are part of a conception of society as more messy, untidy, and hard to see, than in most other accounts.

Of course, life would be easier if society were neater and more straightforward. In the search for patterns and understanding, sociologists move up and down in their levels of analysis, sometimes using greater abstraction to achieve simplification (as in our discussion of social theory as metaphors) and sometimes looking at things in greater detail. Much internal debate arises from this confusion of levels; where we start our analysis is as much a product of personal preferences and circumstances as it is a matter of theoretical orientation.

Social divisions, sociology and social life

Sociologists, like other people, bring to their work their own intellectual and personal baggage. The variety of stances this creates does not however make it impossible to work within a social divisions framework, because there is no need to commit to a single narrow perspective. For example, Reid, whose work was used in Chapter 2 (this volume) operates 'on the assumption that social class is the most fundamental form of social stratification':

> Put as boldly as possible, being Black, female or elderly and middle class is different from being Black, female or elderly and working class... This is not to deny the importance of gender, ethnicity and age either objectively or subjectively, or to suggest that changes in class would necessarily end the differences between them. (1998: 238)

Conversely, Anthias's treatment of social division prioritises gender and ethnicity, but nonetheless lists class as the third division (1998).

It is not the intention of this book to claim that one or other division is the most important (although each of the contributors might well wish to make such a case!). Our highlighting of class, gender and ethnicity does reflect a basic prioritisation, but the inclusion of the other divisions indicates the importance of taking a broad view.

Whichever division(s) is accorded priority, the question remains as to how, given a multiplicity of divisions, they intersect. Reid argues that class takes precedence, while Anthias suggests two possible outcomes: cross-cutting systems of domination may articulate by being 'mutually reinforcing' ('social divisions articulate to produce a coherent set of practices of subordination', Anthias 1998: 531) or may give rise to 'contradictory locations' where individuals dominate within one division but are subordinate in another (*ibid.*: 532). In contrast, our own position as outlined above has tended to stress a *lack* of articulation in a complex of social divisions.

O'Brien and Howard have advocated an alternative approach. While welcoming attempts to move the experience of marginalised groups to the centre of sociological analysis, they support the view that the call for inclusion of race, class, gender and other 'differences'

> has served to point out the weaknesses in attempts to compare sexism with racism or classism (and other 'isms'). Additive approaches to incorporating race, class and gender fail to comprehend how experiences are qualitatively different from others rather than being simply an additional component. (1998: xiii)

As ethnographers, they advocate that the way to understand this is to study how social inequalities and difference are 'done' in everyday life, or in our terms, how systems of social division are manifested on the ground. This places sociological research into situational interactions, rather than at the more macro-level adopted by most of the contributors here.

While O'Brien and Howard start from this different methodological stance, much of their basic view of divisions, as about hierarchy, has a lot in common with our own. This is interesting in that their approach has a quite separate origin in American concerns with affirmative action and the 'celebration of difference'; the attempt to promote acceptance of cultural differences between (mainly) ethnic groups. They find a simplistic reliance on difference unhelpful, as it leaves the 'what' from which things differ, that is, the normative structures of white middle-class male America, unproblematised. Gender, for example, is not just a statement of difference, but one of hierarchy. The celebration of difference, which resonates so directly and strongly in the lives of American students, nonetheless makes those who have 'difference' carry the responsibility for it; this is like blaming the victim for the crime.

The study of divisions is therefore not simply a means of examining a random selection of segments of society. Its coherence lies in the notions of hierarchy, social inequality and social injustice that such a study entails. The way the divisions come together is a difficult sociological problem that we may not have entirely resolved, but we have tried to show that worse errors are likely if one takes the crude perspective that prioritises a single social division. This latter approach may help to simplify but it is unlikely to generate an adequate analysis.

However, social divisions are not just about intellectual problems of sociology but about the way the world we live in is going to operate. Because divisions are persistent, the social injustices they entail are a constant source of frustration and anger for ordinary people. Division is not itself pathological; divisions are the normal state of society. It is the persistence of their associated disadvantages that is the problem, with extremely unequal access to the desirable things in life continually impinging on the same categories of people. The greater the overall availability of desirable things – whether material, cultural or personal – and the more their attainment is promoted as a legitimate goal by advertisers and politicians – the more those excluded will feel their deprivation. While written in the first place as a book for sociologists, one measure of its utility will be how far *Social Divisions* can contribute to a clearer view and improved understanding of the processes of divisions, inequalities and injustices, and so assist in the building of a fairer society.

Bibliography

Abbott, P and Ackers, L. (1997) 'Women and Employment'. In Spybey, T. (ed.) *Britain in Europe*. London: Routledge.

Abbott, P. and Payne, G. (eds) (1990) *New Directions in the Sociology of Health*. London: Falmer Press.

Abbott, P. and Sapsford, R. (1987) *Women and Social Class*. London: Tavistock.

Abbott, P. and Sapsford, R. (1988) *Community Care for Mentally Handicapped Children*. Milton Keynes: Open University Press.

Abbott, P. and Tayler, M. (1995) 'Ethnic Variations in the Female Labour Force: A Research Note'. *British Journal of Sociology*, **46**(3): 339–53.

Abbott, P. and Wallace, C. (1992) *The Family and the New Right*. London: Pluto.

Abbott, P. and Wallace, C. (1996) *An Introduction to Sociology: Feminist Perspectives*. London: Routledge.

Albrow, M. (1993) 'Skills and Capacities in the Sociology Curriculum'. In Payne, G. and Cross, M. (eds) (1994) *Sociology in Action*. London: Macmillan.

Alexander, P. (1988) 'Prostitution: A Difficult Issue for Feminists'. In Delacoste, F. and Alexander, P. (eds) (1988) *Sex Work*. London: Virago.

Allatt, P. and Yeandle, S. (1992) *Youth Unemployment and the Family*. London: Routledge.

Anderson, B. (1996) 'Introduction'. In Balakrishnan, G. (ed.) (1996) *Mapping the Nation*. London: Verso Books.

Anderson, G. (1976) *Victorian Clerks*. Manchester: Manchester University Press.

Anderson, P. (1991) *Imagined Communities*. London: Verso.

Anthias, F. (1998) 'Rethinking Social Divisions'. *Sociological Review*, **46**(3): 505–35.

Anthias, F. and Yuval-Davis, N. (1992) *Racialized Boundaries: Race, Nation, Gender, Colour and Class and the Anti-racist Struggle*. London: Routledge.

Arber, S. (1990) 'Opening the "Black Box": Inequalities in Women's Health'. In Abbott, P. and Payne, G. (eds) (1990) *New Directions in the Sociology of Health*. London: Falmer Press.

Arber, S. and Ginn, J. (1991) *Gender and Later Life: A Sociological Analysis of Resources and Constraints*. London: Sage.

Arber, S. and Ginn, J. (1995) *Connecting Gender and Ageing*. Buckingham: Open University Press.

Archard, D. (1993) *Children, Rights and Childhood*. London: Routledge.

Arensberg, C. and Kimball, S. (1940) *Family and Community in Ireland*. Gloucester, MA: Peter Smith.

Ariès, P. (1962) *Centuries of Childhood*. London: Jonathan Cape.

Armstrong, D. (1994) *Outline of Sociology as Applied to Medicine*. London: Butterworth-Heinemann.

Askham, J., Henshaw, L. and Tarpey, M. (1993) 'Policies and Perceptions of Identity: Service Needs of Elderly People from Black and Minority Ethnic Backgrounds'. In Arber, S. and Evandrou, M. (eds) (1993) *Ageing, Independence and the Life Course.* London: Jessica Kingsley.

Atkinson, A. (1989) *Poverty and Social Security.* Hemel Hempstead: Harvester Wheatsheaf.

Bailey, J. (1998) 'In Front of the Arras: Some New Introductions'. *Sociology,* 31(1): 203–9.

Banton, M. (1967) *Race Relations,* London: Tavistock.

Banton, M.(1977) *The Idea of Race,* London: Tavistock.

Banton, M.(1987) *Racial Theories,* Cambridge: Cambridge University Press.

Banton, M.(1988) *Racial Consciousness,* London: Longman.

Banton, M. and Harwood, J. (1975) *The Race Concept,* Newton Abbot: David & Charles.

Barnes, B. (1995) *The Elements of Social Theory.* London: UCL Press.

Barnes, C. (1990) *Disabled People in Britain and Discrimination: A Case for Anti-discrimination Legislation.* London: Hurst.

Barnes, C., Mercer, G. and Shakespeare, T. (1999) *Exploring Disability: A Sociological Introduction.* Cambridge: Polity.

Barnett, A. (1997) *This Time: Our Constitutional Revolution.* London: Vintage.

Barrett, M. and Phillips, A. (1992) *Destabilising Theory: Contemporary Feminist Debates.* Cambridge: Polity.

Barth, F. (ed.) (1969) *Ethnic Groups and Boundaries.* Bergen: Universitetsforlaget.

Bartkey, S. L. (1990) *Femininity and Domination: Studies in the Phenomenology of Oppression.* London: Routledge.

Barton, L. (ed.) (1996) *Disability and Society.* Harlow: Longman.

Bauman, Z. (1990) *Thinking Sociologically.* Oxford: Basil Blackwell.

Baumann, G. (1996) *Contesting Culture.* Cambridge: Cambridge University Press.

Beck, U. (1992) *Risk Society: Towards a New Modernity.* London: Sage.

Beck, U. (1998) 'Politics of Risk Society'. In Franklin, J. (ed.) (1998) *The Politics of Risk Society.* Cambridge: Polity Press.

Beck, U. and Beck-Gernsheim, E. (1995) *The Normal Chaos of Love.* Cambridge: Polity Press.

Beck-Gernsheim, E. (1996) 'Life as a Planning Project'. In Lash, S., Szerszynski, B. and Wynne, B. (eds) (1996) *Risk, Environment and Modernity: Towards a New Ecology.* London: Sage.

Beechy, V. and Perkins, T. (1986) *A Matter of House: An Investigation of Women's Part-time Employment.* Cambridge: Polity.

Bell, C. and Newby, H. (1971) *Community Studies.* London: George Allen & Unwin.

Bell, M. (1994) *Childerley.* Chicago: University of Chicago Press.

Benedict, R. (1938) 'Continuities and Discontinuities in Cultural Conditioning'. *Psychiatry,* 1(1): 161–7.

Bengston, V. (1996) 'Continuities and Discontinuities in Intergenerational Relationships Over Time'. In Bengston, V. (ed.) (1996) *Adulthood and Aging: Research on Continuities and Discontinuities.* New York: Springer.

Benzeval, M., Judge, K. and Whitehead, M. (eds) (1995) *Tackling Inequalities in Health.* London: Kings Fund.

Berkman, L. and Breslow, L. (1983) *Health and Ways of Living: the Almeda County Study*. Oxford: Oxford University Press.

Bernardi, B. (1985) *Age Class Systems: Social Institutions and Polities Based on Age*. Cambridge: Cambridge University Press.

Berthoud, R. (1997) 'Income and Living Standards'. In Modood, T. and Berthoud, R. (eds) (1997) *Ethnic Minorities in Britain*. London: Policy Studies Institute.

Berthoud, R., Lakey, J. and McKay, S. (1993) *The Economic Problems of Disabled People*. London: Policy Studies Institute.

Blackburn, R. and Prandy, K. (1997) 'The Reproduction of Social Inequality'. *Sociology*, 31(3): 491–509.

Blaikie, A. (1999) *Ageing and Popular Culture*. Cambridge: Cambridge University Press.

Blakemore, K. and Boneham, M. (1994) *Age, Race and Ethnicity*. Oxford: Oxford University Press.

Blaxter, M. (1990) *Health and Lifestyles*. London: Routledge.

Blaxter, M and Paterson, E. (1982) *Mothers and Daughters*. London: Heinemann.

Bloor, M. (1976) 'Professional Autonomy and Client Exclusion'. In Wadsworth, M. and Robinson, D. (eds) (1976) *Studies in Everyday Medical Life*. London: Martin Robertson.

Booth, C. (1901–2) *Life and Labour of the People of London*, 17 Volumes. London: Macmillan.

Bosma, H., Marmot, M., Hemingway, H., Nicholson, A., Brunner, E. and Stansfeld, S. (1997) 'Low Job Control and Risk of Coronary Heart Disease in the Whitehall II (prospective cohort) Study'. *British Medical Journal*, 314: 558–65.

Bourdieu, P. (1984) *Distinction: A Social Critique of the Judgment of Taste*. London: Routledge & Kegan Paul.

Bowling, A. (1997) *Measuring Health*. (2nd edn). Buckingham: Open University Press.

Bradley, H. (1996) *Fractured Identities: Changing Patterns of Inequality*. Cambridge: Polity.

Bradley, H. (1999) *Gender and Power in the Workplace*. London: Macmillan.

Brannen, J. (1995) 'Young People and Their Contribution to Household Work'. *Sociology* 29(2): 317–38.

Braverman, H. (1974) *Labor and Monopoly Capitalism*. New York: Monthly Review Press.

Breen, R. (1998) 'Self Interest, Group Interest and Ethnic Identity'. Florence: Department of Political and Social Sciences, European University Institute (unpublished paper).

British Medical Association (1995) *Inequalities in Health*. BMA Occasional Paper. London: BMA.

Brody, H. (1973) *Inishkillane*. London: Allen Lane.

Brown, A., McCrone, D. and Paterson, L. (1998) *Politics and Society in Scotland*. London: Macmillan.

Brown, B., Burman, M. and Jamieson, L. (1993) *Sex Crimes on Trial: The Use of Sexual Evidence in Scottish Courts*. Edinburgh: Edinburgh University Press.

Brown, C. (1984) *Black and White Britain: The Third PSI Survey*. Aldershot: Gower.

Brown, C. and Gay, P. (1985) *Racial Discrimination: 17 Years After the Act*. London: Policy Studies Institute.

Brown, M. (1995) 'Naming and Framing: The Social Construction of Diagnosis and Illness'. *Journal of Health and Social Behaviour*, 36 (extra issue): 34–52.

Brubaker, R. (1992) *Citizenship and Nationhood in France and Germany*. Cambridge, MA: Harvard University Press.

Brubaker, R. (1996) *Nationalism Revisited*. Cambridge: Cambridge University Press.

Budd, A. and Campbell, N. (1998) *The Roles Of The Public and Private Sectors in the UK Pension System*. London: HM Treasury Web Site <http://www.hm-treasury.gov.uk/pub/html/docs/misc/pensions.html>.

Bulmer, M. (ed.) (1975) *Working Class Images of Society*. London: Routledge & Kegan Paul.

Bury, M. (1997) *Health and Illness in a Changing Society*. London: Routledge.

Butler, J. (1990) *Gender Trouble: Feminism and the Subversion of Identity*. New York: Routledge.

Bytheway, W. (1995) *Ageism*. Buckingham: Open University Press.

Cabinet Office (1999) *Modernising Government*. London: The Stationery Office.

Calnan, M. (1987) *Health and Illness: The Lay Perspective*. London: Tavistock.

Cameron, E. and Bernades, J. (1998) 'Gender and Disadvantage in Health: Men's Health for a Change'. In Bartley, M., Blane, D. and Davey-Smith, G. (eds) (1998) *The Sociology of Health Inequalities*. Oxford: Blackwell.

Cannadine, D. (1998) *Class In Britain*. New Haven: Yale University Press.

Carr-Hill, R. (1990) 'The Measurement of Inequalities in Health'. *Social Science and Medicine*, 31(3): 393–404.

Cartwright, A. and O'Brien, J. (1976) 'Social Class, Variations in Health Care and the Nature of General Practitioner Consultations'. In Stacey, M. (ed.) (1976) *The Sociology of the NHS*. Sociological Review Monograph No. 22. Keele: University of Keele.

Castells, M. (1997) *The Power of Identity*. Oxford: Blackwell.

Cavendish, R. (1982) *Women on the Line*. London: Routledge & Kegan Paul.

Central Statistical Office (1994) *Social Focus on Children*. London: HMSO.

Central Statistical Office (1995) *Social Trends*, 25. London: HMSO.

Chaney, J. (1981) *Social Networks and Job Information: The Situation of Women Who Return to Work*. Report presented to the Equal Opportunities Commission. London: Equal Opportunities Commission.

Clark, C. (1940) *The Conditions of Economic Progress*. London: Macmillan.

Clift, D. and Fielding, D. (1991) *A Survey of Management Morale in the 90s*. London: Institute of Management.

Cobban, A. (1994) *National Self-Determination* (extract reprinted). In Hutchinson, J. and Smith, A. D. (eds) (1994) *Nationalism*. Oxford: Oxford University Press.

Cockburn, C. (1983) *Brothers: Male Domination and Technological Change*. London: Pluto Press.

Cockburn, C. (1991) *In the Way of Women: Men's Resistance to Sex Equality in Organisations*. London: Macmillan.

Cohen, A. (ed.) (1982) *Belonging*. Manchester: Manchester University Press.

Cohen, A. (1985) *The Symbolic Construction of Community*. London: Tavistock.

Cohen, A. (1987) *Whalsay*. Manchester: Manchester University Press.

Cohen, M. (1998) 'A Habit of Healthy Idleness: Boys Underachievement in Historical Perception?'. In Epstein, D., Elwood, J., Hey, V. and Maw, J. (eds) (1998) *Failing Boys: Issues in Gender and Achievement*. Milton Keynes: Open University Press.

Cohen, R. (1994) *Frontiers of Identity: the British and Others*. London: Longman.

Cohen, R., Coxall, J., Craig, G. and Sadiq-Sangster, A. (1992) *Hardship Britain*. London: CPAG/FSU.

Cole, T. (1992) *The Journey of Life: A Cultural History of Ageing in America*. Cambridge: Cambridge University Press.

Colley, L.(1992) *Britons: Forging the Nation, 1707–1837*. New Haven: Yale University Press.

Collison, P. (1963) *The Cutteslowe Walls*. London: Faber & Faber.

Comfort, A. (1977) A *Good Age*. London: Mitchell Beazley.

Connor, W. (1994) *Ethnonationalism: the Quest for Understanding*. New Jersey: Princeton University Press.

Cooper, D. (1995) *Power in Struggle: Feminism, Sexuality and the State*. Buckingham: Open University Press.

Craig, G. and Mayo, M. (eds) (1995) *Community Empowerment*. London: Zed Books.

Crompton, R. (1998) *Class and Stratification: An Introduction to Current Debates*. (2nd edn). Cambridge: Polity.

Crompton, R. and Le Feuvre, N. (1996) 'Paid Employment and the Changing System of Gender Relations: A Cross National Comparison'. *Sociology*, 50(3): 427–45.

Crompton, R. and Mann, M. (1986) *Gender and Stratification*. Cambridge: Polity Press.

Crossick, G. (1977) 'The Emergence of the Lower Middle Class in Britain'. In Crossick, G. (ed.) (1977) *The Lower Middle Class in Britain, 1870–1914*. London: Croom Helm.

Crow, G. (ed.) (1996) *The Sociology of Rural Communities*. London: Edward Elgar.

Crow, G. (1997) *Comparative Sociology and Social Theory*. Basingstoke: Macmillan.

Crow, G. and Allan, G. (1994) *Community Life*. Hemel Hempstead: Harvester Wheatsheaf.

Crow, G. and Allan, G. (1995) 'Community Types, Community Typologies and Community Time'. *Time and Society*, 4(2): 147–66.

CSU (1995) *Labour Force Survey (Winter 1995)*. London: Central Statistical Office Labour Force Survey Quarterly Series, The Stationery Office.

Curtice, J. (1990) 'The Northern Irish Dimension'. In Jowell, R., Witherspoon, S., Brook, L. and Taylor, B. (eds) (1990) *British Social Attitudes: the 7th Report*. Aldershot: Gower.

Czechoslovak Demographic Society (1989) 'Proceedings of the International Population Conference. Ageing of Population in Developed Countries'. *Acta Demographica*. 9 (Special Edition).

d'Houtard, A. and Field, M. (1984) 'The Image of Health: Variations in Perceptions by Social Class in a French Population'. *Sociology of Health and Illness*, 6: 30–60.

Dahlgren, G. and Whitehead, M. (1991) *Policies and Strategies to Promote Social Equity in Health*. Stockholm: Institute for Future Studies.

Dalley, G. (1996) *Ideologies of Caring*. (2nd edn). Basingstoke: Macmillan.

Daniel, W. W. (1968) *Racial Discrimination in England*. Harmondsworth: Penguin.

Davis, D. (1984) *Slavery and Human Progress*. New York: Oxford University Press.

Day, G. and Murdoch, J. (1993) 'Locality and Community'. *Sociological Review*, 41(1): 82–111.

de Beauvoir, S. (1972) *The Second Sex*. Translated by Purskley, H. Harmondsworth: Penguin.

Delphy, C. (1984) *Close to Home: A Materialist Analysis of Women's Oppression*. London: Hutchinson.

Delphy, C. (1993) 'Rethinking Sex and Gender'. *Women's Studies International Forum*, 16(1): 1–9.

Delphy, C. and Leonard, D. (1992) *Familiar Exploitation: A New Analysis of Marriage in Contemporary Western Societies*. Cambridge: Polity Press in association with Blackwell.

Dempsey, K. (1990) *Smalltown*. Melbourne: Oxford University Press.

Dennis, N., Henriques, F. and Slaughter, C. (1956) *Coal Is Our Life*. London: Eyre & Spottiswoode.

Department of Employment (1988) *Family Expenditure Survey 1987*. London: HMSO.

Department of Employment (1998) *Family Expenditure Survey 1997*. London: HMSO.

Department of Health (1998a) *Independent Inquiry into Inequalities in Health*. London: The Stationery Office.

Department of Health (1998b) *Our Healthier Nation*. London: The Stationery Office. Cmd 3852.

Department of Health (1999) *Saving Lives: Our Healthier Nation*. London: The Stationery Office. Cmd 4386.

Department of Social Security (1997) *Press Release 97/192*. London: DSS: 2 October.

Department of the Environment, Transport and the Regions (1998) *Index of Local Deprivation*. London: DETR.

Devine, F. (1992a) *Affluent Workers Revisited*. Edinburgh: Edinburgh University Press.

Devine, F. (1992b) 'Gender Segregation in the Engineering and Science Professions: A Case of Continuity and Change'. *Work, Employment and Society*, 6(4): 557–95.

Dingwall, R. (1976) *Aspects of Illness*. London: Martin Robertson.

Dixon, C. (1996) 'Having a Laugh, Having a Fight. Masculinity and the Conflicting Needs of the Self in Design and Technology'. *International Studies in Sociology of Education*, 6(2).

Donzalot, J. (1978) *The Policing of Families: Welfare versus the State*. London: Hutchinson.

Dowds, L. and Young, K. (1996) 'National Identity'. In *British Social Attitudes: the 13th Report*. Aldershot: Dartmouth.

Doyal, L. (1994) 'Changing Medicine? Gender and the Politics of Health Care'. In Gabe, J., Kelleher, D. and Williams, G. (eds) (1994) *Challenging Medicine*. London: Routledge.

Doyal, L. (1995) *What Makes Women Sick*. London: Macmillan.

Draper, P. (1976) 'Social and Economic Constraints on Childlife among the !Kung'. In Lee, R. and DeVore, I. (eds) (1976) *Kalahari Hunter-Gatherers*. Cambridge, MA: Harvard University Press.

Drever, F. and Whitehead, M. (eds) (1997) *Health Inequalities*. Decennial Supplement. DS Series No. 15. London: The Stationery Office.

Dryler, H. (1998) 'Parental Role Model: Gender and Education Choice', *British Journal of Education*, 49(3): 377–98.

Duffield, M. (1985) 'Rationalization and the Politics of Segregation: Indian Workers in Britain's Foundry Industry, 1945–62'. In Lunn, K. (ed.) (1985) *Race and Labour in Twentieth Century Britain*. London: Frank Cass.

Duncan, S. and Edwards, R. (eds) (1997) *Single Mothers in an International Context*. London: UCL Press.

Duncombe, J. and Marsden, D. (1996) 'Whose Orgasm is This Anyway? "Sex Work" in Long-term Heterosexual Couple Relationships'. In Weeks, J. and Holland, J. (eds) (1996) *Sexual Cultures*. Basingstoke: Macmillan.

Dunleavy, P. (1980) *Urban Political Analysis*. London: Macmillan.

Durkheim, E. (1893/1984) *The Division of Labour in Society*. Basingstoke: Macmillan.

Eade, J. (1989) *The Politics of Community*. Aldershot: Avebury.

Epstein, D., Elwood, J., Hey, V. and Maw, J. (eds) (1998) *Failing Boys: Issues in Gender and Achievement*. Buckingham: Open University Press.

Erikson, R. and Goldthorpe, J. (1993) *The Constant Flux*. Oxford: Clarendon Press.

Etzioni, A. (1993) *The Spirit of Community*. New York: Touchstone.

Eurobarometer (1997) 'Women and Men in Europe: Equality of Opportunity Summary Report'. *Equal Opportunities Magazine*, 2 July.

European Commission (1998) *Employment in Europe 1997*. Luxembourg: Office for Official Publications of the European Communities.

Evans, D. (1993) *Sexual Citizenship: The Material Construction of Sexualities*. London: Routledge.

Featherstone, M. and Hepworth, M. (1989) 'Ageing and Old Age: Reflections on the Postmodern Life Course'. In Bytheway, W. (ed.) (1989) *Becoming and Being Old: Sociological Approaches to Later Life*. London: Sage.

Fennell, G., Phillipson, C. and Evers, H. (1988) *The Sociology of Old Age*. Buckingham: Open University Press.

Fevre, R. (1984) *Cheap Labour and Racial Discrimination*. Aldershot: Gower.

Field, S. (1987) 'The Changing Nature of Racial Discrimination'. *New Community*, 14(1/2): 118–22.

Finkelstein, V. (1996) 'The Disability Movement Has Run Out of Steam', *Disability NOW*. February, 11.

Finnegan, R. (1989) *The Hidden Musicians*. Cambridge: Cambridge University Press.

Firestone, S. (1974) *The Dialectic of Sex: The Case for Feminist Revolution*. New York, Morrow.

Ford, C. and Beach, F. (1952) *Patterns of Sexual Behaviour*. London: Eyre & Spottiswoode.

Fortes, M. (1970) 'Social and Psychological Aspects of Education in Taleland'. In Middleton, J. (ed.) (1970) *From Child to Adult: Studies in the Anthropology of Education*. Austin: University of Texas Press.

Foster, J. (1974) *Class Struggle and the Industrial Revolution*. London: Methuen.

Foster, J. (1999) *Docklands*. London: UCL Press.

Foucault, M. (1981) *The History of Sexuality*, Vol I. London: Allen Lane.

Frankenberg, R. (1957) *Village on the Border*. London: Cohen & West.

Freud, S. (1977) *The Penguin Freud Library*, Vol. 7: *Sexuality*. Harmondsworth: Penguin.

Fulcher, J. and Scott, J. (1999) *Sociology*. Oxford: Oxford University Press.

Fuss, D. (1991) *Inside/Out: Lesbian Theories, Gay Theories*. New York: Routledge.

Gabriel, J. (1998) *Whitewash: Racialized Politics and the Media*, London: Routledge.

Gagnon, J. and Simon, W. (1974) *Sexual Conduct*. London: Hutchinson.

Giarchi, G. (1990) 'Distance Decay and Information Deprivation'. In Abbott, P. and Payne, G. (eds) (1990) *New Directions in the Sociology of Health*. London: Falmer Press.

Giarchi, G. (1996) *Caring for Older Europeans*. Aldershot: Ashgate.

Giddens, A. (1981) *A Contemporary Critique of Historical Materialism*, Vol. I: *Power, Property and the State*. London: Macmillan.

Giddens, A. (1985) *A Contemporary Critique of Historical Materialism*, Vol. II: *The Nation-State and Violence*. London: Polity Press.

Giddens, A. (1990) *The Consequences of Modernity*. Cambridge: Polity Press.

Giddens, A. (1991) *Modernity and Self-Identity: Self and Society in the Late Modern Age*. Cambridge: Polity Press.

Giddens, A. (1992) *The Transformation of Intimacy: Sexuality, Love and Eroticism in Modern Societies*. Cambridge: Polity Press.

Giddens, A. (1997) *Sociology*. (3rd edn). Cambridge: Polity.

Gilborn, D. and Gipps, C. (1996) *Recent Research on the Achievements of Ethnic Minority Pupils*. London, HMSO.

Gilligan, H. (1990) 'Padstow'. In Harris, C. (ed.) (1990) *Family, Economy and Community*. Cardiff: University of Wales Press.

Gillis, J. R. (1974) *Youth in History*. London: Academic Press.

Ginn, J. and Arber, S. (1996) 'Gender, Age and Attitudes to Retirement in Mid-life'. *Ageing and Society*, **16**(1): 27–55.

Glendinning, C. and Millar, T. (1992) *Women and Poverty in Britain in the 1990s*. (2nd edn). Hemel Hempstead: Harvester/Wheatsheaf.

Gluckman, M. (1960) *Custom and Conflict in Africa*. Oxford: Blackwell.

Glucksman, M. (1995) 'Why Work?'. *Gender Work and Organisation*, **2**: 67–9.

Godway, E. and Finn, G. (eds) (1994) *Who is This 'We'?* Montreal: Black Rose Books.

Goffman, E. (1961) *Asylums*. New York: Anchor.

Goffman, E. (1972) *Encounters*. Harmondsworth: Penguin.

Goldthorpe, J. (1964) 'Social Stratification in Industrial Society'. In Halmos, P. (ed.) (1964) *The Development of Industrial Societies. Sociological Review Monograph*, 8. Keele: University of Keele.

Goldthorpe, J. (1980) *Social Mobility and Class Structure*. Oxford: Clarendon Press.

Goldthorpe, J. (1983) 'Women and Class Analysis: In Defence of the Conventional View'. *Sociology*, **17**(4): 465–88.

Goldthorpe, J. and Lockwood, D. (1963) 'Affluence and the British Class Structure'. *Sociological Review*, **11**(1): 133–63.

Goldthorpe, J., Lockwood, D., Bechhofer, F. and Platt, J. (1969) *The Affluent Worker in the Class Structure*. Cambridge: Cambridge University Press.

Goulbourne, H. (1991) *Ethnicity and Nationalism in Post-Imperial Britain*. Cambridge: Polity Press.

Graham, H. (1987) 'Women's Poverty in Caring'. In Glendenning, C. and Miller, J. (eds) *Women and Poverty*. Hemel Hempstead: Harvester/Wheatsheaf.

Gray, P., Elgar, J. and Bally, S. (1993) *Access to Training and Employment for Asian Women in Coventry*. Coventry: Coventry City Council, Economic Development Unit, Research Paper.

Gray, R. (1981) *The Aristocracy of Labour in Nineteenth Century Britain*. London: Macmillan.

Green, J. (1997) *Risk and Misfortune: the Social Construction of Accidents*. London: University College London Press.

Gregory, J. and Lees, S. (1999) *Policing Sexual Assault*. London: Routledge.

Gregory, S. and Hartley, G. (eds) (1991) *Constructing Deafness*. London: Pinter.

Grillis, J. (1987) 'The Case against Chronologization; Changes in the Anglo-American Life Cycle, 1600 to the Present'. *Ethnologia Europaea*, 17(2): 97–106.

Guardian (1998) 'Now I am Old...', interview with John Ezard, G2 Arts: 9, 14 April.

Guillaumin, C. (1995) *Racism, Sexism, Power and Ideology*. London: Routledge.

Guillemard, A. (1989) 'The Trend Towards Early Labour Force Withdrawal and Reorganisation of the Life Course: a Cross-national Analysis'. In Johnson, P., Conrad, C. and Thomson, D. (eds) (1989) *Workers versus Pensioners*. Manchester: Manchester University Press.

Guillemard, A. (1990) 'Re-organising the Transition from Work to Retirement in an International Perspective: Is Chronological Age still the Major Criterion Determining the Definitive Exit?'. Madrid: paper presented to the International Sociological Association Conference.

Guttsman, W. (1963) *The British Political Elite*. London: MacGibbon & Kee.

Hakim, C. (1991) 'Grateful Slaves and Self-made Women: Fact and Fantasy in Women's Work Orientations'. *European Sociological Review*, 7: 101–21.

Hakim, C. (1995) 'Five Feminist Myths about Women's Employment'. *British Journal of Sociology*, 46(4): 424–55.

Hall, S., Held, D. and McLennan, G. (eds) (1992) *Modernity and its Futures*. Cambridge: Polity Press.

Halperin, D. M. (1995) *Saint Foucault: Towards a Gay Hagiography*. Oxford: Oxford University Press.

Halson, J. (1991) 'Young Women: Sexual Harassment and Mixed-sex Schooling'. In Abbott, P. and Wallace, C. (eds) (1991) *Gender, Power and Sexuality*. London: Macmillan.

Hardy, M. (ed.) (1997) *Studying Ageing and Social Change: Conceptual and Methodological Issues*. London: Sage.

Hardy, T. (1902) *The Mayor of Casterbridge*. London: Macmillan.

Hardy, T. (1975) *Jude the Obscure*. London: Macmillan.

Hareven, T. (1994) 'Ageing and Generational Relations – A Historical and Life-course Perspective'. *Annual Review of Sociology*, 20: 437–61.

Harne, L. (1984) 'Lesbian Custody and the New Myth of the Father'. *Trouble and Strife*, 3: 12–14.

Hartman, H. (1981) 'The Unhappy Marriage of Marxism and Feminism: Towards a More Progressive Union'. *Capital and Class*, 8: 1–33.

Hawkes, G. (1996) *A Sociology of Sex and Sexuality*. Buckingham: Open University Press.

Heath, S. (1982) *The Sexual Fix*. London: Macmillan.

Held, D. (1992) 'The Development of the Modern State'. In Hall, S. and Gieben, B. (eds) (1992) *Formations of Modernity*. London: Polity Press.

Hennessy, R. (1995) 'Queer Visibility and Commodity Culture'. In Nicholson, L. and Seidman, S. (eds) (1995) *Social Postmodernism*. Cambridge: Cambridge University Press.

Hennessy, R. (1998) 'Disappearing Capital: The Queer Material of Sexual Identity'. Paper presented at the Centre for Interdisciplinary Gender Studies, Leeds.

Herdt, G. (1981) *Guardians of the Flutes*. New York: McGraw-Hill.

Herzlich, C. (1973) *Health and Illness: A Social Psychological Analysis*. London: Academic Press.

Hetherington, K. and Munro, R. (1997) *Ideas of Difference*. Oxford: Blackwell.

Hill, S. (1976) *The Dockers*. London: Heinemann.

Hillman, M., Adams, J. and Whitlegg, J. (1990) *One False Move: A Study of Children's Independent Mobility*. London: Policy Studies Institute.

Hills, J. (ed.) (1995a) *New Inequalities*. Cambridge: Cambridge University Press.

Hills, J. (1995b) *Income and Wealth: A Summary of the Evidence*. Joseph Rowntree Foundation Inquiry into Income and Wealth, Vol 2. York: Joseph Rowntree Foundation.

Hockey, J. and James, A. (1993) *Growing Up and Growing Old*. London: Sage.

Hoggett, P. (ed.) (1997) *Contested Communities*. Bristol: Policy Press.

Holcombe, L. (1973) *Victorian Ladies At Work*. Newton Abbott: David & Charles.

Holland, J., Ramazanoglu, C., Sharpe, S. and Thomson, R. (1990) *Don't Die of Ignorance – I Nearly Died of Embarrassment: Condoms in Context*. London: Tufnell Press.

Holland, J., Ramazanoglu, C., Sharpe, S. and Thomson, R. (1991) *Pressure, Resistance, Empowerment: Young Women and the Negotiation of Safer Sex*. London: Tufnell Press.

Holland, J., Ramazanoglu, C., Sharpe, S. and Thomson, R. (1994) 'Power and Desire: the Embodiment of Female Sexuality'. *Feminist Review*, **46**: 21–38.

Holland, J., Ramazanoglu, C., Sharpe, S. and Thomson, R. (1998) *The Male in the Head: Young People, Heterosexuality and Power*. London: Tufnell Press.

Homans, G. (1951) *The Human Group*. London: Routledge & Kegan Paul.

Honeyford, R. (1993) 'Why are we still Fed the Myth that Britain is a Racist Society?' *Daily Mail*, 14 April.

Hood, S., Kelley, P., Mayall, B. and Oakley, A. (1996) *Children, Parents and Risk*. London: Social Science Research Unit, Institute of Education.

Hood-Williams, J. (1990) 'Patriarchy for Children: On the Stability of Power Relations in Children's Lives'. In Chisholm, L., Büchner, P., Krüger, H.-H. and Brown, P. (eds) (1990) *Children, Youth and Social Change: a Comparative Perspective*. London: Falmer.

Howlett, B., Ahmad, W. and Murray, R. (1992) 'An Exploration of White, Asian and Afro Caribbean Peoples' Concepts of Health and Illness Causation'. *New Community*, **18**: 281–92.

Hubbock, J. and Carter, S. (1980) *Half a Chance? A Report on Job Discrimination Against Young Blacks in Nottingham*. London: CRE.

Hugman, R. (1994) *Ageing and the Care of Older People in Europe*. Basingstoke: Macmillan.

Hunt, S., McEwen, J. and McKenna, S. (1986) *Measuring Health Status*. London: Croom Helm.

Hyde, M. (1996) 'Fifty Years of Failure: Employment Services for Disabled People in the UK'. *Work, Employment and Society*, **10**(4): 683–700.

Hyde, M. (1998) 'Sheltered and Supported Employment in the 1990s: The Experiences of Disabled Workers in the UK'. *Disability and Society*, **13**(2): 199–215.

Hyde, M., Dixon, J. and Joyner, M. (2000) 'Work for Those That Can, Security for Those That Cannot: The New United Kingdom Social Security Reform Agenda'. *International Social Security Review*.

Iganski, P. and Payne, G. (1996) 'Declining Racial Disadvantage in the British Labour Market'. *Ethnic and Racial Studies,* 19(1): 113–34.

Iganski, P. and Payne, G. (1999) 'Socio-economic Re-structuring and Employment: The Case of Minority Ethnic Groups'. *British Journal of Sociology,* 50(2): 195–216.

Illsley, R. (1955) 'Social Class Selection and Class Differences in Relation to Still Births and Infant Deaths'. *British Medical Journal,* ii: 1520–4.

Illsley, R. (1986) 'Occupational Class, Selection and the Production of Inequalities in Health'. *Quarterly Journal of Social Affairs,* 2: 151–65.

Illsley, R. (1990) 'Comparative Review of Sources, Methodology and Knowledge'. *Social Science and Medicine,* 31(3): 229–36.

Ingraham, C. (1996) 'The Heterosexual Imaginary'. In Seidman, S. (ed.) (1996) *Queer Theory/Sociology.* Oxford: Blackwell.

Isin, E. and Wood, P. (1999) *Citizenship and Identity.* London: Sage.

Jackson, B. (1968) *Working Class Community.* London: Routledge & Kegan Paul.

Jackson, P. and Salisbury, J. (1996) 'Why Should Secondary Schools Take Working With Boys Seriously?'. *Gender and Education,* 8: 103–16.

Jackson, S. (1982) *Childhood and Sexuality.* Oxford: Blackwell.

Jackson, S. (1990) 'Demons and Innocents: Western Ideas on Children's Sexuality in Historical Perspective'. In Money, J. and Musaph, H. (eds) (1990) *Handbook of Sociology.* Vol. VII. Amsterdam: Elsevier.

Jackson, S. (1996) 'Heterosexuality as a Problem for Feminist Theory'. In Adkins, L. and Merchant, V. (eds) (1996) *Sexualising the Social.* Basingstoke: Macmillan.

Jackson, S. (1997) 'Women, Marriage and Family Relationships'. In Richardson, D. and Robinson, V. (eds) (1997) *Introducing Women's Studies.* (2nd edn). Basingstoke: Macmillan.

Jackson, S. (1998) *Contemporary Feminist Theories.* Edinburgh: Edinburgh University Press.

Jackson, S. (1998) *Britain's Population: Demographic Issues in Contemporary Society.* London: Routledge.

Jackson, S. (1999) *Heterosexuality in Question.* London: Sage.

Jackson, S. (2000a) *Concerning Heterosexuality.* London: Sage.

Jackson, S. (2000b) *Childhood and Sexuality Revisited.* Oxford: Blackwell.

Jackson, S and Scott, S. (eds) (1996) *Feminism and Sexuality: A Reader.* Edinburgh: Edinburgh University Press.

Jackson, S. and Scott, S. (1997) 'Gut Reactions to Matters of the Heart: Reflections on Rationality, Irrationality and Sexuality'. *Sociological Review,* 45(4): 551–75.

Jackson, S., Scott, S., Backett-Milburn, K. and Harden, J. (2000) 'Remembering, Rationalising and Reflecting on Risk: How Parents' Childhood Memories Feature in Accounts of Risks to their Children'. Paper presented to BSA Annual Conference, York, April.

James, A. and Prout, A. (1990) *Constructing and Reconstructing Childhood.* London: Falmer.

James, A., Jenks, C. and Prout, A. (1998) *Theorizing Childhood.* Cambridge: Polity Press.

Jeffreys, S. (1997) *The Idea of Prostitution.* Melbourne: Spiniflex.

Jenkins, R. (1986a) 'Social Anthropological Models in Inter-ethnic Relations'. In Rex, J. and Mason, D. (eds) (1986) *Theories of Race and Ethnic Relations*. Cambridge: Cambridge University Press.

Jenkins, R. (1986b) *Racism and Recruitment*, Cambridge: Cambridge University Press.

Jenkins, R. (1996) *Social Identity*. London: Routledge.

Jenkins, R. (1997) *Rethinking Ethnicity*. London: Sage.

Jenks, C. (1996) *Childhood*. London: Routledge.

Jewson, N., Mason, D., Waters, S. and Harvey, J. (1990) *Ethnic Minorities and Employment Practice, a Study of Six Employers*. London: Department of Employment Research Paper, No. 76.

Johnson, M. (1995) 'Interdependency and the Generational Compact'. *Ageing and Society*, 15: 234–65.

Johnson, P. (1985) *The Economics of Old Age in Britain: A Long-Run View 1881–1981*. London: Discussion Paper No. 47. Centre for Economic Policy Research.

Johnson, P., Conrad, C. and Thomson, D. (eds) (1989) *Workers Versus Pensioners*. Manchester: Manchester University Press.

Johnson, T. (1972) *Professions and Power*. London: Macmillan.

Jones, T. (1993) *Britain's Ethnic Minorities*. London: PSI.

Joseph, J. (1974/1987) 'Warning'. In Adcock, F. (ed.) (1987) *The Faber Book of 20th Century Women's Poetry*. London: Faber & Faber. (Originally published in Joseph, J. (1974) *Rose in the Afternoon*. London: Dent).

Joshi, H. (1990) 'The Cash Opportunity Costs of Child Bearing: An Approach to Estimation Using British Data'. *Population Studies*, 44: 52–3.

Jowell, R., Brook, L., Prior, G. and Taylor, B. (eds) (1992) *British Social Attitudes*. 9th Report. Aldershot: Dartmouth.

Kelly, L. (1988) *Surviving Sexual Violence*. Cambridge: Polity Press.

Kempson, E., Bryson, A. and Rowlingson, K. (1994) *Hard Times*. London: Policy Studies Institute.

Klein, J. (1965) *Samples From English Culture*. London: Routledge & Kegan Paul.

Klein, R. (1988) 'Acceptable Inequalities'. In Green, D. (ed.) (1988) *Acceptable Inequalities? Essays on the Pursuit of Equality*. London: Institute of Economic Affairs.

Kohli, M. (1986) 'The World We Forgot: A Historical Review of the Life Course'. In Marshall, W. (ed.) (1986) *Later Life: The Social Psychology of Ageing*. London: Sage.

Kohli, M. (1991) 'Retirement and the Moral Economy: An Historical Interpretation of the German Case'. In Minkler, M. and Estes, C. (eds) (1991) *Critical Perspectives on Ageing: The Political and Moral Economy of Growing Old*. Amityville, New York: Baywood.

Kohli, M., Rein, M., Guillemard, A. and Van Gunstern, H. (eds) (1992) *Time for Retirement: Comparative Studies on Early Exit for the Labour Force*. Cambridge: Cambridge University Press.

Kuhn, T. (1970) *The Structure of Scientific Revolutions*. (2nd edn). Chicago: Chicago University Press.

Kumar, K. (1978) *Prophecy and Progress*. Harmondsworth: Penguin.

Lacan, J. (1977) *Écrits*. London: Tavistock.

Laczko, F. and Phillipson, C. (1991) *Changing Work and Retirement*. Milton Keynes: Open University Press.

Langford, W. (1999) *Revolutions of the Heart: Gender, Power and the Delusions of Love.* London: Routledge.

Laslett, P. (1968) *The World We Have Lost.* London: Methuen.

Laslett, P. and Wall, R. (1972) *Household and Family in Past Times.* Cambridge: Cambridge University Press.

Lawler, S. (1999) 'Why Difference (Still) Makes a Difference: Sociology's Obligations'. Paper presented to the British Sociological Association Annual Conference, Glasgow.

Layton-Henry, Z. (1992) *The Politics of Immigration: Immigration, 'Race' and 'Race' Relations in Post-war Britain.* Oxford: Blackwell.

Lee, P. and Murie, A. (1999) *Literature Review of Social Exclusion.* Edinburgh: Scottish Office Central Research Unit.

Lee, R. and De Vore, I. (1968) *Man the Hunter.* Chicago: Aldine.

Lees, S. (1993) *Sugar and Spice: Sexuality and Adolescent Girls.* Harmondsworth, Penguin.

Lees, S. (1997) *Carnal Knowledge.* London: Penguin.

Lengermann, P. M. and Niebragge-Brantly, J. (1998) *The Women Founders: Sociology and Social Theory 1830–1930.* Boston and London: McGraw-Hill.

Leonard, D. (1990) 'In Their Own Right: Children and Sociology in the UK'. In Chisholm, L., Büchner, P., Krüger, H.-H. and Brown, P. (eds) (1990) *Children, Youth and Social Change: A Comparative Perspective.* London: Falmer.

Levitas, R. (1998) *The Inclusive Society?* Basingstoke: Macmillan.

Liberty (1994) *Sexuality and the State: Human Rights Violations against Lesbians, Gays, Bisexuals and Transgendered People.* London: National Council for Civil Liberties.

Lichterman, P. (1996) *The Search for Political Community.* Cambridge: Cambridge University Press.

Littlejohn, J. (1963) *Westrigg.* London: Routledge & Kegan Paul.

Locke, J. (1693/1989) 'Some Thoughts Concerning Education'. In Yolton, J. and Walton, J. (eds) *John Locke and the Way of Ideas.* Oxford: Clarendon Press.

Lockwood, D. (1958/1993) *The Black-coated Worker.* Oxford: Oxford University Press.

Lockwood, D. (1960) 'The New Working Class'. *European Journal of Sociology*, 1(3): 248–59.

Lockwood, D. (1966) 'Sources of Variation in Working Class Images of Society'. *Sociological Review*, 14(3): 244–67.

Luthra, M. (1997) *Britain's Black Population.* Aldershot: Ashgate Publishing.

Mac an Ghail, M. (1994) *The Making of Men: Masculinities and Schooling.* Buckingham: Open University Press.

Macintyre, S. (1997) 'The Black Report and Beyond: What are the Issues?'. *Social Science and Medicine*, 44(6): 723–45.

Macintyre, S., Hunt, K. and Sweeting, H. (1996) 'Gender Differences in Health'. *Social Science and Medicine*, 42(5): 617–42.

Maclean, C. (1997) *Migration and Social Change in Remote Rural Areas: A Scottish Highland Case Study.* PhD thesis. Edinburgh: University of Edinburgh.

Macleod, A. (1990) 'Social Divisions in a Small Community'. Paper presented to the British Sociological Association Annual Conference, Guildford.

Macleod, A. (1992) *Social Identity, Social Change and the Construction of Symbolic Boundaries in a West Highland Settlement.* PhD thesis, Plymouth: University of Plymouth.

Macleod, A. and Payne, G. (1994) 'Locals and Incomers'. In Baldwin, J. (ed.) (1994) *Peoples and Settlements.* Edinburgh: SSNS.

MacPherson, W. (1999) *The Stephen Lawrence Inquiry: Report of an Inquiry.* London: Home Office, Cm 4262–I.

Malinowski, B. (1929) *The Sexual Life of Savages in North-Western Melanesia.* London: Routledge & Kegan Paul.

Mannheim, K. (1927) 'The Problem of Generations'. In Hardy, M. (ed.) (1997) *Studying Aging and Social Change: Conceptual and Methodological Issues.* London: Sage.

Marcuse, H. (1964) *One Dimensional Man.* London: Routledge & Kegan Paul.

Marcuse, H. (1972) *Eros and Civilization.* London: Abacus.

Marmot, M. and Wilkinson, R. (1999) *Social Determinants of Health.* Oxford: Oxford University Press.

Marmot, M., Davey-Smith, G., Stansfield, S., *et al.* (1991) 'Health Inequalities Among British Civil Servants: The Whitehall II Study'. *Lancet,* 337: 1387–93.

Marmot, M., Shipley, M. and Rose, G. (1984) 'Do Socioeconomic Differences in Mortality Persist after Retirement?'. *British Medical Journal,* 313: 1177–80.

Marquand, D. (1988) *The Unprincipled Society.* London: Fontana.

Marshall, G., Rose, D., Vogler, C. and Newby, H. (1988) *Social Class in Modern Britain.* London: Hutchinson.

Martin, J. and Roberts, C. (1984) *Women and Employment: A Life Time Perspective.* London: HMSO.

Martin, J., Meltzer, H. and Elliot, D. (1988) *The Prevalence of Disability Among Adults.* London: HMSO.

Marx, K. and Engels, F. (1969) *Selected Works, Vol. 1.* Moscow: Progress Publishers.

Mason, D. (1986) 'Controversies and Continuities in Race and Ethnic Relations Theory'. In Rex, J. and Mason, D. (eds) (1986) *Theories of Race and Ethnic Relations.* Cambridge: Cambridge University Press.

Mason, D. (1994) 'On the Dangers of Disconnecting Race and Racism'. *Sociology,* 28(4): 845–58.

Mason, D. (1995/2000) *Race and Ethnicity in Modern Britain.* Oxford: Oxford University Press.

Mason, D. (1996) 'Themes and Issues in the Teaching of Race and Ethnicity in Sociology'. *Ethnic and Racial Studies,* 19(4): 789–806.

Mayall, B. (ed.) (1994) *Children's Childhoods: Observed and Experienced.* London: Falmer.

McCormick, B. (1986) 'Evidence about the Comparative Earnings of Asian and West Indian Workers in Britain'. *Scottish Journal of Political Economy,* 33(2).

McCrone, D. (1992) *Understanding Scotland: The Sociology of a Stateless Nation.* London: Routledge.

McCrone, D. (1998) *The Sociology of Nationalism: Tomorrow's Ancestors.* London: Routledge.

McCrone, D. and Surridge, P. (1998) 'National Identity and National Pride'. In Jowell, R. (ed.) *British Social Attitudes: the 15th Report.* London: Ashgate.

McCrone, D., Brown, A. and Paterson, L. (1998) *Politics and Society in Scotland*. Basingstoke: Macmillan.

McCrone, D., Brown, A., Paterson, L. and Surridge, P. (1999) *The Scottish Electorate*. Basingstoke: Macmillan.

McIntosh, M. (1993) 'Queer Theory and the War of the Sexes'. In Bristow, J. and Wilson, A. R. (eds) (1993) *Activating Theory*. London: Lawrence & Wishart.

McKibbin, R. (1998) *Class and Cultures: England, 1918–1951*. Oxford: Oxford University Press.

McKnight, A., Elias, P. and Wilson, R. (1998) *Low Pay and the National Insurance System: A Statistical Picture*. Manchester: Equal Opportunities Commission.

Meacham, S. (1977) *A Life Apart: The English Working Class 1890–1914*. London: Thames & Hudson.

Meade, K. (1995) 'Promoting Age Equality'. *Generations Review*, 5(3): 7–10.

Meigs, A. (1990) 'Multiple Gender Ideologies and Statuses'. In Sanday, P. and Goodenough, C. (eds) (1990) *Beyond the Second Sex: New Directions in the Anthropology of Gender*. Philadelphia: University of Pennsylvania Press.

Mewett, P. (1982) 'Exiles, Nicknames, Social Identities and the Production of Local Consciousness in a Lewis Crofting Community'. In Cohen, A. (ed.) (1982) *Belonging*. Manchester: Manchester University Press.

Middleton, S., Ashworth, K. and Braithwaite, I. (1997) *Small Fortunes: Spending on Children, Childhood Poverty and Parental Sacrifice*. York: Joseph Rowntree Foundation.

Midwinter, E. (1991) *The British Gas Report on Attitudes to Ageing 1991*. London: British Gas.

Miles, R. (1982) *Racism and Migrant Labour*. London: Routledge & Kegan Paul.

Miles, R. (1993) *Racism after Race Relations*. London: Routledge.

Mills, C. W. (1956) *The Power Elite*. New York: Oxford University Press.

Mills, C. W. (1959/1970) *The Sociological Imagination*. London: Oxford University Press.

Mirza, H. (1992) *Young, Female and Black*. London: Routledge.

Mitsos, C. and Browne, D. (1998) 'Gender Differences in Education: The Underachievement of Boys', *Sociology Review*, 8(1): 27–31.

Modood, T. (1988) 'Black, Racial Equality and Asian Identity', *New Community*, 14(3): 397–404.

Modood, T. (1990) 'Catching Up with Jesse Jackson: On Being Oppressed and On Being Somebody', *New Community*, 17(1): 85–96.

Modood, T. (1992) *Not Easy Being British*. Stoke-on-Trent: Trentham Books.

Modood, T. (1997a) 'Employment'. In Modood, T. *et al.* (eds) (1997) *Ethnic Minorities in Britain*. London: Policy Studies Institute.

Modood, T. (1997b) 'Culture and Identity'. In Modood, T. *et al.* (eds) (1997) *Ethnic Minorities in Britain*. London: Policy Studies Institute.

Modood, T., Berthoud, R., Lakey, J., Nazroo, J., Smith, P., Virdee, S. and Beishon, P. (eds) (1997) *Ethnic Minorities in Britain*. London: Policy Studies Institute.

Montague, A. (1964) *The Concept of Race*. New York: Free Press.

Montague, A. (1974) *Man's Most Dangerous Myth: The Fallacy of Race*. New York: Oxford University Press.

Morris, J. (1974) *Conundrum*. Oxford: Oxford University Press.

Morris, L. (1995) *Social Divisions*. London: UCL Press.

Morris, L. and Ritchie, J. (1994) *Income Maintenance and Living Standards*. York: Joseph Rowntree Foundation/SCPR.

Morris, L. and Scott, J. (1996) 'The Attenuation of Class Analysis'. *British Journal of Sociology*, 47(1): 45–55.

Morris, R. (1990) *Class, Sect and Party: The Making of the British Middle Class, Leeds 1820–1850*. Manchester: Manchester University Press.

Morrow, V. (1994) 'Responsible Children? Aspects of Children's Work and Employment Outside School in Contemporary UK'. In Mayall, B. (ed.) (1994) *Children's Childhoods: Observed and Experienced*. London: Falmer.

Mosca, G. (1896) 'Elementi di Scienza Politica, (1st edn). In Mosca, G.(ed.) (1939) *The Ruling Class*. New York: McGraw-Hill.

Mosca, G. (1923). 'Elementi di Scienza Politica, (2nd edn). In. Mosca, G. (ed.) (1932) *The Ruling Class*. New York: McGraw-Hill.

Murgatroyd, L. and Neuburger, H. (1997) 'A Household Satellite Account for the UK'. *Economic Trends*, 527, October: 63–71.

Murray, C. (1984) *Losing Ground: American Social Policy 1950–1980*. New York: Basic Books.

Murray, C. (1990) *The Underclass*. London: IEA.

Naipul, V. S. (1961/4) *A House for Mr Biswas*. London: Deutsch.

Nairn, T. (1977) *The Break-Up of Britain*. London: New Left Books.

National Association of Citizens Advice Bureaux (1984) *Unequal Opportunities: CAB Evidence on Racial Discrimination*. London: NACAB.

National Children's Home (1991) *Poverty and Nutrition Survey*. London: National Children's Home.

Nazroo, J. (1997) 'Health and Health Services' In Modood, T. and Berthoud, R. (eds) (1997) *Ethnic Minorities in Britain*. London: Policy Studies Institute.

Newby, H. (1975) 'The Deferential Dialectic'. *Comparative Studies in Society and History*, 17(2): 139–64.

Newby, H. (1980) *Green and Pleasant Land?* Harmondsworth: Penguin.

Nisbet, R. (1970) *The Sociological Tradition*. London: Heinemann.

Noon, M. (1993) 'Racial Discrimination in Speculative Applications: Evidence from the UK's Top One Hundred Firms', *Human Resource Management Journal*, 3(4): 35–47.

O'Brien, J. and Howard, J. (eds) (1998) *Everyday Inequalities*. Oxford: Blackwell.

Oakley, A. (1972) *Sex, Gender and Society*. Oxford: Martin Robertson.

Observer (1998) 3rd May.

Office for National Statistics (1997) *Social Trends 27*. London: The Stationery Office.

Office for National Statistics (1998a) *Social Trends 28*. London: The Stationery Office.

Office for National Statistics (1998b) *General Household Survey 1996*. London: The Stationery Office.

Office for National Statistics (1998) *Social Trends 29*. London: The Stationery Office.

Office for National Statistics (1999) *Annual Abstract of Statistics 1999*, No. 135. London: The Stationery Office.

Oliver, M. (1990) *The Politics of Disablement*. London: Macmillan.

Oliver, M. and Barnes, C. (1998) *Disabled People and Social Policy: From Exclusion to Inclusion*. Harlow: Longman.

Oppenheim, C. and Harker, L. (1996) *Poverty: the Facts.* (3rd edn). London: CPAG.

Owen, D. (1992) *Ethnic Minorities in Britain: Settlement Patterns.* Coventry: University of Warwick, Centre for Research in Ethnic Relations, National Ethnic Minority Data Archive, 1991 Census Statistical Paper No. 1.

Owen, D. (1993) *Ethnic Minorities in Britain: Economic Characteristics.* Coventry: University of Warwick, Centre for Research in Ethnic Relations, National Ethnic Minority Data Archive, 1991 Census Statistical Paper No. 3.

Pahl, J. (1983) 'The Allocation of Money and the Structuring of Inequality within Marriage'. *Work, Employment and Society*, 31(2): 237–62.

Pahl, J. (ed.) (1985) *Private Violence and Public Policy.* London: Routledge & Kegan Paul.

Pahl, R. (1993) 'Does Class Analysis Without Class Theory Have a Promising Future?'. *Sociology*, 27(2): 253–8.

Pareto, V. (1916/1963) *A Treatise on General Sociology.* In Livingstone, A. (ed.) (1963) New York: Dover, Four volumes bound as two.

Parkin, F. (1971) *Class Inequality and Political Order.* London: McGibbon & Kee.

Parry, G., Moyser, G. and Wagstaffe, M. (1987) 'The Crowd and the Community'. In Gaskell, G. and Benewick, R. (eds) (1987) *The Crowd in Contemporary Britain.* London: Sage.

Payne, G. (1973) 'Typologies of Middle Class Mobility'. *Sociology*, 7(3): 417–28.

Payne, G. (1987a) *Mobility and Change in Modern Society.* London: Macmillan.

Payne, G. (1987b) *Employment and Opportunity.* London: Macmillan.

Payne, G. (1989) 'Social Mobility'. In Burgess, R. (ed.) (1989) *Investigating Society.* London: Longmans.

Payne, G. (1992) 'Competing Views of Contemporary Social Mobility and Social Divisions'. In Burrows, R. and Marsh, C. (eds) (1992) *Consumption and Class.* London: Macmillan.

Payne, G. (1996) 'Imagining the Community'. In Lyon, S. and Busfield, J. (eds) (1996) *Methodological Imaginations.* Basingstoke: Macmillan.

Payne, G. and Abbott, P. (1990) (eds) *The Social Mobility of Women.* London: Falmer.

Payne, G., Payne, J. and Hyde, M. (1996) 'Refuse of All Classes? Social Indicators and Social Deprivation', *Sociological Research Online*, 1(1): http://www.socresonline. org.uk/socresonline/1/1/3.html.

Payne, G. and Payne, J. (2001) *50 Key Concepts in Social Research.* London: Sage.

Payne, J. (1995) *Interpreting the Index of Local Conditions.* Plymouth Business School: University of Plymouth.

Payne, J. (1999) *Researching Health Needs: A Community-based Approach.* London: Sage.

Phillips, A. and Taylor, B. (1980) 'Sex and Skill: Moves towards a Feminist Economics'. *Feminist Review*, 6: 79–88.

Phillips, S. (1986) 'Natives and Incomers: The Symbolism of Belonging in Muker Parish, North Yorkshire'. In Cohen, A. (ed.) (1986) *Symbolising Boundaries.* Manchester: Manchester University Press.

Phillipson, C. (1998) *Reconstructing Old Age.* London: Sage.

Phillipson, C. and Walker, A. (eds) (1986) *Ageing and Social Policy: A Critical Assessment.* Aldershot: Gower.

Phizacklea, A. (1983) *One Way Ticket: Migration and Female Labour.* London: Routledge.

Pill, R. and Stott, N. (1982) 'Concepts of Illness Causation and Responsibility: Some Preliminary Data from a Sample of Working Class Mothers'. Social Science and Medicine, 16(1): 43–52.

Pill, R., Peters, T. and Robling, M. (1993) 'Factors Associated with Health Behaviour among Mothers of Lower Socio-economic Status: A British Example'. *Social Science and Medicine*, 36(9): 1137–44.

Pinchbeck, I. and Hewitt, M. (1969) *Children in English Society Volume I*. London: Routledge & Kegan Paul.

Pirani, M., Yolles, M. and Bassa, E. (1992) 'Ethnic Pay Differentials'. *New Community*, 19(1): 31–42.

Pocock, P. (1975) 'British History: A Plea for a New Subject'. *Journal of Modern History*: 4: 601–21.

Pollock, G. and Nicholson, V. (1981) *Just the Job*. London: Hodder & Stoughton.

Popay, J., Williams, G., Thomas, C. and Gatrell, A. (1998) 'Theorising Inequalities in Health: The Place of Lay Knowledge'. In Bartley, M., Blane, D. and Davey-Smith, G. (eds) (1998) *The Sociology of Health Inequalities*. Oxford: Blackwell.

Porter, J. (1965) *The Vertical Mosaic*. Toronto: University of Toronto Press.

Porteus, J. (1989) *Planned to Death*. Manchester: Manchester University Press.

Postman, N. (1994) *The Disappearance of Childhood*. New York: Vintage Books.

Power, C., Bartley, M., Davey-Smith, G. and Blane, D. (1996) 'Transmission of Social and Biological Risk across the Life Course'. In Blane, D., Brunner, E. and Wilkinson, R. (eds) (1996) *Health and Social Organisation*. London: Routledge.

Power, S., Whitty, C. and Edwards, T. (1998) 'School Boys and School Work: Gender, Identification and Academic Achievement'. In Epstein, D., Maw, J., Elwood, J. and Hey, V. (eds) *International Journal of Inclusive Education* (special edition on boys' under-achievement), 2: 135–53.

Prandy, K. (1991) 'The Revised Cambridge Scale of Occupations'. *Sociology*, 24(4): 629–56.

Pringle, R. (1989) *Secretaries Talk: Sexuality, Power and Work*. London: Verso.

Punch, S. (1998) 'Negotiating Independence: Children and Young People Growing Up in Rural Bolivia'. Unpublished paper, School of Geography, University of Leeds.

Ram, M. (1992) 'Coping with Racism: Asian Employers in the Inner City'. *Work, Employment and Society*, 6(4): 601–18.

Rattansi, A. and Westwood, S. (1994) *Racism, Modernity and Identity on the Western Front*, Oxford: Polity Press.

Reich, W. (1951) *The Sexual Revolution*. London: Vision Books.

Reid, I. (1998) *Class in Britain*. London: Polity.

Reiser, R. (1995) 'Stereotypes of Disabled People'. In Reiser, R. (ed.) (1995) *Invisible Children*. London: Save the Children.

Rex, J. and Mason, D. (eds) (1986) *Theories of Race and Ethnic Relations*. Cambridge: Cambridge University Press.

Rex, J. and Moore, R. (1967) *Race, Community and Conflict*. London: Oxford University Press.

Rich, A. (1980) 'Compulsory Heterosexuality and Lesbian Existence'. *Signs*, 5(4): 630–60.

Richardson, D. (ed.) (1996) *Theorising Heterosexuality: Telling it Straight*. Buckingham: Open University Press.

Roberts, I. (1993) *Craft, Class and Control*. Edinburgh: Edinburgh University Press.

Robinson, V. (1989) 'Economic Restructuring and the Black Population'. In Herbert, D. and Smith D. (eds) (1989) *Social Problems and the City*. Oxford: Oxford University Press.

Room, G. (ed.) (1995) *Beyond the Threshold: The Measurement and Analysis of Social Exclusion*. Bristol: Policy Press.

Rose, D. and O'Reilly, K. (1998) *The ESRC Review of Government Social Classifications*. London: Office of National Statistics and ESRC.

Rose, N. (1989) *Governing the Soul: The Shaping of the Private Self*. London: Routledge.

Rowntree, S. (1901) *Poverty: A Study of Town Life*. London: Longmans Green.

Royal Commission on Old Age (1999) *With Respect to Old Age*. Report of the Royal Commission, Cm 4192. London: The Stationery Office.

Rubin, G. (1984) 'Thinking Sex: Notes for a Radical Theory of the Politics of Sexuality'. In Vance, C. (ed.) (1984) *Pleasure and Danger: Exploring Female Sexuality*. London: Routledge & Kegan Paul.

Rubinstein, W. (1981) *Men of Property*. London: Croom Helm.

Rubinstein, W. (1993) *Capitalism, Culture and Decline*. London: Routledge.

Ryan, J. and Thomas, F. (1980) *The Politics of Mental Handicap*. Harmondsworth: Penguin.

Salaman, G. (1986) *Working*. London: Tavistock.

Sarre, P. (1989) 'Race and the Class Structure'. In Hamnett, C., McDowell, L. and Sarre, P. (eds) (1989) *The Changing Social Structure*. London: Sage.

Saunders, P. (1990) *A Nation of Home Owners*. London: Unwin Hyman.

Savage, M. (1992) 'Women's Expertise, Men's Authority: Gendered Organisation in the Contemporary Middle Classes'. In Savage, M. and Witz, A. (eds) (1992) *Gender and Bureaucracy*. Oxford: Blackwell.

Savage, M. and Miles, A. (1994) *The Remaking of the British Working Class, 1840–1940*. London: Routledge.

Savage, M., Barlow, J., Dickens, P. and Fielding, T. (1992) *Property, Bureaucracy and Culture: Middle Class Formation in Contemporary Britain*. London: Routledge.

Scambler, G. (ed.) (1997) *Sociology as Applied to Medicine*. (4th edn). London: W. B. Saunders.

Scase, D. and Goffee, L. (1982) *The Entrepreneurial Middle Class*. London: Croom Helm.

Scott, J. (1991) *Who Rules Britain?* Cambridge: Polity Press.

Scott, J. (1994a) 'Class Analysis: Back to the Future'. *Sociology*, 28(4): 933–42.

Scott, J. (1994b) *Poverty and Wealth: Citizenship, Deprivation and Privilege*. Harlow: Longman.

Scott, J. (1996) *Stratification and Power: Structures of Class, Status and Command*. Cambridge: Polity Press.

Scott, J. (1997) *Corporate Business and Capitalist Classes*. Oxford: Oxford University Press.

Scott, S. and Freeman, R. (1995) 'Prevention as a Problem of Modernity: The Example of HIV and AIDS'. In Gabe, J. (ed.) (1995) *Medicine, Health and Risk*. Oxford: Blackwell.

Scott, S. and Jackson, S. (eds) (2000) *Gender: A Sociological Reader*. London: Routledge.

Scott, S. and Morgan, D. (eds) (1993) *Body Matters*. Basingstoke: Falmer Press.

Scott, S. and Watson-Brown, L. (1997) 'The Beast, the Family and the Little Children'. *Trouble and Strife*, 36–40.

Scott, S., Wight, D. and Buston, K. (1997) 'Innocence and Ignorance: Professionals' and Pupils' Discourses of Sex Education'. Paper presented at the Scottish Medical Sociology Conference, Kinloch Rannoch.

Scottish Daily Mail (1998) 20 January.

Scully, D. (1990) *Understanding Sexual Violence: A Study of Convicted Rapists*. London: Unwin & Hyman.

Seager, J. (1997) *The State of Women in the World Atlas*. (Revised edn). Harmondsworth, Penguin.

Seidman, S. (1996) *Queer Theory/Sociology*. Oxford: Blackwell.

Seidman, S. (1997) *Difference Troubles: Queering Social Theory and Sexual Politics*. Cambridge: Cambridge University Press.

Sen, K. (1994) *Ageing: Debates on Demographic Transition and Social Policy*. London: Zed Books.

Senior, M. and Viveash, B. (1998) *Health and Illness*. London: Macmillan.

Shahar, S. (1990) *Childhood in the Middle Ages*. London: Routledge.

Shakespeare, T., Gillespie-Sells, K. and Davies, D. (1996) *The Sexual Politics of Disability: Untold Desires*. London: Cassell.

Sharpe, S. (1995) *Just Like a Girl*. (2nd edn). Harmondsworth: Penguin.

Shy, C. (1997) 'The Failure of Academic Epidemiology'. *American Journal of Epidemiology*, **145**: 479–87.

Simon, W. (1996) *Postmodern Sexualities*. New York: Routledge.

Sinfield, A. (1994) *The Wilde Century*. London: Cassell.

Skeggs, B. (1995) 'Introduction'. In Skeggs, B. (ed.) *Feminist Cultural Theory: Process and Production*. Manchester: Manchester Education Press.

Skelton, C. (1993) 'Women and Education'. In Richardson, D. and Robinson, V. (eds) *Introducing Women's Studies: Feminist Theory and Practice*. London: Macmillan.

Skolnick, A. (1973) *The Intimate Environment: Exploring Marriage and the Family*. Boston: Little, Brown.

Skolnick, A. (1980) 'Children's Rights, Children's Development'. In Empey, L. T. (ed.) (1980) *Children's Rights and Juvenile Justice*. Charlottesville: University of Virginia Press.

Sly, F. (1996) 'Disability and the Labour Market', *Labour Market Trends*. September: 413–24.

Smith, D. (1979) 'A Peculiar Eclipse: Women's Exclusion from Men's Culture'. *Women's Studies International Quarterly*, 1: 281–95.

Smith, D. J. (1974) *The Facts of Racial Disadvantage*, London: Political and Economic Planning.

Smith, D. J. (1981) *Unemployment and Racial Minorities*. London: Policy Studies Institute.

Smith, M. G. (1986) 'Pluralism, Race and Ethnicity in Selected African Countries'. In Rex, J. and Mason, D. (eds) (1986) *Theories of Race and Ethnic Relations*. Cambridge: Cambridge University Press.

Social And Community Planning Research (1999) *Geographical Variations in Health Indicators by Health Authority, 1994–1996*. London: Department of Health.

Solomos, J. and Back, L. (1996) *Racism in Society*. Basingstoke: Macmillan.

Song, M. (1996) '"Helping out": Children's Participation in Chinese Take-away Businesses in Britain'. In Brannen, J. and O'Brien, M. (eds) (1996) *Children in Families*. London: Falmer.

Spybey, T. (ed.) (1997) *Britain in Europe*. London: Routledge.

Stacey, M. (1960) *Tradition and Change: A Study of Banbury*. Oxford: Oxford University Press.

Stacey, M., Batstone, E., Bell, C. and Murcott, A. (1975) *Power, Persistence and Change*. London: Routledge & Kegan Paul.

Stanworth, M. (1984) 'Women and Class Analysis: A Reply to Goldthorpe'. *Sociology*, 18(2): 159–70.

StatBase (1999) <http://www.statistics.gov.uk/statbase>.

Stepan, N. (1982) *The Idea of Race in Science*. London: Macmillan.

Stone, L. and Stone, J. (1984) *An Open Elite?* Oxford: Oxford University Press.

Strong, P. (1990) 'Black on Class and Mortality'. *Journal of Public Health Medicine*, 12: 168–80.

Syme, S. (1996) 'To Prevent Disease: The Need for a New Approach'. In Blane, D., Brunner, E. and Wilkinson, R. (eds) *Health and Social Organisation*. London: Routledge.

Synge, J. M. (1911) *The Playboy Of The Western World*. Dublin: Maunsel.

Tam, M. (1997) *Part-time Employment: A Bridge or a Trap*. Aldershot: Avebury.

Tamir, Y. (1993) *Liberal Nationalism*. New Jersey: Princeton University Press.

Taunton Commission (1868) *Commissioners School Inquiry Report*. 23 Volumes. London: Taunton Commission.

Taylor, I., Evans, K. and Fraser, P. (1996) *A Tale of Two Cities*. London: Routledge.

Taylor, S. and Field, D. (1997) *Sociology of Health and Health Care*. (2nd edn). Oxford: Blackwell.

Tebbutt, M. (1995) *Women's Talk?* Aldershot: Scolar Press.

Thompson, E. P. (1968) *The Making of the English Working Class*. Harmondsworth: Penguin.

Thompson, F. (1963) *English Landed Society in the Nineteenth Century*. London: Routledge & Kegan Paul.

Thomson, R. (1994) 'Moral Rhetoric and Public Health Pragmatism: The Recent Politics of Sexual Education'. *Feminist Review*, 48: 40–60.

Thomson, R. and Scott, S. (1991) *Learning About Sex: Young Women and the Social Construction of Sexual Identity*. London: Tufnell Press.

Thorne, B. (1987) 'Re-visioning Women and Social Change: Where are the Children?'. *Gender and Society*, 1(1): 85–109.

Thorne, B. (1993) *Gender Play: Girls and Boys in School*. Buckingham: Open University Press.

Thorogood, N. (1990) 'Caribbean Home Remedies and Their Importance for Black Women's Health Care in Britain'. In Abbott, P. and Payne, G. (1990) *New Directions in the Sociology of Health*. London: Falmer Press.

Tilly, C. (1992) *Coercion, Capital and European States, AD 990–1992*. Oxford: Blackwell.

Tönnies, F. (1887/1955) *Community and Association*. London: Routledge & Kegan Paul.

Topf, R., Mohler, P. and Heath, A. (1989) 'Pride in One's Country: Britain and West Germany'. In Jowell, R., Witherspoon, S. and Brook, L. (eds) (1989) *British Social Attitudes: Special International Report*. Aldershot: Gower.

Townsend, P. (1957) *The Family Life of Old People: An Inquiry in East London*. London: Routledge & Kegan Paul.

Townsend, P. (1979) *Poverty in the United Kingdom, A Survey of Household Resources and Standards of Living*. Harmondsworth: Penguin.

Townsend, P. (1986) 'Ageism and Social Policy'. In Phillipson, C. and Walker, A. (eds) (1986) *Ageing and Social Policy: A Critical Assessment*. Aldershot: Gower.

Townsend, P., Phillimore, P. and Beattie, A. (1986) *Poverty and the London Labour Market: An Interim Report*. London: Low Pay Unit.

Townsend, P., Davidson, N. and Whitehead, M. (1992) *Inequalities in Health: The Black Report and The Health Divide*. (Revised edn). Harmondsworth: Penguin.

Trudell, B. N. (1993) *Doing Sex Education: Gender, Politics and Schooling*. New York: Routledge.

Tunstall, J. (1962) *The Fishermen*. London: MacGibbon & Kee.

Turnball, C. (1984) *The Forest People* London: Triad/Paladin.

Turnbull, C. (1966) *Wayward Servants: The Two Worlds of the African Pygmies*. London: Eyre & Spottiswoode.

Tyler, M. (1997) *Women's Work as the Labour of Sexual Difference: Female Employment in the Airline Industry*. PhD Thesis. Derby: University of Derby.

Union of Physically Impaired Against Segregation (1976) *Fundamental Principles of Disability*. London: Union of Physically Impaired Against Segregation.

Valentine, G. (1996) 'Angels and Devils: Moral Landscapes of Childhood'. *Society and Space*, 14: 581–99.

van den Berghe, P. (1967) *Race and Racism*, New York: Wiley.

Van Every, J. (1996) 'Heterosexuality and Domestic Life'. In Richardson, D. (ed.) (1996) *Theorising Heterosexuality: Telling it Straight*. Buckingham: Open University Press.

Varo-Watson, D. (1998) 'Does it Work?', *Disability NOW*. April: 13.

Vernon, A. (1998) 'Multiple Oppression and the Disabled People's Movement'. In Shakespeare, T. (ed) (1998) *The Disability Reader: Social Science Perspectives*. London: Cassell.

Victor, C. (1991) *Health and Health Care in Later Life*. Milton Keynes: Open University Press.

Vincent, J. (1995) *Inequality and Old Age*. London: UCL Press.

Vincent, J. (1996) 'Who's Afraid of an Ageing Population?'. *Critical Social Policy*, 16(1): 3–26.

Vincent, J. (1999) *Power, Politics and Old Age*. Buckingham: Open University Press.

Virdee, S. (1997) 'Racial Harassment'. In Modood, T. and Berthoud, R. (eds) (1997) *Ethnic Minorities in Britain*. London: Policy Studies Institute.

Waites, M. (1998) 'Sexual Citizens: Legislating the Age of Consent in Britain'. In Carver, T. and Mottier, V. (eds) (1998) *Politics of Sexuality*. London: Routledge.

Walby, S. (1986) *Patriarchy at Work*. Cambridge: Polity.

Walby, S. (1990) *Theorising Patriarchy*. Oxford: Blackwell.

Walker, A. (1993) 'Wither the Social Contract? Intergenerational Solidarity in Income and Employment'. In Hobman, D. (ed.) (1993) *Uniting Generations: Studies in Conflict and Co-operation*. London: Age Concern England.

Wallman, S. (ed.) (1979) 'Introduction'. In *Ethnicity at Work*. London: Macmillan.

Wallman, S. (1986) 'Ethnicity and the Boundary Process in Context'. In Rex, J. and Mason, D. (eds) (1986) *Theories of Race and Ethnic Relations*. Cambridge: Cambridge University Press.

Walsh, J. (1999) 'Myths and Counter-myths: An Analysis of Part-time Female Employees and their Orientations to Work and Working Hours'. *Work, Employment and Society*, 13(2): 179–203.

Ward, R. and Jenkins, R. (eds) (1984) *Ethnic Communities in Business*. Cambridge: Cambridge University Press.

Ware, J. (1993) 'Measuring Patients' Views: The Optimum Outcome Measure'. *British Medical Journal*, 306: 1429–30.

Warwick, D. and Littlejohn, G. (1992) *Coal, Capital and Culture*. London: Routledge.

Waskler, F. (ed.) (1991) *Studying the Social Worlds of Children*. London: Falmer.

Watney, S. (1987) *Policing Desire*. London: Routledge.

Weber, M. (1914/1968) 'The Distribution of Power Within the Political Community: Class, Status, Party'. In Roth, G. and Wittich, C. (eds) (1968) *Economy and Society*. New York: Bedminster Press.

Weber, M. (1920/1968) 'Status Groups and Classes'. In Roth, G. and Wittich, C. (eds) (1968) *Economy and Society*. New York: Bedminster Press.

Weeks, J. (1989) *Sex, Politics and Society*. Harlow: Longmans.

Weeks, J. (1991) 'Pretended Family Relationships'. In Clark, D. (ed.) (1991) *Marriage, Domestic Life and Social Change*. London: Routledge.

Weeks, J. (1995) *Invented Moralities*. Cambridge: Polity.

Weiner, M. (1981) *English Culture and the Decline of the Entrepreneurial Spirit*. London: Heinemann.

Wellings, K., Field, J., Johnson, A. and Wadsworth, J. (1994) *Sexual Behaviour in Britain*. London: Penguin.

Wellman, B., Carrington, P. and Hall, A. (1988) 'Networks as Personal Communities'. In Wellman, B. and Berkowitz, S. (eds) (1988) *Social Structures*. Cambridge: Cambridge University Press.

Westwood, S. (1984) *All Day Every Day: Factory and Family in the Making of Women's Lives*. London: Pluto Press.

Wetherall, M., Stiren, H. and Potter, J. (1987) 'Unequal Egalitarianism: A Preliminary Study of Discoveries Concerning Gender and Employment Opportunities'. *British Journal of Social Psychology*, 26: 59–71.

Whitefield, G. (1997) *The Disability Discrimination Act: Analysis of Data from an Omnibus Survey*. London: Department of Social Security.

Wight, D. (1993) *Workers not Wasters*. Edinburgh: Edinburgh University Press.

Wight, D., Abraham, C. and Scott, S. (1998) 'Towards a Psychosocial Theoretical Framework for Sexual Health Promotion'. *Health Education Research*, 13(3): 317–30.

Williams, G. and Popay, J. (1994) 'Lay Knowledge and the Privilege of Experience'. In Gabe, J., Kelleher, D. and Williams, G. (eds) (1994) *Challenging Medicine*. London: Routledge.

Williams, R. (1983) 'Concepts of Health: An Analysis of Lay Logic'. *Sociology*, 17(1): 185–204.

Willis, P. (1977) *Learning to Labour*. Farnborough: Saxon House.

Willmott, P. (1986) *Social Networks, Informal Care and Public Policy*. London: Policy Studies Institute.

Wilton, T. (1996) 'Which One's the Man? The Heterosexualisation of Lesbian Sex'. In Richardson, D. (ed.) (1996) *Theorising Heterosexuality: Telling it Straight*. Buckingham: Open University Press.

World Health Organisation (1999) <http://www.who.init/aboutwho/en/definition.html>.

Wright, E. O. (1985) *Classes*. London: Verso.

Wright, E. O. (1989) *The Debate on Classes*. London: Verso.

Wright, E. O. (1993) *Interrogating Inequality: Essays on Class Analysis, Socialism and Marxism*. London: Verso.

Wright, E. O. (1997) *Class Counts*. Cambridge: Cambridge University Press.

Wright, P. (1985) *Living in an Old Country*. London: Verso.

Yeandle, S. (1984) *Women's Working Lives: Patterns and Strategies*. London: Tavistock.

Yinger, J. M. (1986) 'Intersecting Strands in the Theorisation of Race and Ethnic Relations'. In Rex, J. and Mason, D. (eds) (1986) *Theories of Race and Ethnic Relations*. Cambridge: Cambridge University Press.

Yinger, J. M. (1994) *Ethnicity: Source of Strength? Source of Conflict?* Albany: State University of New York.

Young, I. (1986) 'The Ideal of Community and the Politics of Difference'. *Social Theory and Practice*, 12(1): 1–26.

Young, M. and Willmott, P. (1957) *Family and Kinship in East London*. London: Routledge & Kegan Paul.

Yuval-Davis, N. and Anthias, F. (eds) (1989) *Woman-Nation-State*. London: Macmillan.

Zweig, F. (1961) *The Worker in an Affluent Society*. London: Heinemann.

Index

278